Yellow Peril!

University of Hertfordshire UH

College Lane, Hatfield, Herts, AL10 9AB

This item must be returned if reserved.

Fines are charged for the late return of reserved items.

Helpdesk@herts.ac.uk +44(0)1707 284678

Yellow Peril!

An Archive of Anti-Asian Fear

Edited and Introduced by
John Kuo Wei Tchen and Dylan Yeats

VERSO
London • New York

The Asian/Pacific/American Institute at NYU

Published in collaboration with the Asian / Pacific / American Institute, NYU
First published by Verso 2014
© John Kuo Wei Tchen and Dylan Yeats 2014

The moral rights of the authors have been asserted

3 5 7 9 10 8 6 4 2

Verso
UK: 6 Meard Street, London W1F 0EG
US: 20 Jay Street, Suite 1010, Brooklyn, NY 11201
www.versobooks.com

Verso is the imprint of New Left Books

ISBN-13: 978-1-78168-123-7 (pbk)
ISBN-13: 978-1-78168-124-4 (hbk)

British Library Cataloguing in Publication Data
A catalogue record for this book is available from the British Library

Library of Congress Cataloging-in-Publication Data

Yellow peril! : an archive of anti-Asian fear / edited and introduced by John Kuo Wei
Tchen and Dylan Yeats.
    pages cm
ISBN 978-1-78168-123-7 (pbk.) — ISBN 978-1-78168-124-4 (hardcover)
1. Asian Americans in popular culture—History—Sources. 2. Asian Americans—
History—Sources. 3. Xenophobia—United States—History—Sources. 4. Racism—
United States—History—Sources. 5. United States—Race relations—Sources. I.
Tchen, John Kuo Wei, editor, author. II. Yeats, Dylan, editor, author.
E184.A75Y45 2014
973'.0495—dc23
                    2013026694

Typeset in Garamond Pro by MJ & N Gavan, Truro, Cornwall
Printed by CPI Group (UK) Ltd, Croydon CR0 4YY

In Memory of Yoshio Kishi, Him Mark Lai, and Alexander Saxton

"The person who finds his homeland sweet is still a tender beginner; he to whom every soil is as his native one is already strong; but he is perfect to whom the entire world is as a foreign place."

Hugo of St. Victor, *Didascalicon*, c. 1120

"Every nation ... whether Greek or barbarian, has the same conceit that it before all other nations invented the comforts of human life."

Giambattista Vico, *The New Science*, 1744 (Axiom 125)

"The West is not in the West. It is a project, not a place."

Édouard Glissant, *Caribbean Discourse*, 1989

"We are never as steeped in history as when we pretend not to be, but if we stop pretending we may gain in understanding what we lose in false innocence. Naiveté is often an excuse for those who exercise power. For those upon whom that power is exercised, naiveté is always a mistake."

Michel-Rolph Trouillot, *Silencing the Past*, 1995

"Gog and Magog are at work in the Middle East. Biblical prophecies are being fulfilled ... This confrontation is willed by God, who wants to use this conflict to erase his people's enemies before a new age begins."

President George W. Bush to French President Jacques Chirac justifying the U.S. invasion of Iraq, 2003

Contents

Introduction: Yellow Peril Incarnate

[A] veritable octopus had fastened upon England—a yellow octopus whose head was that of Dr. Fu-Manchu, whose tentacles were dacoity, thuggee, modes of death, secret and swift, which in the darkness plucked men from life and left no clew behind.

Sax Rohmer, *The Insidious Dr. Fu-Manchu* (1913)

Paired with the quote by Sax Rohmer, our cover image (Figure 1) is a smirking yellow octopus possessively hugging the globe. The stylish sea creature with the title "The Japanese 'brain trust' and how it plans to act," drawn by Weimar Berlin–based illustrator Erich Schilling, was printed in the German satirical magazine *Simplicissimus* in 1935, at a time Japan was expanding into China.[1] This volume juxtaposes fragments of different times and different places to illustrate connections not otherwise imagined or understood.

Shown alongside this contemporary political cartoon (Figure 2), we suddenly become aware of a continuity of a visual political language. Appearing seventy-five years later, Cologne-based German satirist Heiko Sakurai's commentary on the Google octopus is part of a visual political culture that is still potent, though we may not understand why.

The historical moments are distinct, yet the messages are the same. As we'll discover throughout this volume, there is a long tradition of European-originated visuals representing some part of Asia as competing with and threatening "the West." Sakurai's octopus can be viewed as more benign. Perhaps Schilling's could as well. However, this 1873 railroad monopoly octopus (Figure 3) has no ambiguity—it threatens the virtue of America. And we'll discover in this volume how class conflict has been racialized and sexualized.

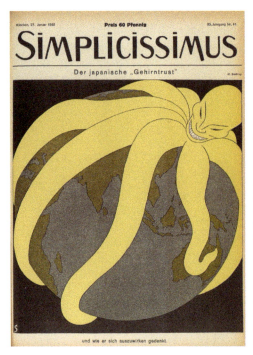

Figure 1. Illustrator Erich Schilling published some 1,500 drawings with the Munich-based satirical magazine *Simplicissimus* between 1907–1944. He was known for his modernist art deco style. This illustration predated the Anti-Soviet Pact signed by Germany and Japan in 1936. Erich Schilling, "The Japanese 'Brain Trust,'" *Simplicissimus*, vol. 39, no. 44 (January 27, 1935). Rare Book & Manuscript Library, Columbia University in the City of New York.

Figure 2. Cologne-based satirist Heiko Sakurai's Google octopus taking back its toys in the face of a bespectacled Chinese octopus said to be hacking online data about Chinese dissidents. Heiko Sakurai, "Octopus Data," *The West German Daily News* (January 14, 2010). © 2010 Heiko Sakurai. Courtesy of the artist. www.sakurai-cartoons.de

Figure 3. Frank Bellew, "The Cephalopod, or Terrestrial Devil Fish—A Monster of Centralization," *New York Daily Graphic* (March 4, 1873), 8. Courtesy of the New York Public Library.

Figure 4. The tentacles represent the railroad monopoly monster entangling Columbia in order to destroy the scrolled U.S. Constitution she is protecting. Detail, "The Cephalopod."

Columbia, a common nineteenth-century female embodiment of the United States perhaps best known as the logo for Columbia Pictures or the Statue of Liberty, is here a "damsel in distress" trying desperately to protect the rolled document labeled "The Constitution" from the monster's extending reach. The "Cephalopod's" tentacles, detailed as railroad cars, represent grabbing monopolistic railroad companies. The monster has already eaten "congressional honor" and now wants to run the nation by destroying its foundational claim to sovereignty.

The dystopic cartoon of Columbia being assaulted can best be appreciated when paired with a romantic painting embodying America's Manifest Destiny to occupy the continent. John Gast's "American Progress" (Figure 5) shows Columbia enlightening the North American continent. Civilization would follow the sun's arc westward, laying the "progress" of cultivated lands, telegraph lines, railroads, and steamships in her wake as "savages" and wild animals flee.

Octopuses had long been the icons of top-down authoritarian power in Europe. In industrializing America, however, a revolutionary nation that

Figure 5. John Gast, "American Progress," Chromolithograph after Gast's painting by George A. Crofutt (1873). Courtesy of the Library of Congress.

imagined itself free of the corruption of Europe also became entangled in monopolies controlling previously unimagined wealth and power. The tension between an expansive empire of promises and a fear of autocrats threatening virtue had been at the core of European-style republics. The result? An internal psychic fear projected outward toward various "others." The uses and abuses of this Other, as we'll see in this volume, relates to the ongoing historical formulation of the normative American Self. Such anxieties, fears, and paranoia have been powerfully captured and conveyed in the development of the colonialist Enlightenment culture of Europe and the U.S.—in its various patrician, expressive, intellectual, commercial, and political forms.

WESTERN CIVILIZATION VIOLATED

The white woman from *The Master Detective* (Figure 6) is scared yet transfixed, ready to scream yet mute. Her Chinese seducer/assaulter has her mesmerized with his steely gaze and threatening claw. The artist of this particular image is not credited in this issue of the detective-fiction weekly, nor do any of the stories contained within involve an Asian villain, protagonist, or even character. No matter—such images sold and that's all that counted.

Sax Rohmer took this bundle of anxieties, investments, and archetypes and combined them with the urban legends of vice, crime, and opium addiction in the London slums to fabricate the fantastic world of Fu Manchu (1913). Fu Manchu desires neither white women (though he uses them to manipulate Scotland Yard), nor fame. He is bizarre, "queer," non-heteronormative. *Horrors! He cannot be bought off!* Instead, the inscrutable Dr. Fu Manchu uses his Western intellect and Eastern cunning to try to destroy Western Civilization and beat it at its own game of world conquest. He organizes the colonized against the British, and picks off colonial administrators who catch on to his plot. This sublimated revenge fantasy helps make sense of why the Devil Doctor seems to take so much pleasure in his ability to outwit and terrify the British. The messy details of Western violence need not complicate the story of Western purity and innocence. In a paranoid political culture, seemingly random disruptions of London's peace can be explained simply and elegantly: The East wants to annihilate the West.

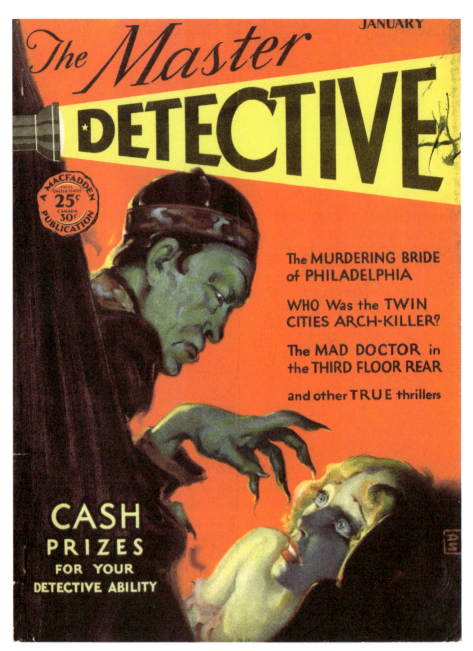

Figure 6. Yoshio Kishi/Irene Yah Ling Sun, *The Master Detective* (January, 1930).
Collection of Asian Americana made possible in large part in memory of Dr. Wei
Yu Chen, MSS 292, Series V, Box 18, folder 12. Courtesy of Fales Library and
Special Collections, New York University.

"This man, whether a fanatic or a duly appointed agent, is, unquestionably, the most malign and formidable personality existing in the known world to-day. He is a linguist who speaks with almost equal facility in any of the civilized languages, and in most of the barbaric. He is an adept in all the arts and sciences which a great university could teach him. He also is an adept in certain obscure arts and sciences which *no* university of to-day can teach. He has the brains of any three men of genius. Petrie, he is a mental giant."

"You amaze me!" I said.

"As to his mission among men. Why did M. Jules Furneaux fall dead in a Paris opera house? Because of heart failure? No! Because his last speech had shown that he held the key to the secret of Tongking. What became of the Grand Duke Stanislaus? Elopement? Suicide? Nothing of the kind. He alone was fully alive to Russia's growing peril. He alone knew the truth about Mongolia. Why was Sir Crichton Davey murdered? Because, had the work he was engaged upon ever seen the light it would have shown him to be the only living Englishman who understood the importance of the Tibetan frontiers. I say to you solemnly, Petrie, that these are but a few. Is there a man who would arouse the West to a sense of the awakening of the East, who would teach the deaf to hear, the blind to see, that the millions only await their leader? He will die. And this is only one phase of the devilish campaign. The others I can merely surmise."

"But, Smith, this is almost incredible! What perverted genius controls this awful secret movement?"

"Imagine a person, tall, lean and feline, high shouldered, with a brow like Shakespeare and a face like Satan, a close-shaven skull, and long, magnetic eyes of the true cat-green. Invest him with all the cruel cunning of an entire Eastern race, accumulated in one giant intellect, with all the resources of science past and present, with all the resources, if you will, of a wealthy government—which, however, already has denied all knowledge of his existence. Imagine that awful being, and you have a mental picture of Dr. Fu Manchu, the yellow peril incarnate in one man."

Sax Rohmer, *The Insidious Dr. Fu-Manchu*
(New York: McBride Nast & Co., 1911, 1913) 23–6.

In *The Mask of Fu Manchu* (1932), the fifth Fu Manchu novel, the Devil Doctor competes with the British Museum to unearth the mask of the

Figure 7. Boris Karloff made up in "yellowface" as Fu Manchu. Note the two circular octopus motifs behind the throne. Film still from *The Mask of Fu Manchu* (1932).

"golden prophet" Mohammed in order to rally Muslims worldwide against British imperialism. Yet when MGM Studios adapted the novel for American audiences that same year, they dropped the colonial history, cleansing the violation of and violence upon a people into a simplistic tale of defense against a horde of costumed extras. Sir Nayland Smith and his party, in this Americanized version, are innocents, as are the American audience. The film replaces the mask of the "golden prophet" with the mask of Genghis Khan—connecting Fu Manchu's terrorizing ambitions to a long (imagined) transhistorical fantasized tradition of Eastern antagonism against the West. In the film, the Devil Doctor (played by Boris Karloff) hypnotizes his white victims, orders large, muscular African guards around, and calls on East, Central, and West Asian peoples of the world to rally behind him as the modern successor of the historic Mongol leader, commanding: "Conquer and breed. Kill the white man and take his women!" Through the magic of American filmmaking, the twelfth-century rise of the Mongol empire, nomads demanding tribute from Central Asia east into China and west as far as Hungary, becomes part of the iconographic living memory of moviegoers. Whereas the far more recent and relevant event that might give Boris Karloff reason to be so bent—the colonial projects in China—are not scripted (Figure 7). Instead, the personification of an ancient pride and a vague vengefulness dominate this storytelling tradition.

Another fragment of a later time and place is New York–based Gahan Wilson's 1979 limited edition print (Figure 8). Wilson's Fu Manchu is retro and knowing, peering at us with a wink and nod. Wilson's black ink on yellow paper is a distilled essence of cartooning. Born in 1930, Wilson lived through the disclosures of the death camps, was familiar with Boris Karloff playing Fu, and fully aware of the 1950s–60s Civil Rights movement.

Look at Wilson's rendering of Fu's hands. The bright yellow, the unmistakable gesture of threat, the long stiletto nails are the optical equivalent of the cephalopod's tentacles. Certainly this Fu is more an alien creature than what's considered proper manliness. But it's the hypodermic needle that is most terrifying here. With hypodermic needle raised, Wilson's wry Fu Manchu is the master of nasty microbes ready to mainline evil into our collective veins. *Wink, wink.* Science is no longer in the trusted hands of an enlightened Western vanguard or John Gast's romantic "American Progress." It is instead in the hands of this monster whose twisted vision

Figure 8. Gahan Wilson, "Fu Manchu," lithograph (1979). © Gahan Wilson 1979.

of progress threatens civilization itself (like Dr. Mengele of the Nazi era or Mary Shelley's mad scientist of the much earlier *Frankenstein* [1818]). In Wilson's hand this pictograph is perversely nostalgic. But is this fear simply in the past, or is it still living? If it still lives, it surely must be subtler and less obvious. These visual fragments certainly remind us how explicit yellow perilist anxieties used to be.

WHERE DID THE "QUEER" COMPOUND "YELLOW PERIL" COME FROM?

"Yellow," as a racial signifier in the Western imagination, has come to represent those now classified as "East Asian." Yet, its first noted usage was applied to South Asians. In the 1684 publication "New Division of the Earth, According to the Different Species or Races of Man that Inhabit it, Sent by a Famous Voyager," cultural and historical difference was reduced to "the exterior form of their bodies ... principally in their faces." Indians of Asia were deemed *jaunes, gelb,* or *olivegelb*.[2] "Yellow" (or "green") to whom? "East" of where? "Yellow" to an emergent whiteness, and yellow to the "black" of whiteness. As yellow came to be used farther and farther eastward in Asia, "brown" became the old yellow for those in between the "far east" and Europe. Yellow has never been pure and absolute but always part of a spectral hybrid of imputed phenotypes. And yellow is part of a visual imaginary that varies in relation to the extension of European colonization into "the Orient." East of Europe became differentiated into "near," "middle," and "far" with the additional vectors of "south" and "southeast" Asia.

"Peril" to whom? Peril is a potential "at your own risk" danger of injury or death. In thirteenth-century Middle English "peril" and "danger" were used interchangeably. Injury or death could be individual and/or social and/or civilizational. It is a future possibility especially frequent when the world of security appears now vulnerable to a larger world of new and unknown dangers. This Anglo-Norman term was associated with the "danger of shipwrecks," "exposure to danger," "perile and drede" (1398 CE), and "to be in perell" (1475). One of the earliest written records of "peril" is associated with Christian morality. In *Ancrene Wisse*, Christian "spiritual temptations" were equated with "a mortal wound" precisely because of the potential of peril or danger. As a form of Christian preventive moral regulation, what *could be* was therefore considered equivalent to *a temptation given into,* the transgression of a taboo.[3] Hence, when this elision to be tempted was as good as sinning, the potential peril was as good as an actual acting out of temptation.

Generally, however, peril lay in the masculinist world of knyghtes (1440), robbynge (1378), pyrates (1576), and travel through seas of "Sharkes" (1634) and "Desarts full of wild Beasts" (1648). Yet, such was the hero's chivalric duty to put oneself in harm's way for the "cause of freedome" (1398). A 1384 Bible wrote of "In perels of flodis [floods], in perels of theues [thieves], … in perils of hethen men."[4]

Many credit German Kaiser Wilhelm II as having coined "die Gelbe Gefahr" or "the Yellow Peril." Wilhelm claimed to have had a prophetic dream of a seated Buddha riding a vicious dragon storm upon Europe. He commissioned Hermann Knackfuss in 1895 to illustrate his dream as gifts to leaders of Europe and America (Figure 9). The painting depicts the Archangel Michael (who leads the just against Satan during the final battle of Armageddon in Bible prophecy) cajoling the various European nations to fight together. An allegorical feminine figure represents each European nation. The painting is titled "Peoples of Europe, Defend Your Holiest Possessions."

The "holiest possessions" of the Kaiser's nightmare, the virtue of white womanhood imagined to be the hallmark of Western Civilization and the related Lockean idea of liberal self-possession, can also be translated into English as "dearest goods." This alternate translation highlights the economic undertones of this phrase, suggesting that the Kaiser's nightmare isn't merely about civilizational clash, but tied to his expansionist ambitions. Not merely threatened by Japanese encroachment into China, the Kaiser sought to use the threat of Japan to avoid an intra-European war over the grab for the remaining Chinese territory (a competition he feared Germany would lose).

The modern usage of "yellow peril" was said to emerge around the time of Kaiser Wilhelm's dream. But as we can see in this brief digging up of philological genealogies in the *Oxford English Dictionary*, the origins are tangled yet consistent. In roughly 1425, Bernard Mandeville wrote, "It es grete peril to pursue be [by] Tartarenes [Tartars of the Mongol armies]." And Lord Macaulay wrote, "Their chiefs, when united by common peril, could bring eighty thousand men into the field" (1841). In an era of tribalism, war against a common foe brought unity. Non-Christian "heathens"

Figure 9. Archangel Michael calls for unity in Christian Europe, each nation represented by women warriors, against the visualized threat of a seated Buddha on a dragon thunderstorm sweeping the landscape below. *Harper's Weekly*, vol. 42, no. 2144 (January 22, 1898), 76. Courtesy of the New York Public Library.

and nomadic warrior Mongols were automatic perils to the settled Christian way of life. Here we arrive at the roots of the compound joining of yellow Asians with an imperiled West. In the contemporary Western world, to evoke Yellow Peril has become synonymous with a looming dread where the potential threat is as good as any actual violation. Today yellow perilism has become an omnipresent haze—a malaise that sometimes coheres around an actual event, a fictitious character, or something else deliciously dangerous to establishment norms.

WHERE DID THE YELLOW PERIL TERM GO?

In the twenty-first century, Yellow Peril is a term that feels a bit out of date. It emerged at a specific moment of crisis and consolidation yet its meaning still haunts us today. That's why we use it to describe the phenomenon we

Figure 10. *The United States Marines*, vol. 1, no. 3 (New York: Magazine Enterprises, 1943). Government Comics Collection, Love Library, University of Nebraska, Lincoln. Courtesy of Richard Graham.

are exploring. The historical precision of the term resonates both with a long history preceding its invention as well as with its continued unspoken relevance.

When the Yanks "scorched" the "Yellow Octopus" in 1945, as in this U.S. Marine Corps comic book (Figure 10), the threat to Western Civilization seemed to have ended, for a brief moment at least. As other perils rose to prominence, the term Yellow Peril fell out of fashion. During the Cold War, as both the U.S. and Soviet Union competed for the allegiance of the former European and Japanese colonies, the Library of Congress featured the subject heading "Yellow Peril" to describe Western–Asian diplomatic relations. However, in 1992, after Japanese American Senator Daniel Inouye and his constituents requested it removed, the phrase disappeared from the classification system. Yet, the archive of books, manuscripts, images, and meanings still continues. While the term itself has faded into semi-obscurity, fears crystalized and embedded in the West of Yellow Peril still remain and flourish.

To illustrate, let's return to the nasty hypodermic needle of Wilson's Fu. Regularly, some Asiatic flu, or an Asian beetle or supposedly Asian-originated fish nibbling up America's natural resources ratchets up U.S. anxieties. The SARS scare made coughing DWA (dangerous while Asian). Indeed, Steven Soderbergh's film *Contagion* (2011) exploits these associations with Asia as the origins of disease, when Gwyneth Paltrow carries the deadly virus from a Hong Kong restaurant to the Midwest, infecting and killing thousands of heartland Americans. Even scarier, however, is the alien Oriental as a mad scientist.

In a post–civil rights era of anxieties about being accused and sued for racial discrimination, such evocations of Yellow Peril have become coded and fly just below the radar. This is the central question of this book. How do Yellow Peril fears survive in the political culture of the U.S., Great Britain, Europe, and "the West"? As Wilson's 1979 commemorative gesture itself indicates, the iconography is deeply held in the American soul. Therein, Westernizing innocence is forever violated by foreign evil. The future is uncertain once again, always. This is why we seek to revive Yellow Peril as an analytical category. Yellow Peril harkens back to Europe's earliest dreams of itself and its others, and still beckons us toward a haunted future. This tradition can be called yellow perilism.

A TRADITION, AN IDEOLOGY, A WAY OF LIFE

Yellow Peril! calls for recognition of this pervasive and multifarious phenomenon so we can begin to unpack it, put it in historical context, and make sense of how it affects our own moment. To do so, we are laying out a long trajectory of how the West differentiated itself from the East, and the roles of fantasy villains and civilizational threats in that process. Herein, we acknowledge a variety of traditions has been necessary to sustain these feelings generation after generation.

In the terms of historian Eric Hobsbawm, this is one of Westernization's longest running "invented traditions," one that even today reappears as if new yet deeply familiar and emotionally resonant.[5] Customs and traditions, as pointed out by Hobsbawm, are infused with inventions, old and recent, that keep social relations as they have been, and *business as usual* intact and more solidified. Images, especially those heavily coded with repeated motifs of threat and fear, hail us on a visceral, often subconscious level. Fu Manchu's hypnotic clawing hand, the yellow octopus's slimy tentacles slithering—these images beckon to us. And we respond back. Call and response is key. These visceral responses appear to be almost primal and "natural." We know not of where such revulsion comes from.

This complex and sweeping genealogy of Yellow Peril, connecting Mongols and Muslims, Jews and Japanese, the West and the East, from the twelfth-century past to a horrific dystopic future, suggests the scale and topography of recurring fears. It is for all times and all places. It is not fettered by historical realities, but appears as a universal "truth." Here historical facts only complicate this larger faith. Fear as a recurrent pattern, as a tradition, becomes part of the politics of a people. It becomes ideology and faith. And like all of what we live with every day, we take such patterns for granted. Recurrent fear becomes naturalized like the bogeyman, imminent injury, or death. Yellow Peril fears become systemic, a part of the political culture of daily life. It becomes yellow perilism—a way of believing, a way of living. This book, as a critical archive, demonstrates the ongoing living ideology of Yellow Peril in the logic and fears, the symbolic universe and material realities, and the domestic and foreign policies of our governing culture. Indeed, yellow perilism is hardwired into the formulation of Western Civilization itself.

German-Jewish cultural critic Walter Benjamin understood a more dynamic way to analyze the visual fragments we've dug up as part of the ruling ideology of any given time. Sometimes fragments of a seemingly distant past appear as a lightning flash in the present. This sudden intense light causes us to look at our surroundings differently and a new configuration of recognition is possible. Rather than believe the past is past, Benjamin argues that ideological blinders prevent us from seeing the pastness of the present.[6] We literally don't notice how the powerful shape our everyday present. It is hidden from sight except at certain moments in which a fragment of the past that captures this struggle for power helps us understand a new pattern of meaning. Suddenly we can literally re-connect or re-member pieces of a puzzle.

With this flash of lightning, as if by magic, the odd fragment of "protecting goods" aligns with Schilling's possession-happy octopus. Within the logic of colonization, any threat to resist such expansion is understood as a potential threat to the goods and quality of life of the empire. At the core of Enlightenment Reason is the imperial logic of global eminent domain. The power of Japanese expansionism was readily recognized, in part because the memory of the Kaiser's "dream" was still alive. Now the Kaiser's meaning can be illuminated more clearly. Note Knackfuss's painting represents Britannia as standing well behind Germania. Her shield is down. The Kaiser's warning chided Great Britain, other European nations, and the United States. The true threat is not Germany, but farther east. Don't put down your defenses from the true threat of the Asiatic races!

Certainly, Indian-born writer of British colonialism Rudyard Kipling had not lowered his guard. His poem "The White Man's Burden," subtitled "The United States and the Philippine Islands" (1899), supported Theodore Roosevelt's move to colonize the Philippines. He advised it was best to take a proactive stance in the "Far East." Soon to frame the rivalry between the British Empire and Russia over Asia as "the Great Game" (1901), Kipling was the intellectual of British patriarchal *imperium* that asserted colonization as a mission of a father civilizing the poor and benighted childlike races. In September 1898, Kipling wrote to Teddy Roosevelt, stating, "Now go in and put all the weight of your influence into hanging on permanently to the whole Philippines. America has gone and stuck a pickaxe into the foundations of a rotten house and she is morally bound to build the house over again from the foundations or have it fall about her ears."[7] That November, Kipling sent his poem to Roosevelt, just after Roosevelt was elected Governor of New York.

This Victor Gillam political cartoon (Figure 11) from *Judge*, a New York–based satirical weekly, caricatures what this "civilizing mission" promised. Following John Bull, Uncle Sam is valiantly rescuing oppressed and barbarized peoples clambering up the rocks of ignorance and superstition toward "Civilization," defined by "education" and "liberty." However, this vision also evoked criticism and laid the foundations of fear (figures 12 and 13). Was "benevolent assimilation" possible? What about the "troubles which may follow an imperial policy"?

These illustrations personalized global dynamics. A sense of direct threat was provoked—making the headlines and word-of-mouth stories circulating in Berlin, or elsewhere, come alive. Such flashes reconfigure the darkness of night.

Figure 11. Victor Gillam, "The White Man's Burden (Apologies to Rudyard Kipling)," *Judge*, vol. 36, no. 911 (April 1, 1899), 200–1. The Ohio State University Billy Ireland Cartoon Library & Museum.

Figure 12. William H. Walker, "The White (?) Man's Burden," *Life*, vol. 33, no. 850 (March 16, 1899), cover. Courtesy of the Library of Congress.

Figure 13. Here, an imagined Filipino congressman demands the passage of an appropriations bill from pro-colonization Speaker of the House Thomas Reed. Charles Nelan, "Troubles Which May Follow an Imperial Policy," *Cartoons of Our War With Spain* (New York: Frederick A. Stokes, 1898). Richard Samuel West Collection, Ohio State University Cartoon Library and Museum.

PRODUCING THE PAST

The production of history expresses political and cultural power while also actively silencing other versions. In this sense the "winner" is a certain noisier version that emerges as a master narrative and a master history. The truism that history is written by the victors is broken down by Michel-Rolph Trouillot into an understanding of history as a production process tied to sociopolitical power. History, writes Trouillot, can be silencing when facts, archives, narratives, and histories are absented at the very moment in which a history is being produced. He identifies "four crucial moments":

> the moment of fact creation (the making of *sources*);
> the moment of fact assembly (the making of *archives*);
> the moment of fact retrieval (the making of *narratives*); and
> the moment of retrospective significance (the making of *history* in the final instance).[8]

Visuality, according to philosopher Immanuel Kant, is a master aesthetic sense. The painter René Magritte put it succinctly: "Thought is what sees and can be described visually." What can be seen appears as a verifiable fact for the European Enlightenment values of classification and order. Rationality and visuality have been tightly linked. As one visual culture theorist has demonstrated, "visuality and its visualizing of history are part of how the 'West' historicizes and distinguished itself from its others."[9]

The visual as a master European sense can also be understood as a sense of surveillance and possession. Certainly this has been true in the development of Westernizing Europe and the spread of European bourgeois Enlightenment cultures through colonial expansion eastward to the Near East and Middle East, but especially South Asia and Southeast Asia, and westward into the Americas and beyond, into the Pacific. The ascription of the skin tone yellow, for example, was first thought to be descriptive of Arabs, then of South Asians, and then farther east to East Asians. The "yellow race" becomes the category of both power and supposed knowledge about "the East." Indeed, with the analytic lens of Westernist visuality one can also discuss the imperial gaze in the Orientalist paintings of Jean-Léon Gérôme or the empire of sight surveyed in the Hudson River landscapes of Asher Brown Durand.

How did such a visuality gain social and political coherence? Jürgen Habermas includes salons, libraries, museums, and coffeehouses as part of the "bourgeois public sphere"—the spaces where newly empowered male elites not under the control of the traditional aristocracy gather, discuss, and debate their ideas more freely and more rationally based on visually-discernible patterns of mankind, nature, and the heavens.[10]

As we celebrate this opening of human knowledge, we also know we cannot be naïve. With European Enlightenment came its own hierarchies: male over female, colonialism, and the racial sciences, to name just a few axes of power. Visuality in this European and Euro-American sense also became evidence of invidious superiority.

In contrast, the proximate senses—those of touch, taste, smell—were deemed the lower "animal senses."[11] The visual became the sense of civilization. What can be seen on the surface of power/knowledge justified notions of class, gender, and racial superiority. Such is the "visual ideology" of what philosopher Charles W. Mills calls the "racial contract."[12]

This form of elite "distinction"—and here we use distinction as the French sociologist Pierre Bourdieu analyzes the term, as a form of differentiation separating the civilized from the masses—becomes the way bourgeois elites distinguish themselves from their own citizens and non-Christian heathens at home and abroad.[13]

The spoken occupied an ambiguous position. For a colonized Indian, either from India or from North America, to speak perfect "English" (in contrast to the expected Indian-accented English of Apu in Matt Groening's *The Simpsons*) has been a "curiosity"—seemingly anomalous, incongruent. In effect, speaking and storytelling is a borderland between the so-called superior sense of sight and the lower senses. Trouillot's framing offers an analysis of this key sensate dimension, that of sound and silence, in terms relevant to what we have done in archiving Yellow Peril fragments and re-presenting them back in the public sphere.

Who has the power to be the record for posterity? The majority of people do not. (This statement recognizes and includes our current romance with the possibilities of online social media.) Hence, silencing and invisibility are also intrinsic to the forensics of those stories excluded from Habermas's bourgeois public sphere. Eve Kosofsky Sedgwick terms these stories a form of "closeted knowledge."[14] They work to produce and sustain master narratives, precisely because they refuse to be recognized as such.

What we do and how we do it are not innocent of power/knowledge relationships. Are we, without realizing it, simply reiterating and reproducing such inequitable power relations? Or are we actively rethinking them?

In so refusing a narrow definition, Trouillot brings in the lived practice of storytelling and what we do in the everyday. We are now in the domain of how we produce and reproduce, as a people of a culture, how we use historical evidence and tell stories, and also how historians within that culture write "history" books.

The process of speaking and the process of listening, once included, is a far more popular and pervasive activity than writing and reading. Indeed, sight including sound, in the forms of exhibitions, film, and electronic and digital media, move us toward a fuller deployment of how Yellow Peril representations are actually embedded at all moments of our everyday life.

And the range suggests how we are complicit and active in such processes, even if we are unaware of our involvement. Trouillot emphasizes here the processes of *public* and *commoning* historical work, not simply the work of historians as specialists writing books elaborating the work of other specialists.

REPRESSION, INNOCENCE, SPECTRES, SURPRISE

The pamphlet tradition of political protest is closer to the sounds of street corner agitation. American Federation of Labor founder Samuel Gompers was attuned to the speeches of sandlot rallies and the responses of the European immigrant and European American working man. This classic item of propaganda "Meat vs. Rice" provoked a gut response in 1902 (Figure 14). That same year, elected politicians extended the Chinese Exclusion Act indefinitely.

This historical artifact comes as a strange piece of ephemera to most U.S. citizens' eyes and ears. What an odd and funny juxtaposition of words! Like Knackfuss's seated Buddha, rice is no longer such an oddity in the American cultural experience. The language of "manhood" appears dated in an age of rhetoric about equal rights for women and lesbians/gays. And the words "Asiatic coolieism" sounds simply archaic.

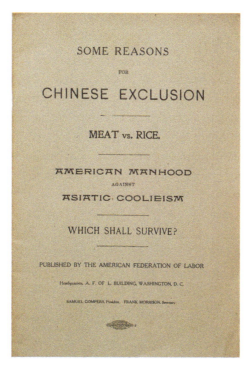

Figure 14. *Some Reasons for Chinese Exclusion, Meat vs. Rice, American Manhood Against Asiatic Coolieism, Which Shall Survive?* (Washington D.C.: American Federation of Labor, 1902). Yoshio Kishi/Irene Yah Ling Sun Collection of Asian Americana made possible in large part in memory of Dr. Wei Yu Chen, MSS 292, Series II, Box 6, folder 42. Fales Library and Special Collections, New York University.

We might distance ourselves from this clearly racist sentiment while not understanding how Americans still live the impact of this reality. Few Americans understand that the Chinese Exclusion Laws, which began in 1882, and were extended to include other Asian nationalities, continued in effect until 1968. This legacy still limits the role of Asian immigrants in the mainstream of U.S. culture today. The lack of sound bites and the obscurity of such visuals is in direct proportion to a lack of public awareness. This ignorance of our history also contributes to the cultivated sense of American innocence in global affairs.

If "Meat vs. Rice" can be understood as the first rumble accompanying Benjamin's lightning bolt, these next two historical fragments constitute the rolling thunder that continues to echo into the present. Louis Glackens's

"A Skeleton in His Closet" (Figure 15) might be legible to those aware of the antiwar and anti-imperialist tradition within the U.S. The spectre of Chinese exclusion comes to haunt Uncle Sam's "Protest Against Russian Exclusion of Jewish Americans."[15] This is a rejoinder to exclusionists—satirical, caustic, and legible in the great American cartooning tradition. It is a slapstick routine about the return of the repressed. Uncle Sam will get his comeuppance for the wrong he did. Just as the tradition of yellow perilism has become distant and silenced, so has the American tradition of anti-exclusion.

Yet today, as a piece of decontextualized ephemera falling across our sightlines, this visual primarily conveys the horror of a grotesque with long hair. The words comparing the two exclusions are exceeded by the visual fright. This skeleton is seeking revenge! If one could figure out that the hair still attached to the skull is a queue, an informed contemporary viewer might realize this haunting is that of a Chinese man. Today, the visual visceral response of "ickiness" is likely more deeply immediate, far more than

Figure 15. Louis Glackens, "A Skeleton in His Closet," *Puck*, vol. 70, no. 1818 (January 3, 1912), 2. Courtesy of the Library of Congress.

a public's legal-literary comprehension of what now appears as obscure historical trivia. Historical silencing works in odd, confounding ways.

The second rolling echo is the response of *Baohuanghui* (the Chinese Empire Reform Association), a translocal network of some 70,000 diasporic Chinese, calling for a boycott of American goods in the ports of Shanghai and Hong Kong from 1903 onward. In June 1905 a boycott handbill, circulated from their branch in Rangoon, Burma, narrates a counter-script to American yellow perilist cries. "The United States has extended the exclusion treaty in order to put an end to Chinese people's livelihood there. This is a national disgrace second to none. Everyone is furious and aggrieved ... Noble-minded people in Shanghai and Hong Kong and the charitable organizations in Guangdong province have all responded enthusiastically ... They communicated with each other through letters and telegrams to encourage one another to do a citizen's duty."[16] These protests were relatively unknown to American ears and eyes at the time and absolutely unknown today. New Yorkers, at the center of U.S. economic power, barely took note. In contrast, the impact in the port cities of China was enormous.

Indeed, Chinese nationalism and anti-imperialism emerged from such translocal struggles. Scholar and activist journalist Liang Qichao described the significance of the boycott in the streets of Shanghai. "In the last month, everyone in Shanghai has been thinking about and talking about the Exclusion Treaty. From millionaires to poor workers, millions of people are of one mind, and we must not stop until we win back our rights."[17] The noisy public talk in the streets of Shanghai was a marked contrast to the quietude and obliviousness in New York.

A third thunderous echo is historian Marc Bloch's insight about why Europe formed and then colonized so much of the Muslim world. The regions, in the sweep of what used to be called the "Dark Ages," increasingly defining themselves as Europe, separate from Eurasia, were "attacked from three sides at once: in the south by the devotees of Islam, Arabs or their Arabized subjects; in the east by Hungarians; and in the North by Scandinavians."[18] Jacqueline Kaye argues that European colonialism was itself a reaction to the Islamic spread, driven by the desire to reclaim lost territories and to invade the territories of Arab colonizers.[19] The Orient of Arabs was conflated with that of the Scythians and Central Asian nomads, and continues to be further conflated with South Asians, Southeast Asians, and Far Eastern Asians. The deafening confusions echo on.

Furthermore, the long-term consequences are quite profound. Anti-Chinese and anti-Asian racism in the "civilized" West continues to drive Asian nationalist movements from Sun Yatsen to Mahatma Gandhi to Ho Chi Minh to Muslim fundamentalists. The anti-Muslim legacy of the Crusades continues to drive a disfigured Western "common sense." Asian nationalist revolutions and ruling military regimes have defined themselves as responses to Western colonialisms and imperialist investments. In stark contrast, the American public's understanding of Chinese and Asian histories is characterized by little to no knowledge of the Asian othered, within and without.[20] Hence our regular naïve surprise at the skeletons in our national closet.

We can't afford to remain aloof and insensate. We must take notice of these ephemeral fragments and turn them into stories we tell, into truer histories we must convey. Our inability to recognize facts, collect archives, tell stories, and write histories of yellow perilism in the making of the West paralyzes those who subscribe to this way of thinking, this perilist ideology, from dealing with the reality of U.S. interventions in and representations of the long-desired and long-feared yet always imagined but not understood "Orient."

Literary scholar Shankar Raman perceptively notes "the West misunderstands itself to the degree that it overlooks what it discovered."[21] Jonathan Gil Harris delights in reminding us "Europeans invented 'Indians' and populated the world with them." We live with that confusion every day. From the translation of a river in what is now Pakistan, the Indus River, the European use of India emerged and then applied to boundaries of the European known world: India, Indonesia, the West Indies, and even to Indiana. Indians appeared everywhere. "Even after Columbus's error was corrected, the peoples of the American New World—their antiquity canceled at the stroke by that 'New'—continued to be known as Indians, as were their counterparts in the 'old' worlds of South and Southeast Asia."[22] The term became so all-purpose it was also used to label Ethiopians, and, as late as the eighteenth century, Polynesian peoples and the Maori in New Zealand. All explanatory power outside of the naming practice's own inadequacy is lost.

Raman, credited with opening up this study of "Indography," describes such reigning metaphors as a historical process in which the two Christian European metaphorical frameworks of "the cosmos" and "the voyage" were tested out by historical experience. "India's 'discovery' in the early modern era impelled a radical reconfiguration of the [Christian European] self and world." Were these inhabitants beyond their known borders "monsters" of some kind? How can they be accommodated by the prevailing cosmologies and maps? "At the same time, the conditions enabling this self-assertion also produced (and concealed) other consequential discontinuities, specifically those separating the newfound Western subject from the colonial others it 'discovered.'"[23] Hence, from the Christian cosmological understanding of the time, all peoples on the edge places of the T-O-mapped European imagination could be logically called Indians—in Asia and in the Caribbean and the Americas. Henceforth, prevailing European metaphors literally mapped themselves, via colonial "discovery" and conquest, onto the naming of "new" worlds.

Raman brings our attention to the brilliant, yet underexamined concept of philosopher Hans Blumenberg's "metaphorology."[24] The master metaphor of "the cosmos" provided early Europeans, from antiquity to the late medieval period, "a powerful metaphor for locating the human subject in relation both to divinity and the material world" that provided a coherent system of theological, astrological, and locational "answers."[25] However, this master narrative was dramatically challenged by "the voyage" of 1492. "In producing a knowledge that the ancients had not possessed, the voyages expressed a practical transformation of the relationship between human subject and world." "Truth and knowledge," consequently, demanded a different way of knowing—a new metaphor, denoting a paradigm shift.[26]

In effect, the cosmos of "the Indies" became the voyage into "the heart of darkness"—a process of colonialist discovery, description, and mastery. In this breach between metaphors, the "dark side" of the Renaissance was also "discovered."[27] Different realities and historical-cultural systems of worldmaking did not simply accept claims of European rights to discovery and possession. "As a consequence, the metaphor of the voyage came to represent a reconfigured understanding of the subject as an active producer of truth and knowledge."[28] In this Manichean colonialist clash, the European male discoverer meets his nemesis—the other Other who refuses, the "genus malignus" intent upon deceiving the superior, highbrowed, European rational man.[29] As "the West" constitutes "the East," that part of "the East" that actively resists becomes represented by an emergent paranoid and dystopic master for metaphor of modernity—that of yellow perilism.

Yet, like the ubiquitous but antiquated naming of all "new" people and places Indian and Indies, yellow perilism conjures ancient, primal fears to the service of colonialist and imperialist dysfunctions. Naïveté and self-denial result in a systemic misunderstanding of what is actually going on in the world. At one moment, somewhere in Asia is still that "Shangri-la" closest to heaven on earth, and at another moment China is pimping America, impeding Manifest Destiny.

HOW TO USE THIS BOOK

Yellow Peril! is an archival ordering of fragments based on the logic of relational historical provenance. Where did such fragments come from? What is the metaphoric, psychological, geostrategic, or immediate political genealogy of such yellow perilist artifacts? Yellow perilism, the practice, is rooted within a European Enlightenment and European colonialist worldview. Hence we are exploring the ramifications of a Eurocentric way of knowing, desiring, and exercising power. Yellow Peril practice is relational. "Yellow" to whom? "Peril" to whom?

What of the provenance of the idea of "the West" itself? Along with the Christian calendar, British imperial intellectuals set the standards against which the world was measured. Time and place for all peoples in the world have come to be dominated and universalized by Greenwich Mean Time and zero degrees longitude. As White Anglo-Saxon Protestant (WASP) political culture became White Anglo-American Protestant (WAAP) political culture, America also became Westernized, hence also gaining fears of the otherness of yellow perilism.

This book documents and comments on an ordered, historical system of how the Westernization process has formulated a villainous Yellow Peril Other to stabilize its own identity. This relational, historical view allows us to recognize the continuity of a tradition, an ongoing reinforced practice that requires updating and reiterating, generation to generation, in order to maintain a coherent nationalist political identity.

Modern archives utilize finding aids to help researchers navigate materials, and these aids help structure, make sense of, and consequently analyze and frame the collections they describe. This volume is a finding aid for the yellow perilist *mentalité* expressed in the records, documents, and things produced by the formation of Western Civilization. It is a disappeared yet omnipresent and omnipotent archive, an archive at this contemporary moment largely hidden from our everyday awareness and scrutiny. In subtle and not-so-subtle ways, it is an archive that invalidates the full humanity of the so-imagined Oriental or Asiatic Other.

It is an archive of counter-identification or disidentification: We are what they are not. As an archive of negating power, it is rude, impolite, and violating. We experience it, but like much racism we are barely aware of it. By outlining the contours of this ordered system of othering, this volume suggests ways of identifying, describing, and navigating through an inheritance of a worldview shot through with propaganda, misrepresentations, and erasures.

Yellow Peril! is divided into three parts. Part One, "The Imagined West," unpacks the mythos of "the West." Chapter One, "Decolonizing Scholarship," is a basic examination of the prevailing Western assumptions of mapping time and place onto the world. The short chapter provides a way to reorient, or better yet re-occident, our bearings in the topsy-turvy world of decolonizing what has become foundational in order to gain insights about how power as a historical process has become realized. By curating a collection of fragments that trace this historical process, via images, documents, and essays, we begin to identify hitherto shadowed moments by which intellectuals and policy makers on the western peninsula of the Eurasian landmass increasingly differentiated the region as "Europe" and "the West." Chapter Two, "Westernizing Europe," delineates how the political-cultural process of Westernization prized a unique historical and civilizational destiny in contradistinction to various lesser Others: nomadic, barbaric, deviant, and monstrous. As the regional history of Greece was later reclaimed as the basis of a Western Civilization, the Greek mapping of the world was also adopted. At that moment, "the East," "the Orient," and "Asia" became fixtures of the European imagination—the antithesis of the Westernization project. The U.S. and the Anglo-settler world have inherited this historical project, with its attending universal claims to time and space, somewhat uncritically. This chapter identifies the early and diverse origins of what was to become yellow perilism, and offers a glimmer of a more nuanced transnational, relational approach to a decolonized global history.

Part Two, "Manifest Destinies," presents how the Westernization of Europe played out conceptually as Europeans expanded their empires into the New World, Asia, the Pacific, and Africa. Chapter Three, "Geo-Racial Mapping," arranges fragments depicting the evolution of schemas of racial science rooted in colonialist Enlightenment maps of the world. Such science made sense of European imperialism and the destiny of the "West" in contrast to imagined barbarous hordes of inferior peoples presumed to be incapable of rational individuality. Many Europeans and Americans believed they had assumed the mantle of a progressive individuality first born in ancient Greece as they built modern empires in the late nineteenth century. Chapter Four, "Anglo America's 'Great Game,'" suggests how the British Empire waged what Kipling called the "Great Game" for Central and South Asia, which was then taken on by the United States after World Wars I and II. The shift from British white Anglo-Saxon Protestant to white Anglo American Protestant ideology undergirds America's "exceptional" ascendency to superpower status over what historians refer to as "the long twentieth century." Yet the seeming triumph of "the West" in this regard has been haunted by deeper fears, whose connections and genealogies have been obscured by fixations on national destiny. This triumphalism and its attending anxieties have shaped our current worldview. By historicizing this development in the context of yellow perilism, we seek to foreground the often unacknowledged role of the Pacific and "the East" in this vision of America's national destiny and its effect on polices at home and abroad. We also emphasize how deeply visceral yellow perilism as an ideology is ingrained in the political culture.

Part Three, "Indispensable Enemies," continues this nationalist history of yellow perilism within the sphere of the U.S. nation-state and U.S. global interests. In Chapter Five, "The Enemy Within," we show how the paranoid othering of various yellowized peoples, goods, and ideas extended the unresolved regional, labor, and equity issues of the U.S. Civil War. Asian laboring bodies within the U.S. were both recruited and reviled. Each was seen as a potential threat. From the passage of Chinese Exclusion in 1882 to present-day Homeland Security policies, the Asian racialized Other still drives and distorts policies, responses, and attitudes. Asians have become synonymous with overwhelming hordes who will take over America. In Chapter Six, "The Coming War," we suggest how yellow perilism provides a framework for the succession of enemies the U.S. has committed itself to countering worldwide since World War II. From Asian imperialism through Oriental Communism to Chinese Nationalism and Islamic Fundamentalism these various and ever-changing perils have maintained a remarkably consistent iconography and narrative. Yellow perilism has let such diverse threats become in effect interchangeable, encouraging the public to accept such war-making as a natural and inevitable component of the American way of life.

The Epilogue, "Uncle Sam and the Headless Chinaman," proposes a Western counter-tradition in which fundamental change can happen. "Interracial justice" requires a deep cultural reckoning, a *reconnaissance* or self-recognition, of the ways in which the paranoid tradition of the American self has to be reworked in order to cease the fantasy of the Yellow Peril. Here we present a variety of approaches challenging the binary logic of property and boundary-making. Decolonizing oneself and recognizing one's relation to Yellow Peril practices is the beginning of a liberatory shift vital to navigating a less divisive, less war-torn future.

This volume is by no means comprehensive, but it is practical, suggestive, and, we hope, inspirational—inspiring our readers to identify Yellow Peril collections and to document such artifacts. We have tried to acknowledge the sheer volume of yellow perilist material, by presenting a sweeping historical arc and including a variety of materials with which to work. In doing so, we present the possibilities of a critical archive to recoup the evidentiary function of preserving and highlighting documents of enduring historical value, but also to recognize the inherent political-analytical function of such a gathering of materials. Our interest and practice in these sorts of critical archival studies is to support a necessary ongoing process of de-silencing the facts, the archives, and the stories we tell, and ultimately decolonizing our history.

Yellow Peril! is also a transnational call for study. In addition to building local and regional archives documenting the particular forms of yellow perilist othering, this volume also makes the case for seeing yellow perilism as a lens or filter, a way of knowing the ongoing struggles of decolonizing scholarship, policies, and our political cultures.

A NOTE ON THE TEXT

We have preserved the original spelling and usage in the excerpts and fragments assembled here, but we have applied modern punctuation for ease of reading and have occasionally condensed and combined footnotes for the same reason and for the sake of space. Editors' notes and citations appear at the back of the volume as endnotes.

Part One: The Imagined West

Any storyteller or professional photographer understands that point of view is everything. What's the angle? How is the story constructed? What point of view is being visualized? If yellow perilism is part of the pervasive yet unrecognized culture of our politics, how far back does it go? And who constitutes the "us" in "us versus them"? Who constitutes the "them"?

Part One, "The Imagined West," traces yellow perilism to a "prehistory," exploring the very roots of how the Eurasian landmass became split within a Westernizing worldview: Europe became the virtuous opposite of an outdated, senilic Asia. Examined will be the local origins of the mapping of "East" and "West." These tidbits of "facts" from extant "archives" tell the "story" and "history" of Western superiority. This is a dominant, omnipresent perception that drives notions of progress and defines notions of enlightenment embedded in Western and colonialist discourses and systems of knowing today.

At the same time, the ability to track human genetic markers generationally and spatially has definitively debunked these very same prevailing notions of racialist difference. Therefore, it must be first said, "race" is a historical-cultural construct with no basis in biology. These findings definitively refute outdated but still lingering beliefs that there are distinct racial subspecies of humankind. None of us are evolutionarily closer to apes. We are not defined by subspecies of the human race. Nor are we of differing racial origins. There was but one "Eve" and "Adam" and they were in what we now call Africa over 150,000 years ago. Migrations into what is considered the "Near East" account for the subsequent various migrations northward, westward, and eastward, settling Mother Earth. Africans migrated along the Indian Ocean rim, including the islands infelicitously called Melanesia. Others migrated from the Near East northeastward across Siberia and Mongolia, ultimately across the land bridge into the Americas. Still others migrated eastward to populate South Asia, Southeast Asia, and the Pacific Islands. These numbers are hard to translate into our everyday lives. We'll unpack the formation and breaking apart of Eurasia in the coming two chapters. The key to keep in mind is that racial metaphors, master stories we tell ourselves and others to explain the world, are not in line with the latest in truth-seeking research and scholarship in bio-history, linguistic anthropology, and archaeology. Nor are colonialist attitudes in line with a global ethics and a commitment to social justice. Yellow perilism, Islamophobia, and other anti-Asian fearmongering (along with other forms of racial scapegoating), nonetheless flourish in our contemporary everyday and in the political culture.

The selected excerpts below are intended to sharply reverse the working assumptions of Western knowledge about itself and the world. The goal here is not to create an opposite truth—this would simply reinscribe a binaried moral fallacy—but to break with what we imagine we know and believe by finding a third space where differences are understood as gradations rather than starkly as "us" versus "them." This break is necessary both to debunk the Western colonial tradition and also to demonstrate that once decolonized, it is a varied history full of alternative pasts, presents, and futures that can engage with different cultures, traditions, and visions. This possibility is the key to envisioning an alternative to the deeply embedded tradition of yellow perilism in the Western imagination. Chapter One seeks to decenter what has become our "common sense" understandings of the world and how we have mapped it conceptually. Analyzing how these boundaries have shifted over time give us historical insights about how seemingly fixed realities have changed dramatically over time and place. Chapter Two offers access to some of the new scholarship that dramatically reframes and challenges what we imagine we already know. Yellow Peril has deep roots in premodern dynamics of settled and nomadic cultures.

Herodotus's fifth-century account of "The Battle of Thermopylae" is one story retold regularly in the West. Zack Snyder's film version *300* (2007), yet again, takes an ancient regional war from the Mediterranean and reintroduces it. This time it is in a powerful graphic-novelized form as a testosterone battle for all times and all places. Romantic norms of Western masculinity are elevated and contrasted to a caricatured, demeaned, binaried opposite. The films *300* (2007) and the sequel *300: Rise of an Empire* (2014) emphasize abhorrent and kinky sexuality, monstrousness, and monomaniacal power in the Persian figure of Xerxes, a nine-foot-tall "god-king" bedecked with jewelry and suggestive makeup. In this retelling of the Battle of Thermopylae, the violent, digital video game–influenced style updates and reinvests the Greek civilizational narrative over regional others into contemporary Western commercial cultural currency.

Why do such representations of Eastern evil persist, getting replayed and revived time and again? Why the fixation? Foundational questions of what we know and how we know it, and questioning how limited these framings have been, are at the heart of developing an understanding of the phenomenon of anti-Asian xenophobia.

1

Decolonizing Scholarship

All cultures tend to place themselves in the middle of their origin stories and their view of the world. In eras of European empires, Asia became its antithesis, its orientalized other. In 1744, Giambattista Vico shrewdly noted: "Every nation ... whether Greek or barbarian, has the same conceit that it before all other nations invented the comforts of human life."[1] Yet, the very formation of a European aristocracy, elites, and their institutions formed much more than an agglomeration of nations. Latin Christendom, though historically complex and fluid, became increasingly used as part of what we are calling a Westernization process. In the times of the Crusades, Christian fundamentalism, as with any warring movement, asserted a foundational purity against and amid inferior heathen and pagan cultures, which had to be won over or defeated. Later Western Atlantic-oriented Europeans during the "Enlightenment," in what J. G. A. Pocock has delineated as the "Machiavellian moment," rediscovered ancient Greek achievements and claimed that tradition, from a distant time and place, as their own.[2] Henceforth, British schoolboys studied Latin and Greek civilization as part of their collectively claimed heritage and colonial education. Part and parcel to notions of Western civilizational progress, was the conceit of racial superiority over non-white, non-Christian (and for many, non-Protestant Christian), non-property owning cultivated others. The art and politics of Latin Christendom and later European mapping encoded the mythos of itself in relation to the world around it, and its ambitious desires to bring back the riches of elsewhere.

In the mid-fifteenth century, Christendom's popes divided up the newly "discovered" non-Christian lands of the world between Portugal and Spain.

Europe's aristocratic and merchant possessions and wealth derived, increasingly, from the entangled and intermingled port and trading cultures of first, the Mediterranean, and then, the Atlantic. European civilizational advance, it was argued and believed, moved as the sun rising in the east and ever-progressing westward toward Europe, from *oriens* to *occidens*. Literal believers of the T-O map fixed a simple three-part divide between land and cultures different from our contemporary satellite notions of geographic accuracy. The sons of Noah became scattered and separated by this schema. The traffic between these divides—the goods exchanged, the peoples in movement, the ideas and practices borrowed—is alluded to. They were brothers and understood each other relationally. But the fixity of the letter "T" within the "O" certainly created a sense of a separate design from both God and aesthetic clarity. Europe was divided clearly from Asia, and both were separate from Africa.

Yet, this angular and separated interpretation of the T-O map of 1472 had not always been dominant. Alternative stories bridging distant places were also told and retold, part and parcel to what became a minor tradition but extant in the archival repertoire. Heaven, after all, appeared to be just beyond Eden, which was farther than the farthest known east. And wasn't Prester John also out there eastward? As Christendom divided the globe for Portuguese and Spanish claims, Asia, Europe, and Africa became distinct and related categories—at once geographic, religious, and civilizational.

To paraphrase legal scholar Boaventura de Sousa Santos, another historical "common sense is possible."[3] This opening chapter draws from recent scholarship that demonstrates how and when "the West" formulated its own self-conception in contradistinction to "the East." This was a long and complex process of Latin Christendom's formulating its own sense of coherence against and with various Others, all historically fluid and with different possible outcomes.[4]

These essays examine and dissect the conceits of the now dominant story of Western civilizational advancement—the march of modern, progressive, inventive societies versus the stasis of stagnant, bounded, inferior racial others; forward versus backward—constructed binary by binary over many moments in many places. Historical insight helps restore the earlier, lived nuanced relationships of these differences. Revealed are the many ways in which local and regional conflicts have led to divides that get amplified and compounded over the decades and centuries. Otherwise these binaries, when unquestioned, uncritically accept the victor's justifications for conquest, colonialism, war, and our lives as we have come to live them.

Critical counter-traditions certainly existed as minority stances, as Vico's opening quote testifies. Perhaps those living in ports, border zones, and intermingled settlements tended not to subscribe to the most vulgar claims of absolute Western superiority, yet dominant frames of reference still privilege a colonial modernist worldview. Opening the *New York Times* or the *Wall Street Journal* one cannot avoid the Western progress narrative infused in the news, coverage of business, the arts, travel, and automobiles. As esteemed Oxford anthropologist Jack Goody makes clear, such frames of reference are infused in our very notions of time, space, and measurement. How can we even write without falling into such traps?

A double strategy is needed here. First, we must understand the nature and history of either/or binaries: West or East, good or bad, civilized or uncivilized, understanding how they have been usefully abused in practices of power and knowledge-making. Reversing unquestioned meanings associated with phrases such as "Western civilization" and "human progress" is a beginning. Second, fixed notions of such universalist claims need to be understood relationally. The Enlightenment cannot be understood, for example, divorced from the age of European colonialism, euphemistically called the "Age of Discovery." Nor can Northern Italy be understood severed from its relations to Persia and the Mediterranean ports that were historically linked to Africa and Asia.

A relational understanding opens up the space for a global historical practice within which the perspectives of civilizations, regions, nations, and groups can be told.

John Kuo Wei Tchen, "Mapping Boundaries of Difference and Shared Spaces, a Visual Essay" (2013)

Mapping a sense of time and spatiality can be understood as a core human activity. This series of maps represents Christendom's T-O mappa mundi tradition that centers around the holy Christian, Jewish, and Muslim city of Jerusalem while also clearly differentiating Asia from Europe and Africa.

This is the first of a series of visual essays mapping the representation of cultural-historical difference. Rather than emphasizing the written word, these essays explicate a series of visual-historical claims and arguments.

Figure 16. T-O map, from Isidore of Seville, "Liber Etimologiarvm" (woodcut), German School, (fifteenth-century edition) f.177v / Newberry Library, Chicago, The Bridgeman Art Library.

The earliest printed example of a classical T-O map was by Günther Zainer in Augsburg, 1472, just decades before Columbus's "discovery" of the new world. Note that the Oriens, or East, is on top. With the coming "age of exploration" signaling various European expansionist ventures, the contemporary rendering of the east-west axis tips this earlier convention on its side. This map shows the continents as domains of the sons of Noah: Sem (Shem), Iafeth (Japheth) and Cham (Ham). This printed version is likely a copy of a copy from a manuscript by Isidore of Seville, who wrote in the sixth century CE. This version streamlines and abstracts other versions such as the far more ornate and detailed world depicted in the Psalter map (c. 1265) below.

The Psalter World Map, a hand-drawn illuminated map illustrating a more open set of borders and bridges, is graphically less angular in the T separations between Europe, Asia, and Africa. The Garden of Eden is herein located eastward, at the top of the map, with Heaven above that. Certainly

Figure 17. Psalter World Map, (c. 1265). Additional Ms 28681, f.9: World Map (vellum), English School, (thirteenth-century edition) / British Library, London / © British Library Board. All Rights Reserved / The Bridgeman Art Library.

these placements suggest a cosmology of East different from what was to develop and dominate. However the Psalter map also prefigured what was to become "racial science." As true with other T-O maps, the Psalter prominently featured "monsters" on its margins near the rightward coast of Africa. Furthermore, the Latinate Christian view embodied here did acknowledge the "antipodes" and wondered if Christ could have visited these distant regions or not.

Figure 18. Detail of Psalter map "monsters" on the outer, right edge of the O.

In the first century CE, Pliny the Elder recounted in his *Natural History* that the outside world was full of remarkable "monsters," including "the Nigroe, whose King hath but one eye," "the Cynamolgi, who have Heads like Dogs," and "the Artabatitae, who wander about like four-footed savage beasts." Blemmyae (men with faces in their chests), the Anthropophagi (cannibals) and the Ascians, or men without shadows. The Plinian races reappeared many times in medieval writings such as that of Isidore of Seville's *Etymologies* and the *Nuremberg Chronicle*.

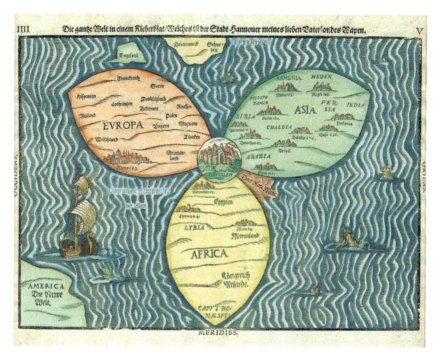

Figure 19. Cloverleaf map of the world. Heinrich Bünting, *Itinerarium Sacrae Scripturae* (1581). Later colorization. Photo: IAM / akg.

Heinrich Bünting, *Itinerarium Sacrae Scripturae*, 1581. Bünting, a Hanover-born Protestant pastor and theologian, produced this book of woodcuts mapping the world in terms of the Holy Scripture. This was a popular text reprinted and translated frequently into the seventeenth century.

Jerusalem is in the center, with America on the lower left margins. Just north of Europa is "Engeland" (England), and "Dennemarck" further above is likely a compound of Denmark and Greenland (long claimed by Denmark). This mapping clearly illustrates the imagined separation of Eurasia into two, Europe from its landed connection to Asia; and a dissolution of the Mediterranean world that linked east/west and north/south. Latin terms mark the directions outside the border of the map.

Note the contrasts between mappings of detail and complexity, making something visually "messy" versus the reductive simplicity of T-O, cloverleaf, and anthropomorphic visualizations.

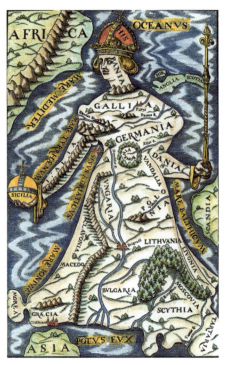

Figure 20. Europa map. Sebastian Münster, *Cosmographia* (1628). Later colorization. Photo: akg-images.

Sebastian Münster map, 1628, comparable to Bünting's earlier map, with the motif of Europa as queen Hispania. Since Bünting's Europa, such representations of Europe as a woman became a common motif of mapmakers—a precedent for European nations also represented as women, as depicted in Kaiser Wilhelm II's illustration of a threatening Japanese Buddha on a stormy dragon (Figure 9). Note, the head and crown rise westward from the lower body of eastern Europe. The dress's hem touches the metaphorical ground of "the Orient." This map-drawing convention is reiterated in Figure 53, the 1889 Great Lakes transportation "Man of Commerce" map. The orientations of where its feet stemmed from—in this case, Asia, and in the U.S. map, Europe—are significant in their reorientation from the West to the East, to the symbolic if not literal advance of Westernization westward with the arc of the sun.

In Figure 21, Bünting represents Asia "minor," "major," and what was understood as the far eastern frontier of India, as the Greek mythological

Figure 21. Pegasus as Asia. Heinrich Bünting, *Itinerarium Sacrae Scripturae* (1581). Later colorization. Courtesy of Wattis Fine Art.

figure of Pegasus.[5] Hesiod linked the name Pegasus with the word for "spring." Subsequent stories have stated wells spouted wherever Pegasus's hooves hit the ground. Hesiod also linked the creature as the bringer of thunderbolts. This layering of Mediterranean classical cosmology in a Christian visual primer also informs the motif underlying Wilhelm II's commissioned drawing—the women nations of Europe are being warned by archangel Michael of the lightning, of the stormy dangers of a Buddha sweeping toward them from the east. The horse's hind end, represented by India, as with Bünting's cloverleaf of Asia, marks the farthest parameters of his imagined cartography.

John Kuo Wei Tchen, "Mapping: Local Gone Global" (2007)[6]

The author discusses the origins of the term "Asia" and how it is represented in the T-O map.

Today "Asia," "Asian," and "Asiatic" are still common, though the latter is far less preferred. Variations such as "Asianic," "Asiaticism," "Asiatise," "Asiatall," "Asiatican," and "Asiatically" are now archaic.

Each of these terms comes loaded with particular spatial orientations rooted in temporal relationships. "Asia" has Arabic, Aramaic, Ethiopian, and Greek origins signifying "was or became beautiful," "to rise" (said of the sun), "burst forth" or "went out," and "to go out." Demetrius J. Georgacas[*] speculates that "Asia" comes from the ancient Greeks, who adopted a cuneiform Hittite word *assuva* when traveling to the western shores of Anatolia (present-day Turkish Asia) around 1235 BCE. *Assuva*, in turn, may have originally been a pre-Persian name referring to a town in Crete with an ancient temple to Zeus, or a "land or country with good soil."[†] Georgacas adds that Greek mariners first articulated a nautical boundary between the lands of the rising sun and those of the setting sun by traversing the saltwater straits of the Aegean through the Dardanelles, the Sea of Marmara, the Bosphorus, the Black Sea through the Straits of Kerch, and ending in the Sea of Azov where the landmass to the north did not have such a divide.[‡] Hence "Asia" as "east" began as a local definition.

"Asia" in these contexts appeared as separated by water from the Greek world, leading to the inaccurate *idée fixe* of a separable landmass and people. The categorization of continents that emerged from this idea reproduced early notions of racial superiority and inferiority. By the fifth century CE "Asiatic" was clearly associated with vulgarity, arbitrary authority, and luxurious splendor— qualities deemed antithetical to Greek values.[§] An early-eleventh-century T-O map reveals a clear religious cosmos of the world. A "T" within a circle divides three continents: Asia, marked "oriens," is over Europe and Africa (or Libya), which are both marked "occidens." The "T" itself represented the Nile River, believed by some to be the divide between Africa, Asia, and the Mediterranean.[¶] Noah's sons, Japheth, Shem, and Ham, were said to have dispersed to Europe, Asia, and Africa, respectively, thereby fixing their characters to geographic

---

* Demetrius J. Georgacas, "The Name *Asia* for the Continent: Its History and Origin," *Names* 17, no. 1 (1969): 33.

† Ibid., 73–5.

‡ Ibid., 71–2.

§ Denys Hay, *Europe: The Emergence of an Idea* (Edinburgh: Edinburgh University Press, 1957), 3.

¶ Ibid., Plate 1b, 54.

spaces. This dispersal suggests two traditions or more. The interconnectedness of the sons through their shared father was also expressed in Prester John stories of a Christian patriarch amid the Muslims and "pagans" of "the Orient." This legend was popular as part of the making of Europe from the twelfth through seventeenth centuries and offered a different pathway to posing Muslims and nomadic Central Asians, embodied by the "hordes" of the Khan's landed conquests. Prester John was a Christian symbol who also represented the church's reach across humanity despite distance and differences. During the centuries of Crusade warfare, this alternative vision had significance.* Indeed, in some narratives, the setting of the sun in the west marked death and decline. Yet the triumphal tradition of Western advance marks the prevailing legacy we need to now unpack.

For Western Christians the split with the Eastern orthodoxy to the east marked a key break further reinforced by the Crusades.† As their city-states became more secular and Westernizers colonized non-Christian lands westward, northward, and southward, Renaissance intellectuals retrospectively redefined "civilization" and "progress" as moving westward like the arc of the sun. A double shift took place: the West became synonymous with Christianity, and Western ideologues claimed direct continuity with Greek civilization.

In this centuries-long process, the appropriation of the word "Europe" for this Western Christian political culture also projected the imagined heathenism affixed to peoples onto the continents of "Asia" and "Africa." Intercultural influences that produced overlapping renaissances in the Mediterranean world were appropriated as *the* (one and only) Renaissance, at once Eurocentric and colonizing. Taxonomist Carl Linnaeus (1708–1778) formulated "the four races of mankind," from primitive Africans to civilized Europeans, with Asians or "Mongoloids" said to be the "semi-civilized" peoples of once-great material civilizations now stifled by despotic rulers.

In 1507 German mapmaker Martin Waldseemüller named "America" after the Italian explorer Amerigo Vespucci's charting of South America. At that moment, a fourth continent upset the tripartite T-O map, and the Americas

---

* Charles Beckingham, *Prester John, the Mongols and the Ten Lost Tribes* (London: Aldershot, 1996); Michael Uebel, *Ecstatic Transformation: On the Uses of Alterity in the Middle Ages* (New York: Palgrave/Macmillan, 2005).

† Norman Housley, *Contesting the Crusades* (Malden, MA: Blackwell Publishing, 2006).

became the place where populations—indigenous, Africans, Europeans, and Asians—would intermingle.

Given this long and complex history, the challenges for American cultural studies scholarship and practice are numerous. A thorough critique of Eurocentric knowledge needs to continue and be extended into curricula. The contestation of values and meanings is critical to our future collective well-being. Like other keywords of these globalized struggles, it is the fate of "Asian" to be contested locally and regionally—in contending, politicized practices of naming.

Jack Goody, "The Theft of History" (2006)[7]

While in his eighties and nineties, anthropologist Jack Goody has produced book after book challenging the assumptions of Eurocentric scholarship. This excerpt from The Theft of History *offers a compelling reframing of western European notions of time, space, and periodization. Goody's work exemplifies how decolonization work can be taken up from many locations—including at the centers of empire's universities.*

Since the beginning of the nineteenth century, the construction of world history has been dominated by western Europe, following their presence in the rest of the world as the result of colonial conquest and the Industrial Revolution …

The current dimensions of both time and space were laid down by the West. That was because expansion throughout the world required time-keeping and maps which provided the frame of history, as well as of geography. Of course, all societies have had some concepts of space and time around which to organize their daily lives. These concepts became more elaborate (and more precise) with the advent of literacy which provided graphic markers for both dimensions. It is the earlier invention of writing in Eurasia that gave its major societies considerable advantages in the calculation of time, in creating and developing maps as compared with oral Africa, for example, rather than some inherent truth about the way the world is organized spatiotemporally.

The very calculation of time in the past, and in the present too, has been appropriated by the west. The dates on which history depends are measured before and after the birth of Christ (BCE and CE). The recognition of other eras, relating to the Hegira, to the Hebrew or to the Chinese New Year, is relegated to the margins of historical scholarship and of international usage. One aspect of this theft of time within these eras was of course the concepts of the century and of the millennium themselves, again concepts of written cultures.

The monopolization of time takes place not only with the all-inclusive era, that defined by the birth of Christ, but also with the everyday reckoning of years, months, and weeks. The year itself is a partly arbitrary division. We use the sidereal cycle, others a sequence of twelve lunar periods ... There is, in fact, nothing more "logical" about the sidereal year, which Europeans use than about the lunar reckoning of Islamic and Buddhist countries. It is the same with the European division into months. The choice is between arbitrary years or arbitrary months. Our months have little to do with the moon, indeed the lunar months of Islam are definitely more "logical." There is a problem for every calendrical system of integrating star or seasonal years with lunar months. In Islam the year is adjusted to the months; in Christianity the reverse holds. In oral cultures both the seasonal count and the moon count can operate independently, but writing forces a kind of compromise.

The week of seven days is the most arbitrary unit of them all. In Africa one finds the equivalent of a "week" of three, four, five, or six days, with markets to correspond. In China it was ten days. Societies felt the need for some regular division smaller than the month for frequent cyclical activities such as local markets, as distinct from annual fairs. The duration of these units is completely conventional. The notion of a day and a night clearly corresponds to our everyday experience but once again the further subdivision into hours and minutes exists only on our clocks and in our minds; they are quite arbitrary.[*]

The different ways of reckoning time in literate society all had an essentially religious framework, offering as their point of reference the life of the prophet, the redeemer, or the creation of the world. These points of

---

[*] Jack Goody, "The Social Organization of Time," in *The Encyclopaedia of the Social Sciences* (New York: Macmillan, 1968).

reference have continued to be relevant, with those of Christianity becoming, as the result of conquests, colonization, and world domination not only the West's but the world's; the seven-day week, the Sunday day of repose, the yearly festivals of Christmas, Easter, Halloween are now international ...

When Britain became internationally dominant, the coordinates of space turned around the Greenwich meridian in London; the West Indies and largely the East Indies were created by European concerns, as well of course as by European orientations, European colonialism, European expansion overseas ...

Mercator (1512–1594) was one of the Flemish mapmakers who profited from the arrival in Florence of a Greek copy of Ptolemy's *Geography*, coming from Constantinople but written in Alexandria in the second century CE. The treatise was translated into Latin and published in Vicenza ... That work arrived at the time of the first circumnavigation of the globe and the coming of the printing press, both important factors in mapmaking. The "distortion of space" ... occurred because orbs have to be flattened for the printed page and the projection is an attempt to reconcile the sphere and the plane.* But the "distortion" took on a specifically European slant that has dominated modern mapmaking throughout the world.

Latitude was defined in relation to the equator. But longitude posed different problems, because there was no fixed starting point. Yet one was needed, because of attempts to reckon time for navigation, which became more urgent with the development of frequent long-distance voyages. Research at the Royal Observatory at Greenwich, near London, facilitated by the work of the clockmaker, John Harrison (1693–1776), who built a clock that was accurate on ships at sea, meant that eventually in 1884 the completely arbitrary meridian of Greenwich was chosen as the basis of the calculation of longitude as well as for the calculation of time (Greenwich Mean Time) throughout the world ...

Until recent centuries, Europe did not occupy a central position in the known world, though it did so temporarily with the emergence of classical Antiquity. Only since the Renaissance, with the mercantile activities of first the Mediterranean and then the Atlantic powers, did Europe begin

---

* Nicholas Crane, *Mercator: The Man Who Mapped the Planet* (London: Phoenix, 2003).

to dominate the world, firstly with its expansion of trade, then through conquest and colonization. Its expansion meant that its notion of space, developed in the context of Christianity, were imposed upon the rest of the world ...

The "theft of history" is not only one of time and space, but of the monopolization of historical periods ... That beginning is understandable because for later Europe the Greek and Roman experience represented the very dawn of "history," with the adoption of alphabetic writing (before writing all was prehistory, the sphere of archaeologists rather than historians)* ... One of the first subjects of Greek writing was the war against Persia which led to the distinction made in evaluative terms between Europe and Asia, with profound consequences for our intellectual and political history ever since.[†] To the Greeks the Persians were "barbarian," characterized by tyranny rather than democracy. This was of course a purely ethnocentric judgment, fuelled by the Greco-Persian war. For example the supposed decline of the Persian empire from the reign of Xerxes (485–465 BCE) arises from the vision centered upon Greece and Athens; it is not borne out by Elamite documents from Persepolis, Akkadian from Babylonia, nor Aramaic documents from Egypt, quite apart from archaeological evidence.[‡] In fact the Persians were as "civilized" as the Greeks, especially among their elite. And they were the main way in which knowledge coming from literate Ancient Near Eastern societies was transmitted to the Greeks.[§]

The very notion that what occurred in the east represented "Asiatic exceptionalism"[¶] and that the Western sequence of events was "normal" embodies an unwarranted European assumption, based on the vantage point of the nineteenth century, which asserts that it pointed to the only

---

* Jack Goody and Ian Watt, "The Consequences of Literacy," *Comparative Studies in Society and History* 5 (1963): 304–45; M. I. Finley, *Early Greece: The Bronze and Archaic Ages* (London: Chatto & Windus, 1970), 6.

† Edward Said, *Orientalism* (New York: Vintage, 1995), 56–7.

‡ Pierre Briant, "History of the Persian Empire, 550–330 BC," *Forgotten Empire: The World of Ancient Persia,* ed. John E. Curtis & Nigel Tallis (London: British Museum, 2005), 14.

§ Alexandra Villing, "Persia and Greece," *Forgotten Empire*, 36.

¶ [Editor's note: Goody's use of "Asiatic exceptionalism" is referred to in this volume with older, even more normative references, such as "Asiatic despotism" and "the Asiatic mode of production."]

road to "capitalism." And that idea arises from a conflation of capitalism, in the broad sense in which the historian Braudel often employed the term, with the development of industrial production, a much more specific economic event, often seen as involving "productive investment" (though that is a general factor even in agricultural societies). While western Europe itself became "exceptional" in the nineteenth century, it is not apparent that earlier on it was out of line with other major civilizations, except in terms of its advantages in the era of the "Great Voyages" perhaps related to technical developments in "guns and sails" and following its adoption of printing long practiced in China, to an alphabetic script using movable type. That development permitted the more rapid circulation (and accumulation) of information, an advantage which the Chinese and Arabic civilizations had earlier enjoyed because of their use of paper, and in the first case of printing.

The effect of differentiating the Ancient from the Asiatic development of post–Bronze Age civilization creates an explanatory problem relating to that supposed divergence. At the same time it pushes back the question of the origin of capitalism to the supposed roots of European culture. Because already in Antiquity, according to many classicists, Europe was pursuing the right path in that direction, whereas Asia had gone astray. Until recently that was the view of the majority of "humanists" who saw European culture as springing from the achievements of Roman and Greek society in a quite unique way. These achievements have sometimes been put down to "Greek genius," as did Burkhardt in a manner that is difficult to discuss from a straightforward historical or sociological point of view. Sometimes they have been seen as connected with the invention of the alphabet in a way that neglects the Asiatic (Semitic) roots of systematic phonetic transcription as well as the very considerable achievements of other systems of writing.[*] Sometimes Greek science (or logic) is given a unique status with regard to later developments, an idea that would seem to have been refuted by Needham's encyclopedic work on *Science and Civilization in China*.[†8] Each of

---

* Jack Goody, *The Domestication of the Savage Mind* (Cambridge: Cambridge University Press, 1977).

† Joseph Needham, ed., *Science and Civilization in China* (Cambridge: Cambridge University Press, 1954); G. E. R. Lloyd, *Magic, Reason and Experience: Studies in the Origin and Development of Greek Science* (Cambridge: Cambridge University Press, 1979).

these factors appeals to some extent to the means of communication and made some contribution to later developments at the time of the Renaissance but it is difficult to accept a categorical distinction in the levels of achievement between East and West, Europe and Asia, before that period. Indeed most would accept that until then cultural and economic attainments were not greatly different and that mercantile "capitalism" urban cultures, and literate activity were present elsewhere at least to the same degree.

"Hemispheres of the Globe" (1910)

In October 1884 delegates from Liberia, Turkey, Great Britain, France, Italy, Austria-Hungary, the Netherlands, Denmark, Germany, Sweden, Switzerland, Spain, Brazil, Colombia, Venezuela, Chile, Santo Domingo, Paraguay, El Salvador, Mexico, Russia, Japan, Hawaii, and the U.S. met in Washington to decide on a universal day and Prime Meridian (0). They chose the Greenwich Meridian running through the Royal Naval Observatory supposedly because more commercial traffic used that meridian for navigational purposes than any other.

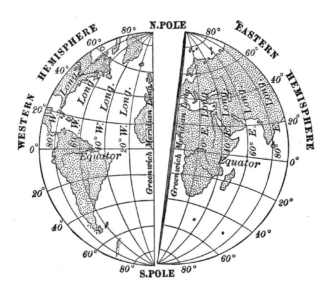

Figure 22. "Hemispheres of the Globe." Ralph S. Tarr and Frank M. McMurry, *New Geographies* (New York: The Macmillan Company, 1910), 203. Courtesy of the New York Public Library.

Martin W. Lewis and Kären E. Wigen, "Where Is The West? Where Is The East?" (1997)[9]

Seeking to formulate a more rigorous and less biased understanding of mapping and geography, Lewis and Wigen further challenge us to reframe our understanding of what has been considered "the East" by "the West." If cartographic mapping has been a tool of colonialist expansion, so too can remapping be a tool of undoing such mythos and challenging prevailing assumptions. Rather than understanding "the West" as a set of absolute, fixed locations, this essay helps us to understand this framing as historically shifting and dynamic. In this sense, Europe became separated from Eurasia in a Westernizing process.

The East-West division is many centuries old,[*] and has had at least three distinct referents. While these referents have followed each other in historical development, all remain in current use. Like other metageographical categories, the spatial designation of the West remains unstable and can be subtly shifted by different authors to fit their particular arguments (see map).[†]

The original and persistent core of the West has always been Latin Christendom, derived ultimately from the Western Roman Empire—with (ancient) Greece included whenever the search for origins goes deeper.[‡] As the Hungarian scholar Jenő Szűcs shows, the most significant historical divide across Europe was that separating the Latin church's *Europa Occident* from the Orthodox lands of the Byzantine and Russian spheres. Since shortly after its inception in the Middle Ages, the "Western" cultural area associated with

---

* Raymond Schwab, *The Oriental Renaissance: Europe's Rediscovery of India and the East, 1680–1880* (New York: Columbia University Press, 1984), 1; Schwab dates the East-West divide back to the period of the Roman Empire.

† Even single authors not uncommonly slide from one vision of the West to another in order to maintain the thread of tenuous arguments. [For example,] Theodore Von Laue usually limits the West to Britain and France (with the United States joining the club after World War I), but at one point he explicitly defines the region as including all of Europe—even though he continues to exclude western (European) Russia in practice; Theodore Von Laue, *The World Revolution of Westernization* (New York: Oxford University Press, 1987), 35.

‡ On the positioning and repositioning of the Greeks along the East-West axis, see Anthony Smith, *The Ethnic Origins of Nations* (Oxford: Blackwell, 1986), 203.

Latin Christianity has encompassed central as well as western Europe.* But as we will see below, central Europe's status in the West has been unstable. In particular, the far eastern frontier of church lands (i.e., Poland, Hungary, Croatia, and environs) has often been seen as a transitional zone between West and East,† and one can trace back to the Enlightenment the notion that all of Europe lying to the east of Germany constitutes a separate buffer zone, intermediary between Asia and the West—and between barbarism and civilization.‡

Following the European diaspora of the sixteenth through nineteenth centuries, in any case, divisions within European Christendom began to recede in importance.§ In their stead, the idea of a supra-European West, encompassing European settler colonies across the Atlantic, increasingly took hold. This sense of an expanded West was greatly strengthened after World War II. The United States and Canada had long been regarded as an overseas annex of European civilization (just as Australia and New Zealand formed distant outposts), but with Europe now sundered by the Iron Curtain, the Atlantic community began to displace western Europe as the primary geographical referent of the West.¶ Leftist opponents of Euro-American neo-imperialism promoted this vision as much as Cold Warriors, shifting the value signs but

---

* Robert Bartlett, *The Making of Europe: Conquest, Colonization, and Cultural Change, 950–1350* (Princeton, NJ: Princeton University Press, 1993).

† Jenő Szűcs, "The Three Historical Regions of Europe," *Acta Historica Academiae Scientiarum* 19 (1983), 133, 156.

‡ Larry Wolff, *Inventing Eastern Europe: The Map of Civilization on the Mind of Enlightenment* (Stanford, CA: Stanford University Press, 1994).

§ During the Protestant Reformation, however, the East-West division was occasionally mapped upon [the] new split within Western Christendom. In Spenser's Protestant imagery, for example, the pope himself was portrayed as a figure of Oriental tyranny [Ellis Goldberg, "Smashing Idols and the State: The Protestant Ethic and Egyptian Sunni Radicalism," in *Comparing Muslim Societies*, ed. Juan R. I. Cole (Ann Arbor, MI: University of Michigan Press, 1992), 217].

¶ Jacques Rupnik, "Central Europe or Mitteleuropa," *Eastern Europe ... Central Europe ... Europe*, ed. Stephen R. Graubard (Boulder, CO: Westview Press, 1991), 233–65; A common post–World War II definition of the West was Europe (less Russia and its allies), the Americas, Australia, and South Africa [see, for example, Alfred Weber, *Farewell to European History (Or the Conquest of Nihilism)*, trans. R. F. C. Hull (New Haven, CT: Yale University Press, 1948), 2].

retaining the category* ... At the same time, however, as David Slater notes, the vision of the West being propagated was based essentially on a "selective reading of the history of [only] the United States and Britain."[†]

Finally, a third and still broader notion of the West has arisen since the 1960s to become widespread in journalism and popular use. This version casts aside all geographical moorings to become simply a proxy for the developed world. Newspaper headlines, for example, occasionally refer to the heads of state in the G7 forum as "Western powers"—overlooking the fact that one member, Japan, is physically and culturally rooted in what used to be considered the extreme East. The implicit contention is that Japan has been Westernized simply by becoming rich and powerful.[‡] Similar assumptions lie behind characterizations of modern technological artifacts as items of "Western culture"—as though automobiles and soft drinks were inherently of the West, wherever they might be produced or consumed. A recent newspaper story, for example, claims that "Western culture flourishes in a changed Cambodia" on the grounds that "Mercedes, Peugeots and Toyotas glide alongside trishaws and water buffalo, running almost all the Spartan Soviet-made Ladas out of town."[§] The only way to make sense of this passage is to accept a dubious definition of non-Westernness as backwardness (manifested in everything from animal-drawn carts to cars made in Russia), while glossing all things modern and sophisticated, including Japanese Toyotas, as Western[¶] ...

---

* Only with the rise of the pacifist Green movement in Germany in the 1980s was this vision seriously challenged. All that these new voices did, however, was to revert to a strictly continental framework (see Rupnik, 255).

† David Slater, "Trajectories of Development Theory: Capitalism, Socialism and Beyond," *Geographies of Global Exchange*, ed. R. J. Johnston et al. (Oxford: Blackwell, 1995), 67.

‡ A recent example of this maneuver can be seen in the geographical work of Gearóid Ó. Tuathail and Timothy W. Luke, "Present at the (Dis)integration: Deterritorialization and Reterritorialization in the New Wor(l)d Order," *Annals of the Association of American Geographers* 84 (1994), 391, who describe Lester Thurow's *Head to Head: The Coming Economic Battle Among Japan, Europe, and America* (New York: Morrow, 1992) as a book contending "that the real conflicts will be over who is 'the best in the West.'"

§ "Western Culture Flourishes in a Changed Cambodia," *Raleigh News and Observer*, May 26th, 1993.

¶ One can, of course, put an opposite moral spin on the same idea. Consider for

Even as Westernness has shifted from a purely spatial to a quasi-temporal category, the other half of this global pair has undergone a similar transmutation, giving rise to that essentially aspatial abstraction, the Third World. This term has its own complicated history, and deserves a more extended treatment than is possible here ... Whenever it is convenient, the term *West* is still contrasted with a supposed *East*, whether that be defined in cultural or geopolitical terms. It is to the tortured history of the latter category that our attention now turns.

The Orient began its career in the eastern Mediterranean, at a time when India was to Europeans the eastern limit of the known world and China little more than a rumor.[10] Its original referent consisted essentially of Southwest Asia. Prior to the arrival of Islam, the Orient effectively comprised the eastern variant of a common cultural and economic region centered on the Mediterranean Sea.[*] After the Arab conquests of the seventh and eighth centuries, however, the Orient took on new meaning as the alien cultural realm against which Europeanness was denied. Its physical location did not immediately change; from the Middle Ages through the Enlightenment, Orientalists were typically philologists who worked with Arabic, Syrian, Coptic, and Hebrew sources (only the more adventuresome setting their sights as far east as Persia). But as the Orient became synonymous with Islam, its referent began to expand out of the eastern Mediterranean. Only thus could Morocco, most of which lies to the west of England, be subsumed under the rubric of Oriental civilization.

It was with the expansion of European colonial networks into the Indian Ocean and South China Sea that the conceptual Orient began to push eastward. To be sure, what is now called Southwest Asia remained for a long time the primary focus of Orientalist scholarship. As recently as 1924, a book entitled *The Occident and the Orient* could discuss only Arabs, Turks, and Indians

---

example, Benjamin Barber's comments on Japanese electronic games: "The Gameboys are stealth cultural networks reaching into Russian homes and children's minds with a steady diet of Western games, comic characters, and attitudes about competition, violence, consumption, and winning" [Benjamin R. Barber, *Jihad vs. McWorld* (New York: Times Books, 1995), 254].

[*] Discussed in John M. Steadman, *The Myth of Asia* (New York: Simon and Schuster, 1969), 42–3.

in the latter category.* But in the course of the 1800s, according to Raymond Schwab,[11] India gradually displaced the Levant as the primary subject of Orientalist research, with China beginning to emerge clearly on the map as well. Encompassing such a vast zone into a single regional category was seldom questioned. While many scholars differentiated the "hither" (more familiar) East of Southwest Asia and North Africa from the "farther" (more exotic) East of India and China, all such distinctions remained secondary to the opposition between the Orient as a whole and the dynamic, restless West ...

A possible cause of this eastward displacement of the Orient may be found in the rise of biological criteria as the basis for partitioning humanity. Most inhabitants of the eastern Mediterranean look more European than Chinese, and in the "racial science" of the early twentieth century, they were increasingly classified as Caucasians (although Turkish-speaking peoples occasionally appeared as "Mongolians"). Oriental peoples, by contrast, came to be defined by most lay observers as those with a single eye fold. It is perhaps on this grounds that Burma (Myanmar) continues to be thought of as Oriental, while India is usually excluded. This pseudo-racial Orient is now well entrenched in public perceptions. In consequence, the lingering scholarly tradition of referring to the area between Morocco and Iran as the Orient has come to seem quaintly archaic.

The portion of the earth denoted by the term *West* varies tremendously from author to author and from context to context. In Figure 23, the area enclosed by a heavy black line is what has been call the West: 1) One extreme incarnation, where the West includes only England ("The Wogs begin at Calais," as an old racist, xenophobic refrain has it). 2) The standard minimal West, which is essentially Britain, France, the Low Countries, and Switzerland. As interpreted by Thomas Mann, this West is basically centered on France. 3) The historical West of medieval Christendom, circa 1250. 4) The West of the Cold War Atlantic alliance, or Europe and its "settler colonies" (with Japan often included as well). 5) The greater "cultural" West. By the criteria of language, religion, and "high culture," Latin America and the areas of concentrated European settlement in South Africa

---

* Valentine Chirol, *The Occident and the Orient* (Chicago: University of Chicago Press, 1924), 5.

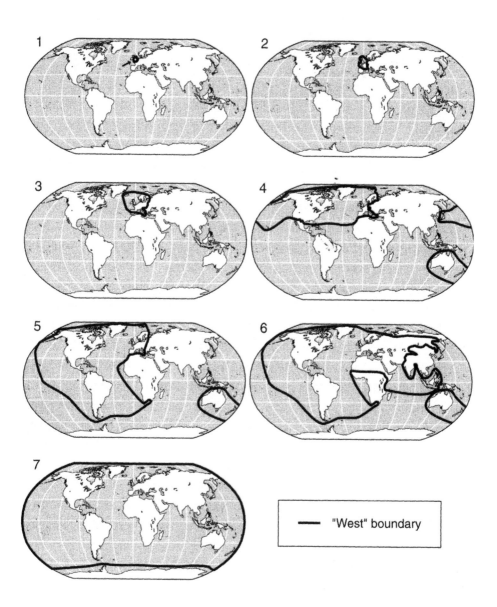

Figure 23. Seven Versions of the "West."

are added to the West. The Philippines is sometimes included here as well. (Those more concerned with "race," on the other hand, are inclined to add only Argentina, Uruguay, and southern Brazil.) 6) The maximum West of the eco-radical and New Age spiritual imagination. In this formulation, all areas of Christian and Islamic heritage are included. 7) The global (future?) West of modernization. See, for instance, Arnold Toynbee's cartography showing the entire globe as under Western hegemony in one form or another, whether political, "associative" (India, Iran, Ethiopia), or "in the heterodox form of Communism."*

Linda Tuhiwai Smith, "Positional Superiority of Western Knowledge" (2012)[12]

Gayatri Spivak famously asked scholars who sought to present the point of view of those at the margins of power and its institutions of higher learning, "Can the subaltern speak?" Part and parcel to this difficulty has been the ways in which systems of knowing and not knowing, evidences and absences, are embedded in hierarchies of what's considered worth knowing and worth archiving. Who speaks, and who is not listened to, is at the root of her provocation. The use of the English language itself to debunk the phenomenon of yellow perilism is itself full of perils that tend to reinscribe stereotypes and standard assumptions. As critics of colonizers, racists, and anti-Semites have long observed, decolonizing implicates the very language of colonizing norms, challenging us to unlock the hidden, unspoken meanings of the same words. Walking this tightrope with much finesse, this excerpt by scholar Linda Tuhiwai Smith offers a foundational critique, from a feminist Maori perspective, of Western knowledge claims and impacts. This excerpt further demonstrates the double and triple critiques necessary in the process of naming, unpacking, and re-envisioning foundational assumptions. Yet, this radically Othered vantage lends Smith extra-critical insight, what scholars refer to as "epistemic privilege" about the Western civilizational project that excludes indigenous grounded knowledge frameworks, past and present.

---

* Arnold J. Toynbee, *A Study of History*, vol. 2 (London: Oxford University Press, 1934–61 [1959]), 192–3.

Notions about the Other, which already existed in the European imagination, were recast within the framework of Enlightenment philosophies, the industrial revolution and the scientific "discoveries" of the eighteenth and nineteenth centuries. When discussing the scientific foundations of Western research, the indigenous contribution to these foundations is rarely mentioned. To have acknowledged their contribution would, in terms of the rules of research practice, be as legitimate as acknowledging the contribution of a variety of plant, a shard of pottery or a "preserved head of a native" to research. Furthermore, according to Bazin, "Europeans could not even imagine that other people could ever have done things before or better than themselves."* The objects of research do not have a voice and do not contribute to research or science. In fact, the logic of the argument would suggest that it is simply impossible, ridiculous even, to suggest that the object of research can contribute to anything. An object has no life force, no humanity, no spirit of its own, so therefore "it" cannot make an active contribution. This perspective is not deliberately insensitive; it is simply that the rules did not allow such a thought to enter the scene. Thus, indigenous Asian, American, Pacific, and African forms of knowledge, which began to be recorded in some detail by the seventeenth century, were regarded as "new discoveries" by Western science.† These discoveries were commodified as property belonging to the cultural archive and body of knowledge of the West.‡

The eighteenth and nineteenth centuries also constituted an era of highly competitive "collecting." Many indigenous people might call this "stealing" rather than "collecting." This included the collecting of territories, of new species of flora and fauna, of mineral resources and of cultures …

The idea that collectors were actually rescuing artifacts from decay and destruction, and from indigenous peoples themselves, legitimated practices which also included commercial trade and plain and simple theft. Clearly, in terms of trade indigenous peoples were often active participants, in some

* Maurice Bazin, "Our Sciences, Their Science," *Race and Class* 34, no. 4 (June 1993), 35–6.

† Susantha Goonatilake, "Colonies: Scientific Expansion (and Contraction)," *Review* (Fernand Braudel Center) V, no. 3 (Winter 1982), 413–36.

‡ Michael Adas, *Machines as the Measure of Men: Science, Technology, and Ideologies of Western Dominance* (Ithaca, NY: Cornell University Press, 1989).

cases delivering "made to order" goods. The different agendas and rivalries of indigenous groups were also known to have been incorporated into the commercial activities of Europeans. Hence, muskets could be traded and then used to pursue traditional enemies or one group of people could be used to capture and assist in the enslavement of another group who were also their traditional rivals ...

It is important to remember, however, that colonialism was not just about collection. It was also about re-arrangement, re-presentation and re-distribution. For example, plant species were taken by Joseph Banks for the Royal Botanic Gardens at Kew—a collection point where they could be "grown, studied, and disbursed to the colonial stations, a center of plant transfers on the scientific level, and of the generation and publication of knowledge about plants."[*] The British Empire became a global laboratory for research and development. New species of plants and animals were introduced to the colonies to facilitate development and to "strengthen" indigenous species. This point is worth remembering as it contrasts with the view, sometimes referred to as a diffusionist explanation, that knowledge, people, flora, and fauna simply disbursed themselves around the world. This botanical colonization had already been successfully carried out in other places: for example, maize, sweet potatoes, and tobacco from South America had been widely distributed. At the centre of this collection and distribution network was the imperial "home" country. The colonies were peripheral satellites which gained access to these new knowledges and technologies through "recourse to the writings of authors in the center."[†] One effect of this system of redistribution was the interference caused by new species to the ecologies of their new environments and the eventual extinction of several species of bird and animal life ... [‡]

Among the significant consequences of ecological imperialism—carried by humans, as well as by plants and animals—were the viral and bacterial diseases that devastated indigenous populations. This devastation or genocide

---

[*] Lucile H. Brockaway, *Science and Colonial Expansion: The Role of the British Royal Botanical Gardens* (New York: Academic Press, 1979), 187.

[†] Goonatilake, "Colonies," 432.

[‡] Alfred W. Crosby, "Biotic Change in Nineteenth-Century New Zealand," *Review* (Fernand Braudel Center) 9, no. 3 (Winter 1986), 325–7.

was, in the accounts of many indigenous peoples, used deliberately as a weapon of war ... There were several ideologies that legitimated the Western impact on indigenous health and well-being. These supported racial views already in place but which in the later nineteenth century became increasingly legitimated by the "scientific" view of social Darwinism. The concept of the "survival of the fittest," used to explain the evolution of species in the natural world, was applied enthusiastically to the human world. It became a very powerful belief that indigenous peoples were inherently weak and therefore, at some point, would die out. There were debates about how this could be prevented, for example, through miscegenation and cultural assimilation, and whether this, in fact, was "desirable." Judgments on these issues circled back or depended upon prior considerations as to whether the indigenous group concerned had souls, could be saved, and also could be redeemed culturally ...

[T]here were also state policies (federal, provincial, and local) of "benign neglect" that involved minimal intervention (the "infected blanket" strategy) while people suffered and died. There were also more proactive policies based around such ideas as "Manifest Destiny" that sanctioned the taking of indigenous lands by any means ... Aboriginal activist Bobbi Sykes has an "acid test" for the Western impact on indigenous health that consists of two lists: one a list of diseases introduced by Europeans to Aboriginal people, the other a list of diseases introduced by Aboriginal people to Europeans. There are no items listed on the second list. That empty space tells a very potent story.*

The globalization of knowledge and Western culture constantly reaffirms the West's view of itself as the center of legitimate knowledge, the arbiter of what counts as knowledge and the source of "civilized" knowledge ... For indigenous peoples ... the real lesson to be learned is that we have no claim whatsoever to civilization. It is something which has been introduced from the West, by the West, to indigenous peoples, for our benefit and for which we should be duly grateful.

---

* Roberta B. Sykes, *Black Majority* (Hawthorn, Australia: Hudson, 1989), 185.

Fernando Coronil, "Occidentalism and Modernity" (1996)[13]

Political anthropologist Fernando Coronil builds upon the insights of Edward Said about Occidentalism and links it to the contemporary realm of neoliberal globalization. Here, Coronil extends the problem of Occidentalism into an analysis that is also useful for North/South Americas' reframings of interrelated political economies and political cultures. This implies a more complex reterritorialized and convoluted era in which international, cosmopolitan "color-blind" elites float above the mass of fragmented, "balkanized" Others living in "pockets" of aspiring middle classes, and various degraded "primitives" and "semi-civilized" cultures.

HISTORY AND THE FETISHIZATION OF GEOGRAPHY

If Occidentalism is an imperial malady, one of its major symptoms is the ongoing reproduction of a colonial Self-Other polarity that mystifies the present as much as the past and obscures its potential for transformation. In his last book, Nicos Poulantzas argued that states establish a "peculiar relationship between history and territory, between the spatial and the temporal matrix."* Taking the nation as his fundamental unit, he characterized the unity of modernity in terms of the intersection of temporal and spatial dimensions: "national unity or modern unity becomes a historicity of a territory and territorialization of a history"† ...

The historicization of territories takes place through the obscuring of their history; territories are largely assumed as the fixed, natural ground of local histories. The territorialization of histories, in turn, occurs through their fixation in nonhistorical, naturalized territories. As a consequence, the histories of interrelated peoples become territorialized into bounded spaces. Since these spaces appear as being produced naturally, not historically, they serve to root the histories of connected peoples in separate territories and to sever the links between them. Thus, the illusion is created that their identities are the result of independent histories rather than the outcome

---

* Nicos Poulantzas, *State, Power, Socialism* (London: New Left Books, 1978), 114.
† Ibid., 114.

of historical relations. There is a dual obscuring. The histories of various spaces are hidden,* and the historical relations among social actors or units are severed.†

In other words, history and geography are fetishized. As with commodities, the results of social-historical relations among peoples appear as intrinsic attributes of naturalized, spatialized, bounded units. Although Poulantzas focused on nations, we could consider these units to be groups of nations or supranational entities: the West, the Occident, the third world, the East, the South, as well as localized intranational subunits, such as peasants, ethnic "minorities," "slum dwellers," the "homeless," forms of "communalism," and so forth. With the generalization of commodity relations, modes of reification involved in commodity fetishism radiate from the realm of the production of things to the production of social identities. Typical markers of collective identities, such as "territory," "culture," "history," or "religion," appear as autonomous entities. Identified by these markers, interconnected peoples come to lead separate lives whose defining properties appear to emerge from the intrinsic attributes of their "histories," "cultures," or "motherlands." As commodity fetishism becomes deeply rooted in society, it works as a cultural schema that permeates other sociocultural domains. As with commodities, the material, thinglike, tangible form of geographical entities becomes a privileged medium to represent the less tangible historical relations among peoples. Through geographic fetishism, space is naturalized and history is territorialized. Thus, the West is constituted as an imperial fetish, the imagined home of history's victors, the embodiment of their power. Every society represents other societies as part of the process of constructing its own collective identity, but each does so in ways that reflect its unique historical trajectory and cultural traditions.

---

* For this discussion, I find useful de Certeau's conception of "space" as a "practiced place"; Michel de Certeau, *The Practice of Everyday Life* (Berkeley, CA: University of California Press, 1988), 117.

† This point is supported by the pioneering work of African and African American scholars who have discussed the erasure of links between Greece and Africa in dominant historiography (for example, C. A. Diop, *The African Origin of Civilization: Myth or Reality?* [Westport, CT: L. Hill, 1974]) as well as by Martin Bernal's forceful argument in *Black Athena* (New Brunswick, NJ: Rutgers University Press, 1987).

What distinguishes Occidentalism as an ethnocentric style of representation is that it is linked to the West's effective global dominance. While this linkage raises a number of questions concerning the relationship between Western knowledge about the world and power over it, it must be noted that this dominance is always partial and that it takes place through processes of transculturation which also transform the West. Westernization entails not the homogenization of the world's societies under the force of capitalism but their reciprocal transformation under diverse historical conditions. In this light, capitalism appears not as a self-identical system that emanates from the West and expands to the periphery but as a changing ensemble of world-wide relations that assumes different forms in specific regional and national contexts.

The nineteenth-century thinkers who insightfully examined the making of the modern world before its categories became second nature initiated a polemical discussion of the relationship between modernity and capitalism. Yet it is striking that even divergent ideological positions often coincide in their assumption that the West is the source and locus of modernity. If we expand our focus so as to bring the West and the non-West within a unified field of vision that encompasses the historical terrain of their mutual formation,[14] the modern world appears larger and more complex, formed by universalizing and innovating impulses that continuously redefine geographical and cultural boundaries and set new against old, Self against Other. If the West is involved in the creation of its obverse and the modern is unimaginable without the traditional, the West's preoccupation with alterity can be seen as being constitutive of modernity itself rather than as an incidental by-product of Western expansionism. The examination of Western representations of Otherness, from the perspective of a critique of Occidentalism, could then be encompassed within an interrogation of why Otherness has become such a peculiarly modern concern.

Premised on a teleology of progress, capitalist development is embodied in reified institutions and categories. Cultural constructs such as the West and the third world come to acquire, like a commercial brand, an independent objective existence as well as the semblance of a subjective life. The West comes to be identified with leading capitalist nations, the economy with the market, democracy with universal elections, difference with Otherness. Embodying the contradictions of capitalist society, these formations help shape the landscape within which, with mesmerizing allure despite its disruptive social consequences, capitalist arrested development parades as modern progress.

2

Westernizing Europe

How do Europeans and European colonial settlements, from their particular times and places, come to imagine, represent, and "know" worlds eastward? And how has this process itself become a means for Europeans to formulate who they are and are not? This is a question many scholars have been tackling in recent decades. Chapter One has provided some hints on the ways the formation of "the West" had mapped the world. We now explore this question in greater historical detail.

The glossy generalizations that public discourse and civics books proffer about "The Orient," "the Asian Century," or "The Asian Challenge" are only as absurd as describing, as we do, "The West," "Europe," and "Western Civilization" as a unitary, transhistorical lump. We do this, but we know such formulations are only so useful. Yet, political discourse and policies are premised on such broad-stroked configurations. The specifics, the particularities of this aspect of Nyonya society, of a moment in the formation of Topkapi Palace, or what happened in the British-waged "opium wars" in China, are deemed devilishly too complicated to grapple with in public and political culture. This is unfortunate because it also means the particularities of our own regional and national narratives—how "the Chinese question" emerged in New York City during the 1870s, how FDR knew there were no security threats from Japanese Americans before he declared Executive Order 9066, and *ad infinitum*—also become deemed too much for serious public discussion. Instead, broad slogans and platitudes dominate our understandings, and this highly manipulable form of knowing is reinforced by what is popular and trendy in the commercial media industries, fiction and nonfiction. Any hot-button issue of the moment is destined to fall foul of our attention deficit as new moments crowd out what just occupied our focus. Yet, certain deeply embedded fixed ideas remain. These fixed ideas are so foundational, we tend to take them for granted. As we'll discover in the subsequent chapters, especially Chapter Six and the Epilogue, if these assumptions were ever a good foundation for knowing in the past, today they are rotted out and dangerous to support any sustainable notion of self and otherness.

Just as we imagine continents to be fixed and forever, we think of people as of fixed races, and "progress" as linear within a hierarchy of "advanced" and "primitive" cultures and peoples. How can we understand phenotypic differences when breakthroughs in human genome studies have calculated that 99.99 percent of our DNA are the same in all *homo sapiens*? If any racial category is a valid descriptor then it is accurate to say we are all one human race. According to pioneering Harvard geneticist Richard Lewontin, the remaining .01 percent (or 1/10,000) of genes accounts for all individual variation. Of that .01 percent, .00009 to .00015 percent (or 9/1,000,000 to 15/1,000,000) of our genes are relevant as individual traits historically ascribed to the outward appearance of racial differences—skin hue, hair texture, nose shape, or eye shape, etc. Only a small number of these different outward traits are linked together, such as skin hue and straight hair. In contrast, the greatest marker of differences within the human population is among individuals, each embodying three million distinctive genes from the next unrelated person. Therefore, individuals are genetically more different from each other than historically ascribed intragroup differences in outward appearances or skin hue.[1]

This chapter seeks to challenge these fixities and help gain some sense of the process of events and societies in flux as they unfolded across different times and places. Just as rival nations make claims about who they are and aren't in relation to their arch-nemesis, so has what is commonly and unfortunately referred to as "Western Civilization" been formulated in terms of "the Orient" and so-called "primitive" cultures. It is important therefore to unpack how a region such as Greece or Persia, or the larger area of the Mediterranean, morph, confound, and reformulate into that Christian, increasingly Protestant assemblage of wealth and power that we now know as the U.S., Western Europe, and "the West."

Our central question in this chapter is: How, then, did Europe and then the Americas become Westernized, as points east (and west) became "Orientalized"? Our second question is: How do we develop a more accurate and less narrow, less nationalist-centered framing of what has happened?

In recent decades revisionist historians have come to discern the long-term patterns, the *longue durée*, of a place like the Mediterranean, where a history of not one triumphant story of empire presides, but many peoples, ports, and interlinked histories are documented and interpreted.[2] The same openings have been made in looking at the related histories of the Atlantic world, where the process of enslavement and colonial trade is understood comparatively and inter-relationally, such as what the point of view of those enslaved might have been, as well as the African tribal leaders who betrayed them. And the same is beginning to develop in understanding the worlds of the Pacific and Indian oceans. What was the perspective of the indigenous Pacific Islander? Once we recognize this new set of facts, archives, stories, and histories, we can also begin to discern the *longue durée* of yellow perilism.

As scholars across national borders have been able to work together, more alternative framings and comparative studies are emerging. A central question of Asian studies scholars, especially those focusing on developments in science and technology, is what has been called "The Great Divergence," when European economies began to outstrip what had been a very dynamic Chinese, Indian Ocean world, and inter-Asian economic system. In addition, documents and scholarship on the hitherto under-examined vast region of Central Asia, and the role of the massive grasslands or steppes stretching through the heartland of the Eurasian landmass, are gaining serious study. Jack Weatherford's two studies have provocatively challenged both a Eurocentric and Sinocentric view of these long-othered pastoral-nomadic peoples. Genghis Khan and his mobile federation of conquered lands, Weatherford argues, opened access to economic flows and technology changes that greatly influenced the development of east and south Asia and also Europe. The intention of this chapter is to open up new lines of inquiry.

Understanding human cultural development and migrations over the *longue durée*, including what we awkwardly and not very usefully refer to as "ancient" and "prehistoric" eras, is critical to opening up a truer history of the world. Writer Spencer Wells offers a primer on how to understand the vast temporal and spatial scale of human movements:

> Imagine, then, that apes appear on New Year's Day. In that case, our first hominid ancestors to walk upright—the first ape-men, in effect—would appear around the end of October. *Homo erectus*, who left Africa around 2 million years ago, would appear at the beginning of December. Modern humans wouldn't show up until around 28 December, and they wouldn't leave Africa until New Year's Eve! In an evolutionary eye-blink, a mere blip in the history of life on our planet, humans have left Africa and colonized the world.[3]

The Homo sapiens Adam and Eve emerged approximately 150,000 years ago in Africa. Their descendants migrated out of Africa about 50,000 years ago. Farming developed in Africa and spread up to the Near East 11,000 years ago. The lush farmlands of what we now know of as the Sahara Desert dried up 10,000 years ago. Domesticating grazing animals and farming in central Asia, moving into Europe and into east Asia, developed 7,000 years ago. This shared humanity of our genetic makeup and our restless migrating spirits set the stage for the introduction to the ancient cultures of Eurasia from which horses, the wheel, and carts emerged—on the immense steppes of Central Asia.

As Europe separated from Asia, the formulation of a technologically superior Western Civilization began to Westernize Europe itself.

St. George and the Dragon (1876)

This is a drawing of the sculpture St. George and the Dragon *by Austrian-born English-educated Sir Joseph Edgar Boehm (1834–1890). Boehm also designed the portrait of Queen Victoria stamped on British coins. The statue was first displayed at the Royal Academy of Arts Exhibition in 1876 and then purchased to grace the entrance to the State Library of Victoria, Australia in 1889. "The most fearsome dragons of the Old Testament are horrible but vague incarnations of evil, darkly outlined opponents of both God and man. They inhabit the depths of the seas and are often employed as apt metaphors of heathen kings hostile to the children of Israel."[4]*

Figure 24. Drawing of J. E. Boehm's *St. George and the Dragon* (1876). *Magazine of Art Illustrated*, vol. 3 (New York: Cassell, Peter and Galopin and Co., 1880), 337. Courtesy of the New York Public Library.

EURASIA

David W. Anthony, "Eurasia: The Horse and the Wheel" (2009)[5]

Jared Diamond has suggested the cultures of Eurasia enjoyed an environmental advantage over those of Africa or the Americas partly because the Eurasian continent with its vast band of grasslands or steppes is oriented in an east-west direction. This made it easier for innovations like farming, herding, and wheeled vehicles to spread rapidly between environments that were basically similar because they were on about the same latitude.[6] Over time and over mountain ranges, the cultures of nomadic and pastoral steppe herders, archaeologist David W. Anthony argues, were key to the domestication of the horse and adaptation of wheel technologies to horse drawn vehicles. This largely un-thought and unrecognized part of the world is precisely where Eurasia flourished. Yet, as anthropologist Eric Wolf has provocatively suggested, the ancient inhabitants of this region are a "people without history," because their story does not fit easily into what later became the set narrative of a distinctive Europe, or into the Renaissance "Machiavellian moment" mythos of European culture emerging from Greek civilization. A growing body of genetic, archaeological, and linguistic evidence, however, suggests this part of the world was central to human historical development. The cultures that Anthony refers to are far from current everyday references, yet are likely to prove more and more central to telling a more accurate story of our shared human heritage.

Innovations in transportation technology are among the most powerful causes of change in human social and political life. The introduction of the private automobile created suburbs, malls, and superhighways; transformed heavy industry; generated a vast market for oil; polluted the atmosphere; scattered families across the map; provided a rolling, heated space in which young people could escape and have sex; and fashioned a powerful new way to express personal status and identity. The beginning of horseback riding, the invention of the heavy wagon and cart, and the development of the spoke-wheeled chariot had cumulative effects that unfolded more slowly but eventually were equally profound. One of those effects was to transform Eurasia from a series of unconnected cultures into a single interacting system …

Most historians think of war when they begin to list the changes caused by horseback riding and the earliest wheeled vehicles. But horses were first domesticated by people who thought of them as food. They were a cheap source of winter meat; they could feed themselves through the steppe winter, when cattle and sheep needed to be supplied with water and fodder. After people were familiar with horses as domesticated animals, perhaps after a relatively docile male bloodline was established, someone found a particularly submissive horse and rode on it, perhaps as a joke. But riding soon found its first serious use in the management of herds of domesticated cattle, sheep, and horses. In this capacity alone it was an important improvement that enabled fewer people to manage larger herds and move them more efficiently, something that really mattered in a world where domesticated animals were the principal source of food and clothing. By 4800–4600 BCE horses were included with obviously domesticated animals in human funeral rituals at Khvalysnk on the middle Volga.

By about 4200–4000 BCE people living in the Pontic-Caspian steppes probably were beginning to ride horses to advance to and retreat from raids. Once they began to ride, there was nothing to prevent them from riding into tribal conflicts. Organic bits functioned perfectly well, Eneolithic steppe horses were big enough to ride (13–14 hands), and the leaders of steppe tribes began to carry stone maces as soon as they began to keep herds of cattle and sheep, around 5200–4800 BCE. By 4200 BCE people had become more mobile, their single graves emphasized individual status and personal glory unlike the older communal funerals, high-status graves contained stone maces shaped like horse heads and other weapons, and raiding parties migrated hundreds of kilometers to enrich themselves with Balkan copper, which they traded or gifted back to their relatives in the Dnieper-Azov steppes. The collapse of Old Europe about 4200–4000 BCE probably was at least partly their doing.

The relationship between mounted steppe pastoralists and sedentary agricultural societies has usually been seen by historians as either violent, like the Suvorovo confrontation with Old Europe, or parasitic, or both. "Barbaric" pastoral societies, hungry for grain, metals, and wealth, none of which they could produce themselves, preyed upon their "civilized" neighbors, without whom they could not survive. But these ideas are inaccurate and incomplete even for the historical period, as the Soviet ethnographer Sergei Vainshtein, the Western historian Nicola Di Cosmo, and our own botanical studies have shown. Pastoralism produced plenty of food—the average nomad probably ate better than the average agricultural peasant in Medieval China or Europe. Steppe miners and craftsmen mined their own abundant ores and made their own metal tools and weapons; in fact, the enormous copper mines of Russia and Kazakhstan and the tin mines of the Zeravshan show that the Bronze Age civilizations of the Near East depended on *them*. For the prehistoric era covered [in my] book, any model based on relationships between the militarized nomads of the steppes and the medieval civilizations of China or Persia is anachronistic. Although the steppe societies of the Suvorovo-Novodanilovka period did seem to prey upon their neighbors in the lower Danube valley, they were clearly more integrated and apparently had peaceful relationships with their Cucuteni-Tripolye neighbors at the same time. Maikop traders seem to have visited steppe settlements on the lower Don and even perhaps brought weavers there. The institutions that regulated peaceful exchange and cross-cultural relationships were just as important as the institution of the raid.

The reconstructed Proto-Indo-European vocabulary and comparative Indo-European mythology reveal what two of those important integrative institutions were: the oath-bound relationship between patrons and clients, which regulated the reciprocal obligations between the strong and the weak, between gods and humans; and the guest-host relationship, which extended these and other protections to people outside the ordinary social circle. The first institution, legalizing inequality, probably was very old, going back to the initial acceptance of the herding economy, about 5200–5000 BCE, and the first appearance of pronounced differences in wealth. The second might have developed to regulate migrations into unregulated geographic and social space at the beginning of the Yamnaya horizon.

When wheeled vehicles were introduced into the steppes, probably about 3300 BCE, they again found their first use in the herding economy. Early wagons and carts were slow, solid-wheeled vehicles probably pulled by oxen and covered by arched roofs made of reed mats plaited together, perhaps originally attached to a felt backing … Wagons permitted herders to migrate with their herds into the deep steppes between the river valleys for weeks or months at a time, relying on the tents, food, and water carried in their wagons. Even if the normal annual range of movement was less than 50 km, which seems likely for Yamnaya herders, the combination of bulk wagon transport with rapid horseback transport revolutionized steppe economies, opening the majority of the Eurasian steppe zone to efficient exploitation. The steppes, largely wild and unused before, were domesticated. The Yamnaya horizon exploded across the Pontic-Caspian steppes about 3300 BCE. With it probably went Proto-Indo-European, its dialects scattering as its speakers moved apart, their migrations sowing the seeds of Germanic, Baltic, Slavic, Italic, Celtic, Armenian, and Phrygian.

The chariot, the first wheeled vehicle designed entirely for speed, first appeared in the graves of the Sintashta culture, in the southern Ural steppes, about 2100 BCE. It was meant to intimidate. A chariot was incredibly difficult to build, a marvel of carpentry and bent-wood joinery. It required a specially trained team of fast, strong horses. To drive it through a turn, you had to rein each horse independently while keeping a backless, bouncing car level by leaning your weight into each bounce. It was even more difficult to throw a javelin accurately at a target while driving a speeding chariot, but the evidence from the Sintashta chariot graves suggests that this is precisely what they did. Only men with a lot of time and resources, as well as balance and courage, could learn to fight from a chariot. When a squadron of javelin-hurling chariot warriors wheeled onto the field of battle, supported by clients and supporters on foot and horseback with axes, spears, and daggers, it was a new, lethal style of fighting that had never been seen before, something that even urban kings soon learned to admire.

This heroic world of chariot-driving warriors was dimly remembered in the poetry of the *Iliad* and the *Rig Veda*. It was introduced to the civilizations of Central Asia and Iran about 2100 BCE, when exotic Sintashta or Petrovka strangers first appeared on the banks of the Zeravshan, probably bouncing along on the backs of the new kinds of equids from the north … Horses and chariots appeared across the Near East, and the warfare of cities became dependent, for the first time, on well-trained horses … From this time forward the people of the Eurasian steppes remained directly connected with the civilizations of Central Asia, South Asia, and Iran, and, through intermediaries, with China. The arid lands that occupied the center of the Eurasian continent began to play a role in transcontinental economies and politics.

CLASSICAL ROUTES

For Western cultures today, notions of Asian difference emerged from how Greek civilization has been abstracted and elevated from its historical regional context to stand in for the origins of that entity we call "Western Civilization." The new scholarship on the Greek seaward empire has explored how ideas of Greek identity have been formulated in a more complex set of relations to competing cultures and notions of otherness. The settled city-state was not like the nomadic Eurasian "Scythians" and "Huns" to the north. Nor did Greeks identify with their arch-nemesis the Persians to the east whom they battled and memorialized by the "first" histories of Herodotus and Aeschylus. Nor were they the same as the Egyptians to the south. Early notions of Asia and "the Orient" (where the sun rises to the east) were formulated from these roots, prefiguring much more fixed West/ East divides later on. However, what new scholarship has also emphasized is how the cultural historical influences of the regions of the Mediterranean, Black Sea, Persian Gulf, and Indian Ocean were highly intermingled.

From another vantage, Eurasia, an earlier regional system, became split in various ways with the developments of the Mediterranean worlds of Greek, Persian, Egyptian, Scythian, Saracen, and other so-named groups. Ultimately, the story of Greek democracy and "Oriental luxuries" corrupting virtue becomes a master narrative of the rise of Western civilizations.

Irene J. Winter, "Homer's Phoenicians" (1995)[7]

Eurasian steppe influences circulated to the south and impacted the ancient and classical cultures of the inland and seafaring communities of the Fertile Crescent and the Mediterranean world. The Silk Route linked to markets and ports creating exchange chains linking the makers, sellers, and consumers of goods in China to the makers, sellers, and consumers of goods in the Levant and the Mediterranean worlds. Phoenicians, for example, inhabited an ancient series of port city-states that maintained advanced maritime trade networks. Located in Canaan and the coastal part of the Fertile Crescent from 1200 to 539 BCE, they produced the dyes of royal purple, spread the basic alphabet, and circulated goods produced from various parts of the Mediterranean.

Irene J. Winter's scholarship is part of a generation of interdisciplinary scholars probing more deeply into various kinds of evidence—reframing archaeological findings and exploring inter-cultural historical understanding of the region. Influenced by Edward Said, she argues that Homer's epic poem The Odyssey (700s BCE) already tilted toward a binary of Greek Occidentalist othering of Phoenicians as Oriental Others.

Seductive though it may be to move from eloquence in a given text to mental image to historical reconstruction, recent work in literary and cultural studies has shown that one can no longer read the Homeric poems, or indeed any literary work, with an innocent assumption of transparency between "the world" and "the word"; archaeological data and other textual studies are necessary as corroboration or corrective. With respect to the Phoenicians, at issue is whether and to what degree one can distinguish historical and ethnographic description from literary construct—"fact" from fiction—in the epics …

In the end, it is the degree of constructedness that is so striking in the texts. At first, moved by the apparent verisimilitude of description, it is indeed tempting to read "The Phoenicians" from the poems, since there are "true" details presented. Then, as one gathers data, one begins to notice the absences: what is *not* being said also becomes revealing, and makes apparent those traits that have been reduced to formulaic stereotype in what *is* represented. Next, as one sees through comparison what elements and attributes are being set in opposition to the Phoenicians, their role as "other" emerges vis-à-vis a purported Greek ideal. But it is only when the sociocultural context is explored as well, that an even subtler role of ambivalent "self" is manifest in Greek attitudes toward the Phoenicians.

How the "self" is culturally constituted with respect to the identification of, *with,* and against an "other" is currently a topic of widespread intellectual attention. Representing the other as opposite—and particularly, as exoticized, sensualized, savage, irrational opposite—is the better understood of these strategies.* Ribichini applied the principle directly to the representation of Phoenicians in Classical sources, observing a general pattern, from Homer to Herodotus, of characterizing in the negative all surrounding populations, which was itself part of a larger cultural design of recuperation and control of the social environment†... Perhaps the clearest exposition is to be found in Todorov's study of the conquest of America, in which he first defines "the other" as "... exterior to interior ... female to male ... poor to rich ... crazy to normal ... or another society to one's own ... near or far ... on the cultural,

---

* Ella Shohat, "Imaging Terra Incognita," *Public Culture* 3 (1991), 59. In this respect, the "ethnic" otherness of the Phoenicians in the Homeric poems plays the same role as racial otherness does in later Western literature—see Kwame A. Appiah, "Race," in *Critical Terms for Literary Studies*, ed. F. Lentricchia and T. McLaughlin (Chicago: University of Chicago Press, 1990), 274–87, esp. 281.

† Sergio Ribichini, "Mito e storia: L'imagine dei fenici nelle fonte classiche," *Atti del I. Congresso Internazionale di studi fenici e punici*, eds. Bartolini and Bondi (Rome: 1983), 446, 448. Tamara Green has suggested that the creation of the "other" in texts like the Homeric epics was a way for Greeks to assert their own view of cultural norms. This is also the theme of the recent book of Francois Hartog, *The Mirror of Herodotus,* the subtitle of which, *The Representation of the Other in the Writing of History,* implies his agenda of cultural constitution. And yet, the ambiguities inherent in the issue should not be obscured. Tamara M. Green, "*Black Athena* and Classical Historiography: Other Approaches, Other Views," *Arethusa*, Special Issue (1989), 55–65.

moral or historical level" and then argues that, in fact, to identify the "exterior" is to discover the "other" in oneself.* It is useful to consider, therefore, whether in the Homeric texts as well it is in relation to the "other" that the ideal "self" is both defined and integrated. In such a view, the Phoenicians would represent what the Greeks need to socialize, what they fear most to be in the new social order, and what they are most mindful of becoming.

A longstanding enmity between Greece and the peoples of Asia is observed by Ribichini in Herodotus and Thucydides as well as in Homer. In this perpetuation of a traditional "other" we see the seeds of an early "orientalism," so powerfully raised with regard to classical scholarship by Bernal,† and responded to in the recent publications of Sarah Morris. One of Morris's principal points is that it is not only classical scholarship in the recent West, but the Classical Greeks themselves, who evinced discomfort in acknowledging, and so often obscured, their enormous debts to the Levant, at the same time as they absorbed, and even admired, so many of its goods and traditions.‡

I would stress that this pattern can be seen already in the Homeric treatment of the Phoenicians. It should probably come as no surprise that an "Orientalizing" period should be one most prone to "orientalism." From Said's important study of 1979 to its myriad offshoots,§ it is clear that a powerful component of orientalism is the attribution of the exotic, of luxury, and even of transgression to a putative "East"—an East constituted in an amalgam of both knowledge and prejudice, in which exoticism and xenophobia, constraint and desire, consumption and denial combine to tell us a great deal more about the "constructing" culture than about the constructed.

Such a pattern is all the more to be expected at critical junctures of nation- or, in this case, *state*-building. It should also not be lost sight of that for the Greeks,

---

* Tzvetan Todorov, *La conquête de l'Amérique, La question de l'autre* (Paris: Seuil, 1982), 11, 252.

† Martin Bernal, *Black Athena: The Afroasiatic Roots of Classical Civilization, Volume I: The Fabrication of Ancient Greece* (New Brunswick, NJ: Rutgers University Press, 1991).

‡ Sarah Morris, "Daidalos and Kadmos: Classicism and 'Orientalism'," *Arethusa*, Special Issue (1989), 39–54.

§ Edward Said, *Orientalism* (New York: Vintage, 1979); Timothy Brennan, "The National Longing for Form," *Nation and Narration*, ed. Homi K. Bhabha (London: Routledge, 1990), 47.

the period of state-building happened to coincide with a period of intensive mercantile development and colonization. In addition to all of the issues discussed thus far, the very fact of the Phoenicians' status in that mercantile world, as well as their already established colonies and mobility as seafarers, needs to be kept in focus. The composite picture presented in the *Odyssey* of the Phoenician king of Sidon acting according to proper rules of behavior, but his people on the seas clearly not observing the rules, leads one to wonder whether this is not an expression of the trepidation the Greeks must have felt anticipating the dispersal of their own population into the colonies and onto the seas of commerce. Seen through the lens of a nostalgia not only for the past but for the integrity of the "homeland," the particular state of Greek social (colonial) and economic, not just political, development becomes a significant factor in the representation of Phoenicians in the Homeric epics.*

Those texts most associated with national "identity" at a time of state-building, such as national myths of origin or epics, often contain highly developed expressions of the constitutive signs conveying "belonging" and "collective values."† In such texts, as in the construction of a national or civic identity itself, the oppositions of civilized versus barbaric, law-based versus lawless, fair versus treacherous come to stand for the choices the socialized "citizen" must make in order to belong, and in order for the society to function.‡ This perspective helps us to read the Homeric construct of honor (and its opposites, shame and dishonor) at the explicit level within the text, and to see the representation of the Phoenicians with respect to Odysseus in particular, and Greeks in general, as a way of articulating Greek values. At the same time, if we understand nationalism, or statism, as a social process maintained at least in part by *not* articulating all of its political ideologies, but rather through allying itself with (an often fabricated) "tradition" that preceded it,§ then the casting of a national text into a heroic past can be seen as part of the very process of state-formation.

---

* Nicholas Purcell, "Mobility and the *Polis*," in *The Greek City from Homer to Alexander*, eds. Oswyn Murray and Simon Price (Oxford: Clarendon Press, 1990), 29–58.

† Brennan, "National Longing for Form," 44–70.

‡ Jonathan Friedman, "Culture, Identity and World Process," *Domination and Resistance*, eds. Daniel Miller, Michael Rowlands, and Chris Tilley (London: Routledge, 1989), 252.

§ Homi K. Bhabha, Introduction, in *Nation and Narration*, ed. Bhabha, 1–7.

Vance's understanding of the texts of Chrétien de Troyes helps to make clear that much can be happening at the nonexplicit level in providing channels or detours for collective energies. By his account, the "really vital problems that arise as the poetic mind reacts to change are expressed *beneath the narrative or thematic surface of a work.*"* For this reason, at the most general level, any work that we call "literary" is by definition "suspect as a document of history."† And in particular, as noted by Runciman, "the *Odyssey* as a work of fiction is a poor guide to the sociological realities of contemporary Greece."‡

That the *Iliad* and the *Odyssey* are indeed "literary" constructs will come as no surprise to literary historians and classicists; but the point must be underscored for those who have optimistically sought to read "history" therein. To come to grips with the full complexity of the representational strategies involved in Phoenicians-as-trope in both the *Odyssey* and the *Iliad,* it is necessary to pursue not only an internal analysis of how they function structurally within the texts, but also an external analysis of how the texts themselves functioned in their contemporary world. Only with such an external analysis do the issues of purposeful selectivity, alterity, and "orientalism" take on a full complement of meaning.

Less a mirror of their time than a deflector, the Homeric texts elevate an ideal of the warrior-hero at the very moment that Greeks were embarking upon mercantile ventures not unlike those of the very Phoenicians whom the texts disparage. If we see the heroic ideal—of Odysseus no less than of Achilles—as a displacement, a detour around current social realities, and see the Phoenicians in terms at once of grudging respect for quality in manufacture, contempt with regard to social values, powerful ambivalence in commercial practice, and suspicion regarding the consequences of dispersal and mobility, then virtually all aspects of the way in which the Phoenicians are represented in the *Iliad* and the *Odyssey* can be accounted for. "Homer's Phoenicians," then, do not represent the world of the Phoenicians; rather, they present a masterful literary construct, at once produced by and working

---

* Eugene Vance, "Signs of the City: Medieval Poetry as Detour," *New Literary History* 4 (1975), 557, emphasis added.
† Ibid.
‡ W. G. Runciman, "Origins of States: The Case of Archaic Greece," *Journal of Comparative Study of Society and History* 24 (1982), 362.

to produce the broader social, political, economic, and symbolic fabric of the early state in Archaic Greece.

Benjamin Isaac, "Isocrates' 'Europe vs. Asia' Rhetoric" (2004)[8]

Isocrates (436–338 BCE) was a Sophist rhetorician, said to be the most influential of his time. He taught orators and politicians how to speak and argue in the fora of Athenian democracy. The wealth of his family declined after the Peloponnesian War. This may account for his virulent anti-Persian stance decrying the slave-like obedience to despotic leaders and the corrupting influences of Asian-associated luxuries. This is an accusation to be carried on again in Renaissance discourse and yet again by the new nation of the U.S. in espoused ideals of "republican simplicity." Such rhetoric is also the rudimentary formulation of "Oriental Despotism" discussed at length later on in Chapter Three, "Geo-Racial Mapping."

Isocrates, *Panegyricus* (380 BCE), writes:

> It is impossible for people raised and governed as they [the Persians] are to have any virtue, and, in combat, to put up a trophy over the enemies. How could there exist a competent commander or a courageous soldier with the habits of these people, of whom the majority is a crowd without discipline or experience of danger, which has lost its motivation for war and is better educated for slavery than our servants? Those who have the highest reputation among them have, without exception, never any care for the interests of other people or the state, but they spend all their time offending some and acting as slaves to others, in the manner whereby people are most corrupted. They indulge their bodies in the luxury of their riches. They have souls humiliated and terrified by the monarchy. They let themselves be inspected at the palace gates, prostrate themselves, practice every form of humility, fall on their knees for a mortal man whom they address as god, caring less for divinity than for men.[*]

[In] Isocrates' *Panegyricus* ... we find, for the first time in Greek rhetoric ... an insistence on presumed oriental deficiencies such as a lack of discipline,

---

[*] Isaac citing Isocrates, *Panegyricus*, 1501.

softness, servility combined with arrogance, luxury, and corruption* ...
[Also expressed] is the Greek insistence on the corrupting influence of
wealth and luxury ... [T]he idea that luxury corrupts and even destroys
empires was a commonplace in antiquity and hence fully accepted in some
late periods such as that of the Enlightenment.[†] In Greek literature it is
the East, Asia Minor, and Persia that suffer from this weakness, not the
Greeks themselves. Roman preoccupation is quite different: Roman moral-
ists accuse Rome itself of being corrupted by Asiatic wealth and luxury.[‡]
According to Isocrates the Persians are also faithless to their friends, are
swindlers, and are impious towards the gods.[§] These deficiencies are found
very often in later ancient sources hostile to peoples from the East ...

There is no doubt in Isocrates' mind that a monarchy, such as that in
Persia, makes it impossible for a nation to produce a good army, an assumption often echoed by modern scholars, although the opposite idea has
also been defended with equal assurance.[¶] Like the fifth-century authors,
Isocrates recalls the destruction of the Athenian temples as a central event in
the war.[**] Unlike them, however, he insists on the need to hate the Persians.[††]
"So naturally comes our hostility to them, that we most enjoy those of
our stories which deal with the Trojan and Persian wars, for through them
we learn of their disasters."[‡‡] "Towards all other peoples with whom [the
Greeks] waged war, they forget their past hostility when they stop fighting, but towards the Asiatics they are not grateful even when they receive
favours."[§§] He constantly repeats that the Greeks should unite to fight Persia.[¶¶]
Interestingly, the same text both calls for war and insists on the inferiority

---

* Edith Hall, *Inventing the Barbarian: Greek Self-Definition through Tragedy* (Oxford:
Oxford University Press, 1989), 128.
† Isaac, *Invention*, chapters 1–3, 189f, 227, 241.
‡ I use the term "Asiatics" as a problematic rendering of several Greek terms.
§ Isocrates, *Panegyricus*, 152.
¶ Léon Poliakov, *Le mythe aryen: essais sur les sources du racisme et nationalisme* (Paris:
Calmann-Lévy, 1991), 45.
** Isocrates, *Panegyricus*, 156.
†† Ibid., 157ff.
‡‡ Ibid., 158.
§§ Ibid., 157.
¶¶ Ibid., 106, 134, 160–6, 168, 181.

of the enemy and the need to punish them for past injuries.* Even in the text written as a "sportive essay" in c. 370 BCE, the *Encomium of Helen*, Isocrates insists on seeing the conflict between the Greeks and Persians as a chronic one, which is really a struggle between Europe and Asia. Moreover, this chronic tension can result in one of two possibilities only: either the Greeks rule Asia or the reverse has to happen. Isocrates, in fact, reinterprets Herodotus in the sense that the Trojan War is represented as the first victory of Europe over Asia. Thanks to the Greek victory over Troy, the Greeks are not slaves of the barbarians.† Finally, it should be observed that Isocrates' hostility towards Persia, fierce as it is, cannot be called "proto-racist" … Although he consistently thinks in terms of an opposition Europe-Asia, his descriptions of the Persians all lie within the social and political spheres. The Persians are inferior because of the way they are ruled and because of their social relationships. The causes are not said to be hereditary or caused by physical traits.

It is clear, then, that in Isocrates we find the bipolar worldview, opposing Asia to Europe, with its contrast between a masculine and free Greece opposed to a weak and slavish Persia fully developed.

Adam Kuper, "Greeks and Multiple Barbarians" (2005)[9]

Scholars unpacking a fixed formulation of Greek civilization have often posed a singular and simple Other. It is especially fascinating to learn of the origin of the term "barbarian" in this context. Hence the Greek Occidental Self versus the Persian Oriental Other. Here Adam Kuper argues for a multilateral set of self/other relations resonant with the regional complexities of the intense state-to-state rivalries amongst Greek-Egyptian-Scythian-Persian. Such complexities, as we will see, further develop in the Renaissance and into our contemporary era.

Thucydides remarked in his *History of the Peloponnesian War* that Homer did not call his heroes Greeks. "He does not even use the term barbarian,"

---

* Cf. Frank W. Walbank, "The Problem of Greek Nationality," in *Selected Papers: Studies in Greek and Roman History and Historiography* (Cambridge: Cambridge University Press, 1985), 1–19, esp. 2f.

† Isocrates, *Helen*, 67f.

he added, "probably because the Hellenes had not yet been marked from the rest of the world by one distinctive appellation."* A sense of Greek unity was forged only when isolated city-states drew together to face the threat posed by Persia under Darius and his son Xerxes in the early years of the fifth century BCE. The Greeks then adopted the description "barbarian" for their common enemy. They pretended that *barbaroi* stammered liked idiots, or babbled like babies, or grunted like animals—*bar bar*. Hence the name. More polite and rarefied terms for foreigners, *heterophone*, "other speech," and *allogloss*, "other tongue," insisted equally on the primacy of Greek. The initial mark of the barbarian was a deficiency of language.

A twin birth, the new ideas of Greeks and barbarians were inextricably linked. "Greek writing about barbarians is usually an exercise in self-definition," Edith Hall writes in her study, *Inventing the Barbarian*, "for the barbarian is often portrayed as the opposite of the ideal Greek."† Athenians were the ideal Greeks, of course, and Persians the prototypical barbarians. Yet both polar types were easily generalized, differences obliterated. A traveler complained in Plato's *Statesman* that just because the Greeks defined Hellenes as one species, they lumped all other nations together as barbarians regardless of differences in language. "Because they have one name they are supposed to be of one species also."

Yet once it was admitted that there were different types of barbarian, the variants might be invoked in order to represent the Greeks more subtly, by way of a more complex play of oppositions ... The Scythians and Egyptians also each stood in a different relationship to the main adversaries of the Greeks, the archetypal barbarians, the Persians. The Egyptians submitted to Darius, the Persian king. The Scythians, like the Greeks, had defeated the Persian army. So Greeks and Scythians were united as freedom fighters against the Persians. However, the Scythians and the Egyptians were contrasted in turn with the Greeks. The Scythians were nomads, who carried their houses with them, while the Greeks insisted that they were autochthonous, natives of their homeland, and urban dwellers. The Egyptians lived in a different climate, on the banks of a unique river and "so they have made

---

* Thucydides, *History of the Peloponnesian War*, Book 1, Chapter 1 (trans. Richard Crawley).

† Edith Hall, *Inventing the Barbarian: Greek Self-Definition through Tragedy* (Oxford: Oxford University Press, 1989), 1.

all their customs and laws of a kind which is for the most part the converse of those of all other men"* ...

Above all, there was a political divide between the Greeks and the barbarians. The Greeks, or at least the Athenians, lived in the ideal state, the democratic *polis*. All Greece resisted tyranny. Barbarians were not democratic. They were either a leaderless rabble or the slaves of tyrannical rulers. The Scythians were homeless anarchists, without leaders. In contrast to the Scythians, the Egyptians were urban and sophisticated. However, they were ruled by an absolute king. The archetypal barbarians, the Persians, were the very model of royal tyranny. "There is a link between barbarianism and royalty," Hartog concludes, "among barbarians, the normal mode for the exercise of power tends to be royalty. And reciprocally, royalty is likely to have something barbarian about it."†

This association of barbarians with tyranny proved to be an enduring characterization of the anti-Greek. "For barbarians, being more servile in character than Hellenes ... do not rebel against a despotic government," Aristotle wrote, a century after Herodotus and Thucydides. Indeed, "among barbarians no distinction is made between women and slaves, because there is no natural ruler among them: they are a community of slaves, male and female. Wherefore the poets say, 'It is meet that Hellenes should rule over barbarians,' as if they thought that the barbarian and the slave were by nature one." Barbarian kingdoms were tyrannies "because the people are by nature slaves."‡ There were slaves in Athens, but they were always foreigners, and so could be classed as barbarians: and according to the logic of Aristotle, as barbarians it was their nature to be slaves.

Not only was the barbarian incapable of independence and devoid of civic values. He lacked the emotional self-control of a mature Greek man. Barbarians represented on the Athenian stage gabbled in strange languages, dressed in skins, ate raw meat, carried bows but not the spears that brave men used for close fighting, and were servile and emotional. Warriors behaved more like women than like self-reliant and restrained

* Herodotus, *History*, 2.35.

† Francois Hartog, *The Mirror of Herodotus: The Representation of the Other in the Writing of History* (Berkeley, CA: University of California Press, 1988) 324.

‡ Aristotle, *Politics*. Book I, Part I, and Book III, Part XIV. Translated by Benjamin Jowett.

Greek men. In the *Persians* of Aeschylus, Xerxes appears as an effeminate tyrant.*

Dramatists might play with the image of the barbarian, and confront audiences with the paradoxical figures of the noble barbarian, and the barbarous Greek,† but in general the two stereotypes were fixed in their proper places, each at the further possible remove from the other. Even if it was admitted that Greeks had once been barbarians themselves, what mattered was that they had moved far beyond this point of departure.

RISE OF WESTERN FUNDAMENTALISM

How did the Bible, notions of belonging and borders, and recycled stereotypes play out during the Renaissance? Rather than accepting the retrospective European Renaissance narrative of the Western modern era emerging from the rebirth of a long "dark ages," U.S., European, and international scholars have been challenging prior evidence, frameworks, and interpretations. The excerpts below are meant to open up some windows into scholarship that seeks to make connections.

The stories, told and retold, of Gog and Magog, emerging from the Old Testament and recycled regularly to the present-day U.S. presidential justification for the invasion of Iraq and the comic-book framing of the "Axis of Evil," delineate a deep pattern of absolute and abject othering. R. I. Moore's pioneering formulation of the European eleventh and twelfth century CE as "the persecuting society" informs this section.[10]

Until the twelfth century, the Muslim and Byzantine world "exercised a true economic hegemony over the West: the only gold coinage still circulating in … Europe came from Greek or Arab mints."[11] European colonialism came out of a need to defend against the various Islamic powers and to regain lands lost in prior centuries. The reconquest of the Iberian Peninsula by Spain and Portugal was linked to excursions into North Africa, sub-Saharan Arica, and Asia to gain lands from Arab colonizers.[12] Out of this the rise of a Westernization culture, usually referred to as the "high Middle Ages," was "an epoch of economic growth, territorial expansion, and dynamic

---

* Edith Hall, "Commentary," *Aeschylus: Persians* (Oxford: Aris & Phillips, 1996).
† Hall, *Inventing the Barbarian*, 211–23.

cultural and social change."[13] Warfare was accompanied by the massive migrations of people to the peripheries: England to Ireland, Germany to its east, and crusaders and colonists to the eastern Mediterranean. These people extended conquering languages, laws, beliefs, and habits from cores to peripheral frontiers. This centralizing movement created a more homogenized and consolidated "European" culture.

This section focuses on how a series of advancements and knowledge claims, arguing for a distinctive purity and disavowing the intermingled Mediterranean world, made for a Westernizing process. Though Yellow Peril was not articulated in its contemporary form at this time, the roots of its logic were clearly in formation. Greek views were reused and fixed at the core of a European rationality that determined who the superior civilizational self was to be. John V. Tolan notes below: "Those who refused to listen to Christian reason must be irrational: the blind Jew, the stubborn heretic, the flesh-bound Saracen." Here, the possessor of the imagined superior European rational mind was superior to and separated from the disabled, body-bounded others living amongst and outside settled city-states. These mappings and orientations became the basis of the rise of the West and Eurocentrism in the era of European colonization and renaissance.

Alexios I Komnenos, "Letter to Pope Urban II" (1094 or 1095)[14]

In 1094 or 1095, Alexios I Komnenos (1056–1118), a Byzantine emperor, sent a letter to the pope, Urban II, and asked for aid from the west against the Seljuq Turks, who had taken nearly all of Asia Minor from him. At the Council of Clermont, Urban addressed a great crowd and urged all to go to the aid of the Greeks and to recover Palestine from the rule of the Muslims. The acts of the council have not been preserved, but we have five accounts of the speech of Urban that were written by men who were present and heard him. This version is excerpted from the chronicler Fulcher of Chartres.

All who die by the way, whether by land or by sea, or in battle against the pagans, shall have immediate remission of sins. This I grant them through the power of God with which I am invested. O what a disgrace if such a despised and base race, which worships demons, should conquer a people that has the faith of omnipotent God and is made glorious with the name of Christ! With what reproaches will the Lord overwhelm us if you do not aid those who, with us, profess the Christian religion! Let those who have been accustomed unjustly to wage private warfare against the faithful now go against the infidels and end with victory this war which should have been begun long ago. Let those who for a long time, have been robbers, now become knights. Let those who have been fighting against their brothers and relatives now fight in a proper way against the barbarians. Let those who have been serving as mercenaries for small pay now obtain the eternal reward. Let those who have been wearing themselves out in both body and soul now work for a double honor. Behold! on this side will be the sorrowful and poor, on that, the rich; on this side, the enemies of the Lord, on that, his friends. Let those who go not put off the journey, but rent their lands and collect money for their expenses; and as soon as winter is over and spring comes, let them eagerly set out on the way with God as their guide.

Matthew Paris, "That Detestable Race of Satan" (1240)[15]

Though oral/aural stories of the conquering horsemen of Genghis Khan are legendary in various parts of old Europe, few authors left documents noting this event at the time. Matthew Paris was one of the few who did. He wrote about the "Tartar" conquests and is credited as having alerted Europeans to Genghis Khan's sweeping advances through Asia and into Europe. Paris (c. 1200–1259) was a Benedictine monk whose Historia Anglorum *(1253) is still considered an important source document. Paris based his history on a variety of sources with no primary documentation, hence embodying a mix of hearsay through the lens of Christian-based logics. Paris wrote this "global" history from his isolated life in rural England in Latin and "condensed all that former writers had said about the times that preceded, and to which all succeeding writers must have recourse for the history of the period in which its author lived."[16]*

There was little knowledge about who these warrior horsemen were and where they came from. It was commonly speculated they had come from Tartarus, of Greek lore, an underworld where monsters were exiled and as a deity of chaos—implying these invaders emanated from the darkness.[17] Based on the Tatar tribe, "Tartars" was also one of the names Europeans mistakenly used

synonymously with Mongols. Huns was another. Paris speculates here on Tartars'
being a lost tribe of Israel seeking vengeance on Christians. This thirst for blood,
both human and animal, is a recurrent representation of Mongols—a variation
of monsters living at the edges of Christianity's mappa mundi *and linked to the*
mythos of cannibals.

In this year, that human joys might not long continue, and that the delights
of this world might not last long unmixed with lamentation, an immense
horde of that detestable race of Satan, the Tartars, burst forth from their
mountain-bound regions, and making their way through rocks apparently
impenetrable, rushed forth, like demons loose from Tartarus (so that they
are well called Tartars, as it were inhabitants of Tartarus); and overrunning
the country, covering the face of the earth like locusts, they ravaged the
eastern countries with lamentable destruction, spreading fire and slaughter
wherever they went.

Roving through the Saracen territories, they razed cities to the ground,
burnt woods, pulled down castles, tore up the vinetrees, destroyed gardens,
and massacred the citizens and husbandmen; if by chance they did spare
any who begged their lives, they compelled them, as slaves of the lowest
condition, to fight in front of them against their own kindred. And if they
only pretended to fight, or perhaps warned their countrymen to fly, the
Tartars following in their rear, slew them; and if they fought bravely and
conquered, they gained no thanks by way of recompense, and thus these
savages ill-treated their captives as though they were horses.

The men are inhuman and of the nature of beasts, rather to be called
monsters than men, thirsting after and drinking blood, and tearing and
devouring the flesh of dogs and human beings; they clothe themselves in
the skins of bulls, and are armed with iron lances; they are short in stature
and thickset, compact in their bodies, and of great strength; invisible in
battle, indefatigable in labour; they wear no armour on the back part of
their bodies, but are protected by it in front; they drink the blood which
flows from their flocks, and consider it a delicacy; they have large and powerful horses which eat leaves and even the trees themselves, and which owing
to the shortness of their legs, they mount by three steps instead of stirrups.

They have no human laws, know no mercy, and are more cruel than lions
or bears; they have boats made of hides of oxen, ten or twelve having one

amongst them; they are skiful [*sic*] in sailing or swimming, hence they cross the largest and most rapid rivers without any delay or trouble; and when they have no blood, they greedily drink disturbed and even muddy water.

They have swords and daggers with one edge, they are excellent archers, and they spare neither sex, age, or rank; they know no other country's language except that of their own, and of this all other nations are ignorant. For never till this time has there been any mode of access to them, nor have they themselves come forth, so as to allow any knowledge of their customs or persons to be gained through common intercourse with other men; they take their herds with them, as also their wives, who are brought up to war, the same as their men; and they came with the force of lightning into the territories of the Christians, laying waste the country, committing great slaughter, and striking inexpressible terror and alarm into every one.

The Saracens, therefore, desired and begged to be allowed to enter into alliance with the Christians, in order that they might, by multiplying their forces, be enabled to resist these human monsters.[18] These Saracens, the memory of whom is detestable, are believed to have been of the ten tribes, who abandoned the law of Moses, and followed after the golden calves; and Alexander also endeavoured to shut them up in the precipitous Caspian mountains by walls cemented with bitumen; but as this work appeared to be beyond human accomplishment, he invoked the aid of the God of Israel; upon which the ridges of the mountains united one with another, and the place became inaccessible and impassable.

Concerning this place Josephus says, "How much will God do for his faithful servants, when he has done so much of infidels. From this it is clear that the Lord was not willing that they should go forth; however, as it is written in the scholastic history, they will come forth at the end of the world to commit great slaughter amongst men."

Indeed it appears doubtful whether these Tartars, who at this time made their appearance, are the people mentioned; for they do not speak in the Hebrew tongue, nor know the Mosaic law, nor do they enjoy, nor are they governed by legal institutes. But the reply to this is, that it nevertheless is probable that they are some of those who were enclosed in the mountains, of whom mention has been before made. And as in the time of the government of Moses their rebellious hearts were perverted to an evil way of thinking, so that they followed after strange gods and unknown customs, so now in a more wonderful manner, owing to the vengeance of God, they were unknown to every other nation, and their heart and language was confused, and their life change to that of the cruel and irrational wild beast.

They are called Tartars, from a river called Tartar, which runs through their mountains, through which they have made their way, in the same way as the river of Damascus is called Farfar.[19]

Scott D. Westrem, "The Story of Gog and Magog" (1998)[20]

As referenced by President George W. Bush in attempting to gain the support of French President Jacques Chirac in 2003 to justify the invasion of Iraq, the uses of "Gog and Magog" have continued into the contemporary era. Scott D. Westrem, in a critical appraisal of the literal claims of where Alexander the Great actually imprisoned barbaric enemies, argues that the Gog and Magog references in Ezekiel were part of a Latin Christian exegetical metaphor for enemies of the Church (and as well as a Muslim metaphor for enemies of Islam thus mirroring Christian abjection). Christian Latin stories were often represented to take place in Asia—a site that posed various possible Gogian-like evils that could imperil Europe.

In this excerpt, Genghis Khan's armies arriving in the Eurasian borderlands of Hungary is notable. Westrem also emphasizes the multiple, varied, and ambivalent readings of Gog and Magog as testimony to the shifting uses of such cosmological metaphors for different purposes at different places and historical moments. The motivational and explanatory uses for which Gog and Magog were deployed can be understood as part of what R. I. Moore has described as European political culture, from the ruler downward: "the formation of a persecuting society" from the eleventh century to the present day. These mappings, explanations, and systematically deployed fears are historically linked to the later development of yellow perilism.

It would be hard to imagine a more excoriated, more exilic figure than Magog, who appears innocently in Genesis as a son of Noah's son Japheth; whose name is appropriated to designate the homeland of Gog, to whom the prophet Ezekiel was commanded by the Lord of Israel to thunder "I am against thee" not once but twice; and who appears in some mortal form at the end of the Revelation of St. John as half of the innumerable

Figure 25. Detail of Gog and Magog from the Ebstorf World Map of 1284. According-ing to the caption: "Alexander enclosed two wild nations, Gog and Magog, who will be the companions of Antichrist. They eat human flesh and drink human blood."

twin forces, with Gog, assembled by Satan from the four quarters of the earth to fight, unsuccessfully, against the saints and the beloved city of Jerusalem.* As if the opposition of Yahweh and the Triune God were not enough, the Qur'an reports Allah's antipathy for Gog and Magog, who ravage a land so remote that its people can "barely understand a word," yet who plead with Alexander the Great (called Dhul-Qarnayn) to help them; he builds a rampart of iron and brass against them, which Allah will level at the end of time, when unbelievers will be cast into hell.†

So far, so evil. As a result of the role they play in Christian, and less distinctly in Islamic, eschatology, however, Gog and Magog take on the oxymoronic character of a welcome enemy, for their movement from the margin to the center of the earth is the necessary prelude to the communion of saints in Paradise ...

[Andrew Runni] Anderson's central argument [is] that the "legend of Alexander's Gate and of the enclosed nation [of Gog and Magog] is in reality the story of the frontier in sublimated mythologized form"‡ ... Writing just over a decade after World War I, Anderson uses "frontier" to signify a defensive buffer zone, a kind of Maginot line ...

As individual Europeans imagined their culture under siege, they identi-fied a series of ethnic groups as Antichrist's allies, including Goths, Huns,

---

*   Genesis 10.2; I Chron. 1.5; Ezekiel 38, 39.

†   Sura 18.83–108.

‡   Andrew Runni Anderson, *Alexander's Gate, Gog and Magog, and the Inclosed Nations* (Cambridge, MA: Medieval Academy of Sciences, 1932), 8.

Figure 26. In the upper-left corner, Gog and Magog are illustrated as two naked, imprisoned anthropophagi behind a rampart of iron and brass. The Ebstorf World Map of 1284, by Gervasius of Tilbury. Facsimile (original destroyed in 1945, Hanover). Photo: bpk, Berlin / Staatsbibliothek zu Berlin / Ruth Schacht, Manuscript Division / Art Resource, NY.

Alans, Khazars, Arabians, Turks, Magyars, Parthians, Mongols, the Ten
Lost Tribes, Scythians, Scandinavians, Terracontans, Essedones, and Jews
(Muslim writers shared several of these interpretations and added to them
Latin Christians).* In addition … European cartographers, between 1100
and 1500, more or less programmatically assigned territory to Gog and
Magog (gradually shifting their haunts to the east)† …

[T]he common denominator of its meanings seems to be little more
specific than "bogeyman" …

One complex of ethnic identifications, made by European writers beginning in the thirteenth century, does deserve some attention, however, because
its formulation was rapid, its influence considerable, and its implications
important. The Mongol invasions of Russia in the 1230s, with attacks as far
west as Silesia during the next decade, elicited a terror in Europe that invited
apocalyptic interpretation. Brother Julian, the Hungarian Dominican who
reported the advance of Batu Khan in late 1237, appears to have been the
first European to link the Mongols to Gog and Magog‡ … Matthew Paris
made a similar connection a few years later …

[T]hirteenth-century Europeans attempted to explain the baffling,
sudden appearance of the Mongols, a race unrecorded in the Bible, by
making them Jewish. Reporting around 1291 on a decade of travels in Asia,
the Dominican Ricold of Monte Croce refered to the "opinion of many"
(they need not necessarily have been Europeans) in identifying the "Tartari"
with the "Ten Tribes of Israel, who were taken captive."

Suzanne Conklin Akbari, "Placing the Jews in Late Medieval English Literature" (2002)[21]

*Historically, from the interrelational vantage of Westernizing Europeans,
Eastern European Jews and Arabs were thought to be Orientals, hence also*

---

* Ibid., 12–14; Daniel J. Boorstin, *The Discoverers* (New York: Random House, 1983), 104.

† Anderson, *Alexander's Gate*, 85, 87–90, 101–4.

‡ Robert E. Lerner, *The Power of Prophecy: The Cedars of Lebanon Vision from the Mongol Onslaught to the Dawn of the Enlightenment* (Berkeley, CA: University of California Press, 1893), 10, 21–2, n. 26.

subjected to othering processes. Understanding these processes help us understand earlier forms of orientalizing that later results in yellow perilism.

Suzanne Conklin Akbari unpacks some of the parallels between anti-Muslim and anti-Jewish prejudice in the context of European Medieval attitudes and practices. Anti-Semitism has been specifically defined as anti-Jewish prejudice, yet historically it references all those of Semitic languages, including Hebrew, Arabic, Phoenician, Aramaic, Maltese, Ge'ez, Amharic, and other Ethiopian Semitic languages, as well as other active and inactive languages located in the Arabian peninsula. The term derives from the biblical story of Noah's son Shem. During the medieval era all Asian peoples were thought to be the children of Shem as illustrated in the T-O map. "Anti-Semitism" is said to have been first coined by Austrian scholar Moritz Steinschneider who used this phrase in 1860 to characterize Ernest Renan's ideas about how "Semitic races" were inferior to "Aryan races."[22] Scholars cited in this excerpt note the comparability and interrelatedness of anti-Jewish and anti-Arab stereotypes.

Christian fundamentalism, as with any fundamentalism, asserts a foundational purity against and amid othered cultures. Purity can be gained from this process of disidentification.[23] This fundamentalist zeitgeist demands a clear delineation of self and other, cleansing the impure self, and projecting the impure outward to others.

In the contemporary political climate, noting the similarities between misperceptions of Jewish and Muslim identity is, sadly, disturbing and even dangerous. Some twenty years ago, Edward Said asserted that anti-Arab polemic is fundamentally the same as anti-Semitic polemic: during the oil embargo of the 1970s, he wrote, caricatures of Arabs with "Semitic" features "were obvious reminders ... that 'Semites' were at the bottom of all 'our' troubles ... The transference of a popular anti-Semitic animus from a Jewish to an Arab target was made smoothly, since the figure was essentially the same"* ... For example, in response to Pat Robertson's claim that Islam is an intrinsically violent religion, and that Muslims in America "want to control, dominate and then, if need be, destroy," Hussein Ibish, a representative of the American-Arab Anti-Discrimination Committee, stated: "We know the word

---

* Edward Said, *Orientalism* (New York: Random House, 1978), 286.

for this. This is called anti-Semitism. It's a resurgent anti-Semitism with the word 'Muslims' instead of the word 'Jews.'"*

It may be that medievalists have something to contribute to this painful debate; long before the development of the term "anti-Semitism" in the late nineteenth century, the image of the Jew and the Muslim were complexly intertwined.† Allan and Helen Cutler argued several years ago that "medieval anti-Semitism … was primarily a function of anti-Muslimism," while Jeremy Cohen has more recently (and more precisely) pointed out that in the medieval "classification of the Jews together with the Muslims," both are merely "subsets in a larger genus of hermeneutically constructed *infideles* who undermined the unity of Christian faith."[24] In canon law, regulations limiting the interactions of Christians with Jews and Muslims treated the latter two as equivalents.‡ Literary texts reflect this interchangeability as well: medieval mystery plays depicting the nativity of Jesus, for example, characterize Herod using the conventions associated with Muslim sultans in the *chansons de geste* and romances. He is opulently dressed, given to violent rages and, most tellingly, invokes the name of his god, Muhammad.§

Both Jews and Muslims were seen by medieval Christians as people who privileged the carnal over the spiritual, not only epistemologically (in their preference for the dead letter of the law above the living spirit of faith) but also behaviorally (in their propensity toward sensuous pleasures and sexual deviance) …

The Siege of Jerusalem, which was written in a northern dialect of Middle English in the last decade of the fourteenth century … is a horrific poem, full of bodily mutilations and wholesale slaughter carried out in the name of God; at

---

* Alan Cooperman, "Robertson Calls Islam a Religion of Violence, Mayhem," *Washington Post,* February 22, 2002, A2.

† It is important to note that "anti-Arab" and "anti-Muslim" are terms that must not be conflated, although they frequently overlap: the former refers primarily to an ethnic identity, the latter to a religious identity.

‡ Shlomo Simonsohn, *The Apostolic See and the Jews, Documents: 492–1404,* Studies and Texts 94 (Toronto: Pontifical Institute of Mediaeval Studies, 1988), passim.

§ "Mahounde full of might" (line 283; cf. 327, 406); "The Vintners Playe," in *The Chester Mystery Cycle,* eds. R. M. Lumiansky and David Mills [Early English Text Society], supplementary series 3 (Oxford: Oxford University Press, 1974), 156–74.

the same time, the Siege contains many passages notable for their poetic beauty, including some of the most horrific scenes of carnage ...

In order to understand the relationship between Jewish and Muslim identity as depicted in the *Siege of Jerusalem,* it is necessary to examine more closely how communities are constituted in the poem, and how their borders are defined. It is certainly true that the Jews of the *Siege* are characterized, in certain respects, in terms that evoke the Muslims of contemporary Crusade literature. Strangely, however, the Jews are simultaneously characterized in terms that are not merely "sympathetic"* but that explicitly identify them with the Christian protagonists of the Crusade chronicles—not the Muslim antagonists. This ambivalence creates a peculiar economy in the poem in which the Jews are simultaneously the object of identification for the Christian reader and that which must be abjected. The genre of the siege poem lends itself especially well to this ambivalent characterization; siege poems in general are centrally concerned not with conversion, but with the integrity of the community† ...

In the *Siege of Jerusalem,* Jewish bodies are repeatedly shown in the act of being torn to pieces: in the bodies that fly apart as they are struck by hurled stones,‡ in the bodies of Jewish prisoners that are cut open by Christian soldiers eager to find the gold coins concealed in their "gottes,"§ in the bodies of the Jewish priests flayed into "rede peces."¶ This is not only a fragmented community, but a community that is in the act of eating itself up, as is powerfully symbolized in the mother who eats the body of her child, ordering him to "turn around, and go back in where you came out."** Steven Kruger has shown that several other late medieval English texts, including the Croxton

---

* Elisa Narin van Court, *"The Siege of Jerusalem* and Augustinian Historians: Writing About Jews in Fourteenth-Century England," *Chaucer Review* 29 (1995), 227–48; Bonnie Millar, *The* Siege of Jerusalem *in its Physical, Literary, and Historical Contexts* (Dublin: Four Courts, 2000), 141–80.

† Suzanne Conklin Akbari, "Incorporation in the *Siege of Melayne"* in *Pulp Fictions of Medieval England: Essays in Popular Romance,* ed. Nicola McDonald (Manchester: Manchester University Press, 2004), 22–44, esp. 31–2.

‡ *The Siege of Jerusalem,* eds. Eugen Kölbing and Mabel Day, EETS 188 (Oxford: Oxford University Press, 1932) 822–8.

§ Ibid., 1163.

¶ Ibid., 702.

** Ibid., 1083–4.

Play of the Sacrament and Chaucer's *Prioress's Tale*, depict Jewish bodies as ending, inevitably, in "dismemberment and disintegration." Kruger argues that Jewish bodies are presented in this way in order to symbolize the fragmentation of the diasporic Jewish community, which functions as a mirror image of the Christian community whose integrity is reaffirmed daily in the sacrifice of the Mass.* Christian wholeness, then, is necessarily built on the ground of Jewish fragmentation. Here, then, is the crucial distinction between the depiction of Jews and Muslims in medieval literature, which otherwise correspond in many respects: the Muslim community is located outside, on the outer borders of the Christian community, and therefore is repudiated, as it were, at a distance; the Jewish community, by contrast, is located both outside and inside, within the Christian community itself, and must therefore be repudiated by being abjected from within.† The Jewish community is defined as internal to the Christian community based not only on the actual presence of Jewish communities within the cities of western Europe (at least until the expulsions of the later Middle Ages),‡ but also on the virtual presence of Judaism as a shadowy presence prior to Christianity.

The author *of Mandeville's Travels* pursues a number of different strategies to impose order upon the heterogeneous world, ranging from the geographical (all the rivers of the world are said to flow from the four rivers of paradise) to the genealogical (all the people of the earth are said to be descended from the three sons of Noah). The genealogical schema employed in the work is rather unusual, however, as Benjamin Braude has shown in his survey of the

---

* Steven F. Kruger, "The Bodies of Jews in the Late Middle Ages" in *The Idea of Medieval Literature: Essays on Chaucer and Medieval Culture in Honor of Donald R. Howard*, eds. James M. Dean and Christian K. Zacher (Newark, DE: University of Delaware Press, 1992), 301–23, quotation from 318.

† Kruger makes a similar distinction with regard to twelfth-century perspectives: "The Muslim 'other' is conceived not, like the Jews … as a scattered presence within a Christian hegemony, but as a hegemony of its own." Steven F. Kruger, "Medieval Christian (Dis)identifications: Muslims and Jews in Guibert of Norgent," *New Literary History* 28 (1997), 185–203; quotation from 194.

‡ For a useful survey of the presence of Jewish communities in England before the expulsion of 1290, see Robert C. Stacey, "Jews and Christians in Twelfth-Century England: Some Dynamics of a Changing Relationship" in *Jews and Christians in Twelfth-Century Europe*, eds. Michael A. Signer and John Van Engen (Notre Dame, IN: University of Notre Dame Press, 2001), 340–54.

manuscript evidence.* While medieval *mappa mundi* conventionally divide
the world into the three continents of Asia, Africa, and Europe, assigning each
of them to Shem, Ham, and Japheth respectively,† *Mandeville's Travels* reallo-
cates the continents so that "[Ham] toke the gretter and the beste partie toward
the est, that is clept Asye. And Sem toke Affryk. And Iapheth toke Europe."‡
More extraordinary, however, is his description of their descendants: the sons
of Ham are the "dyuerse folk" of India, the sons of Shem are the Saracens, and
the sons of Japheth include not only "wee [that] duellen in Europe," but also
"the peple of Israel."§ It is entirely conventional to identify the Saracens as the
offspring of Shem and to identify the Europeans as the offspring of Japheth;¶ but
to couple "the peple of Israel" (that *is*, the descendants of Jacob, rather than the
inhabitants of a certain land) with the Europeans is something quite extraordinary. One might be forgiven for optimistically believing, for a moment,
that the author is suggesting that there is a kinship between the Europeans
and the Jews, that they share a common birthright. Instead, however, it soon
becomes clear that the purpose of the anomaly is to lay the groundwork for
another innovative account of Jewish genealogical descent; that is, the identification of the Jews with the unclean, enclosed tribes of Gog and Magog, who
are conventionally described as the offspring of Japheth.**

---

* Benjamin Braude, "The Sons of Noah and the Construction of Ethnic and
Geographical Identities in the Medieval and Early Modern Periods," *William and
Mary Quarterly* 54 (1997), 103–42, esp. 116–20.

† My assessment of the conventions of the *mappa mundi* differs slightly from Braude's;
see Akbari, "From Due East to True North: Orientalism and Orientation," in *The
Postcolonial Middle Ages*, ed. Jeffrey Jerome Cohen (New York: St. Martins, 2000), 22.

‡ *Mandeville's Travels*, ed. M.C. Seymour (Oxford: Claredon Press, 1967), 24;
160.10–12; this is the Cotton manuscript, and is cited by chapter, page, and line
number in the text.

§ *Mandeville's Travels*, 24; 161.1–10.

¶ Among the sons of Shem: "Ismael fihus Abraham, a quo Ismaelitae, qui nunc
corrupto nomine Saraceni, quasi a Sarra, et Agareni ab Agar." Isidore, *Etymologiarum
sive Originum,* ed. W. M. Lindsay, 2 vols. (Oxford: Clarendon Press, 1911), 9.2.6.
With regard to Japheth: "Haec sunt gentes de stirpe Iaphet, quae a Tauro monte
ad aquilonem mediam partem Asiae et omnem Europam usque ad Oceanum
Brittanicum possident." Isidore, *Etymologiarum,* 9.2.37.

** Isidore, *Etymologiarum,* 9.2.27; 14.3.31. The association of the Jews with the tribes
of Gog and Magog were first connected in the ninth century by Christian of Stavelot.

In *Mandeville's Travels,* the Jews inhabit a peculiar space in the world: they belong nowhere, yet are found everywhere. Their proper place is not Jerusalem and its environs, for the Holy Land is the rightful "heritage"* of Christians. If the Jews do have a proper place, it is in the confines of the northern mountains, the prison from which they will emerge only in the last days, with the advent of Antichrist. The Jews are simultaneously within Western Christendom, in the ghettoes or "jeweries" of the cities, and outside, banished to the remotest regions of the world map.† The medieval prehistory of Orientalism is intertwined with the construction of Jewish identity, which functioned both as a typological prefiguration of Christian identity and as a template for other groups destined to be cut off from the body of the European, Christian community.

The place of the Jews, in the end, is plural, both in terms of physical location and symbolic position. Physically, they belong nowhere, having "no proper land of their own," as the author of *Mandeville's Travels* puts it; yet they are found throughout Christendom, "in all lands." They are even found, along with other ethnic and religious groups, in Jerusalem itself, but not because they belong there: their only home, such as it is, is in the prison of the northern mountains. Symbolically, the place of the Jew is in the past, providing a template for the foundation of Christian identity, a mold that, after use, must be broken. Simultaneously, however, the place of the Jew is perpetually in the present, whether in the reedification of Jerusalem by the Muslims or in the contemporary cities of western Europe. Jewish identity is thus at once tightly contained in a confined area (whether the besieged city or the enclosure within the mountains)‡ and disseminated widely throughout time and space. This plural position generates the phenomenon of what Steven Kruger describes as the "spectral Jew," a figure that haunts Christians: "the attempt to conjure Jews away also serves to conjure them up, into a certain presence."§ Edward Said

---

* *Mandeville's Travels,* Prologue, 2.24, 29, 32.

† Andrew Fleck, "Here, There, and In Between: Representing Difference in the *Travels* of Sir John Mandeville," *Studies in Philology* 97 (2000), 379–400, esp. 395–9, quotation from 396.

‡ In both the besieged city and the mountain dwelling, the Jews are said to be "enclosed" (*Siege of Jerusalem,* 688; *Mandeville's Travels,* chap. 29; 192.8).

§ Steven F. Kruger, "The Spectral Jew," *New Medieval Literatures* 2 (1998), 9–35; quotation from 17.

uses a similar metaphor when he characterizes the Arab as a kind of spectre or "shadow that dogs the Jew."* In this hall of mirrors, it seems that identity is only provisional, and origins recede infinitely into the distance.

John V. Tolan, "Christians on Saracens" (2003)[26]

This analysis of a Christian view on "Saracens" gives us a feel for the early formation of a perilist tradition at work that eventually becomes codified in terms of the contemporary diagnosis of Islamophobia. A moment of facing Islam and engaging with it, however limited, during what has been conventionally considered a "dark age" is contrasted with Europe's "turning its back" to Islam from the 1300s into the "early modern" era. Here we gain insights into how an othering process informs fundamentalist purification and self-identity. Engagement and complexities are displaced with simplistic juxtapositions and either/or binaries. With the careful approach John V. Tolan exemplifies here, case-by-case studies of the fear of Arabs, fear of Muslims, and yellow perilism can be understood comparatively and as episodic, interrelated phenomena linked historically over a wide range of time and geographies—a tradition of anti-Oriental xenophobia appearing in various guises throughout the ages.

In the fourth century, Marcellinus wrote that Saracens were "desert dwellers," connoting a people living on the edges of settled society. Here the image of the tented Bedouin is firmly fixed to describe a whole diasporic mix of people and types of habitats. Like the nomadic Scythians to the north of the Fertile Crescent, the norm was presumed to be a certain type of settled homebound Greekness, and not a life in movement. Trade route exchanges brought peoples of different environments into active relation, whereas self-referential civilizational discourses argued for fundamental differences. Tolan delineates European Renaissance attempts to convert Muslims and other Othered with their sense of reason; yet when unsuccessful, the barrage of anti-Muslim stereotypes was resurrected. Carefully contextualizing author by author in his survey, Tolan notes the importance of rigorous historical scholarship before coming to such broader conclusions. In case after case, the process of recycling judgments across diverse places perpetuated notions of fundamentalist virtues of the Chosen versus Others beyond virtue.

---

* Said, *Orientalism*, 286.

In 1542, as the armies of Sulayman the Magnificent prepared to invade Hungary, a Swiss publisher named Johann Herbst found himself in jail in Basel. The crime he had committed, along with his accomplice Theodor Buchman, was to publish the Qur'an in Robert of Ketton's Latin translation of the 1140s, along with Riccoldo da Montecroce's *Contra legem Sarracenorum* and other medieval polemical works against Islam. The Basel municipal council judged that it was dangerous to publish the "fables and heresies" of the Qur'an. Help came to the embattled humanists in the form of a letter to the council from none other than Martin Luther himself, who declared his support for the project, saying that there was no better way to injure Muhammad and the Turks than to publish their "lies and fables" for all to see.* Earlier the same year Luther himself had completed his German translation of Riccoldo's *Contra legem Sarracenorum*. When Martin Luther and his contemporaries sought to comprehend Islam and to engage in polemics against it, they turned naturally to translations and texts produced between the twelfth and the early fourteenth centuries.

The ideological responses to Islam that I examine in this book were redeployed countless times in medieval and modern Europe. Europeans would not again expend the same intellectual effort against Islam as did their forbears to explain, refute, convert. Rather, the intellectual weapons forged in the twelfth and thirteenth centuries were reused, anthologized, translated, published[†] ... Little truly new was written about Islam between 1300 and the Enlightenment. There were occasional exceptions, the best known being that of Juan de Segovia, whose grand project was a trilingual Qur'an: the Arab text alongside new translations into Latin and Spanish.[27] Yet for the most part the humanists turned their back on Islam: Arab and Muslim culture were parts of the "Gothic" accretion that they wished to shed in order to return to a pure, antique wisdom. The old stereotypes of barbaric invaders, now couched in the vocabulary of humanism, flowed easily from

* Martin Luther, letter dated 27 October 1542 in Karl Hagenbach, "Luther und der Koran vor dem Rate zu Basel," *Beitrage zur vaterlandischen Geschichte* 9 (1870), 291–326, cited by Kritzeck, *Peter the Venerable and Islam*, viii n. 3. For a brief discussion with bibliography, see Kritzeck, vii–ix; Merigoux, introduction to Riccoldo da Montedroce, *Contra legem Sarracenorum*, 56–8.

† John V. Tolan, *Petrus Alfonsi and His Medieval Readers* (Gainesville, FL: University of Florida Press, 1993), 108–10.

their pens: gone was any sense that Islam could be a serious intellectual or theological adversary.*

The portrayals of Islam presented in this book found their first expression in the defensive ruminations of Christian *dhimmis* subjected to a vigorous new Muslim empire. The earliest Christian authors to describe the Muslim conquest and dominion of the Christian Roman empire reiterated the standard topoi used since the Hebrew prophets to explain their subjugation: the Muslim invader was a scourge sent by God to punish his wayward flock. As Christians got to know Islam better, and as they saw with growing alarm that their coreligionaries were converting to Islam, they portrayed the rival faith as a Christological heresy, a worldly religion cleverly crafted by the cunning heresiarch Muhammad to dupe an uncouth and lascivious people into following him. This image of Saracen idolatry provided a useful caricature with which the Christian author could justify and glorify the killing of Muslims and the conquest of Muslim territories. By creating a largely imaginary enemy outside the bounds of Christian Europe, the *chansons de geste* could revel in the knightly violence that was in reality more often directed at internal Christian enemies.

This caricature of Saracen paganism was untenable for those with even a rudimentary familiarity with Islam, many of whom portrayed Islam as a Christian heresy. For Guibert de Nogent, chronicling the first Crusade, Muhammad was merely the latest and most nefarious of a long line of oriental heresiarchs: the success of Islam was proof of the oriental penchant for heresy, calling for the intervention of vigorous and stolid Latins. The image of Islam as heresy, an image forged by *dhimmis* in the Near East and Spain, came to northern Europe at a time when Latin Christians were increasingly in contact with Muslims and when they were increasingly preoccupied with the supposedly nefarious influence of other non-Christians, Jews and heretics. The association between these various enemies of the faith is crucial for understanding the Christian perceptions of Muslims (or, for that matter, of Jews or heretics) in the following centuries ...

The development of scholastic theology in the twelfth and thirteenth centuries went hand in hand with the new forms of argumentation used

---

* Nancy Bisaha, "'New Barbarian' or Worthy Adversary? Humanist Constructs of the Ottoman Turks in Fifteenth-Century Italy" in *Western Views*, eds. David Blanks and Michael Frassetto (New York: St. Martin's, 1999), 185–205.

against infidels. If Catholic doctrine was based on reason, it should be possible to prove it to Jews, heretics, and Muslims through logical exposition and argumentation …

The widespread failure of the missionary movements had become clear by the early fourteenth century, as the fall of Acre and the conversion of the Mongols to Islam made manifest. If the infidels were impervious to the subtle reasoning and clear arguments of the missionaries, the fault must lie with the infidels themselves: the obstinate Jews, lascivious Saracens, and barbarous Mongols, all too obsessed with the literal and carnal to understand the intellectual or the spiritual. Peter of Cluny contrasted the learned, logical Arabs with the obdurate Jews whose failure to accept Christian reason led him to wonder whether they really could be rational humans, rather than insensate beasts. Increasingly, as Muslims proved as impervious to "rational" polemics as Jews, the two groups were lumped together as stubborn and irrational infidels. Missionaries such as William of Rubruck and Riccoldo da Montecroce painted the Oriental, Muslim or not, as a foreign, lethargic being unfit for rational argumentation. Because of this irrationality, it was entirely appropriate to use coercion and force with these infidels: to treat them forcefully, as one would treat children or animals, compelling them to submit to Catholic authority, to listen quietly to missionary sermons, and so on.

This phenomenon of lumping together the enemies of the Catholic faith should not be exaggerated. It was one thing to be forced to listen to a Dominican sermon in one's Barcelona mosque or synagogue, something else entirely to be massacred as a Cathar by the Albigensian crusaders. The same authors who associated Jews, Muslims, and heretics as the devil's minions could distinguish their different social and legal statuses. There is a fundamental distinction between violence aimed at the eradication of a deviant group (the Cathar heretics) and coercion aimed at enforcing and maintaining the inferior social status of accepted groups (such as Jews and Muslims) …

The goal, rather than to dole out posthumous prizes for "tolerance" or castigations for intolerance, is to understand what motivated individual writers to portray Saracens as pagan idolaters or to paint Muhammad as a debauched heresiarch—or, on the contrary, to argue that Islam was as legitimate (or nearly so) as Christianity. Only by carefully examining the specific contexts in which medieval authors worked can we understand what motivated them to portray Islam as they did. Among the various motivations exposed are the desire to justify a war against or an alliance with a Muslim state, an attempt to dissuade Christians from converting to Islam, and a need to justify the rule of Christian princes over Muslim subjects. Only by paying close attention to the contexts and motivations of individual writers can we understand what they say about Islam, not by attempting to string them together to produce a narrative of growing intolerance.

Perhaps indeed European denigration of the other is the back side of Christian universalism. As European Christian ideology crystalized and hardened in the twelfth and thirteenth centuries, there was less and less room for dissent. The increasing use of reason to justify this ideology aggravated the situation: those who refused to listen to Christian reason must be irrational: the blind Jew, the stubborn heretic, the flesh-bound Saracen. Well into the thirteenth century, the Saracen indeed had a better reputation than the non-Christians closer to home. The Saracen was reputed for his learning, seen as eminently rational; he (like the Jew) became the object of philosophical polemics and impassioned preaching. When, toward the end of the thirteenth century, it became clear that the Saracen was (like the Jew) impermeable to such "rational" argument, he was relegated to the subrational world of carnal, semibeastly humans. The Saracen (and more generally the non-Christian, be he Jew or Cathar or, in the centuries that followed, an African animist or an Inca priest) was different, was inferior, precisely because he refused the universal and rational message of Christianity.

John Kuo Wei Tchen, "Latin Christendom's 'Doctrine of Discovery': Papal Bulls, 1452, 1455, 1493" (2013)

The formulation of an "us versus them" binary is foundational to perilist thinking and practices. Christendom's dividing the world for Portuguese and Spanish discovery, conquest, and possession embodied incredible papal arrogance and was foundational in the mapping of the world as we know it. Perhaps no three declamations had greater impact than what two popes commanded in the space of a scant forty years for how we still divide the world today.

The year before Eastern Christendom become Ottoman, Pope Nicholas V issued the papal bull *Dum Diversas*, 1452, authorizing King Alfonso V of Portugal to reduce any "Saracens (Muslims) and pagans and any other unbelievers" to perpetual slavery.* This facilitated the Portuguese slave trade from West Africa. As a follow-up to the *Dum Diversas*, Nicholas also wrote the bull *Romanus Pontifex*, 1455, to the same Alfonso. It extended Christendom's dominion over all "discovered" lands. Along with sanctifying the seizure of non-Christian lands, it encouraged the enslavement of native, non-Christian peoples in Africa and the New World.

> We weighing all and singular the premises with due meditation, and noting that since we had formerly by other letters of ours granted among other things free and ample faculty to the aforesaid King Alfonso—to invade, search out, capture, vanquish, and subdue all Saracens and pagans whatsoever, and other enemies of Christ wheresoever placed, and the kingdoms, dukedoms, principalities, dominions, possessions, and all movable and immovable goods whatsoever held and possessed by them and to reduce their persons to perpetual slavery, and to apply and appropriate to himself and his successors the kingdoms, dukedoms, counties, principalities, dominions, possessions, and goods, and to convert them to his and their use and profit— by having secured the said faculty, the said King Alfonso, or, by his authority, the aforesaid infante, justly and lawfully has acquired and possessed, and doth possess, these islands, lands, harbors, and seas, and they do of right belong and pertain to the said King Alfonso and his successors.†

In 1493 Pope Alexander VI issued the bull *Inter Caetera* stating one Christian nation did not have the right to establish dominion over lands previously dominated by another Christian nation, thus establishing a colonially-determined "Law of Nations."

The *Dum Diversas*, the *Romanus Pontifex* and the *Inter Caetera*, among many bulls, came to serve as the basis and justification for the "Doctrine

---

* Jonathan Locke Hart, *Comparing Empires: European Colonialism from Portuguese Expansion to the Spanish-American War* (New York: Palgrave Macmillan, 2003), 18.

† Frances Gardiner Davenport, ed., *European Treaties Bearing on the History of the United States and its Dependencies to 1648* (Washington: The Carnegie Institution of Washington, 1917), 23.

of Discovery," the global slave trade of the fifteenth and sixteenth centuries, and European imperialism. Columbus's imagined "discovery" of the Indies in the western Atlantic Ocean in 1492 further aggravated the monarchial claims of Portugal versus Spain, already competing along the Atlantic African coast for many years. The 1493 papal bull *Inter Caetera* and the 1494 Treaty of Tordesillas remapped Christendom's division of the world.

Although these centuries-old decrees appear antiquated to contemporary secular understandings, their historical legacy remains absolutely inscribed in the very lands, water, and air of the Americas. Native peoples of the Americas continue to organize and protest around these issues. In 2000, they mounted a campaign to repeal the *Inter Caetera.** This doctrine also formulates the basis of the westernizing right of land claims and expansion later expressed in the U.S. formulation of Manifest Destiny. Kaiser Wilhelm II's conjuring of a heathen yellow perilism was squarely within this tradition of Christian colonial logics.

The Treaty of Tordesillas (1494)[28]

This 1494 treaty effected the papal rulings. It divided the newly discovered lands outside Europe between the Crown of Portugal and the Crown of Castile (Spain) in a longitudinal line west of the Cape Verde islands (off the west coast of Africa). This line of demarcation was about halfway between the Cape Verde Islands (already Portuguese) and the islands discovered by Christopher Columbus on his first voyage (claimed for Spain). The lands to the east would belong to Portugal and the lands to the west to Spain. The treaty was ratified by the Crown of Castile (Spain). The other side of the world would be divided a few decades later by the Treaty of Zaragoza in 1529. Originals of both treaties are kept at the Archivo General de Indias in Spain and at the Arquivo Nacional da Torre do Tombo in Portugal.

Like the division of the world between Asia to the east of the Straits of Marmara and Europe to the west noted earlier, this dividing just a scant few centuries apart is also a global history-making mapping of epic proportions. The

---

* John L. Allen Jr., "Indigenous Demand Revocation of 1493 Papal Bull," *National Catholic Reporter*, October 27, 2000.

latter signals the rise of the great naval powers of Spain and Portugal dividing up the globe into domains in which they can respectively "for the sake of peace and concord" "despatch expeditions of discovery, conquest, and trade." This difference marks the raised stakes of technology and ambition, but also the difference of an imagined divinely-sanctioned right soon to be encoded by systems of knowledge and legal apparatus justifying colonial possessions and properties. Territorial hubris preceded what scholars and technicians were then instructed to rationalize. According to Article 3 of the Treaty: "each one of the said parties shall send certain persons in them, to wit, pilots, astrologers, sailors, and any others they may deem desirable" to "determin[e] the line and boundary" between the two Catholic naval powers. Thus, an ensemble of respective Empire-bound specialists skilled at providing such documentation were deployed and continued to play a role in surveillance and knowledge-accumulation for their respective rulers.

[1.] That, whereas a certain controversy exists between the said lords, their constituents, as to what lands, of all those discovered in the ocean sea up to the present day, the date of this treaty, pertain to each one of the said parts respectively; therefore, for the sake of peace and concord, and for the preservation of the relationship and love of the said King of Portugal for the said King and Queen of Castile, Aragon, etc., it being the pleasure of their Highnesses, they, their said representatives, acting in their name and by virtue of their powers herein described, covenanted and agreed that a boundary or straight line be determined and drawn north and south, from pole to pole, on the said ocean sea, from the Arctic to the Antarctic pole. This boundary or line shall be drawn straight, as aforesaid, at a distance of three hundred and seventy leagues west of the Cape Verde Islands, being calculated by degrees, or by any other manner as may be considered the best and readiest, provided the distance shall be no greater than abovesaid. And all lands, both islands and mainlands, found and discovered already, or to be found and discovered hereafter, by the said King of Portugal and by his vessels on this side of the said line and bound determined as above, toward the east, in either north or south latitude, on the eastern side of the said bound provided the said bound is not crossed, shall belong to, and remain in the possession of, and pertain forever to, the said King of Portugal and his successors. And all other lands, both islands and mainlands, found or to be found hereafter, discovered or to be discovered hereafter, which have been discovered or shall be discovered by the said King and Queen of Castile, Aragon, etc., and by their vessels, on the western side of the said bound, determined as above, after having passed the said bound toward the west, in either its north or south latitude, shall belong to, and remain in the possession of, and pertain forever to, the said King and Queen of Castile, Leon, etc., and to their successors.

[2.] Item, the said representatives promise and affirm by virtue of the powers aforesaid, that from this date no ships shall be despatched—namely as follows: the said King and Queen of Castile, Leon, Aragon, etc., for this part of the bound, and its eastern side, on this side the said bound, which pertains to the said King of Portugal and the Algarves, etc.; nor the said King of Portugal to the other part of the said bound which pertains to the said King and Queen of Castile, Aragon, etc.—for the purpose of discovering and seeking any mainlands or islands, or for the purpose of trade, barter, or conquest of any kind. But should it come to pass that the said ships of the said King and Queen of Castile, Leon, Aragon, etc., on sailing thus on this side of the said bound, should discover any mainlands or islands in the region pertaining, as abovesaid, to the said King of Portugal, such mainlands or islands shall pertain to and belong forever to the said King of Portugal and his heirs, and their Highnesses shall order them to be surrendered to him immediately. And if the said ships of the said King of Portugal discover any islands and mainlands in the regions of the said King and Queen of Castile, Leon, Aragon, etc., all such lands shall belong to and remain forever in the possession of the said King and Queen of Castile, Leon, Aragon, etc., and their heirs, and the said King of Portugal shall cause such lands to be surrendered immediately.

[3.] Item, in order that the said line or bound of the said division may be made straight and as nearly as possible the said distance of three hundred and seventy leagues west of the Cape Verde Islands, as hereinbefore stated, the said representatives of both the said parties agree and assent that within the ten months immediately following the date of this treaty their said constituent lords shall despatch two or four caravels, namely, one or two by each one of them, a greater or less number, as they may mutually consider necessary. These vessels shall meet at the Grand Canary Island during this time, and each one of the said parties shall send certain persons in them, to wit, pilots, astrologers, sailors, and any others they may deem desirable.

But there must be as many on one side as on the other, and certain of the said pilots, astrologers, sailors, and others of those sent by the said King and Queen of Castile, Aragon, etc., and who are experienced, shall embark in the ships of the said King of Portugal and the Algarves; in like manner certain of the said persons sent by the said King of Portugal shall embark in the ship or ships of the said King and Queen of Castile, Aragon, etc.; a like number in each case, so that they may jointly study and examine to better advantage the sea, courses, winds, and the degrees of the sun or of north latitude, and lay out the leagues aforesaid, in order that, in determining the line and boundary, all sent and empowered by both the said parties in the said vessels, shall jointly concur. These said vessels shall continue their course together to the said Cape Verde Islands, from whence they shall lay a direct course to the west, to the distance of the said three hundred and seventy degrees, measured as the said persons shall agree, and measured without prejudice to the said parties. When this point is reached, such point will constitute the place and mark for measuring degrees of the sun or of north latitude either by daily runs measured in leagues, or in any other manner that shall mutually be deemed better. This said line shall be drawn north and south as aforesaid, from the said Arctic pole to the said Antarctic pole. And when this line has been determined as abovesaid, those sent by each of the aforesaid parties, to whom each one of the said parties must delegate his own authority and power, to determine the said mark and bound, shall draw up a writing concerning it and affix thereto their signatures. And when determined by the mutual consent of all of them, this line shall be considered as a perpetual mark and bound, in such wise that the said parties, or either of them, or their future successors, shall be unable to deny it, or erase or remove it, at any time or in any manner whatsoever. And should, perchance, the said line and bound from pole to pole, as aforesaid, intersect any island or mainland, at the first point of such intersection of such island or mainland by the said line, some kind of mark or tower shall be erected, and a succession of similar marks shall be erected in a straight line from such mark or tower, in a line identical with the above-mentioned bound. These marks shall separate those portions of such land belonging to each one of the said parties; and the subjects of the said parties shall not dare, on either side, to enter the territory of the other, by crossing the said mark or bound in such island or mainland.

[4.] Item, inasmuch as the said ships of the said King and Queen of Castile, Leon, Aragon, etc., sailing as before declared, from their kingdoms and seigniories to their said possessions on the other side of the said line, must cross the seas on this side of the line, pertaining to the said King of Portugal, it is therefore concerted and agreed that the said ships of the said King and Queen of Castile, Leon, Aragon, etc., shall, at any time and without any hindrance, sail in either direction, freely, securely, and peacefully, over the said seas of the said King of Portugal, and within the said line. And whenever their Highnesses and their successors wish to do so, and deem it expedient, their said ships may take their courses and routes direct from their kingdoms to any region within their line and bound to which they desire to despatch expeditions of discovery, conquest, and trade. They shall take their courses direct to the desired region and for any purpose desired therein, and shall not leave their course, unless compelled to do so by contrary weather. They shall do this provided that, before crossing the said line, they shall not seize or take possession of anything discovered in his said region by the said King of Portugal; and should their said ships find anything before crossing the said line, as aforesaid, it shall belong to the said King of Portugal, and their Highnesses shall order it surrendered immediately. And since it is possible that the ships and subjects of the said King and Queen of Castile, Leon, etc., or those acting in their name, may discover before the twentieth day of this present month of June, following the date of this treaty, some islands and mainlands within the said line, drawn straight from pole to pole, that is to say, inside the said three hundred and seventy leagues west of the Cape Verde Islands, as aforesaid, it is hereby agreed and determined, in order to remove all doubt, that all such islands and mainlands found and discovered in any manner whatsoever up to the said twentieth day of this said month of June, although found by ships and subjects of the said King and Queen of Castile, Aragon, etc., shall pertain to and remain forever in the possession of the said King of Portugal and the Algarves, and of his successors and kingdoms, provided that they lie within the first two hundred and fifty leagues of the said three hundred and seventy leagues reckoned west of the Cape Verde Islands to the above-mentioned line-in whatsoever part, even to the said poles, of the said two hundred and fifty leagues they may be found, determining a boundary or straight line from pole to pole, where the said two hundred and fifty leagues end.

Likewise all the islands and mainlands found and discovered up to the said twentieth day of this present month of June by the ships and subjects of the said King and Queen of Castile, Aragon, etc., or in any other manner, within the other one hundred and twenty leagues that still remain of the said three hundred and seventy leagues where the said bound that is to be drawn from pole to pole, as aforesaid, must be determined, and in whatever part of the said one hundred and twenty leagues, even to the said poles— they that are found up to the said day shall pertain to and remain forever in the possession of the said King and Queen of Castile, Aragon, etc., and of their successors and kingdoms; just as whatever is or shall be found on the other side of the said three hundred and seventy leagues pertaining to their Highnesses, as aforesaid, is and must be theirs, although the said one hundred and twenty leagues are within the said bound of the said three hundred and seventy leagues pertaining to the said King of Portugal, the Algarves, etc., as aforesaid.

Cantino Planisphere (1502)

The Cantino planisphere, 1502, is the earliest surviving map showing Portuguese land claims. Maps like this, used in colonization, were far more precise than the

Figure 27. Cantino Planisphere (1502). Photo: Universal History Archive/UIG / The Bridgeman Art Library.

T-O maps. The Cantino map portrayed the Brazilian coast, "discovered" in 1500 by the Portuguese Pedro Álvares Cabral, and the African coastline with accuracy and detail, in contrast to cosmographic maps. This type of new mapping approach was indebted to Arab mathematics, navigation, and mapmaking.

Gerard Delanty, "The Westernization of Europe" (1995)[29]

Political sociologist Gerard Delanty traces the decisive "epochal moment" in which "the West" breaks with "the East." The year 1492 is pivotal, in which "the ascending European powers in their conquest of the Americas" supplanted "the older ambivalence between Christendom and Europe" with the cultural politics of "Europe and the West," the latter having become the epicenter of a new European imperial world. The break of Europe from Asia, what Paul Valéry described in 1919 as "a little promontory of the continent of Asia," is critical for the Americas' ideology of the westward progressive march of civilization away from the East toward western frontiers.[28] Western Europe at this moment becomes the hinge from which the past ("the Orient") and future (the Americas) are determined. At the same time, a fundamentalist European purification process about who Europeans were and were not worked at wiping away the historical, social, and cultural interminglings of Christians, Jews, Muslims, and various other groups.

Until the late fifteenth century the idea of Europe was principally a geographical expression and subordinated to Christendom which was the dominant identity system in the West. The idea of Europe as the West began to be consolidated in the foreign conquests of the age of "discovery." Europe then begins to shed itself of its association with Christendom and slowly becomes an autonomous discourse. As a result of the fall of Constantinople to the Turks in 1453 and the subsequent colonial expansion of the western European powers after 1492, the idea of Europe became linked to a system of what was coming to be regarded as specifically European values, though these did not become fully articulated as a European identity until the late seventeenth century. It was thus in the encounter with non-European peoples and in resistance to Ottoman expansion that the idea of Europe itself became the focus for the construction of a specifically European identity.

What we are therefore witnessing … is the transformation of the idea of Europe into a European identity whereby Europe refers not merely to a geographical area but a system of "civilisational" values. In this movement the idea of Europe supplanted Christendom as the cultural frame of reference for new processes of identity formation and the rise of new centres of power. In doing so, however, a tension emerged between the cultural idea of Europe and the geographical framework to which it referred. As a cultural framework Europe became the normative idea of a civilisation that was in the process of expanding overseas, but as the name of that civilisation's geographical territory it was faced with the problem that a considerable part lay under Ottoman suzerainty. This tension could not easily be reconciled, and so we find that the idea of Europe tended to be overshadowed by the hegemonic notion of the West, which became the driving force of the ascending European powers in their conquest of the Americas. The older ambivalence between Christendom and Europe was thus replaced by a new one with Europe and the West as the shifting signifiers of a rapidly expanding world-system with its epicentre in western Europe.

With expansion in the East for a time closed off, the lands beyond the seas provided room for European expansionary zeal. The age of discovery was a renewal of the crusading idea but with the difference that it was primarily western bound and the product of the new absolutist regimes and Counter-Reformation Roman Catholicism. In this transformation a new being was born: the European. The acquisition of the New World greatly strengthened a sense of European superiority at a time when the West had failed to defeat the Muslim Orient. In its colonising thrust across the Atlantic a myth was created. This was the European myth of the West, which was in subsequent centuries to become an important part of the identity of North America in the myth of the limitless frontier of the West. And, Europe, as the Old World, became the cultural repository of the New World. The myth of European civilisation was thus given substance.

In this period Europe emerged to become a clearly defined region, the centre of what Wallerstein* has called a "world-system," and acquired an enduring identity based on its westward thrust. Up until the sixteenth century there

---

* Immanuel Wallerstein, *The Modern World System* (New York: Academic Press, 1974) and *The World System II* (New York: Academic Press, 1980).

were several world-systems, of which the European was relatively insignificant.[*] What may have been of greater significance was the Oriental-western world-system in the thirteenth and fourteenth centuries and the Mediterranean civilisation of the sixteenth century.[†] It may therefore have been, as Marshall Hodgson[‡] once suggested, that European modernity was "the outcome of a breakdown of the common historical conditions on which rested the pre-modern Afro-Eurasian historical complex as a whole." It is important to appreciate that the "unity of Europe" which was constituted in this transformation was an invented unity. To imagine Europe involves the privileging of a particular discourse over others. In the Middle Ages this was Christianity against Islam; in the early modern period it was the victory of civilisation over nature ...

Western Europe never reached the same degree of unity as other world empires had. Islam, for instance, like Christianity, is a religion of unity, but unlike Christianity it claims that all laws derive directly from God.[§] It is possible that the diversity of Europe was precisely as a result of the failure of the Church to unite western Europe into a single bloc. The answer that Europe found to the problem of cultural uniformity was the creation of what could be called a central institution in the form of the Church, which had succeeded in devising master codes for the organisation of knowledge according to a differentiated and rationalised world-view, but a world-view, it must be added, that failed to control political life. So, a civilisation such as India, in contrast, failed to develop unifying master codes to deal with its own diversity.[¶] The problem, then, is in using the idea of Europe to describe what are, in fact, structures of polymorphous diversity and manifold opposition to power. The "unity" of Europe was more the pose of elites than a political reality.

Cultural diversity within Christendom ensured that the unity that Europe

---

[*] Fernand Braudel, *Afterthoughts on Material Civilization and Capitalism* (Baltimore, MD: Johns Hopkins University Press, 1979), 80–5.

[†] Janet L. Abu-Lughod, *Before European Hegemony: The World-System A.D. 1250–1350* (New York: Oxford University Press, 1989).

[‡] Marshall Hodgson, "The Interrelations of Societies in History," *Comparative Studies in Society and History* 5 (1962/3), 250.

[§] Anthony Black, "Classical Islam and Medieval Europe: A Comparison of Political Philosophies and Cultures," *Political Studies*, XLI (1993), 58–69.

[¶] Satish Saberwal, *India: The Roots of Crisis: Interpreting Contemporary Indian Society* (Oxford: Oxford University Press, 1986), 23.

was to find was in foreign conquest and a focus of hostility beyond its frontiers. The hegemony Roman Catholicism eventually achieved should not blind one to the fact of the essential disunity of the Middle Ages. As Braudel has remarked, Europe is diversity itself.* The One Hundred Years War (1337–1453) between England and France, for instance, prevented the unification of the two countries and the formation of a mega-bloc in western Europe. For much of the fourteenth century there was a major schism in the Church with the popes resident in Avignon. Nor should we forget the long tradition of anti-Roman Catholicism that eventually culminated in the Protestant Reformation.

As we have seen, the year 1453 was a turning point. After the fall of the Byzantine empire, the Latin West began to look westwards. The great defeat that the Turkish seizure of Constantinople signalled for the West was compensated for within four decades. The year 1492 was symbolically an important one in the formation of a European identity. In that year the Reconquest begun in the twelfth century was completed with the seizure of Granada from the Muslims, their last stronghold in the West. The Jews were expelled from Spain and the Muslims were forcibly converted to Christianity. The Christianised Muslims, the Morescos, were finally expelled from Spain in the early seventeenth century. This event in the history of Europe gave rise to the doctrine of the purity of the blood, which became the core of European racism in subsequent ages and a major legitimation of "ethnic cleansing."† The destruction of the mosques, the burning of Moorish libraries and the establishment of the Inquisition in the late fifteenth century further enhanced the homogeneity of western civilisation as a Christian polity.

After the late twelfth century the segregation of the Jews established a fear of pollution in Europe. According to R. I. Moore and Cohen, Europe became a persecuting society in the early twelfth century when the new apparatus of government turned to minorities for a focus of hostility: heretics and Jews, for instance.‡ The repression and persecution of minorities thus became a central

---

* Fernand Braudel, *The Mediterranean and the Mediterranean World in the Age of Philip II*, vols. 1 and 2 (London: Fontana, 1990), 190.

† Léon Poliakov, *The Aryan Myth: A History of Racist and Nationalist Ideas in Europe* (New York: Basic Books, 1974), 137.

‡ R. I. Moore, *The Formation of a Persecuting Society: Authority and Deviance in Western Europe 950–1250* (Oxford: Blackwell, 1987); Norman Cohn, *Europe's Inner Demons: The Demonization of Christians in Medieval Christendom* (London: Pimlico, 1993).

component in European modernisation. It is possible that the split in Latin Christianity that occurred with the Reformation was projected onto scapegoats such as the Jews and women. This could explain the mass exodus of Jews from Central Europe and the increased witch-hunting which accompanied the zenith of the Reformation and Counter-Reformation.* With the deliverance of Europe from the external enemy following the final retreat of Islam from the Iberian peninsula, the function of the victim, Europe's Other, was transferred onto the internal enemy, the Jews. This is also a demonstration that European unity was often the result of violent homogenisation.

The ascendant absolute monarchy in Spain required the cultivation of a myth of legitimation based on universal Catholic monarchy in which there could be no room for even the traces of earlier civilisations. From being a frontier land, Spain became a bulwark of a revived and imperialist Roman Catholicism. "Europe conquered the Peninsula," Braudel has written, "by way of the Pyrenees and by the Atlantic and Mediterranean shipping routes: along this frontier zone it defeated Islam with the victories of the Reconquest which were victories for Europe."† Europe became subordinated to the notion of the West in the wake of the reconquest of the Iberian peninsula. Until the Reconquest Spain, being under Muslim rule, was not in the "West" for Christendom. Prior to the Age of Discovery, the West as the Occident was defined by reference to the eastern frontier, that is, in opposition to Islam. After 1492 the ground had been prepared for the invention of a new myth of the West: Columbus replaced Charlemagne as the harbinger of the new age. The notion of the West became transformed into an outward movement.

---

* Jonathan Israel, *European Jewry in the Age of Mercantilism 1550–1750* (Oxford: Oxford University Press, 1985), 6–7.

† Braudel, *The Mediterranean*, 824.

Part Two: Manifest Destinies

How do we unpack the impact of colonialism on the development of Western thinking? What can we do to identify assumptions that limit our thinking? The first step is to identify this history, not run away from it. Part Two seeks to open up inquiry with the hope of provoking further research on yellow perilism.

The "Age of Discovery" heralded an expansionist West with boundless global possibility. In search for wealth and power, merchants, traders, missionaries, and soldiers created markets and systems of exchange. They engaged in what Adam Smith later formulated as the secrets to wealth-making—trading coveted goods from afar in exchange for more plentiful goods nearby. As the passions for luxuries in Europe and its colonies escalated, these chains of exchange drove the plundering of Africa, the Spice Islands, and the colonization of the Americas. Once unleashed, these unruly passions could not be easily contained by older forms of governmentality.[1]

According to economist Albert Hirschman, "capitalist forms owed much to an equally desperate search for a way of avoiding society's ruin, permanently threatening at the time because of precarious arrangements for internal and external order." The expansion of commerce and industry was welcomed by "the intellectual, managerial, and administrative elite" of the seventeenth and eighteenth centuries "not because money-making activities were approved in themselves" (as Weber has emphasized) but "because they were thought to have a most beneficial side effect: they kept the men who were engaged in them 'out of mischief,' as it were, and had, more specifically, the virtue of imposing restraints on princely caprice, arbitrary government, and adventurous foreign policies." This social system of individuals making money helped to consolidate the national interest. It turned "passions into interests."[2]

The promise of shared political power, in the form of granting the vote to larger circles of a property-owning citizenry, became another primary strategy to tame passions regularly aroused to new heights by the unprecedented wealth and luxuries of competitive industrialization and competitive colonialism. In the *Two Treatises*, Locke's formulation of these ideals as "Freedom of Men under Government" meant such individuals were "not to be subject to the inconstant, uncertain, unknown, arbitrary will of another man."[3] This freedom, freedom to own oneself, freedom to actualize individual potential, was defined against others imagined to be stagnant and therefore unfree to seize upon the promise of progress. Within these racially and sexually delimited social contracts, white women were deemed unable to represent themselves; the savage New World indigenous was deemed unfit to own land; the barbaric enslaved African was deemed unfit to own his own labor; and the semi-civilized Oriental was deemed unfit to lead enlightened civilization. Seventeenth- and eighteenth-century colonial expansion created new elites who asserted their rights to govern by pointing to their ownership of land, women, and slaves. This settler-colonial liberalism spawned constitutional monarchy in the British dominion and new republics founded on colonial expropriations.[4]

Psychoanalyst Ashis Nandy has described colonialism as the armed version of modernity.[5] Basking in the glow of the liberatory promise of colonial expansion, Occidentalist knowledge-makers built a modern conception of "the West" as entitled, if not destined, to rule and lead the rest of the world. In an updated, secularized version of the tripartite logic of Christendom's T-O map, Africa represents the enslaved primitive, Asia represents the unfree "semi-civilized," and Europe represents the apogee of civilization and the hope for mankind. This language of essential racial differences, the progress of modernity, and the justification for colonialism still haunts us.

While Americans rejected what they saw as the decadence and despotism of European monarchy, colonialism, and court intrigue, they did not question the fundamental political philosophies and practices of their British forebears. Literal ownership as a justification for political participation morphed into a mass politics rooted in racial and gendered properties.

The supposedly exclusive purchase on manliness, rationality, taste, and the capacity for self-betterment entitled white men alone to formal American citizenship. In this way, an emerging political system purportedly founded upon equality, individuality, and self-actualization was transmuted to an equal entitlement to white male supremacy.[6]

But this fragile political identity, imagined in biological and cultural terms, depended on a fantasy of limitless growth, an expanding field of opportunity that could harness every white man's passions and potential. The promise of the Manifest Destiny of white individualist progress could hardly withstand the economic turmoil such expansionism unleashed. Colonial frontiers and racial segregation provided temporary "relief valves" from this contradictory dynamic, provoking greater and greater expansion abroad but also greater restriction, rationalization, and segregation at home. With the collapse of local moral economies, the symbolic political power of the individual whitened man over his own destiny, often thwarted in reality, was recast as the abstract attitudinal power of the white race to determine the fate of the world.[7]

It is here that Yellow Peril took on its modern valence. Competitive empire building dragged European states into war against each other many, many times. By the late nineteenth century this global conflict posed a paired set of "questions" about who would control Asia—the Russians or the British. "The Eastern Question" referred to who would control access between Central Asia and the Mediterranean, including the Persian Gulf and the Black, Caspian, and Red seas. "The Far Eastern Question" referred to who would control access to the Korean peninsula, the Yellow Sea, and the Sea of Japan. The Ottoman and Chinese empires ostensibly controlled these two questioned strategic sites respectively, but analysts argued these empires had "stagnated." French, German, American, and then Japanese players scrambled to join the British and Russians in claiming control over Asia.[8]

Furthermore, when Japan announced itself as a player in this game of empire in China during the Sino-Japanese War of 1895, it conjured Kaiser Wilhelm II's dream noted in the introduction. Wilhelm's Chancellor Otto von Bismarck had hosted the Berlin Conference in 1884, where the European powers divided up Africa. The Kaiser's dream following Japan's victory over the Chinese was that this Asian threat might help Europeans join together and avoid more wars over Chinese territory.[9] In an anxiously divided and militaristic Europe, Wilhelm's political cartoon, arguing for a civilizational protective reaction policy, caught on like wildfire, especially after the Japanese defeated white Russians in a war over access to the Korean peninsula in 1904. In this context a prominent French journalist noted:

> The "yellow peril" has entered already into the imagination of the people, just as represented in the famous drawing of the Emperor William II: in a setting of conflagration and carnage, Japanese and Chinese hordes spread out over all Europe, crushing under their feet the ruins of our capital cities and destroying our civilizations, grown anemic due to the enjoyment of luxuries and corrupted by vanity of spirit. Hence, little by little there emerges the idea that even if a day must come (and that day does not seem near) when the European peoples will cease to be their own enemies and even economic rivals, there will be a struggle ahead to face and there will rise a new peril, the yellow man. The civilized world has always organized itself before and against a common adversary: for the Roman world, it was the barbarian; for the Christian world, it was Islam; for the world of tomorrow, it may well be the "yellow man." And so we have the reappearance of this necessary concept, without which peoples do not know themselves, just as the "Me" only takes conscience of itself in opposition to the "non-Me": the enemy.[10]

Japanese imperialism posed a new question for anxious European imperialists: What if Asians had their own Manifest Destiny? To many European observers it seemed that rather than bring the progressive spirit of civilization across the globe, Asian empires would bring carnage. They would sink the world into a sea of blood and skulls (Figure 28). Western civilizational advance and a destiny that celebrated divine expansion and technological progress as the unique inheritance of Europeans could not accommodate the reality of geostrategic contests. The Ethiopian victory over the Italians at Adwa in 1896, the Boer near-victory over the British in 1900, and of course the Japanese victory over the Russians all upset the racial logic of liberatory expansionism. There had always been resistance to empire. European American colonists were constantly racked with anxiety over slave revolts and natives attacking in the night. But the Japanese embrace of the promise of expansionism called into question the already fragile assumptions of

Figure 28. Georges Bigot, "The Asian Empire" (Paris: Z.T.N., 1904–1905), Leonard A. Lauder Collection of Japanese Postcards, Museum of Fine Arts, Boston. Photograph © 2013 Museum of Fine Arts, Boston.

white supremacy and helped crystalize a set of fears around a new term that
could be read back into history or projected onto the future: the Yellow
Peril.

The two chapters in Part Two suggest how yellow perilism haunted
the Westernization of Europe and the U.S. Chapter Three, "Geo-Racial
Mapping," offers nineteenth-century excerpts that illustrate the role of
visions of Asian degeneracy in the development of a European sense of self
and the long tradition of mapping immutable racial differences as a way of
making sense of the world. Chapter Four, "Anglo-America's 'Great Game,'"
plays off Rudyard Kipling's term to describe the geostrategic "survival of
the fittest" struggles in order to show how the political psychology of colonialism betrayed its own limitations and fears. Both these chapters sketch
out the ways in which fantasies of epic grandeur and elementary difference trap us in binaries that cannot be reconciled. We hope that by laying
bare these provocative fragments of yellow perilism we can begin to see our
way out.

3

Geo-Racial Mapping

Inspired by the account book, the printing press, and the map, Encyclopedists like Diderot and Naturalists like Linnaeus sought to carve the world's knowledge into bits and rearrange, combine them to see what they could reveal. Some Western scholars attempted to organize the world's people by skin color, phenotype, and imagined immutable character. They mapped these characteristics onto a fanciful simplified history of linear development and believed these patterns suggested a unique, progressive racial destiny. The supposed inferiority of others seemed to explain European power, and the fear of racial degeneracy justified colonial conquest. In 1824, the French naturalist Julien-Joseph Virey asserted, "The European, called by his high destiny to rule the world, which he knows how to illuminate with his intelligence and subdue with his courage, is the highest expression of man and the head of the human race. The others, a wretched horde of barbarians, are, so to say, no more than its embryo." Virey here identified one of the central faultiness between the West and the "rest." Some people were rational individuals who together could forge a national and racial destiny befitting their distinguished past and manly aptitudes. Other people were stagnant, undifferentiated hordes who would impede global progress.[1]

Nineteenth-century Americans, for example, made this divide perfectly clear, and it helped them make sense of what we often imagine today to be the contradictory dynamics of a society founded on the principles of freedom and the practice of slavery.[2] In the 1850s, John Bachman, Lutheran minister in Charleston, South Carolina, fused his belief in racial science to the Christian doctrine that all humans descended from Adam and Eve. He ascribed to the view that the problematic category of Caucasians were the blessed descendants of Noah's son Shem, Mongolians were the descendants of Japheth, and Africans the descendants of Ham. This biblical typology fit into Bachman's belief in human progress and the promise of science. "We have been irresistibly brought to the conviction that in intellectual power the African is an inferior variety of our species. His whole history affords evidence that he is incapable of self-government."[3] Harvard historian Francis Parkman explained the obvious inverse of this racial mapping. "The Germanic race, and especially the Anglo-Saxon branch of it, is perfectly masculine and, therefore, peculiarly fitted for self-government. It submits its actions habitually to the guidance of reason, and has the judicial faculty of seeing both sides of a question."[4]

Enlightenment scientists, scholars, and policy makers measured, typologized, and classified the world. Racial classification as a master organizing principle has characterized the human dimensions of this work. The races of mankind were systematically organized hierarchically by appearance, skull sizes, forehead angles, mental capacity, ad nauseam. Racial science attempted to unlock the mysteries of humankind. Where did Homo sapiens first emerge? Were there multiple sites or just one? When did this happen? Eighteenth- and nineteenth-century racial science still informs Anglo American common sense today. Africans are a primitive people. Asians had a once great civilization but their advance stalled. "The West" is the most advanced, and its individuals the most free and brilliant. Oriental males, whether Arab, Muslim, or East Asian, are patriarchal and oppressive.

These thinkers juxtaposed the inherent despotism of Orientals against the promise of individuality and civilization they believed stemmed from the Greeks, and would remain an exclusive European possession. Mirroring the biological arguments of their contemporaries, they believed that something special, exceptional even, lent Europeans the ability to progress, to individuate, with liberatory consequences. European superiority let individualism break out from the chains of natural degradation, and allowed Europeans and Americans to dominate others justly.

The very metrics that had justified European imperialism seemed also to favor the Japanese over Europeans in Asia. Fantasies of Oriental Despotism and hordes of hive-minded drones led many analysts to believe the Japanese, and all Asians, were better suited for industrial modernity and military order than Europeans. Elaborate geo-racial mapping suggested that Asians fared better in the semi-tropical climates where European colonialism was least secure. Fantasies of what Theodore Roosevelt termed "race suicide"—the lower birthrates that accompanied the emergence of an industrial proletariat and educated bourgeoisie—suggested that Asians might be more fertile than whites. Such fears were exacerbated by colonial fantasies. Europeans and Americans imagined dwindling populations of indigenous Africans, Native Americans, and Aboriginal Australians would give way to superior European colonizing stock. But if Asians were better suited to the climate and practice of modern imperialism, would they instead inherit the world?

This chapter assembles fragments to present three overlapping elements of this geo-racial mapping as it relates to yellow perilism. First, we trace the hierarchical logic of nineteenth-century racial science where the classification of humans seemed to suggest that some were more predestined for greatness than others. Then we present an ensemble of key European thinkers invested in the idea of Oriental Despotism and its meaning for the freedom of the world. Finally, we explore histories and fantasies of the Mongol hordes that stood in the way of progressive expansion, and the fears that they might jeopardize the civilizing project.

Carl Linnaeus, "Five Categories of Homo Sapiens" (1758)[5]

Carl Linnaeus (1707–1778) was a Swedish botanist and physician who pioneered modern taxonomy. In 1735–39, he published the first edition of Systema Naturae *and subsequent editions enlarged and refined his systematic naming and organization of flora and fauna. Among his foundational achievements was the naming of "mammals" after their mammary glands and "Homo sapiens" as an animal species. Linnaeus based his findings on actual fieldwork. He collected samples and sent out trained students to collect samples on colonial ships from around the world. Daniel Solander, for example, joined botanist Daniel Banks on Captain James Cook's voyage into the Pacific Ocean on the* Endeavour *(1768–71). This more empirical approach however, was still fraught with Greek and Renaissance notions of group differences. In the tenth edition (1758) Linnaeus identified five categories of Homo sapiens "varying in education and situation": the Wild Man, the American, the European, the Asiatic, and the African. The Asiatic was said to be "severe, haughty, covetous …*

Governed by opinions." In contrast, the European was "gentle, acute, inventive.... Governed by laws." Earlier representations of Oriental/Asiatic otherness were now translated into modern, scientific form. Though Linnaeus only differentiated humans by "education and situation," he apparently considered skin color a fundamental differential, as the first distinguished feature cited for all.

Wild man. Four-footed, mute, hairy.

American. Copper-coloured, choleric, erect.

Hair black, straight, thick; *nostrils* wide; *face* harsh; *beard* scanty; *obstinate*, content free. *Paints* himself with fine red lines. *Regulated* by customs.

European. Fair, sanguine, brawny.

Hair yellow, brown, flowing; *eyes* blue; *gentle*, acute, inventive. *Covered* with close vestments. *Governed* by laws.

Asiatic. Sooty, melancholy, rigid.

Hair black; *eyes* dark; *severe*, haughty, covetous. *Covered* with loose garments. *Governed* by opinions.

African. Black, phlegmatic, relaxed.

Hair black, frizzled; *skin* silky; *nose* flat; *lips* tumid; *crafty*, indolent, negligent. *Anoints* himself with grease. *Governed* by caprice.

Johann Friedrich Blumenbach, "Five Races of Mankind" (1795)

Johann Friedrich Blumenbach (1752–1840) was a German physician, physiologist, and anthropologist at the University at Göttingen. His focus on comparative anatomy led him to argue for human diversity along lines of racial differences as evidenced by skulls' shapes and measurements. He claimed to have scientifically proven there were five races of humankind. One metric of Blumenbach's classification was the line of the forehead, said to be higher among "Caucasians" and lower among "Mongolians" and "Ethiopians." and this is the origin of the still common usage of "high brow" and "low brow." Blumenbach also added "Malayan" and "Caribbean" as racial types in the 1795 edition of his On the Natural Variety of Mankind. *He was also the first to associate these races with fixed colors: white, yellow, black, brown, and red. He based his Malayan classification on a single skull he secured from Captain James Cook's second voyage (1772–75), and named the "most handsome and becoming" racial type after his favorite skull, that of a female Georgian. Blumenbach's colleague Christoph*

Plate III.

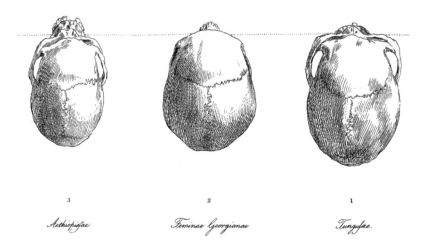

Figure 29. Following the older tradition of the T-O map, Blumenbach initially divided mankind into three "types" with descending head size from Asians, through Europeans, to Africans. *The Anthropological Treatises of Johann Friedrich Blumenbach* (London: Anthropological Society of London, 1865), plate III. Courtesy of the New York Public Library.

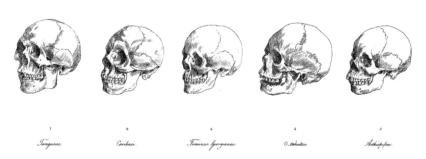

Figure 30. "The Five Races of Mankind," Tungusan (referencing the Amur River in China and referring to all Asians), Caribbean (referring to all Native Americans), Female Georgian ("Caucasian" Europeans and North Africans), Tahitian (referring to Pacific Islanders and later translated as Malay), and Ethiopian (referring to all sub-Saharan Africans). *The Anthropological Treatises of Johann Friedrich Blumenbach* (London: Anthropological Society of London, 1865), plate IV. Courtesy of the New York Public Library.

Meiners argued that the Caucasus Mountains near Georgia was the dividing line between Europeans and Asians, and the name stuck. Blumenbach argued "high browed" Adam and Eve were Caucasian and other groups degenerated due to sun and poor diet.[6]

Robert Chambers, "The Development of Color" (1844)[7]

Robert Chambers (1802–1871) was a Scottish journal editor, publisher, geologist, and phrenologist. Ninety years after Linnaeus, Chambers published this pre-Darwinian theory of human development anonymously in an accessible popular form—in part inspired by the work of the Edinburgh Phrenological Society. Vestiges of the Natural History of Creation *became an international best seller. Prince Albert reportedly read it aloud to Queen Victoria in 1845. The single origins of mankind were herein linked with racial characteristics as the lead indicator of progressive human development. The theory established a rationalist justification for a range of Eurocentric practices, from colonization and Manifest Destiny to social Darwinism, Eugenics, and Aryanism.*

The human race is known to consist of numerous nations, displaying considerable differences of external form and colour, and speaking in general different languages. This has been the case since the commencement of written record. It is also ascertained that the external peculiarities of particular nations do not rapidly change. There is rather a tendency to a persistency of type in all lines of descent, insomuch that a subordinate admixture of various type is usually obliterated in a few generations. Numerous as the varieties are, they have all been found classifiable under five leading ones:—1. The Caucasian, or Indo-European, which extends from India into Europe and Northern Africa; 2. The Mongolian, which occupies Northern and Eastern Asia; 3. The Malayan, which extends from the Ultra-Gangetic Peninsula into the numerous islands of the South Sea and Pacific; 4. The Negro, chiefly confined to Africa; 5. The aboriginal American. Each of these is distinguished by certain general features of so marked a kind, as to give rise to a supposition that they have had distinct or independent origins. Of these peculiarities, colour is the most conspicuous: the Caucasians are generally white, the Mongolians yellow, the Negroes black, and the Americans red. The opposition of two of these in particular, white and black, is so striking, that of them, at least, it seems almost necessary to suppose separate origins. Of late years, however, the whole of this question has been subjected to a rigorous investigation, and it has been successfully shown that the human race might have had one origin, for anything that can be inferred from external peculiarities ...

The probability may now be assumed that the human race sprung from one stock, which was at first in a state of simplicity, if not barbarism. As yet we have not seen very distinctly how the various branches of the family, as they parted off, and took up separate ground, became marked by external features so peculiar. Why are the Africans black, and generally marked by coarse features and ungainly forms? Why are the Mongolians generally yellow, the Americans red, the Caucasians white? Why the flat features of the Chinese, the small stature of the Laps, the soft round forms of the English, the lank features of their descendants, the Americans? All of these phenomena appear, in a word, to be explicable on the ground of *development*. We have already seen that various leading animal forms represent stages in the embryotic progress of the highest—the human being. Our brain goes through the various stages of a fish's, a reptile's, and a mammifer's brain, and finally becomes human. There is more than this, for, after completing the animal transformations, it passes through the characters in which it appears, in the Negro, Malay, American, and Mongolian nations, and finally is Caucasian. The face partakes of these alterations. "One of the earliest points in which ossification commences is the lower jaw. This bone is consequently sooner completed than the other bones of the head, and acquires a predominance, which, as is well known, it never loses in the Negro. During the soft pliant state of the bones of the skull, the oblong form which they naturally assume, approaches nearly the permanent shape of the Americans. At birth, the flattened face, and broad smooth forehead of the infant, the position of the eyes rather towards the side of the head, and the widened space between, represent the Mongolian form; while it is only as the child advances to maturity, that the oval face, the arched forehead, and the marked features of the true Caucasian, become perfectly developed."* *The leading characters, in short, of the various races of mankind,*

---

* Lord's Popular Physiology, explaining observations by M. Serres.

are simply representations of particular stages in the development of the highest or Caucasian type. The Negro exhibits permanently the imperfect brain, projecting lower jaw, and slender bent limbs, of a Caucasian child, some considerable time before the period of its birth. The aboriginal American represents the same child nearer birth. The Mongolian is an arrested infant newly born. And so forth. All this is as respects form;* but whence colour? This might be supposed to have depended on climatal agencies only; but it has been shewn by overpowering evidence to be independent of these. In further considering the matter, we are met by the very remarkable fact that colour is deepest in the least perfectly developed type, next in the Malay, next in the American, next in the Mongolian, the very order in which the degrees of development are ranged. *May not colour, then, depend upon development also?* We do not, indeed, see that a Caucasian fœtus at the stage which the African represents is anything like black; neither is a Caucasian child yellow, like the Mongolian. There may, nevertheless, be a character of skin at a certain stage of development which is predisposed to a particular colour when it is presented as the envelope of a mature being. Development being arrested at so immature a stage in the case of the Negro, the skin may take on the colour as an unavoidable consequence of its imperfect organization. It is favourable to this view, that Negro infants are not deeply black at first, but only acquire the full colour tint after exposure for some time to the atmosphere. Another consideration in its favour is that there is a likelihood of peculiarities of form and colour, since they are so coincident, depending on one set of phenomena. If it be admitted as true, there can be no difficulty in accounting for all the varieties of mankind. They are simply the result of so many advances and retrogressions in the developing power of the human mothers, these advances and retrogressions being, as we have formerly seen, the immediate effect of external conditions in nutrition, hardship,† and also, perhaps, to some extent, of the suitableness and

---

* Conformably to this view, the beard, that peculiar attribute of maturity, is scanty in the Mongolian, and scarcely exists in the Americans and Negroes.

† Of this we have perhaps an illustration in the peculiarities which distinguish the Arabs residing in the valley of the Jordan. They have flatter features, darker skins, and coarser hair than other tribes of their nation; and we have seen one instance of a thoroughly Negro family being born to an ordinary couple. It may be presumed that the conditions of the life of these people tend to arrest development. We thus see how

unsuitableness of marriages, for it is found that parents too nearly related tend to produce offspring of the Mongolian type, that is, persons who in maturity still are a kind of children. According to this view, the greater part of the human race must be considered as having lapsed or declined from the original type. In the Caucasian or Indo-European family alone has the primitive organization been improved upon. The Mongolian, Malay, American, and Negro, comprehending perhaps five-sixths of mankind, are degenerate. Strange that the great plan should admit of failures and aberrations of such portentous magnitude! But pause and reflect; take time into consideration: the past history of mankind may be, to what is to come, but as a day. Look at the progress even now making over the barbaric parts of the earth by the best examples of the Caucasian type, promising not only to fill up the waste places, but to supersede the imperfect nations already existing. Who can tell what progress may be made, even in a single century, towards reversing the proportions of the perfect and imperfect types? And who can tell but that the time during which the mean types have lasted, long as it appears, may yet be thrown entirely into the shade by the time during which the best types will remain predominant?

Samuel George Morton, "Types of Mankind" (1854)

Samuel George Morton (1799–1851), President of the Philadelphia Academy of Sciences, assembled a collection of more than 1,000 skulls, believed to be the largest in existence at that time. Morton collected his skulls in a time of imperial expansion. He received the skulls of slain Seminole warriors from the U.S. Army following the Second Seminole War to remove the Florida tribe in 1835, and those of indigenous Liberians resisting colonial settlement by African Americans there in the 1840s. Medical doctors in Cuba and the Dutch East Indies sent him skulls of coerced plantation laborers who had died in the field. Morton, a follower of Blumenbach and a student of Scottish phrenologist George Combe, scrupulously measured these skulls and concluded that the five human races were in fact separate species. In his influential Crania Americana *(1839) Morton*

---

an offshoot of the human family migrating at an early period into Africa, might in time, from subjection to similar influences, become Negroes.

argued that the Caucasian race was "distinguished for the facility with which it attains the highest intellectual endowments." In his time Morton's theories were celebrated at Harvard and the Smithsonian, but twentieth-century biologist Stephen Jay Gould has illustrated the misunderstanding of human intelligence expressed by early scientists like Morton and also identified how Morton's quantitative analysis was itself skewed by his racial assumptions.[8]

While Morton never argued that his findings justified slavery or colonialism, his acolytes did. South Carolina physician Josiah Clark Nott and British Egyptologist George Robin Gliddon published Types of Mankind *based on Morton's notes after his death. Nott and Gliddon used Morton's work to defend slavery and empire, and their work was cited on the Senate floor. "Dark-skinned races," according to Nott and Gliddon, were "only fit for military governments." Abolitionist and political activist Frederick Douglass publically challenged the logic of polygenesis and racial hierarchy, calling it heretical to Christian brotherhood and "scientific moonshine."*[9]

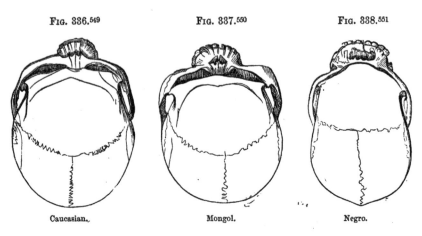

Fig. 336.[549] Fig. 337.[550] Fig. 338.[551]

Caucasian. Mongol. Negro.

Figure 31. "Comparative Anatomy of Races." *Types of Mankind: or, Ethnological Researches, Based Upon the Ancient Monuments, Paintings, Sculptures, and Crania of Races, and Upon their Natural, Geographical, Philological, and Biblical History*, eds. Josiah Clark Nott, George Robin Gliddon, et al. (Philadelphia: Lippincott, Grambo, & Co., 1854), 457. Courtesy of the New York Public Library.

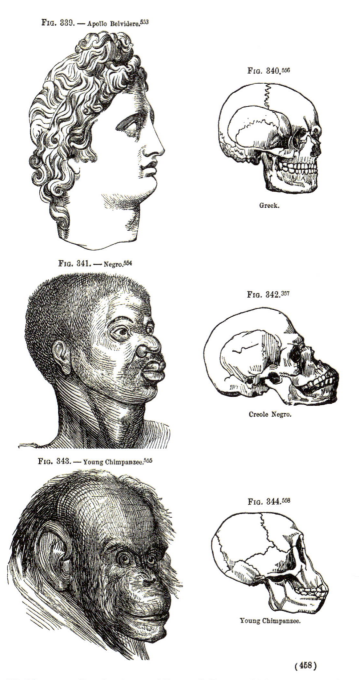

FIG. 339. — Apollo Belvidere.[553]

FIG. 340.[556]

Greek.

FIG. 341. — Negro.[554]

FIG. 342.[357]

Creole Negro.

FIG. 343. — Young Chimpanzee.[555]

FIG. 344.[556]

Young Chimpanzee.

(458)

Figure 32. "Comparative Anatomy of Races," *Types of Mankind*, 458. Courtesy of the New York Public Library.

Phrenological Journal (1870)

Samuel R. Wells (1820–1875) edited and published the American Phrenological Journal *(Figure 33) dedicated "to all those progressive measures calculated to Reform, Elevate, and Improve Mankind." The diagram at the center attributes various functions to the different areas of the brain. Note how Wells located the mental functions associated with "History" and "Individuality" at the base of the brow. This cover also presents Blumenbach's five races with none other than George Washington representing Caucasians at the center. The supposedly "lower-browed" Indian, Mongolian, Negro, and Malay races were not personified by influential individuals. Pioneering Scottish phrenologist George Combe published his own journal in Edinburgh in which he argued that phrenological research made sense of imperialism: "we conclude that among nations … the larger-headed nations manifest their superior power, by subjecting and ruling their smaller-headed brethren—as the British in Asia, for example."[10]*

Ernst Haeckel, "Descendants of the Great Apes" (1876)

Originally published in German as a response to Darwin's theories, Ernst Haeckel (1834–1919) argued for polygenesis, the multiple strands of human evolution, as opposed to Darwin's theory (since confirmed) that all humans emerged from a single source in Africa. This chart (Figure 34) shows Haeckel's six races of mankind and their relationship to six regional primates from which he believed each race descended.

"The Jolly Giant's Artist Agrees with Darwin" (1874)

This cartoon (Figure 35) from a San Francisco satirical weekly magazine playfully reflected the popularity of Charles Darwin's evolutionary theory in America. This illustration demonstrates familiarity with one of Darwin's central concepts, that human evolution waas not an obvious linear progression. Here we see a chart demonstrating the Chinese as a "missing link" between the monkey and the pig.

Figure 33. *Phrenological Journal and Packard's Monthly*, vol. 1, no. 4 (April 1870). Courtesy of the Wong Ching Foo Collection.

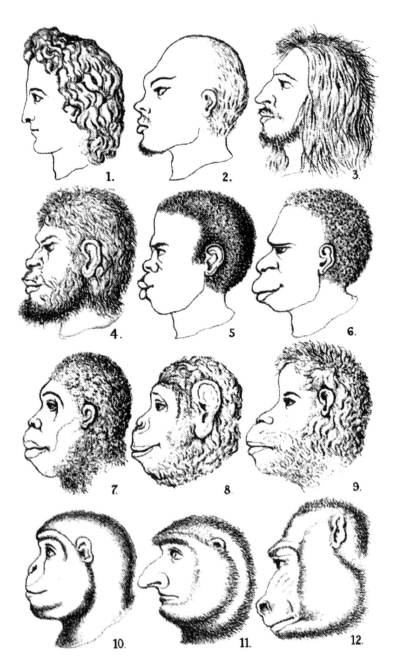

Figure 34. "Descendants of the Great Apes." Ernst Haeckel, *Natürliche Schöp-fungsgeschichte* (Berlin: Georg Reimer, 1868), frontispiece. Courtesy of the New York Public Library.

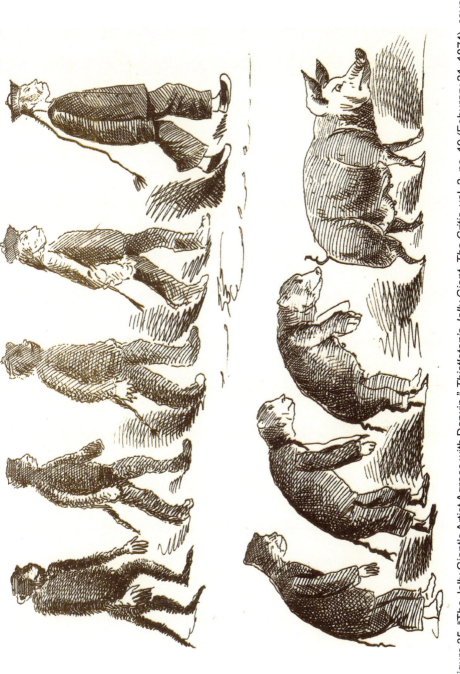

Figure 35. "The Jolly Giant's Artist Agrees with Darwin." *Thistleton's Jolly Giant*, *The Critic*, vol. 2, no. 19 (Feburary 21, 1874), cover. Courtesy of the Wong Ching Foo Collection.

Henry Fairfield Osborn, "Existing Facts of Human Ascent" (1926)

Pioneering paleontologist Henry Fairfield Osborn (1857–1935) prepared this chart in response to the 1925 trial of public school teacher John Scopes for violating the Butler Act passed that year to prevent the teaching of evolutionary theories in Tennessee public schools. Proponents of the law argued that the teaching of evolution violated student's religious freedom by challenging the account of human origins in Genesis. While the trial focused mainly on Darwin's theories of natural selection, as the chart indicates, Osborn embraced theories that

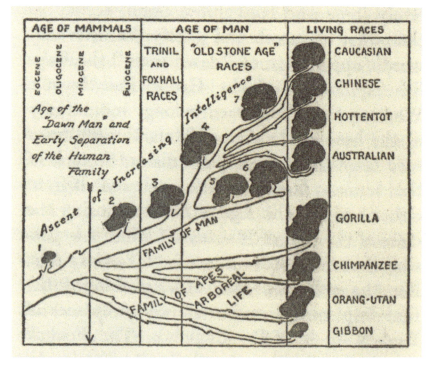

Figure 36. "Existing Facts of Human Ascent: 1, 2. Dawn stage of human prehistory. 3. First known walking stage, the erect Trinil race of Java. 4. Piltdown race of Sussex. 5, 6. The low-browed Heidelberg-Neanderthal race. 7. Cro-Magnon and related races of high intelligence. The races 3, 4, 5, 6, 7 are scattered throughout the entire period of the Age of Man, conservatively estimated at 500,000 years. Altogether, upward of 136 skulls and skeletons of the fossil men of this period are known." Henry Fairfield Osborn, *Evolution and Religion in Education: Polemics of the Fundamentalist Controversy of 1922 to 1926* (New York: Charles Scrbners Sons, 1926), 206. Courtesy of the New York Public Library.

seemed to suggest the division of mankind into essentially separate species, which also went against Christian theology. Note the hierarchical arrangement of the graphics from "Caucasian" at the top, followed by "Chinese," "Hottentot" (an archaic and derogatory name for Southern Africans), "Australian," and lastly the lower primates. Osborn was president of the American Museum of Natural History in New York and a prominent champion of immigration restriction and the eugenic sterilization of the socially and biologically unfit.[11]

G. W. F. Hegel, "Hither and Farther Asia" (1837)[12]

The moorings for yellow perilism were formulated from the heights of European philosophical thought as the absolute "other" against which progressive civilization must be forever vigilant in defending itself. The ultimate great fear? In the age of colonialist mobility, it was the possibility of the unfree to migrate, invade, and infect homelands of free Occidentals. In the following excerpt, another variation of the mapping divide is formulated.

In this excerpt Hegel (1770–1831) maps the European break with patriarchal, authoritarian, unfree Asia as the signal achievement of the rise of Western freedom. He gave these lectures every two years from 1822 to 1830. After his death his notebooks were published as The Philosophy of History *(1837). Hegel's divide is delineated between "Hither and Farther Asia"—the former racialized as "Caucasian," the latter racialized as "Mongolian." Hegel articulates what becomes a standard claim: the capacity for individual freedom is not possible in "Mongolian" "Farther Asia," the boundary of which is the Indus River (the same boundary literary scholar Shankar Raman identifies as the origin of the systemic misuse of India, Indies, and Indians that framed "India" as a global metaphor, as noted in the introduction). In this schema China and India are "islands," and not part of human development or of history. For Hegel the Persians and Egyptians are included in Caucasian "Hither Asia," so they have the possibility of light, but only at the level of society as a whole. Only in Greek civilization did individuals themselves develop the capacity for light. Hence, the arc of individual freedom embodied as external, universal light literally moving westward like the arc of the sun, only became internalized by classical Greek civilization. Unlike the Persians, the Greeks were able to instill their conquered territories with the spirit of freedom and unite their empire under this ethos.*

Asia separates itself into two parts—Hither and Farther Asia; which are essentially different from each other. While the Chinese and Hindoos—the two great nations of Farther Asia, already considered—belong to the strictly Asiatic, namely the Mongolian Race, and consequently possess a quite peculiar character, discrepant from ours; the nations of Hither Asia belong to the Caucasian, i.e. the European Stock. They are related to the West, while the Farther-Asiatic peoples are perfectly isolated. The European who goes from Persia to India, observes, therefore, a prodigious contrast. Whereas in the former country he finds himself still somewhat at home, and meets with European dispositions, human virtues, and human passions—as soon as he crosses the Indus (i.e., in the *latter* region), he encounters the most repellent characteristics, pervading every single feature of society.

With the Persian Empire we first enter on continuous History. The Persians are the first Historical People; Persia was the first Empire that passed away. While China and India remain stationary, and perpetuate a natural vegetative existence even to the present time, this land has been subject to those developments and revolutions, which alone manifest a historical condition. The Chinese and the Indian Empire assert a place in the historical series only on their own account and for us (not for neighbors and successors). But here in Persia first arises that light which shines itself, and illuminates what is around; for *Zoroaster's* "Light" belongs to the World of Consciousness—to Spirit as a relation to something distinct from itself. We see in the Persian World a pure exalted Unity, as the essence which leaves the special existences that inhere in it, free;—as the Light, which only manifests what bodies are in themselves;—a Unity which governs individuals only to excite them to become powerful for themselves—to develop and assert their individuality. Light makes no distinctions: the Sun shines on the righteous and the unrighteous, on high and low, and confers on all the same benefit and prosperity. Light is vitalizing only insofar as it is brought to bear on something distinct from itself, operating upon and developing that. It holds a position of antithesis to Darkness, and this antithetical relation opens out to us the principle of activity and life. The principle of development begins with the history of Persia. This therefore constitutes strictly the beginning of World-History; for the grand interest of Spirit in History, is to attain an unlimited immanence of subjectivity—by an absolute antithesis to attain complete harmony.

Thus the transition which we have to make, is only in the sphere of the Idea, not in the external historical connection. The principle of this transition is that the Universal Essence, which we recognized in Brahm, now becomes perceptible to consciousness—becomes an object and acquires a positive import for man. Brahm is not worshipped by the Hindoos: he is nothing more than a condition of the Individual, a religious feeling, a non-objective existence—a relation, which for concrete vitality is that of annihilation. But in becoming objective, this Universal Essence acquires a positive nature: man becomes free, and thus occupies a position face to face as it were with the Highest Being, the latter being made objective for him. This form of Universality we see exhibited in Persia, involving a separation of man from the Universal essence; while at the same time the individual recognizes himself as identical with [a partaker in], that essence. In the Chinese and Indian principle, this distinction was not made. We found only a unit of the Spiritual and the Natural. But Spirit still involved in Nature has to solve the problem of freeing itself from the latter. Rights and Duties in India are intimately connected with special classes, and are therefore only peculiarities attaching to man by the arrangement of Nature. In China this unity presents itself under the conditions of *paternal* government. Man is not free there; he possesses no moral element, since he is identical with the external command (obedience is purely *natural,* as in the filial relation—not the result of reflection and principle). In the Persian principle, Unity first elevates itself to the distinction from the merely natural; we have the negation of that unreflecting relation which allowed no exercise of mind to intervene between the mandate and its adoption by the will. In the Persian principle this unity is manifested as Light, which in this case is not simply light as such, the most universal physical element, but at the same time also *spiritual* purity—the Good. Speciality—the involvement with *limited* Nature—is consequently abolished. Light, in a physical and spiritual sense, imports, therefore, elevation—freedom from the merely natural. Man sustains a relation to Light—to the Abstract Good—as to something objective, which is acknowledged, reverenced, and evoked to activity by his Will. If we look back once more—and we cannot do so too frequently—on the phases which we have traversed in arriving at this point, we perceive in China the totality of a moral Whole, but excluding subjectivity;—this totality divided into members, but without independence in its various portions.

We found only an external arrangement of this political Unity. In India, on the contrary, distinctions made themselves prominent; but the *principle* of separation was unspiritual. We found incipient subjectivity, but hampered with the condition, that the separation in question is insurmountable; and that Spirit remains involved in the limitations of Nature, and is therefore a self-contradiction. Above this purity of Castes is that purity of Light which we observe in Persia; that Abstract Good, to which all are equally able to approach, and in which all equally may be hallowed. The Unity recognized therefore, now first becomes a principle, not an external bond of soulless order. The fact that everyone has a share in that principle, secures to him personal dignity …

The solution and liberation of that Oriental Spirit, which in Egypt had advanced so far as to propose the problem, is certainly this: that the Inner Being [the Essence] of Nature is Thought, which has its existence only in the human consciousness. But that time honored antique solution given by Oedipus—who thus shows himself possessed of knowledge—is connected with a dire ignorance of the character of his own actions. The rise of spiritual illumination in the old royal house is disparaged by connection with abominations, the result of ignorance; and that primeval royalty must—in order to attain true knowledge and moral clearness—first be brought into shapely form, and be harmonized with the Spirit of the Beautiful, by civil laws and political freedom.

The *inward* or ideal transition, from Egypt to Greece is as just exhibited. But Egypt became a province of the great Persian kingdom, and the *historical* transition takes place when the Persian world comes in contact with the Greek. Here, for the first time, an historical transition meets us, viz. in the fall of an empire. China and India, as already mentioned, have remained— Persia has not. The transition to Greece is, indeed, internal; but here it shows itself also externally, as a transmission of sovereignty—an occurrence which from this time forward is ever and anon repeated. For the Greeks surrender the sceptre of dominion and of civilization to the Romans, and the Romans are subdued by the Germans. If we examine this fact of transition more closely, the question suggests itself—for example, in this first case of the kind, viz. Persia—why it sank, while China and India remain. In the first place we must here banish from our minds the prejudice in favor of duration, as if it had any advantage as compared with transience:

the imperishable mountains are not superior to the quickly dismantled rose exhaling its life in fragrance. In Persia begins the principle of Free Spirit as contrasted with imprisonment in Nature; mere natural existence, therefore, loses its bloom, and fades away. The principle of separation from Nature is found in the Persian Empire, which, therefore, occupies a higher grade than those worlds immersed in the Natural. The necessity of advance has been thereby proclaimed. Spirit has disclosed its existence, and must complete its development. It is only when dead that the Chinese is held in reverence. The Hindoo kills himself—becomes absorbed in Brahm—undergoes a living death in the condition of perfect unconsciousness—or is a present god in virtue of his birth. Here we have no change; no advance is admissible, for progress is only possible through the recognition of the independence of Spirit. With the "Light" of the Persians begins a spiritual view of things, and here Spirit bids adieu to Nature. It is here, then, that we first find (as occasion called us to notice above) that the objective world remains free— that the nations are not enslaved, but are left in possession of their wealth, their political constitution, and their religion. And, indeed, this is the side on which Persia itself shows weakness as compared with Greece. For we see that the Persians could erect no empire possessing complete organization; that they could not "inform" the conquered lands with their principle, and were unable to make them into a harmonious Whole, but were obliged to be content with an aggregate of the most diverse individualities. Among these nations the Persians secured no inward recognition of the legitimacy of their rule; they could not establish their legal principles of enactments, and in organizing their dominion, they only considered themselves, not the whole extent of their empire. Thus, as Persia did not constitute, politically, *one* Spirit, it appeared weak in contrast with Greece. It was not the effeminacy of the Persians (although, perhaps, Babylon infused an enervating element) that ruined them, but the unwieldy, unorganized character of their host, as matched against Greek organization; i.e., the superior principle overcame the inferior. The abstract principle of the Persians displayed its defectiveness as an unorganized, incompacted union of disparate contradictories; in which the Persian doctrine of Light stood side by side with Syrian voluptuousness and luxury, with the activity and courage of the sea-braving Phoenicians, the abstraction of pure Thought in the Jewish Religion, and the mental unrest of Egypt;—an aggregate of elements, which awaited their idealization, and could receive it only in *free Individuality*. The Greeks must be looked upon as the people in whom these elements interpenetrated each other: Spirit became introspective, triumphed over particularity, and thereby emancipated itself.

Brendan O'Leary, "Race and the Asiatic Mode of Production" (1989)[13]

Political scientist Brendan O'Leary pieces together an intellectual history of European nineteenth-century political theory that has Oriental Despotism hardwired into its notions both of human progress and of obstacles to such linear advance. These framings favor stages and formulas of universal advance—norms against which the non-white races of mankind are always found lacking.

The idea of oriental despotism, as opposed to mere despotism, has gone through multiple vicissitudes in the evolution of Western political thought …* [T]here are four core components of oriental despotism which recur with persistent regularity up to the eighteenth century. First, there is the idea of an untrammeled agrarian emperor; that is, the notion of a monarch or despot with power of such plenitude and autonomy as to be effectively free of political restraints. Second, there is the empirical belief that such despots were to be found principally in the Orient, in the land-based empires of Asia. Third, there is the associated assumption that the despot's apparatus of control was an administrative elite, dependent upon the despot for authority, office and revenue, in stark contrast to the independent European aristocracies. Finally, the subjects of such despots, especially the "nobility," were regarded as being, to all intents and purposes, slaves …

[T]he traditional concept of oriental despotism is largely a mythical categorization of preindustrial regimes—the arbitrary power of the despot was largely restricted to control over the immediate coercive apparatus, and even this power was by no means secure.

Political thinkers of the early Enlightenment remained within the typological comparisons established by Aristotle—whether they believed in oriental

---

* Richard Koebner, "Despot and Despotism: Vicissitudes of a Political Term," *Journal of the Warburg and Courtauld Institutes* 14, no. 3–4 (1951), 275–302.

despotisms or not—and were also constrained by the belief that the "laws" of political forms were universal and immutable. Their political philosophies were still based on the essentially static milieu of agrarian societies. The move towards philosophies of history which embraced the idea of progress, characteristic of the late Enlightenment, shattered the empirical and normative framework of Aristotelian discourse. The typology of regimes survived in new guises but theoretical attention was now focused upon locating despotism and other political forms as stages in a scale of human progress. Philosophers of progress gradually came to share the rejection of the belief that all forms of government rested on stable, stationary orders, and also the rejection of simple cyclical theories of the rise and decline of regimes and empires. The thinkers of the late Enlightenment hovered between what have been aptly described as *episodic* and *world-growth* stories of progress.*

In episodic conceptions of progress there is one episode, one transition from a bad state of affairs to one good state, whereas in world-growth or evolutionist theories progress is perpetual, whether it takes place continuously or discontinuously. In episodic conceptions despotisms, and oriental despotisms in particular, came to be regarded as states of evil, unenlightened, superstitious, tyrannous, primordial unfreedom, still in the pre-transition infantile condition. By contrast in evolutionist conceptions despotisms came to be regarded as a necessary steps on the ladder by humanity, a step up from barbarism on the journey towards freedom …

The first inklings of this shift in intellectual orientation are evident in the writings of Turgot who, together with Adam Smith, is rightly credited with the independent creation of the "four stages" theory of historical development (1776).† The four stages theory was based upon the idea of successive modes of subsistence—hunting, pasturage, agriculture and commerce—to which corresponded functionally appropriate political institutions, manners and morals. Turgot thought the Orient a backward and halted version of the agricultural stage. After some initial progress the Orient had stagnated at a low level of development (as we would express his ideas today) … He did not explain why the Orient had stagnated after early promise, and simply

---

* Ernest Gellner, *Thought and Change* (London: Weidenfeld and Nicolson, 1964), 1–32.

† Ronald L. Meek, "Smith, Turgot, and the 'Four Stages' Theory," *History of Political Economy* 3, no. 1 (1971), 9–27.

suggested that the Orient had developed too early; it had not ripened slowly enough for the full moral, political, economic, and scientific development which had taken place in the Occident.

Turgot's ideas were influential in France, feeding through into both physiocratic and philosophical circles. The most spectacular, fideistic example of the *philosophes'* conversion to the doctrine of progress is found in a book which was partially indebted to Turgot, Condorcet's *Esquisse d'un tableau historique des progrès de l'esprit humain* (1795),* which outlined ten stages of human intellectual progress. The accumulation of knowledge was the motor of history in this philosophy. If unimpeded by religious superstition, the sequential and ordered development of knowledge would bring virtue and freedom to all of humanity. In Condorcet's account the third stage in the mind's progress was represented in the despotic empires of Asia, notably China, where prejudice had halted scientific and technological growth. The backward political regimes of the contemporary world provided a visible archaeology in which human progress could be charted. Turgot and Condorcet's philosophies of progress and their theories of stages of development became important components of French intellectual culture and were primary antecedents of the philosophies of Saint-Simon (and his disciple Comte) whose impact upon Marx and Engels is unquestionable.

Philosophies of progress and the location of despotisms as early stages in "Man's" growth-story were especially prevalent in the German branch of the late Enlightenment, at the end of the eighteenth and turn of the nineteenth century—notably in the writings of Kant, Herder, and Hegel. Kant described the various states of Asia as despotic and shared the emergent Sinophobia of the late German enlightenment, which was virulently expressed by Herder in his *Outlines of a Philosophy of the History of Man* (1803). Herder's thought shared many of the presuppositions of Montesquieu, Turgot, and Condorcet. He described Asiatic states as despotic and criticized Voltaire for his absurd admiration of Confucian China, which he condemned as an embalmed mummy wrapped in silk, a sleeping old ruin on the edge of the world where superstitious dogmatism had induced stagnation. But he also associated agricultural work, and the prevalence of the agricultural phase of human development, with despotism—the political and economic systems

---

* Literally: "Sketch for an historical picture of the progress of the human mind."

were symbiotically connected. And, like Montesquieu, Herder believed that climatic conditions in Asia were conducive to despotism. Thus, towards the end of the creative periods of the German and French Enlightenments, despotism and Asia had become firmly established, as twinned concepts, tied together in geographical space, but also placed in time since they were situated as relics, fossils, and reminders of humanity's first steps towards progress.

Nowhere is this emergent philosophy of history more dramatically expressed than in Hegel's *Philosophy of History* (1837) [which] rests on the premise that history ... is the development of the world spirit towards freedom. Human history is not the deliberate product of the intended actions of actors; rather it takes place behind their backs—where "the cunning of reason" operates. The suffering in the world is explained as the byproduct of the world spirit's dialectical evolution towards freedom. The rhythm of the Hegelian dialectic is well known. In the beginning is undifferentiated unity. Then there is the stage of conflict or contradiction. And finally there is the stage of harmonious reconciliation, of differentiated unity, when the contradictory stage is superseded and unity is regained but with the knowledge and benefits derived from the conflictual stage intact. Successive human cultures are the vehicles, through which the world spirit's progress can be charted.

The civilizations of the Orient mark the first irruptions of the journey of the world spirit, but here, "Since Spirit has not yet attained subjectivity, it wears the appearance of spirituality still involved in the conditions of Nature."[*] History begins in the theocratic despotisms of the oriental world ... Hegel even equivocated over whether India and China were in any sense part of the world spirit's journey towards perfection, since they "lie ... still outside the World's History, as the mere presupposition of elements whose combination must be waited for to constitute their vital progress."[†]

Hegel's detailed description of India and Hindus is the most withering hymn of hatred and contempt sung about the Orient in occidental social

---

[*] G. W. F. Hegel, *The Philosophy of History*, trans. John Sibree (New York: Dover, 1956), 112. My understanding of this typical passage of Hegelese is that in the Orient individualism is not yet developed, humanity still partly in a natural state.
[†] Ibid., 116.

philosophy. India for him was "a region of phantasy and insensibility."* The dream was the generic principle of the Hindu nature, and India was above all else a land of dreams, a world of "voluptuous intoxication in the merely natural,"† governed by a "despotism without a principle, without any rule of morality and religion."‡ It is therefore not surprising that the Hindu was deceitful and cunning: "Cheating, stealing, robbing, murdering are with him habitual."§ Given this lack of dynamism and moral individualism it was not surprising that "all political revolutions … are matters of indifference to the common Hindoo, for his lot is unchanged"¶…

Despite his generally optimistic philosophy of progress, it is intriguing that Hegel believed that despotism remained a general threat to modern societies. There was a potentially dark side to the dialectic. Progress was not a simple highway—many culs-de-sac were present. Hegel's critique of the Jacobins' political philosophy and the course of the French Revolution sharply demonstrated these beliefs. Modern societies could suffer disastrous setbacks when individualism and egalitarianism were pushed to their limits; despotism was a potential outcome of democratic enthusiasms. Hegel's themes, divested of their idealist expression, were to become standard components of conservative and liberal political sociology in the nineteenth and twentieth centuries[14] …

The notion of oriental despotism was evidently a stereotype constructed from unreliable sources—or, worse, from a selective reading of sources—to serve as a parable for political sermons in the Occident … At best the Aristotelian notion of oriental despotism was a forerunner of the ideal-type contrast now frequently drawn between the political systems of occidental feudalism and the service nobilities found more frequently, if not exclusively, in the Orient. However, the despotic powers attributed to all oriental monarchs were highly questionable.

---

* Ibid., 139.

† Ibid., 157.

‡ Ibid., 158.

§ Ibid., 158.

¶ Ibid., 154.

Robert Kurfirst, "John Stuart Mill's Asian Parable" (2001)[15]

John Stuart Mill (1806–1873) was a British philosopher, economist, and politician. His political philosophy emphasized individual freedom in opposition to unlimited state control—embodying debates within British society. During Mill's term in Parliament (1865–68) he was appointed Lord Rector of the University of St. Andrews. A key relevant thematic of Mill's On Liberty *(1859) is the principle of harm. Individuals should be able to exercise their liberty as long as they do not harm others. If an action is self-harming only, the state has no right to intervene. Exceptions to this ethic are children and those of "backward states of society." Here Chinese are compared to "automatons" and "machinery" because of their suffering of despotic rule. In this excerpt, political scientist Robert Kurfirst presents Mill's warning about the possibility of the tyranny of majority opinion in democracies, an insight Noam Chomsky and Edward Herman develop as "manufacturing consent."[16]*

While certainly not the first to portray Asian civilizations as stagnant societies, John Stuart Mill was quite adept at using the concept of Oriental Despotism to warn the West that it might suffer a similar fate if its distinguishing features of individuality and political pluralism fell into a state of neglect. Such a state was imminent, Mill believed, because the tyranny of majority opinion had already begun to hold sway in most Western cultures, and centralized bureaucratic socialism appeared ready to take root in some of them. Also problematic was the fact that the democratic franchise had spread too far and too fast in his lifetime, as had a single-minded focus on material gain. Taken together, Mill feared, these last two features threatened to trap the West in a leaderless age of transition for decades and, perhaps, generations.

Mill offers China as an example of a society with this particular imperfection. It is "a nation of much talent … with a particularly good set of customs," yet its people have not "discovered the secret of human progressiveness." Consequently, they "have become stationary [and] have remained so for thousands of years." The cardinal difficulty in China and throughout Asia is that despotic rulers "have succeeded beyond all hope … in making all people alike, all governing their thoughts and conduct by the same maxims and rules."* Mill evaluates the "Order" and "Obedience" obtained

---

* J. S. Mill, "On Liberty," *Collected Works of John Stuart Mill*, vol. 18, *Essays on Politics*

in and through despotic government in the second chapter of *Representative Government*. He observes here that the stability associated with deference to established authorities, moral and political, is necessary "in every society, whether stationary or progressive" and, further, that "there are different degrees of obedience, and it is not every degree that is commendable." Particularly reprobate are the exigencies of order in the "unmitigated despotism" which "demands that the individual citizen shall obey unconditionally every mandate of persons in authority."* In despotic regimes, the security provided by order "does not mean stupid tranquility, with security against change for the worse; it often means being overrun, conquered, and reduced to domestic slavery" in an existential as well as a political sense, for "there can be no doubt that the passive type of character is favoured by the government of one or a few."†

China may be justly praised as "a nation of much talent" blessed not only with "a particularly good set of customs," but also with a "remarkable" capacity "for impressing as far as possible, the best wisdom they possess upon every mind in the community." Still, the order attained there leaves human beings "cramped and dwarfed" and unable to develop fully "their capabilities of comprehension, of action, and of enjoyment." Mill concedes that under a despotism of this kind the human being "might be guided in some good path, and kept out of harm's way," but the momentous question, in his opinion, is "what will be his comparative worth as a human being." In this regard, he objects that even though "the customs be both good as customs, and suitable to him, yet to conform to custom, merely as custom, does not educate or develop in him any of the qualities which are the distinctive endowment of a human being."‡

The end result of blind obedience to custom, Mill maintains, is a rendering of the individual's feelings and character "inert and torpid, instead of active and energetic." The person "whose desires and impulses are his

---

and Society, edited by John M. Robson (Toronto: University of Toronto Press, 1977), 273.

* J. S. Mill, "Considerations on Representative Government," *Collected Works*, vol. 19, *Essays on Politics and Society*, ed. John M. Robson (Toronto: University of Toronto Press, 1977), 384.

† Mill, "Representative Government," 400–1.

‡ Ibid., 262.

own—are the expression of his own nature, as it has been developed and modified by his own culture—is said to have character." In contrast, the "automatons in human form" bred by the despotism of custom have "no need of any other faculty than the apelike one of imitation" and exhibit "no more [character] than a steam-engine"* ...

What troubled Mill most was the prospect of a prolonged entrapment of Western civilization in a "transitional" era. He worries that the wave of democratization will crest prematurely there, leaving the masses without guidance and enabling "dabblers," "dilettantes," and "demagogues" to carry the day. One essential prerequisite for the redemption of his age, he insists, is the presence of "near ... unanimity among the instructed, on all the great points of moral and political knowledge," precisely that quality he found wanting in his own era. Moreover, given that it is a nascent democratic era of which we speak, included among the unanimous principles that must be embraced and advanced by moral and political leaders are a commitment to the education, material enrichment and moral improvement of the masses, and the preservation and promotion of the liberty and individuality necessary to ensure that a single party, with even the most progressive forces at hand, shall not attain absolute, unchallenged authority. Instead, all Mill found around him was consensus about the appropriateness of a life consumed with material pursuits and a political system in which mediocrity was the order of the day. The only "settled" opinion that "can be considered anything like universal," he remarked as early as 1836, is a desire for material wealth which consumes "nearly the whole of the energy of character" and confines it "within the narrow sphere of the individual's money-getting disputes." Evidence of the other "inducements to call forth energy of character," namely "the passion of philanthropy" and "the love of active virtue," was absent.†

Thus, just as the paternal despotisms of Asia exemplify the consequences of unchecked moral, intellectual, and political authority in a "natural" social state, the commercial age exhibits qualities equally deplorable, given that pedestrian cultural attitudes have been translated via the democratic franchise into juridico-political and economic truisms that rival the obstinacy

---

* Mill, "On Liberty," 273, 265, 263, 262, 262, 264.
† Mill, "Civilization," *Collected Works*, 129–30.

of Eastern institutions and customs. Often forgotten, however, is Mill's insistence that, if properly constituted, neither democratic nor socialist societies would threaten the type of cultural and political despotism he abhors. Though he is certain that the former must be established before we can entertain seriously the implementation of the latter, it is only when democracy or socialism are introduced precipitously that we need fear for individuality, liberty, and political and cultural pluralism.

Gregory Blue, "Gobineau on 'China as Menace' " (1999)[17]

Count Joseph Arthur Comte de Gobineau (1816–1882), a French man of letters and novelist, advocated a racist anti-colonialism to prevent further degradation of Aryan purity from yellow and Slavic intermixing. His most famous publication is An Essay on the Inequality of the Human Races *(1853–55) in which he analyzed China. In contrast to Mill's liberal elitism, Gobineau argued for protecting established aristocratic power against what he deemed the degenerative nature of democracy. The count became an ally and friend of composer Richard Wagner who later incorporated his theory into eugenics arguments about scientifically controlling undesirable racial populations. Gobineau argued Europeans should not colonize the lands of inferior races lest they risk being overwhelmed by them. Gregory Blue's description of Gobineau's poem* Amadis *in this excerpt is telling: "The Aryan heroes, though standing to the end unbeaten in actual fighting, are finally drowned in the sea of the corpses of those they have slain."*

One finds Gobineau returning to draw an explicit parallel between China and the French politics of his day in a late essay attacking the Third Republic. In that work he maintained that for most people the word *republic* symbolized the "chimera" of "equality" as represented by "the rule of merit," the opportunity to succeed through one's own abilities. This "principle of 1789," he again stated, was exactly what had long existed in China, where it had produced the mandarinate—a political system run by universal competition and requiring, precisely for that reason, a dictatorship at the top that would ultimately spell the end of liberty.*

---

* Arthur de Gobineau, *Selected Political Writings*, ed. Michael Biddiss (London: J. Cape, 1970), 211–13; this essay was from 1877.

In 1881, a year before his death, Gobineau contributed to Wagner's *Bayreuther Blätter* an article published under the title "Ein Urteil über die jetzige Weltlage," which carried an introduction by the composer and was translated by Cosima.* In this the count first gave a summary of world history as seen from his racial perspective, and then he constructed on that foundation an analysis of world politics since the "opening" of China in the First Opium War. A crucial role in the historical survey was played by the yellow destroyer Attila, whom Gobineau credited with delivering the decisive death-blow to a Roman empire rotten from a profusion of black blood that had been introduced through a long process of "semitization." However, as most of Attila's troops were depicted as being of rude Germanic stock, the so-called "Hunnic" invasions actually set the stage in Gobineau's script for a new flowering of Aryan culture in medieval Europe. When he turned to current international trends, Gobineau drew particular attention to recent Chinese emigration overseas and raised the specter of a Chinese wave that would eventually flood into Europe through the new railways of the expanding Russian empire. Gobineau legitimized white opposition to Chinese immigration to California, Hawaii, and the British dominions on the grounds that racial antipathy was natural, but he forecast that ultimately Europe itself would be overcome by hordes from the East, as its own social structure and racial character had become far too degraded to be able to withstand the flow for long. His vision was that of a "new fifth century," this one involving an invasion in which "yellow" hordes would "explode" upon a Europe far more racially decadent than it had been at the end of the Roman Empire. In his view, the modern invasion would thus mean the demise of the last vestiges of Aryan civilization in Europe at the hands of masses of Chinese motivated by self-interest and narrow commercial gain.†

Gobineau gave this vision artistic expression in his last literary work, the incredibly ponderous, five-hundred-page tragic poem *Amadis,* some 12,000

---

* Arthur de Gobineau, "Ein Urteil über die jetzige Weltlage," SB 4 (1881), 121–40; this translates as "An Assessment of the Current State of the World," but the German *Urteil* may have been intended to carry connotations of religious judgment.

† Michael D. Biddiss, ed., *Selected Political Writings by Gobineau* (London: J. Cape, 1971), 241–7, especially 243 and 246; see Arthur de Gobineau, *Oeuvres,* ed. J. Gaulmier et al. (Paris: Gallimard, 1983–87), xlvi–ii on the new fifth century.

verses in all, the final version of which was published posthumously in 1887.*
Amadis centers on a final cosmic conflict between white and yellow races. It
features a noble elite of white heroes who have created and long upheld civilization and social order. In time they are subverted from within by a revolution
of commoners led by the ethnically mixed middle classes, who in turn are
faced with rebellion by the racially inferior lower orders. In such a weakened
state, Europe is a vulnerable prey, irresistible to the predators waiting vora-
ciously beyond its frontiers. The nobility of the white race emerges one final
time to resist the inevitable invasion of innumerable yellow (or more precisely,
Chinese) hordes aided by half-Asiatic Slavs.† The Aryan heroes, though standing to the end unbeaten in actual fighting, are finally drowned in the sea of the
corpses of those they have slain.‡

One aspect of Gobineau's late writings that is worth noting is the marked
coincidence between his historiography and his eschatology. This is displayed
in the clear parallel between the *Essai's* depiction of the disruption of the Aryan
homeland by yellow hordes at the dawn of history and the portrait of civilization's last days in *Amadis*. A second aspect of the late writings that deserves
mention (and is consistent with his earlier politics) is that Gobineau's racial
analysis led him not to support for imperialist expansion, but to a racist anti-
colonialism. He thus referred to Asia as a tempting fruit that would poison
whoever ate of it, and he warned of long-term negative effects of European
expansion into Asia, and especially of Russian expansion into north China.§
If such reservations about Europe's "civilizing mission" were ostensibly out of
step with the mood of the "new imperialism" of the 1880s, however, the main

---

* Arthur de Gobineau, *Amadis* (Paris: Plon, 1887); a partial version was published in
1876 in a limited edition.

† Ludwig Schemann, *Gobineaus Rassenwerk. Aktenstucke und Betrachtungen zur
Geschichte und Kritik des "Essai sur l'inegalite des races humaines."* (Stuttgart: Fromanns
Verlag, 1910), 485, 490; Schemann held *Amadis* to be the author's crowning achievement and maintained that Gobineau had there recognized the Chinese threat, but
had not yet been able to grasp the role of Japan.

‡ *Amadis* has been left out of the recent critical edition of Gobineau's works.

§ Gobineau's often cited metaphor of Asia as a poisonous fruit (which naturally
evoked the fall of Adam and Eve in Genesis) was deployed in his widely read *Trois ans
en Asie*, published in 1859 following his tour as secretary to the French diplomatic
mission to Persia; see Gobineau, *Oeuvres*, vol. 2, 369.

anti-Asian thrust of his analysis proved quite compatible with the dominant thinking. By his death in 1882, and despite his hopes and efforts, the *Essai sur l'inégalité des races humaines** had languished without republication for three decades. Yet it went into its second edition and then immediately into its third in 1884, the year that France, tightening its hold on Vietnam, initiated hostilities in the Franco-Chinese War.[†] The French original of his 1881 German article raising the specter of a Chinese invasion of Europe finally appeared in print the following year in Paris.

Given his opposition to modern empire building, Gobineau's version of Yellow Peril theory need not be collapsed into the corpus of texts justifying colonial expansion, but important aspects of his philosophically pessimistic vision of a final white-yellow race antagonism do seem to have been adopted and critically integrated into the later standard discourse that optimistically promoted European imperialism. It is interesting to note that the relationship between Gobineau's yellow perilism and the standard imperialistic optimism parallels the relationship between his overall racial analysis and the eugenicist appropriation of his theory by the Wagner circle in particular and by the pan-Germanic movement in general ...

[I]f Gobineau demonstrates that opposition to progress and modernity did not necessarily lead to throwing off conventional disdain for China, his writings also show that his opposition to those concepts did not stop him from sharing many of the categories for interpreting China that were widely accepted in his day among thinkers of other ideological persuasions. He thus remained within the consensus of nineteenth-century Western opinion that identified China essentially with mediocrity, despotism, and lack of freedom. He did so, it is true, by interpreting those categories through the lens of his racial theory: they were for him typical characteristics of "the masses" and "Revolution." China was thus a striking example of democratic despotism and "progress" as he conceived it, and of the consequences he saw flowing from these—namely, slavery, stagnation, and eventual doom. His subversion of the conventional categories for thinking about China seems

---

* Arthur de Gobineau, *Essai sur l'inégalité des races humaines* (Paris: Firmin-Didot, 1853–55).

† Gobineau's correspondence shows that until the mid-1870s he planned to do a major revision of the *Essai,* in which he intended to "smash" the "objectionable" parts of Darwin's theory. See Gobineau, *Oeuvres,* vol. 1, 1170.

therefore to have been more an aggravation than a repudiation of the existing logic of intercultural antagonism.

William Z. Ripley, "World Cephalic Index" (1897)

MIT economics professor William Z. Ripley (1867–1941) compiled data to make this map (Figure 37) as part of a larger project to scientifically classify America's immigrants for the Immigration Restriction League. The patrician members of the League sought to halt the immigration of what Ripley termed "the great horde of Slavs, Huns, and Jews." This map depicts the world based on the "cephalic index" of regional inhabitants. The cephalic index was a number created to indicate the relative broadness of a skull as compared to its volume and length. Totally discredited today, this phrenological science suggested that narrow skulls were superior, unless they sloped as in the case of many sub-Saharan Africans and aboriginal Australians. This map illustrates the supposed diffusion of broad-headed Mongoloids across Asia and the Americas. While "broad-heads" might not be as smart as "narrow-heads," they were more resilient, according to Ripley. As an economist, he believed in the necessity of European expansion into Africa and Asia but feared "a great menace to the feeble attempts of Europeans to colonize the tropics may exist in the surpassing aptitude of the great Mongol horde, which is perhaps the most gifted race of all in its power of accommodation to new climatic conditions."[18]

"Color Map of the World" (1903)

This map (Figure 38) depicts the view of the world argued by Charles Henry Pearson (1830–94) in his widely influential National Life and Character *(1893). Pearson was a globally recognized Anglo-Australian educational reformer. Cole (1832–1918) gave voice to pervasive fears in his* White Australia *(1903) that the Japanese were more biologically fit to colonize Australia than the British had been. Cole argued that the Japanese had a higher birthrate and fared better in semi-tropical conditions and therefore would likely, and rightly, someday seek to annex Australia for themselves.*

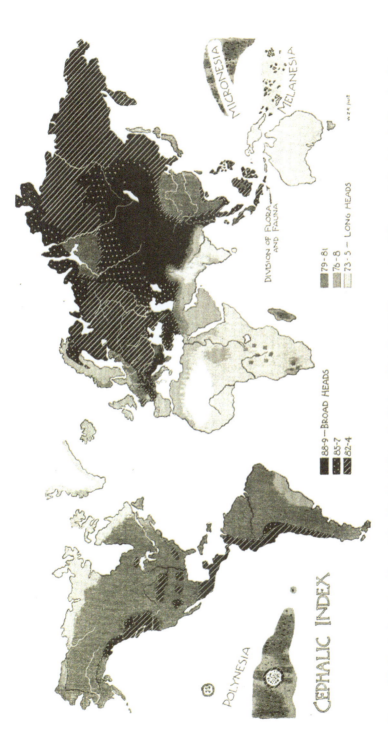

Figure 37. Cephalic Index Map of the World. William Z. Ripley, "The Racial Geography of Europe," *Appleton's Popular Science Monthly*, vol. 50 (March 1897), 582. Courtesy of the New York Public Library.

Figure 38. "Color Map of the World." E. W. Cole, *The White Australia Question* (Melbourne: E. W. Cole Book Arcade, 1903), 27. Special Collections, University of California Library, Davis.

As shown in the diagram, the whole of Africa, called the "darkest continent" lies in the tropics or semi-tropics. In the center, where it is the hottest place on earth, the people are black. In the extreme north and south of the continent, where it is cooler, the people are brown, except in the case of immigrants. Australia lies in the tropics and semi-tropics, and, consequently, all her people must become more or less colored. Therefore, a permanent White Australia is a physical impossibility.

Dylan Yeats, "Civilization Stands Up to the Horde, a Visual Essay" (2013)

European artists and illustrators translated colonialist Enlightenment thinking into a meaningful iconography. As Europeans in an age of empire began constructing an emotionally evocative history of the West, they looked back to the Battle of Thermopylae (480 BCE) where the Spartans under Leonidas defended Greece from the onslaught of Xerxes' Persian forces, and the Battle of Poitiers (732 CE) where Frankish King Charles Martel repelled the armies of the Emir of Cordoba Abd al-Rahman al-Ghafiqi, as central origin myths. Edward Gibbon famously quipped in his Decline and Fall of the Roman Empire *(1776–78) that had Martel not prevailed, "Perhaps the interpretation of the Koran would now be taught in the schools of Oxford."*

By the early nineteenth century, French artists developed a school of historical painting that celebrated brave European individuals defending civilization from inferior hordes. The iconography developed circulated

Figure 39. Eugene Delacroix, *The Battle of Poitiers*, oil on canvas (1830). Paris, Musée Du Louvre. Photo: akg / De Agostini Pic.Lib.

widely and shaped American depictions of their own epic confrontation with "hordes."

This classic example (Figure 39) of the French school of romantic histori-cal painting, commissioned by the Duchesse de Berry, depicts the John le Bon's heroic if doomed last stand at another Battle of Poitiers in 1356, this one against the British. Edward, the "Black Prince," invaded the heart of France as part of the broader Anglo-French Hundred Year's War. Valiantly defending his homeland against an overwhelming force to the last man, le Bon was captured, imprisoned, and ransomed in England. While unlike Leonidas and Martel before him, le Bon was not victorious, this painting helped solidify le Bon as a mythical symbol of manly patriotic sacrifice and established a compelling visual logic of embattled nationalism. Two years after painting the *Battle of Poitiers*, Delacroix traveled to Morocco after which he became a major figure establishing Orientalist themes in French painting.[19]

Figure 40. Cassilly Adams, *Custer's Last Fight* (1884). Color lithograph by Otto Becker rendered in 1895 for Aneheuser Busch Brewery of St. Louis. Private Col-lection / Peter Newark American Pictures / The Bridgeman Art Library.

Figure 41. Robert Jenkins Onderdonk, *The Fall of the Alamo*, oil on canvas (1903). Friends of the Governor's Mansion, Austin, TX.

Cassilly Adams (1843–1921) trained at the National Academy of Design in New York where he learned the principles of European history painting. No contemporary accounts suggest that Custer's 1873 charge against the Sioux at Little Bighorn, Montana (renamed his "last stand" in the popular press) was anything other than miscalculated aggression toward a superior force. However, by the late nineteenth century many Americans invested in the ideal of the manly "lone hero" saw Custer's death as a noble sacrifice in the service of the White Man's Burden to civilize the world. Budweiser Beer distributed a lithograph of this painting to bars throughout the U.S.[20]

Dallas businessman James T. DeShields commissioned this painting of *Davy Crockett's Last Stand* more than seventy years after the Anglo revolutionaries lost this first battle for independence from Mexico. "Remember the Alamo!" cried Crockett's compatriots as they continued the fight. Since then the Battle of the Alamo has assumed enormous symbolic importance for Americans in Texas. In 1891 they erected a monument to those fallen at the Alamo on the Capitol in Austin with the inscription: "Thermopylae had her messenger of defeat: the Alamo had none."[21]

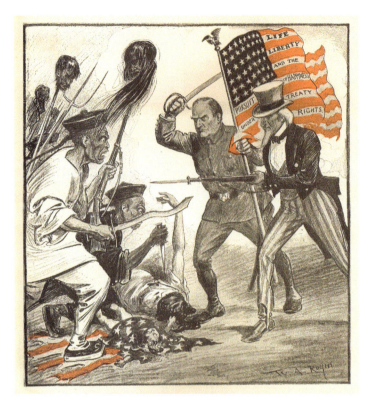

Figure 42. William A. Rogers, "Is this Imperialism?," *Harper's Weekly*, vol. 44, no. 2275 (July 28, 1900), cover. The Ohio State University Billy Ireland Cartoon Library and Museum.

This cover for *Harper's Weekly* answers the question of whether U.S. President William McKinley's decision to send U.S. troops into China to suppress the Boxer Rebellion there was imperialism: no. The Boxers, a secret organization critical of their government's decision to grant European and American missionaries and merchants access to the Chinese market, sought to drive the foreigners out themselves. The U.S. sent veterans of the Indian Wars to brutally avenge the slaying of American missionaries and resecure the authority of the Qing monarchy, who then reimbursed Americans for the lives and property destroyed during the revolt. This prompted anti-imperialists like Samuel Clemens (aka Mark Twain) to argue that perhaps white Americans, not the "inferior races," were the people sitting in the darkness of savagery.[22]

"He Vomits the Yellow to Swallow the White" (1904)

In this French postcard referencing the Russo-Japanese War (1904) a dragon ogre vomits up hordes of yellow demons onto Korea. One German commentator saw what he thought to be the world-historical significance of the Japanese victory:

Figure 43. The caption reads: "He Vomits the Yellow to Swallow the White." *L'Ogre d'Orient* [The Ogre of the Orient] (1904–1905). Leonard A. Lauder Collection of Japanese Postcards, Museum of Fine Arts, Boston. Photograph © Museum of Fine Arts, Boston, 2013.

The idea of world power is not confined to the Caucasian race alone; the Mongoloids can also refer in their history to the fact that they several times succeeded in shaking the Western world in its foundations, and that three times they came near to establishing a powerful world empire—under Attila, Genghis Khan, and Tamerlane.

As soon as the Mongoloids were set in a belligerent direction, they always showed fighting characteristics for which we use the French expression élan— they knew no retreat, even when the bodies piled as high as hills. Exactly like the Japanese. Here, as there, we find that uncanny, wild bravery, incomprehensible to the European mind, which sets the value of the individual at naught.

The clever Japanese, with the knowledgeable Mikado at their head, have enough understanding of historical matters to interpret Mongoloid history, and from this understanding to draw the conclusion that as soon as the mighty will of an energetic ruler set in motion the elementary nationalist fervor of the Mongoloid people, they were irresistible.[23]

H. J. Mackinder, "The Pressure of Asia" (1904)[24]

Sir Halford John Mackinder (1861–1947) was appointed the first Reader in Geography at Oxford in 1887 with the backing of the Royal Geographic Society where he sought to develop imperial policies through "science." Mackinder organized the first European scientific expedition to the summit of Mount Kenya in 1899, helped found the Oxford School of Geography and London School of Economics, and put his ideas into practice as a Member of Parliament and High Commissioner to South Russia. The imperial geopolitical framework Mackinder developed in this excerpt, known as the "heartland" thesis, suggests that Europeans must use their "sea power" to prevent the development of rival Asian "land power." Mackinder's view was rooted in a mind-set that saw the history of Eurasia as a history of antagonism between East and West over control of Central Asia, which Mackinder considered to be the "pivot" on which world history turned. This Great Game theory greatly influenced the Treaty of Paris in 1919 as well as the Cold War strategy of "containment," and serves as the basis for U.S. strategy in Afghanistan today.[25]

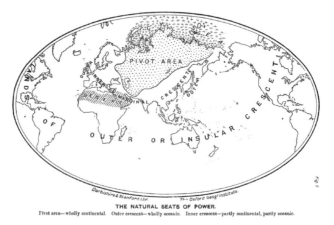

THE NATURAL SEATS OF POWER.
Pivot area—wholly continental.   Outer crescent—wholly oceanic.   Inner crescent—partly continental, partly oceanic.

Figure 44. "The Natural Seats of Power."

The late Prof. [Edward Augustus] Freeman held that the only history which counts is that of the Mediterranean and European races. In a sense, of course, this is true, for it is among these races that have originated the ideas which have rendered the inheritors of Greece and Rome dominant throughout the world. In another and very important sense, however, such a limitation has a cramping effect upon thought. The ideas which go to form a nation, as opposed to a mere crowd of human animals, have usually been accepted under the pressure of a common tribulation, and under a common necessity of resistance to external force. The idea of England was beaten into the Heptarchy by Danish and Norman conquerors; the idea of France was forced upon competing Franks, Goths, and Romans by the Huns at Chalons, and in the Hundred Years' War with England; the idea of Christendom was born of the Roman persecutions, and matured by the Crusades; the idea of the United States was accepted, and local colonial patriotism sunk, only in the long War of Independence; the idea of the German Empire was reluctantly adopted in South Germany only after a struggle against France in comradeship with North Germany. What I may describe as the literary conception of history, by concentrating attention upon ideas and upon the civilization which is their outcome, is apt to lose sight of the more elemental movements whose pressure is commonly the exciting cause of the efforts in which great ideas are nourished. A repellent personality performs a valuable social function in uniting his enemies, and it was under the pressure of external barbarism that Europe achieved her civilization. I ask you, therefore, for a moment to look upon Europe and European history as subordinate to Asia and Asiatic history, for European civilization is, in a very real sense, the outcome of the secular struggle against Asiatic invasion ...

For a thousand years a series of horse-riding peoples emerged from Asia through the broad interval between the Ural mountains and the Caspian sea, rode through the open spaces of southern Russia, and struck home into Hungary in the very heart of the European peninsula, shaping by the necessity of opposing them the history of each of the great peoples around—the Russians, the Germans, the French, the Italians, and the Byzantine Greeks. That they stimulated healthy and powerful reaction, instead of crushing opposition, under a widespread despotism, was due to the fact that the mobility of their power was conditioned by the steppes, and necessarily ceased in the surrounding forests and mountains ... Their realm is limited northward by a broad belt of sub-artic forest and marsh, wherein the climate is too rigorous, except at the eastern and western extremities, for the development of agricultural settlements. In the east the forests extend southward to the Pacific coast in the Amur [River] land and Manchuria. Similarly in the west, in prehistoric Europe, forest was the predominant vegetation. Thus framed in to the northeast, north, and northwest, the steppes spread continuously for 4,000 miles from the Pusstas of Hungary to the Little Gobi of Manchuria, and, except in their westernmost extremity, they are untraversed by rivers draining to an accessible ocean …

The hordes which ultimately fell upon Europe in the middle of the fourteenth century gathered their first force 3,000 miles away on the high steppes of Mongolia. The havoc wrought for a few years in Poland, Silesia, Moravia, Hungary, Croatia, and Servia was, however, but the remotest and the most transient result of the great stirring of the nomads of the East associated with the name of Ghenghiz Khan … [A]ll the settled margins of the Old World sooner or later felt the expansive force of mobile power originating in the steppe. Russia, Persia, India, and China were either made tributary, or received Mongol dynasties. Even the incipient power of the Turks in Asia Minor was struck down for half a century …

Mobility upon the ocean is the natural rival of horse and camel mobility in the heart of the continent. It was upon navigation of oceanic rivers that was based the Potamic stage of civilization, that of China on the Yangtse, that of India on the Ganges, that of Babylonia on the Euphrates, that of Egypt on the Nile. It was essentially upon the navigation of the Mediterranean that was based what has been described as the Thalassic stage of civilization, that of the Greeks and Romans. The Saracens and the Vikings held sway by navigation of the oceanic coasts.

The all-important result of the discovery of the Cape road to the Indies was to connect the western and eastern coastal navigations of Euro-Asia, even though by a circuitous route, and thus in some measure to neutralize the strategical advantage of the central position of the steppe-nomads by pressing upon them in rear. The revolution commenced by the great mariners of the Columbian generation endowed Christendom with the widest possible mobility of power, short of a winged mobility. The one and continuous ocean enveloping the divided and insular lands is, of course, the geographical condition of ultimate unity in the command of the sea, and of the whole theory of modern naval strategy and policy as expounded by such writers as Captain [Alfred Thayer] Mahan and Mr. Spencer Wilkinson. The broad political effect was to reverse the relations of Europe and Asia, for whereas in the Middle Ages Europe was caged between an impassable desert to south, an unknown ocean to west, and icy or forested wastes to north and northeast, and in the east and southeast was constantly threatened by the superior mobility of the horsemen and camelmen, she now emerged upon the world, multiplying more than thirty-fold the sea surface and coastal lands to which she had access, and wrapping her influence round the Euro-Asiatic land-power which had hitherto threatened her very existence. New Europes were created in the vacant lands discovered in the midst of the waters, and what Britain and Scandinavia were to Europe in the earlier time, that have America and Australia, and in some measure even Trans-Saharan Africa, now become to Euro-Asia. Britain, Canada, the United States, South Africa, Australia, and Japan are now a ring of outer and insular bases for sea-power and commerce, inaccessible to the land-power of Euro-Asia ...

But the land power still remains, and recent events have again increased its significance. While the maritime peoples of Western Europe have covered the ocean with their fleets, settled the outer continents, and in varying degree made tributary the oceanic margins of Asia, Russia has organized the Cossacks, and, emerging from her northern forests, has policed the steppe by setting her own nomads to meet the Tartar nomads. The Tudor century, which saw the expansion of Western Europe over the sea, also saw Russian power carried from Moscow through Siberia. The eastward swoop of the horsemen across Asia was an event almost as pregnant with political consequences as was the rounding of the Cape, although the two movements long remained apart ...

As we consider this rapid review of the broader currents of history, does not a certain persistence of geographical relationship become evident? Is not the pivot region of the world's politics that vast area of Euro-Asia which is inaccessible to ships, but in antiquity lay open to the horse-riding nomads, and is today about to be covered with a network of railways? There have been and are here the conditions of a mobility of military and economic power of a far-reaching and yet limited character. Russia replaces the Mongol Empire. Her pressure on Finland, on Scandinavia, on Poland, on Turkey, on Persia, on India, and on China, replaces the centrifugal raids of the steppemen. In the world at large she occupies the central strategical position held by Germany in Europe. She can strike on all sides and be struck from all sides, save the north. The full development of her modern railway mobility is merely a matter of time ...

The oversetting of the balance of power in favour of the pivot state, resulting in its expansion over the marginal lands of Euro-Asia, would permit of the use of vast continental resources for fleet-building, and the empire of the world would then be in sight ... Were the Chinese, for instance, organized by the Japanese, to overthrow the Russian Empire and conquer its territory, they might constitute the yellow peril to the world's freedom just because they would add an Oceanic frontage to the resources of the great continent, an advantage as yet denied to the Russian tenant of the pivot region.

Theodore Roosevelt, "With Faces like the Snouts of Dogs" (1904)[26]

Teddy Roosevelt (1858–1919) wrote this endorsement of Jeremiah Curtin's The Mongols *(1904) while he was president of the United States. Roosevelt, who was a reform police commissioner of New York City (1895–97), Rough Rider in the Spanish-American War (1898), New York State Governor (1898–1901), and twenty-sixth president of the U.S. (1901–09), argues for the ongoing relevance of Curtin's book in terms of the epic battle between East and West. Herein he expresses his robust "aggressive masculinity," both admiring and abhorring the effectiveness of Genghis Khan. Roosevelt's judgment is not ambiguous. The West must triumph. Jeremiah Curtin dedicated* The Mongols *to Theodore Roosevelt and concludes his history with: "Remarkable as has been the part played by the Mongols in history, the part to be played by them yet may be far greater. How great and how varied it may be and of what character is the secret of the future."[27]*

Roosevelt, educated at Harvard, carried on the mantle of European civilization. He negotiated the peace agreement in the Russo-Japanese War (1904) and championed the U.S. colonization of the Philippines (1898). Notable is his comparing Mongols to North American Comanches and Apaches "of the nineteenth century," thus linking the global threat of nomadic peoples to expansionist settlers. Curtin (1835–1906) was also a Harvard graduate, served as a translator in Russia, and returned to the U.S. to work for the Bureau of Ethnology in 1878—a time when native peoples were being pushed off their lands and onto reservations. He was a translator of native North American and Slavic languages. Roosevelt credits Curtin with knowing over seventy languages,[28] unlikely to be true, but as evident in this excerpt, interpretive positions can shape one's sense of reality.

[I]t is extraordinary to see how ignorant even the best scholars of America and England are of the tremendous importance in world history of the nation-shattering Mongol invasions. A noted Englishman of letters not many years ago wrote a charming essay on the Thirteenth Century—an essay showing his wide learning, his grasp of historical events, and the length of time that he had devoted to the study of the century. Yet the essayist not only never mentioned but was evidently ignorant of the most stupendous fact of the century—the rise of Genghis Khan and the spread of the Mongol power from the Yellow Sea to the Adriatic and the Persian Gulf. Ignorance like this is partly due to the natural tendency among men whose culture is that of Western Europe to think of history as only European history and of European history as only the history of Latin and Teutonic Europe. But this does not entirely excuse ignorance of such an event as the Mongol-Tartar invasion, which affected half of Europe far more profoundly than the Crusades.

Into this world burst the Mongol. All his early years Genghis Khan spent in obtaining first the control of his own tribe, and then in establishing the absolute supremacy of this tribe over all its neighbors. In the first decade of the thirteenth century this work was accomplished. His supremacy over the wild mounted herdsmen was absolute and unquestioned. Every formidable competitor, every man who would not bow with unquestioning obedience to his will, had been ruthlessly slain, and he had developed a number of able men who were willing to be his devoted slaves, and to carry out his every command with unhesitating obedience and dreadful prowess. Out of the Mongol horse-bowmen and horse-swordsmen he speedily made the most formidable troops then in existence. East, west, and south he sent his armies, and under him and his immediate successors the area of conquest widened by leaps and bounds; while two generations went by before any troops were found in Asia or Europe who on any stricken field could hold their own with the terrible Mongol horsemen, and their subject-allies and remote kinsmen, the Turko-Tartars who served with and under them. Few conquests have ever been so hideous and on the whole so noxious to mankind. The Mongols were savages as cruel as they were brave and hardy. There were Nestorian Christians among them, as in most parts of Asia at that time, but the great bulk of them were Shamanists; that is, their creed and ethical culture were about on a par with those of the Comanches and Apaches of the nineteenth century. They differed from Comanche and Apache in that capacity for military organization which gave them such terrible efficiency; but otherwise they were not much more advanced, and the civilized peoples who fell under their sway experienced a fate as dreadful as would be the case if nowadays a civilized people were suddenly conquered by a great horde of Apaches. The ruthless cruelty of the Mongol was practised on a scale greater than ever before or since. The Moslems feared them as much as the Christians. They put to death the Caliph, and sacked Bagdad, just as they sacked the cities of Russia and Hungary. They destroyed the Turkish tribes which ventured to resist them with the merciless thoroness [*sic*] which they showed in dealing with any resistance in Europe. They were inconceivably formidable in battle, tireless in campaign and on the march, utterly indifferent to fatigue and hardship, of extraordinary prowess with bow and sword. To the Europeans who cowered in horror before them, the squat, slit-eyed, brawny horsemen, "with faces like the snouts of dogs," seemed as hideous and fearsome as demons, and as irresistible by ordinary mortals. They conquered China and set on the throne a Mongol dynasty. India also their descendants conquered, and there likewise erected a great Mongol empire. Persia in the same way fell into their hands. Their armies, every soldier on horseback, marched incredible distances and overthrew whatever opposed them. They struck down the Russians at a blow and trampled the land into bloody mire beneath their horses' feet. They crushed the Magyars in a single battle and drew a broad red furrow straight across Hungary, driving the Hungarian King in panic flight from his realm. They overran Poland and destroyed the banded knighthood of North Germany in Silesia. Western Europe could have made no adequate defense; but fortunately by this time the Mongol attack had spent itself, simply because the distance from the central point had become so great. It was no Christian or European military power which first by force set bounds to the Mongol conquests; but the

Turkish Mamelukes of Egypt in the West, and in the East, some two score years later, the armies of Japan.

In a couple of generations the Mongols as a whole became Buddhists in the East and Moslems in the West; and in the West the true Mongols gradually disappeared, being lost among the Turkish tribes whom they had conquered and led to victory. It was these Turkish tribes, known as Tartars, who for over two centuries kept Russia in a servitude so terrible, so bloody, so abject, as to leave deep permanent marks on the national character. The Russians did not finally throw off this squalid yoke until thirty years after the conquest of Constantinople by the Ottoman Turks, the power of the Tartars waning as that of the Ottomans approached its zenith. Poland was now rising high. Its vast territory extended from the Baltic to the Black Sea. It was far more important than Muscovy. In the "Itinerary" of that widely travelled Elizabethan, Fynes Morrison, we learn that the Turks dreaded the Polish armies more than those of Germany, or of any other nation; this was after the Hungarians had been conquered. The scourge of the Mongol conquests was terrible beyond belief, so that even where a land was flooded but for a moment, the memory long remained. It is not long since in certain churches in Eastern Europe the litany still contained the prayer, "From the fury of the Mongols, good Lord deliver us." The Mongol armies developed a certain ant-like or bee-like power of joint action which enabled them to win without much regard to the personality of the leader; a French writer has well contrasted the great "anonymous victories" of the Mongols with the purely personal triumphs of that grim Turkish conqueror whom we know best as Timour the Tartar, or Tamerlane. The civil administration the Mongols established in a conquered country was borrowed from China, and where they settled as conquerors the conduct of the Chinese bureaucracy maddened the subject peoples almost as much as the wild and lawless brutality of the Mongol soldiers themselves. Gradually their empire, after splitting up, past away and left little direct influence in any country; but it was at the time so prodigious a phenomenon, fraught with such vast and dire possibilities, that a full knowledge of the history of the Mongol people is imperatively necessary to all who would understand the development of Asia and of Eastern Europe.

Jack London, "The Yellow Peril" (1904)[30]

Jack London (1876–1916) was one of America's most popular novelists in the early twentieth century. He celebrated the vigor of white masculinity and is best known for his Call of the Wild *(1903) and* White Fang *(1906), both set amid the gold rush on the Yukon frontier. London traveled to Korea to cover the Russo-Japanese War (1904) as a correspondent for William Randolph Hearst's* San Francisco Examiner, *where he wrote this excerpt. Hearst's* Examiner *became an ardent advocate for military confrontation with Japan right up until the Japanese attack on Pearl Harbor in 1941. London illustrated the potential danger of Asian hordes addressed here in a future-war short story entitled "The Unparalleled Invasion," in 1910. In that story, following the Russo-Japanese War, the Japanese give China the industrial technology it needs to support unlimited population growth. By 1975 China has a billion people and floods the world with immigrants as a form of invasion. To stem this tide an American scientist develops a poison to drop on the Chinese, exterminating them completely, and the rest of the world carves up China's empty territory for settlement. Literary scholar Colleen Lye argues that London's yellow perilism reflected his profound anxieties about industrial modernity's erosion of the "White Man's Way" (the title of one of London's other stories).[30]*

The menace to the Western world lies, not in the little brown man, but in the four hundred millions of yellow men should the little brown man undertake their management. The Chinese is not dead to new ideas; he is an efficient worker; makes a good soldier, and is wealthy in the essential materials of a machine age. Under a capable management he will go far. The Japanese is prepared and fit to undertake this management. Not only has he proved himself an apt imitator of Western material progress, a sturdy worker, and a capable organizer, but he is far more fit to manage the Chinese than are we. The baffling enigma of the Chinese character is no baffling enigma to him. He understands as we could never school ourselves nor hope to understand. Their mental processes are largely the same. He thinks with the same thought-symbols as does the Chinese, and he thinks in the same peculiar grooves. He goes on where we are balked by the obstacles of incomprehension. He takes the turning which we cannot perceive, twists around the obstacle, and, presto! is out of sight in the ramifications of the Chinese mind where we cannot follow.

The Chinese has been called the type of permanence, and well he has merited it, dozing as he has through the ages. And as truly was the Japanese the type of permanence up to a generation ago, when he suddenly awoke and startled the world with a rejuvenescence the like of which the world had never seen before. The ideas of the West were the leaven which quickened the Japanese; and the ideas of the West, transmitted by the Japanese mind into ideas Japanese, may well make the leaven powerful enough to quicken the Chinese.

We have had Africa for the Afrikaner, and at no distant day we shall hear "Asia for the Asiatic!" Four hundred million indefatigable workers (deft, intelligent, and unafraid to die), aroused and rejuvenescent, managed and guided by forty-five million additional human beings who are splendid fighting animals, scientific and modern, constitute that menace to the Western world which has been well named the "Yellow Peril."

4

Anglo America's "Great Game"

Americans like to believe they are exceptional and exist outside the historical trajectory of the Old World. But just how outside can America be, and what is lost in this exceptionalist narrative?

The Bard of British Imperialism himself, Rudyard Kipling (who you'll remember popularized the terms the Great Game and White Man's Burden) spent half a decade living in Brattleboro, Vermont. He wrote the *Jungle Book* there. Edmund Wilson has argued that Kipling's time in the U.S. pushed him to embrace imperialism in ways he never had before as a young man in British India. According to Wilson, Kipling—having been raised in a rigidly status-conscious colonial setting—couldn't stand the lack of deference and social hierarchy he encountered in America, and found solace in imperial order upon his return to England in 1896.[1]

But America played versions of the Great Game, far more than acknowledged. U.S. presidents Thomas Jefferson and James Monroe sought to extend an "empire of liberty" across the continent, which could extend the promise of propertied freedom farther than ever before. They boldly declared that the newly independent Republics of the Americas would assume the mantle of civilization for themselves over their Old World imperial rivals in the region. However, for all their political differences, the geopolitical results of what Americans came to call their Manifest Destiny were quite similar to the machinations of their European forebears and competitors. As the U.S. pushed south into Cherokee, Chickasaw, Seminole, and Spanish territory, and west into Mexico, the British in India pushed east from their base in Bengal to China, and west to Afghanistan and Persia. The U.S. played its own games with the Caribbean and Latin America, but also played the

Great Game proper in the Far East. The U.S. Navy "opened" Japan in 1852, and helped the British reopen China in the Second Opium War. America is even pictured in Kaiser Wilhelm II's illustration discussed in the Introduction. At the turn of the century, the U.S. Army occupied parts of China following the Boxer Rebellion and as much of the Philippines as they could. America supported Japan's imperial claims to Korea that is, until the United States followed the British in backing the Russians over the Japanese in 1907.[2]

The longing for liberty at the heart of liberal expansionism lent a desperate air of grandiosity to visions of the white man's destiny. The massacres at the Battle of the Alamo (1836) and Elphinstone's retreat from Kabul (1842) felt like betrayal, not the thwarting of aggressive expansion by committed locals. This is in part because expansionists depicted President General Antonio López de Santa Anna in Mexico and Dost Mohammad Khan in Afghanistan as arch-despots abusing property, but also as racialized figures lacking true martial valor. Teddy Roosevelt declared the Filipino, Cuban, and Puerto Rican resistance to U.S. rule "insurrections." He felt these peoples were unfit to govern themselves, even though they won their own independence from the Spanish.[3]

The disconnect between the lofty principles of the White Man's Burden and the brutal practice of Great Game imperialism haunts the European American imagination. As early as 1808, Washington Irving quipped that by the logic of those who would clear America of Indians, if Moon Men with advanced technology were to come to Earth, they would be justified in treating white Americans as kindly as the whites had treated the Indians before them, that is to say with disregard and wanton violence.[4] Irving's warning, no doubt was in part inspired by the recent Haitian Revolution, which was itself inspired by the French Revolution's rhetoric of "liberty, equality, fraternity." It terrified the Atlantic world and hastened the abolition of slavery in the British colonies. Such resistance laid bare the hypocrisy and limits of Enlightenment colonialism.

Like the example of Irving suggests, fiction was a crucial space in which to explore and rework the fears that accompanied the promise of empire. The psychological underpinnings of this imperial worldview lent itself toward ever escalating cycles of violence, and a grandiosity reflected in the hyperbolic inhuman depravity assigned to obstacles of European progress.

Confronted by its own hypocrisy, any resistance to this sort of game became an epic confrontation, justifying harsher and harsher punishments, and more and more elaborate justifications to mask hysterical injustices and preserve the fantasy of European moral superiority. Since white expansionary progress was predestined, how could anti-colonial resistance be just? But what if the classification metrics were incorrect? What if whites weren't the ones destined to rule the world? What if whites were the savages?

As much as Japanese imperialism presented a material threat to Anglo American interests in East Asia, they symbolized much more. The Japanese launched their own version of Kipling's plea, not only in their call for an anti-European imperialist "Asian co-prosperity sphere," but through their actions, propaganda, and sometimes direct support encouraging indigenous independence movements in India, the Philippines, and across the colonized world.[5] Like the Haitian Revolution a century before, such movements struck fear into the hearts of Europeans and Americans invested in white supremacy, or perhaps those just scared that their fantasies of retribution might come true. As with Irving's imagined Moon Men, would *they* enslave the Europeans as the Europeans had sought to enslave others?

If imperialism was a progressive Christian benevolent project that proved the superiority of European culture, what did Japan's empire mean? Some elite Europeans and Americans worried that superior civilization had made their own peoples soft. These elites jealously marveled at what they saw as the regimented and devoted masculine martial culture of Japan, and the hardworking tenacity of Asian peoples. Japanese imperialism, celebrated by many Europeans initially, also mirrored the violence at the heart of the fantasy of the benevolent imperial project itself. Given the history of European and American fixations on racial classification and destiny, the modern Asian empire led many proponents of white supremacy to imagine themselves on the other side of the colonial equation with startling clarity. Fixations on the barbarism of Japanese imperialism offered Europeans and Americans a safe way to express their outrage and disbelief in their own violence, but it did not calm the fears such violence breeds.

As Europeans and Americans invested more and more cultural and psychic resources justifying their own rightful and benevolent rule across the globe, they were troubled by their own past actions. Unable to admit past wrongs, and increasingly afraid such a past might literally come back to bite them, imperialists bound the world into a powder keg. This is the logic of protective reaction and the preemptive strike.

The point is not to figure out who the real "good guys" or "bad guys" are—often, there are none. The point is, instead, to decolonize our under-standing of history and the yellow perilism shot through it, so as not to be lured into the same vicious cycles again and again. In this chapter we present fragments of literature alongside images of imperial expansion to suggest how the expressive culture reflected and reinforced a racialized Anglo American Protestant common sense. We also meet the "Devil Doctor" Fu Manchu again as a master-organizer of these slippery identifications.

"Justice" and "The Indian Revolt" (1857)

On May 10, 1857, a major rebellion rocked northern India. The British press went wild, fixating on the savagery of what they termed the Sepoy Mutiny. The name itself implied a betrayal and reinforced and normalized British authority in Bengal. In the aftermath of the rebellion the British East India Company disbanded and the Crown assumed direct colonial management in South Asia. This marked the beginnings of formal colonialism there, as annexation replaced alliances and tribute with local rulers.[6]

Karl Marx (1818–1883) was at the time the London correspondent for the New York Tribune *and covered the story. Marx was a political-economic phi-losopher who developed a Hegelian-style theory of linear development in which the dialectic propelling world history forward was not a dialectic of spirit, but of material conditions. In his "Communist Manifesto" (1848) Marx had embraced European imperialism as a necessary stage in historical development because it broke Asian societies out of their supposed slumber and into a pro-gressive world development. However, after the Indian uprising in 1857 and the opening of the Second Opium War (1856), Marx increasingly embraced an anti-colonialist position and altered, somewhat, his theories on the devel-opment of the global economy. Marx identified an alternate Asiatic mode of production to his European model and abandoned his notion of Asia as stag-nant. However, these evolving views were still infused with a vision of Oriental Despotism and have been heavily criticized since. Nevertheless, over the course of his career Marx developed a sensitivity and commitment to anti-colonial organizing, and such commitments continued to reshape his economic and political theories.*[7]

Figure 45. "Justice," *Punch* (September 12, 1857), 109. Courtesy of the New York Public Library.

Karl Marx, "The Indian Revolt" (1857)[8]

The outrages committed by the revolted sepoys in India are indeed appalling, hideous, ineffable—such as one is prepared to meet only in wars of insurrection, of nationalities, of races, and above all of religion; in one word, such as respectable England used to applaud when perpetrated by the Vendeans on the "Blues," by the Spanish guerrillas on the infidel Frenchmen, by Serbians on their German and Hungarian neighbours, by Croats on Viennese rebels, by Cavaignac's Garde Mobile or Bonaparte's Decembrists on the sons and daughters of proletarian France. However infamous the conduct of the Sepoys, it is only the reflex, in a concentrated form, of England's own conduct in India, not only during the epoch of the foundation of her Eastern Empire, but even during the last ten years of a long-settled rule. To characterize that rule, it suffices to say that torture formed an organic institution of its financial policy. There is something in human history like retribution: and it is a rule of historical retribution that its instrument be forged not by the offended, but by the offender himself.

The first blow dealt to the French monarchy proceeded from the nobility, not from the peasants. The Indian revolt does not commence with the Ryots, tortured, dishonoured, and stripped naked by the British, but with the Sepoys, clad, fed, petted, fatted, and pampered by them. To find parallels to the Sepoy atrocities, we need not, as some London papers pretend, fall back on the middle ages, not, even wander beyond the history of contemporary England. All we want is to study the first Chinese war, an event, so to say, of yesterday. The English soldiery then committed abominations for the mere fun of it; their passions being neither sanctified by religious fanaticism nor exacerbated by hatred against an overbearing and conquering race, nor provoked by the stern resistance of a heroic enemy. The violations of women, the spittings of children, the roastings of whole villages, were then mere wanton sports, not recorded by Mandarins, but by British officers themselves ...

An officer in the civil service, from Allahabad, writes: "We have power of life and death in our hands, and we assure you we spare not." Another, from the same place: "Not a day passes but we string up from ten to fifteen of them (noncombatants)." One exulting officer writes: "Holmes is hanging them by the score, like a 'brick.'" Another, in allusion to the summary hanging of a large body of the natives: "Then our fun commenced." A third: "We hold court-martials on horseback, and every nigger we meet with we either string up or shoot." From Benares we are informed that thirty Zemindars were hanged on the mere suspicion of sympathizing with their own countrymen, and whole villages were burned down on the same plea. An officer from Benares, whose letter is printed in the London *Times*, says: "The European troops have become fiends when opposed to natives."

And then it should not be forgotten that, while the cruelties of the English are related as acts of martial vigor, told simply, rapidly, without dwelling on disgusting details, the outrages of the natives, shocking as they are, are still deliberately exaggerated. For instance, the circumstantial account first appearing in *The Times*, and then going the round of the London press, of the atrocities perpetrated at Delhi and Meerut, from whom did it proceed? From a cowardly parson residing at Bangalore, Mysore, more than a thousand miles, as the bird flies, distant from the scene of action. Actual accounts of Delhi evince the imagination of an English person to be capable of breeding greater horrors than even the wild fancy of a Hindoo mutineer. The cutting of noses, breasts, &c., in one word, the horrid mutilations committed by the Sepoys, are of course more revolting to European feeling than the throwing of red-hot shell on Canton dwellings by a Secretary of the Manchester Peace Society, or the roasting of Arabs pent up in a cave by a French Marshal, or the flaying alive of British soldiers by the cat-o'-nine-tails under drum-head court-martial, or any other of the philanthropical appliances used in British penitentiary colonies …

The frantic roars of the "bloody old *Times*," as Cobbett used to call it— its playing the part of a furious character in one of Mozart's operas, who indulges in most melodious strains in the idea of first hanging his enemy, then roasting him, then quartering him, then spitting him, and then flaying him alive—its tearing the passion of revenge to tatters and to rags—all this would appear but silly if under the pathos of tragedy there were not distinctly perceptible the tricks of comedy. The London *Times* overdoes its part, not only from panic. It supplies comedy with a subject even missed by Molière, the Tartuffe of Revenge. What it simply wants is to write up the funds and to screen the Government. As Delhi has not, like the walls of Jericho, fallen before mere puffs of wind, John Bull is to be steeped in cries for revenge up to his very ears, to make him forget that his Government is responsible for the mischief hatched and the colossal dimensions it has been allowed to assume.

William Ward Crane, "The Year 1899" (1893)[9]

This fanciful future-history by journalist William Ward Crane (n.d.) is representative of numerous stories from the late nineteenth and early twentieth centuries depicting the unification of colonized peoples under a Fu Manchu-like Asian leader. Crane wrote this story before the Japanese invasion of China or the U.S. invasions of Cuba, Puerto Rico, and the Philippines, and yet he clearly illustrates the fears and fantasies attending these imperialisms. In the early

twentieth century, these types of stories were a key component of the military pre-
paredness movement, and one year before the year his future-war scenario was
to take place Crane himself wrote that the "value of these fanciful predictions of
war is not affected by their being unlike, in detail, what really happens, or even
by their not coming true in any sense, for they may help to prevent their own
fulfillment."[10] *In 1929,* Chicago Tribune *foreign correspondent Floyd Gibbons*
wrote a nearly identical future-history entitled The Red Napoleon. *In that*
novel Mongolian Karakhan of Kazan takes over the Soviet Union to wage war
against the free world. These fantasies reworked the imagined legacy of Asian
race hate against the West and projected them upon present and future fears.[11]

In April 1898, a man named Stanhope appeared in Washington and gained
notoriety as "a rabid crank." The reporters said he looked like an Indian,
and talked wildly about the Chinese Government, and somebody or something he called Kara Hoolakoo. After he had haunted the State Department
for about two weeks, his dead body was found floating in the Potomac. It
was thought then that he had committed suicide. There is little doubt now
that he was murdered.

A little later the movements of the Chinamen in this country began
attracting general attention. Singly, or in small parties they were leaving
the North and West and the Pacific Coast, and moving southward. They
would say nothing about their intentions, but it was soon known that they
were settling on the marshy coasts of the South Atlantic and Gulf States.
They did not compete with the negroes as laborers, but rented or squatted
on swampy, unused lands, and went to work diligently to make them fit
for cultivation. They built clusters of mud huts, which became the favorite
resorts of all the idle negroes for miles around. The Chinamen bought fish,
game, and stolen poultry from their African friends, and they capped the
climax by giving them the titles "Mista" and "Missee." Negroes began using
queer nasal words in their improvised chants, and when asked about what
they meant, would say, "Dunno, 'spec' it muss be some kin' o' Chinee talk."

A white refugee from Jamaica wrote to a New Orleans paper that in
passing by night near one of the Chinese hamlets he had seen a band of
negroes going through a strange ceremony, while the Asiatics sat and looked
on, showing their teeth like rats. An old black woman, who might have
been a Voodoo sorceress, went to the fire, turned around, and screamed.

"One, two, free!" All the other negroes sprang up, and one of them shouted back the same formula. Then the whole gang broke out together:

"One, two, free! I tells you true! De culied man, de Chinee man, de Kolli-holli-koo!"

This was instantly followed by demonic yells and shrieks, and the company began dancing around the fire like their savage ancestors getting ready for a raid after slaves.

The Jamaican remembered the words he had heard the negroes sing while he was flying through the darkness from his burning house—the same words his father had told him were sung by the Jamaica slaves in their insurrection, just before the British government set them free:

"One, two, tree! All de same! White, black, red! All de same!"

"How did this form of the Jamaica negro's Carmagnole reach Louisiana?" asked the refugee. "I don't know how harmless a member of society the Kolli-holli-koo may be, but the other two in the triad certainly need watching."

No special attention was given to this letter, and when three of our consuls in the West Indies sent home word that the blacks were talking of invading the United States, it was thought a good joke.

In February 1899, the government was notified by Colonel Mays, the head-chief of the Cherokees in Indian Territory, that two Chinese strangers had tried to induce him to join a league of Chinamen, negroes, and Indians against the whites of the United States. They said that reservation Indians had generally entered into the plot, and that the Southern negroes had also gone into the league in vast numbers. It was to rise in arms as soon as a great Asiatic confederacy, organized by the Chinese Emperor, had sent an army of a million men to land on our western coast. At the same time, the negroes of the West Indies were to invade the Gulf States, in the vessels they had seized or were then building. The Cherokee chief was offered the command of all the Indian forces, and urged to use his influence in bringing the civilized tribes into the plot. Colonel Mays questioned the men closely, and after learning the particulars of the scheme arrested them both, and held them for the authorities ...

Close detective work at home brought no evidence of any recent organization among the colored people of the North and West; but in the South, and especially in the Gulf States, it was evident that some unusual movement was going on. A large number of clubs had been formed, which denied having any political object, but conducted all their operations secretly. Few of the most respectable colored people had joined these clubs, but the rest were evidently unwilling or afraid to talk about them.

Meanwhile, someone in the State Department at Washington remembered that a document submitted by the unfortunate Stanhope was lying unread in its pigeon-hole. Being brought to light this paper showed what the whole scheme meant.

The writer said he had lived twenty-eight years in Chinese Tartary, engaged in the border-trade between Kiakhta and Maimatchin. He had adopted the Tartar dress and habits, and, as he was partly of Indian descent, had been generally taken for a native of some part of Asia. In 1898 he noticed a violent excitement among the people of Maimatchin, and, gaining the confidence of a Chinese official agent, he found out what had caused it …

Wherever a Tartar had his home there were songs sung and stories told of the great Temugin—or Jenghis Khan—and his mighty sons, before whom the nations far and near were forced to bow down in the dust. But in Mongolia these songs and legends were considered not more a picture from the past than a presage of the future. Every Mongolian believed that, sooner or later, the time would come for the men of his country to go forth again in the van of a great host of Altaic warriors to subjugate the world …

It was determined at Pekin that the Jenghis of our day should be the Emperor of China. Descended from the Manchu family that reimposed the Tartar rule on China after the line of Kublai had been driven out, he already stood as the champion and chief of the Tartar race. Being the civil head of the Lama religion, he claimed reverent allegiance from all the Buddhists in the world; and as Lamaism is a composite religion, the Shamaists and Shivaists also owed him religious homage. No other man could so easily unite the whole Altaic stock and induce other Asiatics to join it, and the prospect of seeing all Asia marching under his leadership to crush and destroy the *Fan-kwoi* in their own homes would be more captivating to the Chinese people than the hope of placing one of their race on the throne.

The first thing to be done was to find some fanatic who could arouse the Tartars. Among the priests who swarmed around the sacred *lama* at Oorga, in Mongolia, was one bearing the name Hoolakoo. He was a monomaniac, claiming descent from the Shaman priest who consecrated Temugin at the great koorooltai in 1205. One of his fancies was to dress entirely in black, as a symbol of the nummud, and from this he was called *Kara* (black) Hoolakoo. He it was who was chosen as the herald of the coming storm. Mohammedan, Brahminical, and Buddhist leaders would be found to excite religious frenzy among the Turks, Turkomans, Arabs, Persians, Siamese, Burmese, Cochin Chinese, Malays, and Hindoos, and it was expected that the whole of Asia and Malaysia and all northern Africa would join in a holy war against the white race everywhere.

Ashis Nandy, "The Psychology of Colonialism" (1988)[12]

Indian psychoanalyst Ashis Nandy argues colonialism is a political-psychological system that affects both the colonized and the colonizing. In this excerpt Nandy discusses Rudyard Kipling (1865–1936), the Anglo-Indian poet and author of The Jungle Book *(1894) and many other immensely popular English tales. Kipling famously implored the U.S. to colonize the Philippines in 1899 with a poem dedicated to President Theodore Roosevelt entitled "The White Man's Burden." Ten years prior Kipling published "The Ballad of East and West," echoing Roosevelt's contention in the first volume of his own* Winning of the West *(1889) that Anglo-Saxons in America earned their dominance through regenerative violence on colonial frontiers. Kipling's poem depicts a British officer proving his worthiness to occupy the Khyber Pass in Afghanistan by earning the respect of a horse-thief from across the border whom he tracks down, races, and fights. The poem opens and closes with the stanza:*

> *Oh, East is East, and West is West, and never the twain shall meet,*
> *Till Earth and Sky stand presently at God's great Judgment Seat;*
> *But there is neither East nor West, Border, nor Breed, nor Birth,*
> *When two strong men stand face to face, though they come from the ends of the earth!*[13]

For Kipling and Roosevelt, the savage warfare of expansion prevented civilized societies from becoming decadent and effete. Instead of celebrating this culture of imperialism, Nandy analyzes the great psychological cost of such social and political investment in martial masculinity.[14]

As folk wisdom would have it, the only sufferers of colonialism are the subject communities. Colonialism, according to this view, is the name of a political economy which ensures a one-way flow of benefits, the subjects being the perpetual losers in a zero-sum game and the rulers the beneficiaries. This is a view of human mind and history promoted by colonialism itself. This view has a vested interest, in denying that the colonizers are at least as much affected by the ideology of colonialism, that their degradation, too, can sometimes be terrifying. Behind all the rhetoric of the European intelligentsia on the evils of colonialism lay their unstated faith that the gains from colonialism to Europe, to the extent that they primarily involved material products, were real, and the losses, to the extent they involved social relations and psychological states, false. To venture a less popular interpretation of colonialism—which I hope is relatively less contaminated by the ideology of colonialism—I shall produce examples from the experience of one of the world's stablest and most subtly-managed colonial polities of all times, British India …

The impact of colonialism on India was deep. The economic exploitation, psychological uprooting and cultural disruption it caused were tremendous.* But India was a country of hundreds of millions living in a large land mass. In spite of the presence of a paramount power which acted as the central authority, the country was culturally fragmented and politically heterogeneous. It could, thus, partly confine the cultural impact of imperialism to its urban centers, to its Westernized and semi-Westernized upper and middle classes, and to some sections of its traditional elites. That was not the case for the rulers from a relatively more homogeneous small

---

* The political and economic dislocation is of course well known and well documented. For an early discussion of the economic exploitation under British colonialism, see for example R. C. Dutt, *Economic History of India in the Victorian Age* (London: Routledge, 1903) and Dadabhoi Naoroji, *Poverty and Un-British Rule in India* (New Delhi: Publications Division, 1969 [1901]). For instances of cultural and psychological pathology produced by colonization in India, see *British Paramountcy and Indian Resistance*, part 2, eds. R. C. Majumdar et al. (Bombay: Bharatiya Vidya Bhavan, 1965). For a case study of a specific cultural pathology under the Raj, see for instance, Ashis Nandy, "Sati: A Nineteenth-Century Tale of Women, Violence and Protest" in *At the Edge of Psychology* (Delhi: Oxford University Press, 1980), 1–31.

island. They were overwhelmed by the experience of being colonial rulers. As a result, the long-term cultural damage colonialism did to the British society was greater.

Firstly, the experience of colonizing did not leave the internal culture of Britain untouched. It began to bring into prominence those parts of the British political culture which were least tender and humane. It de-emphasized speculation, intellection, and *caritas* as feminine, and justified a limited cultural role for women—and femininity—by holding that the softer side of human nature was irrelevant to the public sphere. It openly sanctified—in the name of such values as competition, achievement, control, and productivity—new forms of institutionalized violence and ruthless social Darwinism.* The instrumental concept of the lower classes it promoted was perfectly in tune with the needs of industrial capitalism and only a slightly modified version of the colonial concept of hierarchy was applied to the British society itself. The tragedy of colonialism was also the tragedy of the younger sons, the women, and all "the etceteras and and-so-forths" of Britain ...

Secondly and paradoxically, the ideology of colonialism produced a false sense of cultural homogeneity in Britain. This froze social consciousness, discouraging the basic cultural criticism that might have come from growing intellectual sensitivity to the rigid British social classes and subnational divisions, and from the falling quality of life in a quickly industrializing society. Colonialism blurred the lines of social divisions by opening up alternative channels of social mobility in the colonies and by underwriting nationalist sentiments through colonial wars of expansion or through wars with other ambitious European powers seeking a share of colonial glory. The near-total cultural dominance of a small elite in Britain was possible because the society shunted off to the colonies certain indirect expressions of cultural criticism: social deviants unhappy with the social order and buffeted by the stresses within it. I have in mind the criminality which

---

* Some of these emphases are compatible with the 'standard' description of the authoritarian syndrome deriving from the Frankfurt School of Marxists, elaborated empirically in Theodor Adorno et al., *The Authoritarian Personality* (New York: Harper & Row, 1950). On the culture of social Darwinism in Britain, see Raymond Williams, "Social Darwinism," in *Problems in Materialism and Culture* (London: New Left Books, 1980), 86–102.

comes from the rage of the oppressed, displaced from the rulers to the co-oppressed* ...

Thirdly, there was what E. M. Forster called the "undeveloped heart" in the British which separated them not merely from the Indians but also from each other.† This undevelopment came both in the form of isolation of cognition from affect—which often is a trigger to the "banal" violence of our times—and in the form of a new pathological fit between ideas and feelings. The theory of imperialism did not remain an insulated political position in Britain; it became a religious and ethical theory and an integral part of a cosmology. It not only structured the inner needs of the changing British society but also gave grotesque expression to a "primitive" religious and social consciousness that had acquired immense military and techno-logical power and was now operating on a global scale. Richard Congreve, Bishop of Oxford, once said, "God has entrusted India to us to hold it for Him, and we have no right to give it up"‡ ...

Finally, as Francis Hutchins and Lewis D. Wurgaft have so convincingly argued in the context of India, colonialism encouraged the colonizers to impute to themselves magical feelings of omnipotence and permanence.§ These feelings became a part of the British selfhood in Britain too. And the society was sold the idea of being an advanced techno-industrial society where science promised to liberate man from his daily drudgery, an advanced culture where human reason and civilized norms had the great-est influence, and—for the sake of the radical internal critics of the society

---

* Frantz Fanon in his *The Wretched of the Earth* (London: Penguin, 1967) seems to recognize this displacement.

† Forster's *A Passage to India* (London: Arnold, 1967) of course examines this separa-tion only in the context of the British society in India.

‡ Quoted in Kanatur Bhaskara Rao, *Rudyard Kipling's India* (Norman, OK: University of Oklahoma, 1967), 26. See an interesting treatment of this moral dimension in Lewis D. Wurgaft, "Another Look at Prospero and Caliban: Magic and Magical Thinking in British India" *Psychohistory Review* 6, no.1 (1977), 2–26 and Octave Mannoni, *Prospero and Caliban: The Psychology of Colonization*, trans. Pamela Powers (New York: Frederick A. Praeger, 1964).

§ Francis Hutchins, *The Illusion of Permanence: British Imperialism in India* (Princeton, NJ: Princeton University Press, 1967); Wurgaft, "Another Look at Prospero and Caliban."

who took to the idea like fish to water—a polity farthest on the road to revolutionary self-actualization. Britannia not only ruled the waves; for its inhabitants and for its many admirers in Europe it also ruled the future of human self-consciousness ...

[Rudyard] Kipling probably was the most creative builder of the political myths which a colonial power needs to sustain its self-esteem. The psychological coordinates of his imperialist ideology have often been the coordinates of the West's image of the non-West in our times. Elsewhere ... I have described Kipling's early experiences and worldview to show that he was something more than a rabid imperialist with an integrated identity. He was, I have argued, a tragic figure seeking to disown in self-hatred an aspect of his self identified with Indianness—which in turn was identified with victimization, ostracism, and violence—because of a cruel first encounter with England after an idyllic childhood in India. In this state, Kipling reproduced in his personal life both the painful cultural changes that had taken place in his society and the history of British colonialism in India from Robert Clive to Winston Churchill.

Since about the seventeenth century, the hyper-masculine over-socialized aspects of European personality had been gradually supplanting the cultural traits which had become identified with femininity, childhood, and later on, "primitivism." As part of a peasant cosmology, these traits had been valued aspects of a culture not wedded to achievement and productivity. Now they had to be rejected as alien to mainstream European civilization and projected onto the "low cultures" of Europe and onto the new cultures European civilization encountered. It was as part of this process that the colonies came to be seen as the abode of people childlike and innocent on the one hand, and devious, effeminate and passive-aggressive on the other. The positive qualities of childlikeness, Kipling argued, were attributes of the good savages—for instance, the devoted, obedient martial races of India, the Gunga Dins—and those of the good-hearted, patriotic lower classes of Britain supplying the Raj with "Tommies" who dutifully went to their untimely death in distant lands. Childish or feminine passive-aggression was the attribute of the effete nationalists and fake sahibs or babus drawn from the non-martial races and that of the uninformed, shallow, British liberals supporting the former. It was also the attribute of whatever apparent civilization India, as opposed to the "savage" Africans, seemed to have.

This was the ultimate meaning of the spirit of colonialism and its civilizing mission mounted on behalf of modernity and progress. Kipling merely
produced new myths to consolidate these cultural ideas as a part of his
own search for an integrated selfhood. To use an overworked expression
of Herbert Marcuse's, it was an instance of internal repression mirroring
an externally repressive system. Kipling's idea of the effeminate, passive-
aggressive, and "half-savage-half-child" Indian was more than an Anglo-
Indian stereotype: it was an aspect of Kipling's authenticity and Europe's
other face.

The *denouement* for Kipling came in his old age, when his literary success
with generations of young readers had very nearly established his superiority over his critics in India as well as in the West. It came when his only
son died defending the cause of the Empire Kipling held so dear. Kipling,
neither a clear-cut product of the self-confident colonialism of the nineteenth century nor at home with modern wars based on mega-technology
and mega-death, was broken. The fear of loss of nurture had always haunted
him. The characters in his stories … sometimes sought that nurture through
a reversal of roles: they secured nurture from their wards, from children and
from the childlike aliens they befriended or protected. In the process, they
presumably ensured for their creator a similar nurture from the children
among—and the children in—his readers. That fantasy world of nurture
from below, perhaps compensating loss or deprivation of parental nurture,
collapsed with the death of Kipling's son.

Edmund Wilson sensitively captures the spirit of this Kipling, broken as
much by the imperialism he so admired as by his self-repression.[*] Wilson
does so by quoting the defeated imperialist—lonely, depressed, and fearful
of insanity in his old age:

> I have a dream—a dreadful dream—
> A dream that is near done,
> I watch a man go out of his mind,
> And he is My Mother's Son.

---

[*] Edmund Wilson, "The Kipling That Nobody Read" in *Kipling's Mind and Arts*, ed.
Andrew Rutherford (Stanford: Stanford University Press, 1964), 17–69.

Gary Okihiro, "Perilous Frontiers" (1994)[15]

U.S. historian Gary Okihiro argues that Yellow Peril fears emerge from the very precariousness of white dominance, and the myriad forms of resistance to it. As a result, domestic repression and geopolitical aggression shaped both domestic and global Yellow Peril fears. These internal and external imperial contests represent very real conflict, but also perpetuate a paranoid worldview that structures mainstream understandings of future crises.

American history, as told by the founding fathers, was a progressive account of triumph over the perils of the forests and its beasts, of change from a lesser to a greater good, of growth from the simple to the complex, of evolution from savagism to civilization. America's Indians stood in the way of progress and, in fact, represented the past. "To study him [the Indian] was to study the past," wrote Pearce. "To kill him was to kill the past. History would thus be the key to the moral worth of cultures; the history of American civilization would thus be conceived of as three-dimensional, progressing from past to present, from east to west, from lower to higher." In addition, those historical dimensions related directly to the confrontation between whites and Asians, in that Indians were widely seen as descendants of Asians, and in that America's westward march continued into the Pacific, extending to Asia, where the "Far East" became the nation's "Far West"* …

Repression at home, of immigrants, workers, socialists, African Americans, and women, complemented America's expansion abroad and created, in the words of historian Walter LaFeber, the "new empire." In the pursuit of that empire, there arose "a vastly increased emphasis on race," aligning white America with the European colonial powers and African Americans with other people of color in the Third World, prompting W. E. B. Du Bois's well-known insight: "The problem of the twentieth century is the problem of the color-line." Domestic crises and expansion abroad demanded "an identity as well as an identity of interest" that excluded America's racial and

---

* Roy Harvey Pearce, *Savagism and Civilization: A Study of the Indian and the American Mind* (Baltimore, MD: Johns Hopkins University Press, 1965), 3–49, 49. From John Hay's reflections, see Walter LaFeber, *The New Empire: An Interpretation of American Expansion, 1860–1898* (Ithaca, NY: Cornell University Press, 1963), 5.

ethnic minorities and helped create transnational identities of white and nonwhite.*

The idea of the yellow peril contributed to those global identities. English historian Charles H. Pearson was perhaps the most influential architect of the modern yellow peril. His book *National Life and Character*, published in 1893, ostensibly inspired Wilhelm II's call to European nations to defend their faith and home and articulated the intellectual foundations of the modern danger. Pearson's vision was global. Whites, he maintained, had expanded to the farthest reaches of the temperate zones and no more frontiers remained except in the tropics, where a densely populated band of black and yellow peoples lived and where whites could not settle permanently. At the same time, whites desired tropical products and thus colonized those areas, bringing technology and medicines that enabled more efficient production, but also lengthening the lives of nonwhites and introducing them to Western science and industry. The inevitable result, predicted Pearson, would be a tremendous population explosion among the peoples of color and a dramatic increase in their power, marshaled and led by Asians. The resurgent masses, he warned, would challenge white rule and would spread and expand beyond the tropical band into the temperate, more desirable zones, and thereby threaten the very heart of the white homeland.[†]

Brooks Adams, descendant of two U.S. presidents and born of a bedrock Yankee family renowned for public service, constructed an American version of the yellow peril that underscored a global economic competition and provided an intellectual rationale for imperialism. Like Pearson, Adams believed that European imperialism had stirred recumbent Asia, but he went on to explain that the extraction of Asia's wealth, which enriched the metropoles and impoverished the colonies, resulted in cheap labor among Asia's masses, with the consequence that Asian manufactures and goods would compete with and ultimately supplant European products. "The cheapest form of labour is thus being bred on a gigantic scale," argued Adams, and as competition intensifies, "nature begins to sift the economic minds themselves, culling a favoured aristocracy of the craftiest

---

* LaFeber, *The New Empire*; Nell Irvin Painter, *Standing at Armageddon: The United States, 1877–1919* (New York: W. W. Norton, 1987), 168, 390.

† Richard Austin Thompson, *The Yellow Peril, 1890–1924* (New York: Arno Press, 1978), 4, 18–21.

and the subtlest types; choosing, for example, the Armenian in Byzantium, the Marwari in India, and the Jew in London." Eventually, the "centre of exchanges" will pass from Europe to Asia, because of the "progressive law of civilization" by which vigorous, tenacious barbarians supersede bloated, opulent civilized peoples. Imperialism, westward expansion, and colonialism will toughen soft America, tame the Asiatic economic beast, and reverse the "progressive law of civilization." Adams's study, wrote historian Charles A. Beard, should be counted among "the outstanding documents of intellectual history in the United States and, in a way, the Western World," and Adams's contemporaries such as Theodore Roosevelt, Alfred T. Mahan, and Homer Lea urged American expansion on the basis of his organic analogy about the birth, rise, decline, and revitalization of civilizations. The global themes of imperialism, migration, and economic competition set forth by Pearson and Adams laid the foundation for "yellow perilism"[*] …

The logic of that twentieth-century racial discourse derived from nineteenth-century Europeans, who had promoted the ascendance of science and Darwinism, industrial development and commerce, and imperialism. But it also sought to explain the global subjugation of nonwhite by white and the threats posed to that racial hierarchy by unruly nonwhites in the colonies and by nonwhite migration from the torrid to the temperate zones. The white man's burden had awakened the slumbering colored masses, given them weapons with which to resist the colonizer and created sea-lanes that brought not only tropical products but also "new barbarians" into the homeland. Like the tarantula hidden among the bunches of bananas, the empire had struck back. "The subjugation of white lands by colored armies may, of course, occur, especially if the white world continues to rend itself with internecine wars," argued white supremacist writer Lothrop Stoddard after World War I. "However, such colored triumphs of arms are less to be dreaded than more enduring conquests like migrations which would swamp whole populations and turn countries now white into colored man's lands irretrievably lost to the white world"[†] …

---

[*] Charles A. Beard, "Introduction," in Brooks Adams, *The Law of Civilization and Decay: An Essay on History* (New York: Macmillan, 1895), 286–93, vii; Thompson, *Yellow Peril*, 27.

[†] Lothrop Stoddard, *The Rising Tide of Color Against White World-Supremacy* (New York: Scribner, 1921), vi.

Contrary to most of the literature on anti-Asianism, I do not believe that racism or the idea of the yellow peril is irrational or fantastic; instead, I hold that they are constructed with a purpose in mind and function to sustain the social order. Historian Richard Austin Thompson observed that "the common denominator among yellow perilists was a fear of change," change within the relationship between Europe (and America) and Asia, which was becoming increasingly more intimate and equal.* The idea of the yellow peril, as we have seen, helped to define that challenge posed by Asia to Europe's dominance and was inscribed within the colonialist discourse as a justification for the imposition of whites over nonwhites, of civilization/Christianity over barbarism/paganism. Like Orientalism, however, yellow peril discourse was hegemonic but not all-powerful, breaking down or changing when confronted with Asian resistance. The fear, whether real or imagined, arose from the fact of the rise of nonwhite peoples and their defiance of white supremacy. And while serving to contain the Other, the idea of the yellow peril also helped to define the white identity, within both a nationalist and an internationalist frame …

Whether threatening the state through armed insurrection or invasion, the economy through cheap labor and foreign trade, the race through miscegenation and rape, or the culture through paganism and barbarism, nonwhites served as both object and subject in Europe's defense of its holiest possessions. But the yellow peril was not the only enduring icon of white supremacy, nor was it free of ambiguity and contradiction. Europe's colonization of Asia, as foreseen by Pearson, created Asian versions of European polities and economies, under the tutorship of the West. Those copies were ludicrous, flattering, and threatening all at once. They were seen as cheap imitations (mimicries), as products of admiration (as children emulate parents), and as subversions of the original text (grotesque representations of the European identity). Those meanings gave rise to a complementary, benign image of Asians, called today the "model minority" …

[T]he concepts of the yellow peril and the model minority, although at apparent disjunction, form a seamless continuum. While the yellow peril threatens white supremacy, it also bolsters and gives coherence to a problematic construction: the idea of a unitary "white" identity. Similarly, the

---

* Thompson, *Yellow Peril*, 37.

model minority fortifies white dominance, or the status quo, but it also poses a challenge to the relationship of majority over minority. The very indices of Asian American "success" can imperil the good order of race relations when the margins lay claim to the privileges of the mainstream. As sociologist [Robert] Park put it, "The Japanese, the Chinese, they too would be all right in their place, no doubt. That place, if they find it, will be one in which they do not greatly intensify and so embitter the struggle for existence of the white man."* But Asians can work too hard, study overmuch, stick together and form a racial bloc, and thereby "flood" our markets and displace workers, "flood" our schools and displace students, and "flood" our land with concentrations of Chinatowns, Japantowns, Koreatowns, Little Saigons, Manilatowns. "Model" Asians exhibit the same singleness of purpose, patience and endurance, cunning, fanaticism, and group loyalty characteristic of Marco Polo's Mongol soldiers, and Asian workers and students, maintaining themselves at little expense and almost robotlike, labor and study for hours on end without human needs for relaxation, fun, and pleasure, and M.I.T. becomes "Made in Taiwan," and "Stop the Yellow Hordes" appears as college campus graffiti, bumper stickers, and political slogans ...

It seems to me that the yellow peril and the model minority are not poles, denoting opposite representations along a single line, but in fact form a circular relationship that moves in either direction. We might see them as engendered images: the yellow peril denoting a masculine threat of military and sexual conquest, and the model minority symbolizing a feminized position of passivity and malleability. Moving in one direction along the circle, the model minority mitigates the alleged danger of the yellow peril, whereas reversing direction, the model minority, if taken too far, can become the yellow peril. In either swing along the arc, white supremacy is maintained and justified through feminization in one direction and repression in the other.

* Keith Osajima, "Asian Americans as the Model Minority: An Analysis of the Popular Press Image in the 1960s and 1980s," in *Reflections on Shattered Windows: Promises and Prospects for Asian American Studies*, eds. Gary Okihiro et al. (Pullman, WA: Washington State University Press, 1988), 165–74; Robert E. Park, "Introduction" in Jesse Frederick Steiner, *The Japanese Invasion: A Study in the Psychology of Inter-racial Contacts* (Chicago: A. C. McClurg & Co., 1917), xiv.

Albert Jeremiah Beveridge, "The March of the Flag" (1898)[16]

Republican Party plans to annex the Philippines in the wake of the Spanish American War tore at the fabric of American society. Anti-imperialists questioned the legal and moral basis of incorporating a densely inhabited distant territory with no provisions for it becoming a state or its inhabitants becoming citizens. Beveridge (1862–1927) opened his campaign for U.S. Senate with this speech on September 16, 1898 as Filipino nationalist forces formed a congress to draw up the constitution for the First Philippine Republic. Beveridge saw access to Asian markets as a way to maintain social stability in an era of high unemployment. His appeal to the Manifest Destiny of American expansion helped him win the election, and he supported the military takeover of the islands from America's former Filipino allies against the Spanish. After serving two terms as Senator from Indiana, Beveridge chaired the breakaway Progressive Party or Bull Moose Party that nominated Theodore Roosevelt as presidential candidate in 1912.[17]

It is a noble land that God has given us; a land that can feed and clothe the world; a land whose coastlines would enclose half the countries of Europe; a land set like a sentinel between the two imperial oceans of the globe, a greater England with a nobler destiny.

It is a mighty people that He has planted on this soil; a people sprung from the most masterful blood of history; a people perpetually revitalized by the virile, man-producing working folk of all the earth; a people imperial by virtue of their power, by right of their institutions, by authority of their Heaven-directed purposes—the propagandists and not the misers of liberty.

It is a glorious history our God has bestowed upon His chosen people; a history heroic with faith in our mission and our future; a history of statesmen who flung the boundaries of the Republic out into unexplored lands and savage wilderness; a history of soldiers who carried the flag across blazing deserts and through the ranks of hostile mountains, even to the gates of sunset; a history of a multiplying people who overran a continent in half a century; a history of prophets who saw the consequences of evils inherited from the past and of martyrs who died to save us from them; a history divinely logical, in the process of whose tremendous seasoning we find ourselves to-day.

Therefore, in this campaign, the question is larger than a party question. It is an American question. It is a world question. Shall the American people continue their march toward the commercial supremacy of the world? Shall free institutions broaden their blessed reign as the children of liberty wax in strength, until the empire of our principles is established over the hearts of all mankind?

Have we no mission to perform, no duty to discharge to our fellow man? Has God endowed us with gifts beyond our deserts and marked us as the people of His peculiar favor, merely to rot in our own selfishness, as men and nations must, who take cowardice for their companion and self for their deity—as China has, as India has, as Egypt has?

Shall we be as the man who had one talent and hid it, or as he who had ten talents and use them until they grew to riches? And shall we reap the reward that waits on our discharge of our high duty; shall we occupy new markets for what our farmers raise, our factories make, our merchants sell— aye, and, please God, new markets for what our ships shall carry?

Hawaii is ours, Puerto Rico is to be ours; at the prayer of her people Cuba finally will be ours; in the islands of the East, even to the gates of Asia, coaling stations are to be ours at the very least; the flag of a liberal government is to float over the Philippines, and may it be the banner that Taylor unfurled in Texas and Frémont carried to the coast.

The Opposition tells us that we ought not to govern a people without their consent. I answer, the rule of liberty that all just government derives its authority from the consent of the governed, applies only to those who are capable of self-government. We govern the Indians without their consent, we govern our territories without their consent, we govern our children without their consent. How do they know that our government would be without their consent? Would not the people of the Philippines prefer the just, human, civilizing government of this Republic to the savage, bloody rule of pillage and extortion from which we have rescued them?

And, regardless of this formula of words made only for enlightened, self-governing people, do we owe no duty to the world? Shall we turn these peoples back to the reeking hands from which we have taken them? Shall we abandon them, with Germany, England, Japan, hungering for them? Shall we save them from those nations, to give them a self-rule of tragedy?

They ask us how we shall govern these new possessions. I answer: Out of local conditions and the necessities of the case methods of government will grow. If England can govern foreign lands, so can America. If Germany can govern foreign lands, so can America. If they can supervise protectorates, so can America. Why is it more difficult to administer Hawaii than New Mexico or California? Both had a savage and an alien population; both were more remote from the seat of government when they came under our dominion than the Philippines are today.

Will you say by your vote that American ability to *govern* has decayed; that a century's experience in self-rule has failed of a result? Will you affirm by your vote that you are an infidel to American power and practical sense? Or will you say that ours is the blood of government; ours the heart of dominion; ours the brain and genius of administration? Will you remember that we do but what our fathers did—we but pitch the tents of liberty farther westward, farther southward—we only continue the march of the flag? ...

So Hawaii furnishes us a naval base in the heart of the Pacific; the Ladrones another, a voyage further on; Manila another, at the gates of Asia—Asia, to the trade of whose hundreds of millions American merchants, manufacturers, farmers, have as good right as those of Germany or France or Russia or England; Asia, whose commerce with the United Kingdom alone amounts to hundreds of millions of dollars every year; Asia, to whom Germany looks to take her surplus products; Asia, whose doors must not be shut against American trade. Within five decades the bulk of Oriental commerce will be ours ...

Wonderfully has God guided us. Yonder at Bunker Hill and Yorktown His providence was above us. At New Orleans and on ensanguined seas His hand sustained us. Abraham Lincoln was His minister and His was the altar of freedom the Nation's soldiers set up on a hundred battle-fields. His power directed Dewey in the East and delivered the Spanish fleet into our hands, as He delivered the elder Armada into the hands of our English sires two centuries ago. The American people can not use a dishonest medium of exchange; it is ours to set the world its example of right and honor. We can not fly from our world duties; it is ours to execute the purpose of a fate that has driven us to be greater than our small intentions. We can not retreat from any soil where Providence has unfurled our banner; it is ours to save that soil for liberty and civilization.

Victor Gillam, "It Ought to Be a Happy New Year" (1899)

F. Victor Gillam (1858?–1920) was the artistic director for Judge, *a satirical illustrated magazine based in New York. Gillam also drew "The White Man's Burden (Apologies to Kipling)" cartoon in the introduction. British by birth, Gillam celebrated the promise of the American experiment, but also relished in the Great Rapprochement between the two nations following British support for the Spanish-Philippine-American War. Together the English-speaking peoples would, in Gillam's words, "boss the whole world."*[18]

Figure 46. Victor Gillam, "It Ought to Be a Happy New Year. Uncle Sam and his English Cousin Have the World Between Them," *Judge*, vol. 36, no. 899 (January 7, 1899), cover. The Ohio State University Billy Ireland Cartoon Library & Museum.

Luther Bradley, "Trying On Her New Necklace" (1907)

As the U.S. imperial project brought American interests into conflict with an expanding Japan, Roosevelt sent a "Great White Fleet" of battleships across the Pacific. This tour was largely symbolic, but sent a clear message. The aggression of this act made many Americans uncomfortable, though proponents for expanding American civilization into Asia suggested such acts were for the good of the world and a form of what Laura Wexler has termed "tender violence." Luther Bradley (1853–1917) supported American imperialism and his cartoon registers this view, albeit ambivalently. America as a dainty global power tries on a fleet of Pacific battleships as if they were a string of pearls. She smiles across a continent and hemisphere, where Alaska (annexed in 1867) adorns her head like an evening cap.[19]

Figure 47. Luther Bradley, "Trying On Her New Necklace," *Chicago News,* reprinted in *Literary Digest,* vol. 35 (December 2, 1907), 972. Courtesy of the New York Public Library.

The Yellow Danger (1898)

From his vantage point in the British Caribbean, M. P. Shiel (1865–1947) penned this imperial romance in the aftermath of the Sino-Japanese War (1895). Fu Manchu's predecessor Yen How, a Heidelberg-educated genius medical doctor of both Chinese and Japanese descent studying in England, seeks to avenge Ada Stewart's scorn of his romantic advances by destroying the white race and conquering the world for Orientals. Yen manipulates intra-European rivalries over control of China to foment warring among Europeans, which in turn destroys Western Civilization and leaves Europe vulnerable to invading hordes.[20]

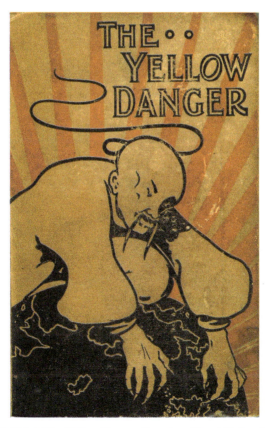

Figure 48. M. P. Shiel, *The Yellow Danger* (London: Grant Richards, 1898). Fales British Collection, Fales Library and Special Collections, New York University.

Unknown (1939)

From the 1920s to the 1940s, fantasies of Asian invasions were mainstays of the emerging genre of science fiction. Such tales and their accompanying iconography (Figure 49) used imagined Asians to play out fantasies of race hate, revenge, and militarist aggression rooted in mainstream American and European politics.[21]

James L. Hevia, "Specters of the Great Game" (1998)[22]

The British launched a bureaucratic quest for "total knowledge" in their imperial contest against the Russians over an "inscrutable" Orient. Historian of China James L. Hevia illustrates how the tenuous fantasy of what he terms the weaponized "archive state" provoked widespread anxiety about the superiority of European information systems. If Europeans had no monopoly on knowledge, or worse, if those inscrutable to Europe could themselves scrutinize Europe, then the empire and its civilizational justification were doomed. Hevia reads this context into the popular Fu Manchu stories of the time.

As U.S. influence replaced European imperialism in Asia in the late twentieth century, Americans too adopted massive surveillance operations at home and abroad. The terror of enduring failures to understand and predict shifting Oriental enemies has produced greater and greater efforts to achieve "total knowledge." Secretary of Defense Donald Rumsfeld summed up this outlook as he secretly oversaw the National Security Administration's warrantless wiretapping of U.S. citizens and the adoption of "enhanced interrogation techniques" for enemy combatants worldwide following the attacks of September 11, 2001.[23]

"Reports that say that something hasn't happened are always interesting to me, because as we know, there are known knowns; there are things we know we know. We also know there are known unknowns; that is to say we know there are some things we do not know. But there are also unknown unknowns—the ones we don't know we don't know. And if one looks throughout the history of our country and other free countries, it is the latter category that tend to be the difficult ones."[24]

After the defeat of the Sikh armies of the Punjab in 1848, Great Britain found itself engaged with imperial Russia in strategic warfare in the "Near"

Figure 49. *Unknown*, vol.1, no.1 (1939). © Penny Publications LLC/Dell Magazines 2013. Reprinted with permission of the publisher. Special Collections Research Center, Syracuse University Library.

and "Far" East. After a brief flurry of open hostilities from 1854 to 1856 (the Crimean War), Great Britain settled into a war of position designed to check or contain Russian expansion into Central Asia and to protect British interests in the Mediterranean, on the southern edges of Eurasia, and in the eastern provinces of China. As a number of contemporary participants, popularizers of empire like Rudyard Kipling, and some recent historians have observed, this sort of limited warfare was less about muscle and armaments than it was a contest of wits, a Great Game. The game was played out in that vast expanse of territory stretching in an arc from the Amur River region of Manchuria, along the border regions of Mongolia and Chinese Turkestan, to Afghanistan in the southwest.[*]

It was precisely the assertion that Great Game operations required superior mental, rather than physical capacities, that made an information-oriented system of warfare attractive to British imperial strategists. In order to contain Russia, they needed the sort of local knowledge and knowledge about the activities of rivals that epistemological projects had already begun to produce. It is no surprise then that Great Britain, perhaps more than any other imperial power of the nineteenth century, perfected this kind of warfare. Those familiar aspects of European imperialism in Africa and Asia that involved the military occupation of territory and the definition of skirmishes along geographical borders appear of less significance in the context of the subtle practices of the Great Game. Far more important for Great Game strategizing was the construction of immutable mobiles,[†] the building of networks to guarantee their uninhibited flow to centers of

---

[*] The conquest of the Punjab in 1848 (The Second Sikh War) extended the British Indian empire to the borders of Afghanistan. See Byron Farwell, *Queen Victoria's Little Wars* (New York: W. W. Norton, 1972), 37–60. For the Great Game see Michael Edwardes, *Playing the Great Game: A Victorian Cold War* (London: Hamilton, 1975); Peter Hopkirk, *The Great Game* (New York: Kodansha International, 1992).

[†] Bruno Latour coined the term "immutable mobiles" to describe standardized inscription practices that allowed imperialists to translate, transport, and compare experiences of real subjects and objects around the world such as maps, census data, and ethnological descriptions. See Bruno Latour, "Drawing Things Together" in *Representations in Scientific Practice*, eds. Michael Lynch and Steve Woolgar (Cambridge, MA: MIT Press, 1990) 9–68; for immutable mobiles specifically, 26–35.

calculation, and the capacity to bring power to bear at strategic points when necessary ...

If the epistemological empire created by the archive state[25] was designed to manipulate native populations and penetrate new regions while warding off rivals, specters, Thomas Richards tells us, nevertheless haunted the project* ... What if a similar project, an alien archive, were to solve the contradiction between certainty and acceleration, and do so by combining its own properties with those of the imperial archive? The resulting combinations might subvert or pollute the British epistemological networks, either severing connections between the centre and its peripheries or creating suspicion about the quality of information on the network. And, since the archive was imagined as the interface between knowledge and the imperial state, the entire empire was at risk if the archive's network was compromised ...

Apprehensions about the stability of imperial networks resonated with more widely diffused fears of hybridity, creating among other things anxieties over the wholesomeness of elements flowing through the coding networks. Great Britain's links to China provide a case in point. Since at least the end of the eighteenth century, when the opium trade with China increased and opium became more widely available in England, apprehensions had been voiced over a possible backlash to the British presence in China. These concerns became even more plausible when British military forces broke open China's doors in 1840 and 1860 to protect the opium trade. By the second half of the century, the small Chinese migrant community in London could raise specters of clever "Chinamen" using opium as a means for retaliation against British aggression. Meanwhile, the growth of the "Coolie" trade in British colonies fueled "Yellow Peril" anxieties, conjuring visions of the imperial network being flooded and overwhelmed by Asiatic hordes[†] ...

---

* Thomas Richards, *The Imperial Archive* (New York: Verso, 1993), 43–57; C. C. Eldridge, *England's Mission* (Chapel Hill, NC: University of North Carolina Press, 1973), 200–5.

† On hybridity, see Robert Young, *Colonial Desire: Hybridity in Theory, Culture, and Race* (London: Routledge, 1995), especially 1–28. On the trade in Chinese labor, see Persia Campbell, *Chinese Coolie Emigration to Countries Within the British Empire* (London: P.S. King & Son, 1923). Snow recounts a panic that ensued in South Africa when Chinese laborers mixed with Africans, raising fears of a super race; see Philip

It is with these overdetermined imaginings and the powerful modes of cultural production to which they were tied that we may begin to understand the nature of the threat Fu-Manchu posed to the archive state. Spawned in the feverish imagination of Sax Rohmer, and the central and shadowy figure in thirteen of his novels published between 1913 and 1959, Fu-Manchu has functioned for much of this century as the very embodiment of deep-seated anxieties over global cross-cultural relations. For many Europeans and Americans, he has stood as the sign of a world fundamentally, and perhaps irreconcilably, divided between East and West—as Nayland Smith, Rohmer's protagonist put it, Fu-Manchu was not only "the yellow peril incarnate in one man," he threatened to inundate the West with even greater numbers of yellow, black and brown aliens than had already made their way there*...

Like other members of his "race," he was clever, cunning, insensitive to his own pain and that of others, cruel, industrious and pragmatic. In addition to these racial characteristics associated with all "Chinamen," Fu-Manchu was also well educated, sophisticated, aloof, arrogant, and convinced, in spite of the many military defeats suffered at the hands of Western powers, of his own and China's superiority ... What separated him from his race and class, as well as from Englishmen, was his command of esoteric Eastern knowledge ... and modern Western scientific knowledge, the combination of which gave him unique powers over nature, making him "seemingly ... immune from natural laws."† As a result of this combination, the danger which Fu-Manchu posed was more disturbing than the classic European fantasy of barbarian invasions from the East and more profound than an inundation of cheap Chinese labor into Europe and North America. His fusion of Eastern and Western knowledge had the potential to undermine

---

Snow, *Star Raft: China's Encounter with Africa* (Ithaca, NY: Cornell University Press, 1988), 45–55.

* Quoted in Sax Rohmer (Arthur Ward), *The Insidious Dr. Fu Manchu* (New York: Pyramid Books, 1975 [1913]), 17. For a particularly distasteful description of a multiethnic London, see Rohmer, *The Return of Dr. Fu Manchu* (New York: Pyramid Books, 1975 [1916]), 62. A comparison between rats from merchant vessels docked in London and humans from Africa and Asia is drawn in Rohmer, *The Hand of Fu Manchu* (New York: Pyramid Books, 1976 [1917]), 99–103.

† Rohmer, *The Hand of Fu Manchu*, 49.

the structure of empire and of global white supremacy, and could conceivably topple the British and other Western empires like a row of dominoes ...

If Fu-Manchu is understood as a product of early twentieth-century British fears projected on to China, he is also something more. By working the symbolically rich representations of China-knowledge and Great Gamesmanship into the structure of the Fu-Manchu stories, Rohmer literally fixed a set of narrative elements that became staples in the succession of paranoid fantasies that have sustained the archive state in this century. Threats would always be total, the prize would always be the world, victories would never be complete, the danger could never be entirely eliminated. Fu-Manchu could be shot through his prodigious brain at the end of one novel and return restored in the next ...

Such anxieties have become a part of our collective culture, infusing the descendants of the British imperial archive—the United States and its North Atlantic allies—with a permanent sense of unease, of a world perpetually on the brink of chaos, of an endless repetition of global crises ... Thus, just as the Chinese mind constructed by diligent British agents in nineteenth-century China remains relatively stable, so does the project of the archive state. Monotonously linked together, they produce a seemingly interminable repetition of Rohmer's endlessly repeated scenario—the danger of an alien archive and the necessity for determined efforts to contain it ... Rohmer's creation might be understood as an objective—and all-too-necessary—hallucination produced by the archive itself, a kind of self-haunting that was generated at the interface between knowledge and the state. In this sense, the phantoms of the archive that Richards points to are no more than a product of the archive state's mania for total knowledge—an obsession which served, in turn, to reconfigure the relationship between the realities of empire and fantasies about global administration, and to propel it and its border disputes through the twentieth century.

Urmila Seshagiri, "Modernity's (Yellow) Perils" (2010)[26]

While drawing heavily on British imperial concerns, the Fu Manchu books were extremely popular in the U.S., where numerous films, comics, and derivative stories flourished for more than fifty years. Many Americans feared that modern industrial society sapped the lifeblood and vigor of "old stock" Americans, while unfairly advantaging supposedly less "manly" immigrants like the Chinese and the Jews. Jonathan Freeman has argued that Rohmer based Fu Manchu in part on George Du Maurier's 1894 character Svengali a mysterious and effeminate Jewish musician who hypnotizes his beautiful female student Trilby to seduce and manipulate her away from the British male protagonist. Freeman links the fears associated with such Oriental villains to fears of an American society and economy that privileged less manly forms of labor.[27] Here, literary scholar Urmila Seshagiri identifies the vampiric nature of alienated wage work and the boundary-disruptions of an increasingly interconnected global economy as bolstering the popularity of Fu Manchu novels.[28]

When *The Mystery of Dr. Fu-Manchu* was published in London in 1913, Sax Rohmer catapulted from literary obscurity into astonishing fame that lasted for almost fifty years. Over the decades that witnessed two World Wars, the emerging Cold War, and rapid scientific and technological change, Rohmer's thirteen novels about a Chinese "devil doctor" captivated massive readerships in England and America. The central recurring conflict of these thrillers—Dr. Fu-Manchu's schemes for global domination—rewrote the master narrative of modern England, inverting the British Empire's racial and political hierarchies to imagine a dystopian civilization dominated by evil Orientals. Although the rhetoric of these novels exalts twentieth-century England as a fount of progress, knowledge, and virtue, Dr. Fu-Manchu's near-total appropriation of sociopolitical and technological systems points to the negative capabilities of industrialization and modernization. By paralyzing English heroes and giving a Chinese villain limitless authority over the metropole, Sax Rohmer's novels overturn the tropes of imperial-era popular fiction and echo the complex treatments of urban modernity in the experimental literature of high modernism. Metropolitan alienation and dehumanization—modernism's signature discontents—become, in the Fu-Manchu tales, conditions expressed through an irrefragable racial anxiety. And rather than illustrating imperial Britain's unassailable authority, these best-selling thrillers unwittingly reveal the very emptiness of twentieth-century technocratic utopianism that constitutes the focus of much modernist thought ...

The race paranoia that suffuses the Fu-Manchu novels unfolded in the context of imperial Britain's varied reactions to transformative political events in China at the turn of the century. In 1900, the slaughter of hundreds of English officials in China during the Boxer uprisings portended the collapse of the imperial Christian West's decades-long control over China; the motto of the Boxer rebels was "Preserve the dynasty; destroy the foreigners," a fierce defense of China's native cultural traditions against Western economic and religious interference.* China's bloody rebellion further destabilized England's already-shaky confidence about its own strength; the British army's recent heavy losses at the hands of the Boers in South Africa had stirred wide cultural unease about the physical deterioration of white English bodies. Vociferous debates about the British Empire's physiological and ideological soundness saturated the English press, along with moral indignation at the barbarity and cruelty of the Chinese.† When Rohmer penned the first of the Fu-Manchu serials in 1911, he declared, "Conditions for launching a Chinese villain on the market were ideal … The Boxer Rebellion had started off rumors of a Yellow Peril which had not yet died down."‡ Indeed, the Fu-Manchu novels reply directly to the Boxers: just as the Boxers killed Westerners to rid China of unwanted foreign influence, Rohmer's stories describe valiant struggles to expel Fu-Manchu and his Asiatic hordes from England. Filled with gory details about Fu-Manchu's calculated cruelties, the novels capitalize on British prejudice against China's antimodernity …

It is precisely this racializing of modernity's crises that invites us to read the Fu-Manchu thrillers against the more subtle, nuanced racial dialectics of the modernist literary canon. As Rohmer's novels sensationalize an impending Yellow Peril's impact on London and gesture toward the changing face of

---

* See Henry Keown-Boyd, *The Fists of Righteous Harmony: A History of the Boxer Uprising in China in the Year 1900* (London: Leo Cooper, 1991) and Paul Cohen, *History in Three Keys: The Boxers as Event, Experience, and Myth* (New York: Columbia University Press, 1997).

† For a historical overview of the scientific culture of racial degeneration in fin-de-siècle Britain, see Nancy Stepan, *The Idea of Race in Science: Great Britain 1800–1960* (Hamden, CT: Archon Books, 1982); see also William Greenslade, *Degeneration, Culture, and the Novel: 1880–1940* (Cambridge: Cambridge University Press, 1994).

‡ Cay Van Ash and Elizabeth Sax Rohmer, *Master of Villainy: A Biography of Sax Rohmer* (Bowling Green, OH: Bowling Green University Popular Press, 1972), 75.

modern China, they reconfigure experimental modernism's obsession with fragmented metropolitan existence as well as its concomitant investment in the wholeness of the Empire's colonial peripheries.* Reverse colonization in the Fu-Manchu novels provocatively racializes the metropolitan alienation that characterizes high modernist literature; urban anomie becomes a function of Western racial inadequacy in the face of a politically and technologically ascendant East. Perhaps most arrestingly, Fu-Manchu's unrestricted circulation through the metropole suggests a racially threatening version of Baudelaire's flâneur. As a corrupt "artist of modern life" who simultaneously participates in and remains detached from his surroundings, Fu-Manchu perpetually reinvents the ideological and material architectures of the present moment for the future Yellow Empire. The totality of modern life—its mosaic of quotidian rituals and its consciousness of the future that awaits—becomes the domain of Fu-Manchu's despotic, Oriental flânerie. Indeed, Rohmer's Chinese villain symbolizes a monstrous pastiche of several modern-era literary characters, an alien warlord who perverts the well-established modes and tropes of urban existence. For example, Dr. Fu-Manchu violently rescripts the legacy of adventure and conquest he inherits from Conrad's Marlow and assumes control of the Thames, using the river for "his highway, his line of communication along which he moved his mysterious forces." The great English river that has transported white English colonizers and their instruments of power now becomes a conduit for Chinese villainy as Fu-Manchu smuggles dead bodies, scientific equipment, and foreign henchmen on the boats and barges that cruise the Thames. Then, like Stoker's Dracula, Fu-Manchu has the power to disappear in a crowd and reappear at will; Dr. Petrie compels us to fear "the wonderful and evil man who once walked, by the many unsuspected, in the midst of the people of England." And like Kipling's hybrid, culturally porous hero Kim, Fu-Manchu's fluency in Eastern and Western languages facilitates his control over the international communities that he assembles in London†...

Recruited from "the darkest places of the East," Fu-Manchu's pan-Asian "murder-gang" includes Negro and mulatto henchmen, Burmese thugs,

---

* I am here indebted to Fredric Jameson's essay "Modernism and Imperialism" in *Nationalism, Colonialism, and Literature* (Minneapolis, MN: University of Minnesota Press, 1990), 43–66.

† Sax Rohmer, *The Mystery of Fu Manchu*, reprinted in *The Fu Manchu Omnibus* (London: Allison and Busby, 1998), 126, 155.

Chinese martial artists, Malaysian dacoits (thieves), Indian lascars (seamen), phansigars (stranglers), hashishin (assassins), and houris (Muslim virgins). In *The Mystery of Dr. Fu-Manchu*, for example, an Indian dacoit who holds a knife to Dr. Petrie's throat evokes "pure horror" because of his "wicked, pock-marked face, with wolfish fangs bared, and jaundiced eyes squinting obliquely." Similarly, in *The Si-Fan Mysteries*, Nayland Smith tries to escape from "the repellent figure" of a Chinaman who "approached, stooping, apish, with a sort of loping gait," and "perched between his shoulders—bending forward—the wicked yellow fingers at work, tightening—tightening— tightening the strangle cord!" Such characters frighten because they stand for a coalesced, mingled East that challenges Western authority; the literal crowding of their foreign bodies around Nayland Smith and Petrie portends the larger encroachment of the Yellow Empire on the West. When Nayland Smith and Petrie kill anonymous members of Fu-Manchu's cohort, as they do in nearly every episode, they comply with a melodramatic imperative to reassert the purity of white Englishness. But while Rohmer's protagonists kill or enact violence against these dark foreign bodies, they remain power-less to combat Dr. Fu-Manchu, the elusive mastermind who commands the henchmen*...

Dr. Fu-Manchu himself becomes the "juggernaut" of modernity: his complete control over time, space, technology, languages, and social systems makes him a monstrous reflection of the very Western civilization he threatens to subsume, and his racial alterity makes literal the alienat-ing, unknowable character of modern urban life. Despite frequent textual insistences that modern England is a white-dominated nation whose white-ness must be preserved, Fu-Manchu's access to seminal cultural discourses and technologies keeps the relationship between racial identity and modernity unstable ...

Each episode in which the Chinese doctor outwits his British pursuers lays bare the conflict that haunts canonical modernist authors and theorists of modernity alike: that state-sponsored democratic and humanistic institu-tions, and the culture that worships them, can breed indescribable brutality,

---

* Sax Rohmer, *The Devil Doctor*, reprinted in *The Fu Manchu Omnibus*, 356; *The Fu Manchu Omnibus*, 129, 552. For a description of the Western fear of the Yellow Peril, see V. G. Kiernan, *The Lords of Human Kind* (Boston: Little, Brown, 1969), 172.

corruption, and violence. Three decades before the Second World War and the Holocaust, Sax Rohmer's Fu-Manchu novels warned readers that the hallmark virtues of the modern era—access to information, individual agency, respect for scientific progress—might produce a killing machine, a brilliant and efficient path to mass death.

By displacing white English agency and manufacturing visions of an Oriental civilization in the West, Sax Rohmer's Fu-Manchu novels chart twentieth-century technocratic utopianism as a series of hollow promises. At a time when so much popular fiction functioned as a transparent, unmediated showcase for imperialist ideology, Rohmer's narratives, albeit unwittingly, expose the limitations of a Western imperial state and its white subjects. In these best-selling thrillers, the discontinuities of race provide a nexus for the broader discontinuities of a modern imperial nation whose global mastery is determined by the acquisition and dissemination of knowledge. When knowledge ceases to be the province and defining characteristic of the West, neither patriotic narrative bluster nor the resources of the *patria* itself can guarantee a racial victory over Fu-Manchu. And as the imperial metropole becomes a pawn of the discourses and technologies it prides itself on authoring, the very idea of progress ceases to be England's yardstick for measuring the world and forms the weapon of its own downfall.

The Rising Tide of Color (1921)

Lothrop Stoddard (1883–1950) was a Harvard-trained historian who argued that rivalries between Europeans for the spoils of empire distracted the white race from a greater threat: the Yellow Peril. This peril was that of Asian competition, for Stoddard believed that Asians were better suited to modern life, which had already encouraged a white materialistic "malaise" that undermined white racial solidarity. Japan's victory over Russia in 1904 marked the "ebb" of white supremacy for Stoddard. He claimed the Japanese victory was a literal and symbolic affront to white superiority that inspired inferior races everywhere to claim modernity for themselves. To preserve the white race, Stoddard advocated abandoning all plans to dominate Asia and the Middle East, and concentrating on preventing Asian immigration to Africa, Australia, and the Western Hemisphere.

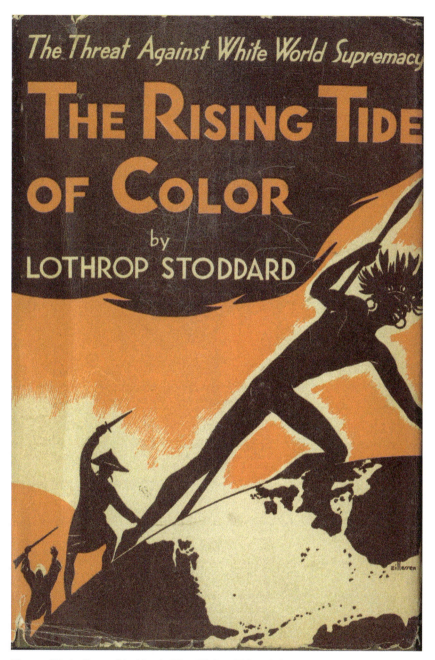

Figure 50. Lothrop Stoddard, *The Rising Tide of Color Against White World-Supremacy* (New York: Scribner, 1921). Courtesy of the Wong Ching Foo Collection.

The nightmare scenario for Stoddard was an embittered alliance between "colored" races, such as Chinese support for Pan-Islamist calls for independence or Japanese stewardship for independent African nations with rich natural resources. Stoddard simultaneously published a book on the Pan-Islamist threat to British authority in the Persian Gulf entitled The New World of Islam *(1921) alongside* Rising Tide of Color, *and the next year wrote* The Revolt Against Civilization: The Menace of the Under Man *(1922), a treatise on the threat of Communism and the Soviet Union.*

Amazing Stories (1927)

H. G. Wells's fantasy The War of the Worlds *(1898) revolutionized the emerging genre of science fiction and has remained popular to this day. In Wells's novel, written on the eve of the Boer War in South Africa, advanced imperialist Martians invade and destroy London in large metallic octopus-like robots. However, these industrial and imperial invaders are themselves infected and destroyed by their own aggression. They catch the colds of the innocent British they colonize and slaughter.*

This reprint dates from the early days of mass-market science fiction magazines. Cover artist Frank Paul was born in Vienna in 1884 and studied art there as well as in Paris and London before immigrating to New York in 1906. Paul is widely recognized as having been the "father" of science fiction illustration. In the more than 200 covers he created for various science fiction magazines as well as the earliest Marvel comics, Paul defined the style and iconography of the emerging genre.

Futuristic Oriental enemies were also mainstays of the mid-century science fiction. The year after this issue was published, Amazing Stories, *one of the most influential science fiction magazines, published the first Buck Rogers stories. Rogers fights Han Chinese half-breeds in a dystopic Yellow Peril future.[29] When Orson Wells turned* The War of the Worlds *into a radio play in 1938, three years before the Japanese attack on Pearl Harbor, some Americans believed the broadcast was the opening salvo of a Japanese invasion.[30]*

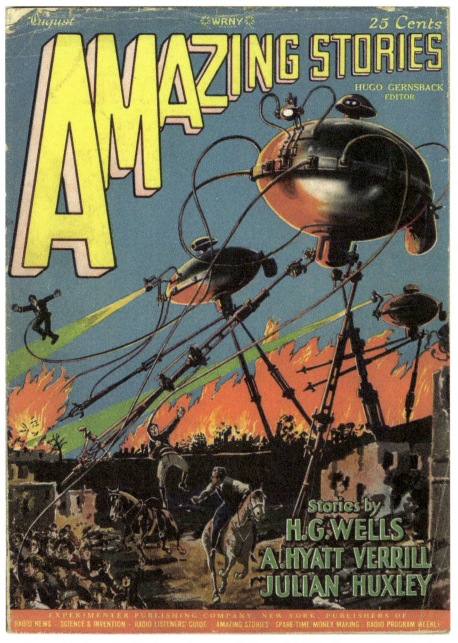

Figure 51. *Amazing Stories*, vol. 2, no. 5 (August 1927). Cover art by Frank R. Paul. *Amazing Stories* is a registered trademark of Steve Davidson and the Experimenter Publishing Company. Reprinted with the acknowledgment and courtesy of the Frank R. Paul Estate.

Part Three: Indispensable Enemies

How can America deliver on its promise of the liberal individualist dream? Placing American traditions into a broader analysis of yellow perilism helps us connect discordant strands of U.S. history together, shedding light on how fears about internal and external enemies reinforce each other and serve as a driving, but repressive, force in U.S. history.

Nineteenth-century white Americans inherited a colonial Enlightenment liberal tradition that defined manly individuality against internal and external hordes, U.S. expansion westward, and Americanized and whitened generations of "pioneers." Political elites promised these migrants that the frontier would offer them a new beginning. But in the face of brutal working conditions, political corruption, and a destabilizing "boom and bust" economy, European American and European immigrant men sought to attain their aspirations against railroad monopolists and against Chinese laborers. "Down With Monopolies! The Chinese Must Go!"

Michael Rogin has argued that fractious tensions between fantasies of republican political equality and the rigid social hierarchy of a society rooted in liberal individualism have haunted white American cultural and political citizenship. Rather than confront these divisive and destabilizing contradictions from within, many proponents of liberal democracy projected these desires and fears outside the imagined fraternity of whitened men.[1] In this Manifest Destiny journey, even the Irish, that lowly, racialized other of the British Empire, became whitened. Chinese in America, racialized and emasculated, became the scapegoats for the failures of the nineteenth-century white Anglo American Protestant promise.

The late nineteenth-century anti-Chinese movement sought to define who and what was "American" and established the traditions and regulations of national identity boundary control that has impacted national demographics and national "character" ever since. Historian Alexander Saxton understood Chinese migrants as "the indispensable enemy."[2] But the exclusion and segregation of the Chinese in the U.S. did little to quell the fears of an Anglo American Protestant political culture.

Americans have come up with many explanations for the perpetual deferments of their dreams. If only a rational, informed citizenry would prevail … If only the tyranny of the mob could be broken … If only the immigrants weren't so degraded … If only the world would let the promise break free. Even after politicians moved to block the peril of Chinese labor competition by closing the door to immigrants, Americans looked to the opening of Chinese markets as a form of salvation. At the turn of the twentieth century, overproducing American industrialists believed that if only the Chinese could become good consumers they would shop America out of its woes. Now, at the beginning of the twenty-first century, this promise has been reversed. The Chinese are overproducing and the Americans are too good at consuming. While this is in some ways a reversal, it's also more of the same: *they* are always to blame.[3]

And the *they* is always changing. In the 1960s, it was the Russian communists. In the 1980s, it was the Japanese capitalists. At each moment the *they* makes sense, for each moment produces its own *they.* These *they* help justify why the American Dream hasn't delivered on its promises despite relentless expansion and an accompanying upheaval in the pursuit of liberty and prosperity. The truth is there really is not a *they*, or at least there doesn't have to be. That is not to say there aren't real conflicts of interest—there are, and there always will be. But conflicts of interests are different from epic civilizational contests between imagined diametrically opposed foes.

While many could easily believe that Americans of Japanese dissent were sleeper agents for Imperial Japan in the 1940s, they were much less aware of just how central U.S. racism against Japanese Americans was to the rhetoric of Imperial Japan itself. Japanese militarists regularly framed their own expansionary project as a response to European and American racism.[4] While American racists did not cause Japanese imperialism, the interconnected nationalisms of the U.S. and Japan (as well as many other places) betray the limits of an "us vs. them" analysis. Instead, such thinking masks the anxieties that accompany the presence of unfair power dynamics within a supposedly equal society. At some level we can all understand how those discriminated against would want to seek revenge.

This sort of thinking led to the racially driven internment of almost 70,000 American citizens of Japanese ancestry. Congressional investigations at the time revealed Japanese Americans posed no security threat. (And many scholars have argued that local land interests and racist resentments motivated Executive Order 9066 more than fears of sabotage.) But Lieutenant General John L. DeWitt's response was simple, "A Jap is a Jap."[5] DeWitt's words are often taken to mean he assumed the Japanese hordes couldn't change: their immutable racial allegiance was stronger than their loyalty to their adopted home. DeWitt no doubt did think that, but his phrasing also reveals a telling analysis of American racism. Given a century of American discriminatory legislation seeking to exclude the "Japs" from immigrating, voting, owning land, marrying outside their race, or sending their children to public school, how could white supremacists imagine such people would be loyal?

This culture of white supremacy also provoked reactions that symbolically connected various groups to the powder kegs of global politics. For example, in the 1940s young people of color in Los Angeles embraced a Zoot Suit culture that included using the symbol of Imperial Japan as part of a critique against American racism. The Zoot Suiters flaunted American WASP cultural conventions with flashy style and bold assertiveness well beyond the established norms of segregated America. The equation of Zoot Suiters with the enemy Japanese was part of what prompted American servicemen to launch a riot in 1943 that left hundreds injured. These whitened servicemen, sometimes with the approval of their superiors and local police, hunted down Zoot Suiters to tear off their clothes and cut their hair, eventually inspiring a municipal ban on the style itself. These servicemen were rightly anxious about their impending deployments. They were also likely jealous, ashamed, and enraged at the fact that the Mexicans, Filipinos, and African Americans flaunting a seemingly anti-American attitude didn't have to fight for "their" country. (It must be noted that many Zoot Suiters were ineligible for citizenship and the military was all white.)[6]

Two decades later, former Zoot Suiter Malcolm X became a perceptive observer of how brutal U.S. Cold War policies abroad came back to haunt their authors. When U.S. President John F. Kennedy, the embodiment of so much promise, was assassinated, Malcolm X scandalously suggested that this was just deserts. Kennedy had authorized the covert assassination of democratically elected left-leaning Patrice Lumumba in the Congo as part of America's global war against Communism, and in Malcolm X's words: "the chickens had come home to roost."[7] The Cold War waged against Communist and specifically Vietnamese enemies abroad were ultimately deployed at home against antiwar groups and others who questioned mainstream authority. Fantasies of "outside agitators" and "subversives" kept the promise machine hobbling.[8]

Most Japanese Americans were loyal and committed to America despite the long history of racial discrimination. Most Zoot Suiters did not necessarily see their support for Japanese anti-imperialism as antithetical to their dreams for and investment in America. This illustrates the very bind such an imperial worldview placed on the analysis of those invested (sometimes unwittingly) in structures of white supremacy. The desire to separate, classify, and label others with one's own projected fears and fantasies is no way forward.

The reliance on scapegoats to protect the deferment of the promise is at the core of American political culture: biological and cultural deficiencies, not market capitalism, are to blame for the violence and despair accompanying social inequality; and those who resist the underdevelopment and violence accompanying liberalism's perpetual expansion are dismissed as external enemies motivated by psychotic jealousy or hate. This popular perception holds as much for America's supposed internal enemies as it does for the external, but this analytical frame is paralyzing and inaccurate. We know things are more complicated.

So what is the status of the promise today? In response to a prompt by *The Atlantic* magazine on "the future of the American idea" in 2007, Hungarian-born, American-based illustrator Istvan Banyai submitted this cartoon (Figure 52) of what appears to be the Statue of Liberty wearing an *abaya* and a *niqab*. Banyai's perceptive and playful use of visual logic defines his critically acclaimed style. The image is striking, likely off-putting to some and humorous to others, but it deftly appropriates and recycles the visual language of our moment.

For starters, where is this? Has the promise spread? Or have the hordes come home to roost? This image is quite striking in the context of the "Ground Zero

Mosque" controversy and the French banning of *hijabs* in public schools in 2005, not to mention America's failed or doomed or sham projects to spread democracy in the Middle East collapsing across the headlines every day. In any event, wherever this scene takes place, over there or over here, it is as far away from the America we knew as the moon (which Kennedy beat the Soviets to and put up our flag!). Can America spread democracy? But perhaps the cartoon references something else. Could an "indigenous" Muslim Democracy lead the hordes out of the darkness in ways the Americans couldn't?

Historian Joan Scott argues that the French fantasy of Muslim women's "veils" threatens a pervasive cultural logic that colonized women should be

Figure 52. Istvan Banyai, "Muslim Democracy," *The Atlantic* (November, 2007). © Istvan Banyai 2007. Courtesy of the artist. www.ist-one.com.

available and knowable to European men. Scott argues that French attacks on women's public displays of religious beliefs are a way to articulate a sense of French identity in relation to that nation's failed colonial legacy. The tragedy is that these attacks on religious expression provoke the civilizational clashes and cultural alienation they are intended to defend against. Lady Liberty (a French invention after all) in a "veil" registers a widely felt sense that these images can't go together.[9]

Part Three explores how the yellow perilism outlined in the previous chapters has shaped American history, and how this history continues to reproduce the trap of a paranoid, race-based worldview. America's inability to confront its own uneasy past, and connect itself to the rest of the world, leaves the U.S. vulnerable to haunting demons of its own making. Chapter Five, "The Enemy Within," proposes a repressed tradition of yellow perilist scapegoating at the heart of American political culture, designed not only to manage people of color, but American society more broadly. Chapter Six, "The Coming War," presents excerpts that suggest how yellow perilist cycles of betrayal and revenge frame American responses to foreign policy questions. Key to these chapters is the idea that Yellow Peril is not built in to America's cultural and political DNA so much as an indispensable tradition that frames but also rewards the reproduction of Yellow Peril over the generations. In order to escape the devastating binary logic of this inheritance, we must first identify the tradition and chart its myriad forms. Part Three serves as a collection of provocative work and historical documents that, when taken together, can serve as an opening attempt.

5

The Enemy Within

Society-wide fearmongering breeds political scapegoating. Throughout U.S. history, politicians and pundits have reshaped the meaning of "America" amid moral panics and national dilemmas. Depicting Chinese immigrants as potential threats to national security in the 1880s secured Congress's exclusive Constitutional right to regulate immigration as a function of its war powers, internal and external. This became the policy precedent for subsequent immigration exclusion laws and culture wars. Rooting the institutional origins and political logic of the idea of "unassimilable" foreigners (be they racially and/or ideologically unfit for participation in American democracy) in this earlier history helps us carry analysis of the role of yellow perilism forward through the subsequent mid-century variations of the "Red Scare" and more recent calls for excluding "undesirable" and "un-American" groups.[1] Maintaining a narrow notion of proper Americanism, in the face of these supposed threats, has profoundly shaped U.S. political culture.

Over the nineteenth century, the extension of popular democracy and the development of industries provoked a fear of "the mob." Elite Americans looked on anxiously at what they considered to be the excesses of the French Revolution and its disregard for life and property. At home, the boisterous parades that typified the Revolutionary period morphed into more formalized political parties holding orderly conventions.[2] Immigration complicated this already fraught situation. Samuel Morse saw unregulated immigration as a "conspiracy," for Catholic emigrants were "but obedient instruments in the hands of their more knowing leaders, to accomplish the designs of their foreign masters."[3] Critics also regularly compared Mormons to Oriental fanatics, or a "tribe of locusts" whose "swarm of emigrants from their pestilent hive" threatened the free American experiment.[4] Carroll Wright considered French Canadian millworkers in New England "the Chinese of the Eastern States … a horde of industrial invaders, not a stream of stable settlers."[5]

This racial civilizational logic led to Chinese Exclusion in 1882 and set the stage for a broader culture of political scapegoating. Eugenicists, for example, claimed inferior races infused with "primitive" African and "semi-civilized" Mongol blood degraded workplaces and neighborhoods, and threatened the stability of the entire social system. Reformers sought to assimilate new European immigrants into "American" standards of living, blaming poor living conditions and crime on Old World cultures, not the poverty of the industrializing machine. Japanese, Korean, Indian, Italian, Russian, and Jewish hordes joined the Chinese as the targets of exclusion in the early twentieth century.[6] When Attorney General Michael Palmer described the "lopsided faces, sloping brows, and misshapen features" of supposedly dangerous radicals in 1919, he linked the American eugenics movement, which dismissed social problems and political opposition as rooted in cultural and biological depravity, to American anti-Communism.[7]

This institutional exclusion of dangerous and intermingling Oriental peoples and ideas provided a framework for understanding the challenges ahead. Under the banner of anti-Communism, the federal government waged war against homosexuality, labor-organizing, civil rights, and antiwar activists.[8] Today, U.S. political parties compete over who is tougher on terrorism and China. A tight-knit network of think tanks mobilize disaffected Americans around the newly fabricated "heathen" threat of Sharia Law and Muslim American "radicalization." FBI informants pressure angry youth on the margins of society to plot "terrorist" acts so they can arrest them. Government operatives infiltrate mosques and antiwar groups to observe and disrupt lawful assemblies.[9] Though ultimately fanciful, these fear-mongering techniques have real effects. They silence opposition from the most vulnerable communities, and they focus the anxieties of millions of Americans away from the problems haunting liberalism and onto easy-to-hate scapegoats.

Arab "control" of oil prices, Japanese "unfair" competition, and the Chinese "manipulation" of currency help politicians and pundits protect Americans from understanding the glaring domestic policy failures underpinning their economic woes. This civilizational-clash framework, built over generations of misinformation, justifies the request for Americans to give up the promise once again. It is no longer the "Asiatic mode of production" or Asian Communism but Asian Capitalism that threatens "the American way of life." U.S. deficit spending, once necessary to fight Communism, now imperils the nation. The only constant amid these shifting and contradictory threats to the American Dream, is that Oriental enemies, not U.S. government actions nor corporate practices, are always to blame.[10]

Yellow perilist scapegoating obscures the effective analysis of U.S. political debates, but also ostracizes, silences, and sometimes sacrifices individuals and communities on the altar of American fantasy. State repression and vigilante violence has suppressed myriad efforts by communities of color to organize for their survival and success. At the same time, the politics of resentment and suspicion provoke some, desperate to hold on to what they imagine to be theirs, to harass, discriminate, and attack their "un-American" neighbors. This chapter lays out fragments of this tradition to suggest how various internal and external threats can all be understood within an overarching yellow perilist framework.

Dylan Yeats, "The Promise and the Peril, a Visual Essay" (2013)

This pairing of images (figures 53 and 54) depicting America anthropomorphized into a large man suggests the promise and the perils of Manifest Destiny. In the first, with sure footing in Western Europe and loins rooted in New England, America peeks his head over the Rocky Mountains and reaches across the Pacific. In the second, "American Labor" travels like Gulliver to expand his possibilities only to be tied down by a horde of tiny men wielding railroad spikes and cheap labor.

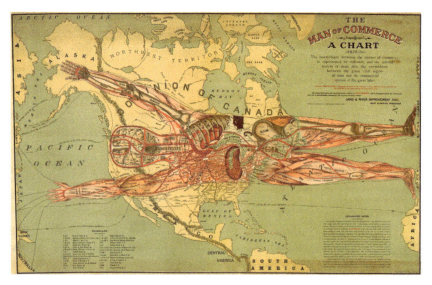

Figure 53. "The Man of Commerce: A Chart" (Superior, WI: Land & River Improvement Company, 1889). From the American Geographical Society Library, University of Wisconsin-Milwaukee Libraries.

Figure 54. "The American Gulliver and Chinese Lilliputians," *Some Reasons for Chinese Exclusion, Meat vs. Rice, American Manhood Against Asiatic Coolieism, Which Shall Survive?* (Washington D.C.: American Federation of Labor, 1902) frontispiece. Yoshio Kishi/Irene Yah Ling Sun Collection of Asian Americana made possible in large part in memory of Dr. Wei Yu Chen, MSS 292, Series II, Box 6, folder 42. Fales Library and Special Collections, New York University.

George Frederick Keller, "A Statue for *Our* Harbor" (1881)

Keller (?–1883) drew this cartoon as New Yorkers debated how to fundraise to build the pedestal for the Statue of Liberty. This was also at the height of the first mobilization to pass a national Chinese Exclusion bill, and Keller, a recent immigrant from Germany, drew the anti-America he imagined would emerge were the Chinese to keep coming. The year before, Keller had illustrated Arizona newspaper editor Pierton Dooner's best-selling book predicting the Chinese take-over of American institutions, entitled The Last Days of the Republic *(1880). Dooner described immigration as a "vicious conspiracy" against the U.S. by the Chinese, and illustrated his point with Keller's drawings including what he considered to be the ultimate threat to American liberty should immigrants continue to come: a democratically-elected Chinese American Governor of California.*

Figure 55. George Frederick Keller, "A Statue for *Our* Harbor," *The Wasp*, vol. 7, no. 276 (November 11, 1881), 320. The Ohio State University Billy Ireland Cartoon Library & Museum.

Saum Song Bo, "A Chinese View of the Statue of Liberty" (1885)[11]

This letter, written by a Chinese American shortly after the passage of the 1882 Chinese Exclusion Act, condemns the hypocrisy of an exclusionary theory of liberty. Ironically, Emma Lazarus had famously celebrated the promise of the "huddled masses yearning to breathe free" in America in Joseph Pulitzer's (also an immigrant) New York World *that same year as part of the campaign to finance the construction of the Statue of Liberty pedestal. Saum Song Bo (n.d.) connects his own exclusion from American citizenship with French imperialism in Southeast Asia.*

Sir:

A paper was presented to me yesterday for inspection, and I found it to be specially drawn up for subscription among my countrymen toward the Pedestal Fund of the Bartholdi Statue of Liberty. Seeing that the heading is an appeal to American citizens, to their love of country and liberty, I feel that my countrymen and myself are honored in being thus appealed to as citizens in the cause of liberty. But the word liberty makes me think of the fact that this country is the land of liberty for men of all nations except the Chinese. I consider it an insult to us Chinese to call on us to contribute toward building in this land a pedestal for a statue of Liberty. That statue represents Liberty holding a torch which lights the passage of those of all nations who come into this country. But are the Chinese allowed to come? As for the Chinese who are here, are they allowed to enjoy liberty as men of all other nationalities enjoy it? Are they allowed to go about everywhere free from the insults, abuse, assaults, wrongs, and injuries from which men of other nationalities are free?

If there be a Chinaman who came to this country when a lad, who has passed through an American institution of learning of the highest grade, who has so fallen in love with American manners and ideas that he desires to make his home in this land, and who, seeing that his countrymen demand one of their own number to be their legal adviser, representative, advocate, and protector, desires to study law, can he be a lawyer? By the law of this nation, he, being a Chinaman, cannot become a citizen, and consequently cannot be a lawyer.

And this statue of Liberty is a gift to a people from another people who do not love or value liberty for the Chinese. Are not the Annamese and Tonquinese Chinese, to whom liberty is as dear as to the French? What right have the French to deprive them of their liberty?

Whether this statute against the Chinese or the statue to Liberty will be the more lasting monument to tell future ages of the liberty and greatness of this country, will be known only to future generations.

Liberty, we Chinese do love and adore thee; but let not those who deny thee to us, make of thee a graven image and invite us to bow down to it.

"The Chinese Exclusion Case" (1889) [12]

Americans have always defended themselves against discriminatory legislation and fought for equal protection under the Constitution. The Chinese Exclusion Act never really worked, for immigrant laborers found ways to circumvent the law that rendered them illegal. As a result, Congress sought to tighten the law such that no Chinese could reenter the U.S. even if they had entered prior to the enactment of Exclusion. Chae Chan Ping (n.d.) traveled to China to attend to his father's death before the Exclusion Act was tightened and left his family in California. Immigration authorities would not let him return under the newly expanded act. Ping challenged that Congress could not deport a Chinese citizen entitled to reside in the U.S. under the Burlingame Treaty of 1868. The resulting decision, excerpted below, justified legislative oversight over immigration irrespective of treaty obligations as an extension of Congressional war powers. This decision serves as the basis of all immigration law in the U.S. to this day. [13]

That the government of the United States, through the action of the legislative department, can exclude aliens from its territory is a proposition which we do not think open to controversy. Jurisdiction over its own territory to that extent is an incident of every independent nation. It is a part of its independence ...

To preserve its independence, and give security against foreign aggression and encroachment, is the highest duty of every nation, and to attain these ends nearly all other considerations are to be subordinated. It matters not in what form such aggression and encroachment come, whether from the foreign nation acting in its national character, or from vast hordes of its people crowding in upon us. The government, possessing the powers which are to be exercised for protection and security, is clothed with authority to determine the occasion on which the powers shall be called forth, and its determinations, so far as the subjects affected are concerned, are necessarily conclusive upon all its departments and officers. If, therefore, the government of the United States, through its legislative department, considers the presence of foreigners of a different race in this country, who will not assimilate with us, to be dangerous to its peace and security, their exclusion is not to be stayed because at the time there are no actual hostilities with the nation of which the foreigners are subjects. The existence of war would render the necessity of the proceeding only more obvious and pressing. The same necessity, in a less pressing degree, may arise when war does not exist, and the same authority which adjudges the necessity in one case must also determine it in the other ...

The exclusion of paupers, criminals, and persons afflicted with incurable diseases, for which statutes have been passed, is only an application of the same power to particular classes of persons, whose presence is deemed injurious or a source of danger to the country. As applied to them, there has never been any question as to the power to exclude them. The power is constantly exercised; its existence is involved in the right of self-preservation ...

Dylan Yeats, "A Peaceful Invasion, a Visual Essay" (2013)

Nineteenth-century Americans who considered themselves the vanguard pioneers of a new robust Western civilization on the Pacific coast connected their struggles to an imagined tradition of a European civilization under constant threat from Oriental hordes:

Civilization in Europe has been frequently attacked and imperiled by the barbaric hordes of Asia. If the little band of Greeks at Marathon had not beaten back ten times their number of Asiatic invaders, it is impossible to estimate the loss to civilization that would have ensued. When we contemplate what modern civilization owes to the two centuries of Athenian life, from which we first learned our lessons of civil and intellectual freedom, we can see how necessary it was to keep the Asiatic from breaking into Europe. Attila and his Asiatic hordes threatened central Europe when the Gauls made their successful stand against them. The wave of Asiatic barbarism rolled back and civilization was again saved. The repulse of the Turks, who are of the Mongolian race, before Vienna finally made our civilization strong enough to take care of itself, and the danger of extinction by a military invasion from Asia passed away. But a peaceful invasion is more dangerous than a war-like attack. We can meet and defend ourselves against an open foe, but an insidious foe under our generous laws would be in possession of the citadel before we were aware. The free immigration of Chinese would be for all purposes an invasion by Asiatic barbarians, against whom civilization in Europe has been frequently defended, fortunately for us. It is our inheritance to keep it pure and uncontaminated, as it is our purpose and destiny to broaden and enlarge it. We are trustees for mankind.

Federation on Chinese Exclusion, "Memorial to Congress" (1901)

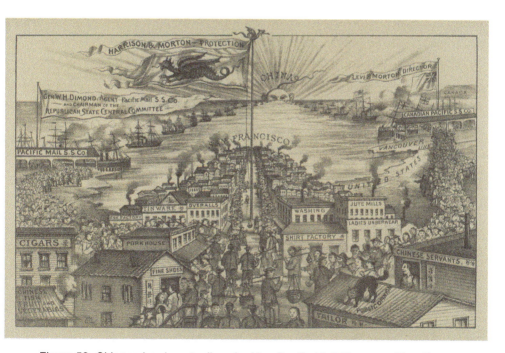

Figure 56. Chinese immigrants disembarking Pacific Mail Steamers (San Francisco: no date [c. late 1860s]). Courtesy of The Bancroft Library University of California, Berkeley.

Figure 57. This cartoon positions the viewer on the northern border of the continental U.S., with the Atlantic Ocean to the left and the Pacific to the right, with the soon-to-be-completed transcontinental railroads in the background. As the Irishman travels west and the Chinaman travels east, they first consume Uncle Sam—then the Chinaman consumes his Irish counterpart. "The Great Fear of the Period—That Uncle Sam May Be Swallowed by Foreigners. The Problem Solved" (San Francisco: White & Bauer Lithographers, late 1860s). Courtesy of the Library of Congress.

Karen Shimakawa, "National Abjection" (2002)[14]

Performance studies scholar Karen Shimakawa argues that Asians have historically threatened the imagined national "body" of the U.S. akin to the mode of germs or vices. Historian Nayan Shah has similarly described the way in which San Francisco's Chinatown was tagged as a site of disease: literally by blaming Chinese immigrants exclusively for plague, syphilis, and typhoid; and symbolically through Chinatown's supposed threat to (white) American morals in the form of available drugs, gambling, and interracial sex. Such rhetoric of disease

displaced the blame for phenomena that made middle class whites uncomfort-
able onto a disenfranchised community. This tradition continues to shape U.S.
policies and culture in the form of racialized panics surrounding AIDS, SARS,
Bird Flu, and Swine Flu.[15]

Asian Americanists have argued that the literal and symbolic exclusion of Asians
(among other groups deemed undesirable) has been fundamental to the formation of (legal and cultural) U.S. Americanness. "In the last century and a half,"
writes Lisa Lowe, "the American citizen has been defined over against the Asian
immigrant, legally, economically, and culturally," Lowe argues that discursive
manipulation of the categories of (Asian) "immigrant" and "citizen" (and material control over their respective bodies) has been foundational in the production
of U.S. American citizenship, both legal and symbolic, often by defining them as
mutually exclusive.* The conceptual U.S. citizen-subject comes into being, in other
words, through the expulsion of Asianness in the figure of the Asian immigrant ...

As David Palumbo-Liu argues, exclusionist and anti-miscegenation psycholo-
gists, sociologists, and jurists found a particularly effective synthesis in the "science"
of eugenics/ethnology and the rhetorical politics of racial exclusion in the early
twentieth century, conceptualizing the body of the nation as one in dire need of
protection from infection: "A particular discursive formation evolved [during the
1920s and 1930s] that blended science with politics, economics with sociology,
national and international interests, within which the nation was imagined as a
body that must, through fastidious hygienic measures, guard against what passes
from the exterior, excise the cancerous cells that have already penetrated it, and
prevent any reproductive act that would compromise the regeneration of its
species in an increasingly massified and mobile world."[†]

The bodily discourse that fueled the anti-immigrant, anti-immigration legislation of the late nineteenth and early twentieth centuries (and that arguably
resurfaced in the 1990s, as evidenced by the passage of anti-immigrant legislation such as California's Proposition 187) constructed the figurative "national
body" as an organism that must be protected from contamination or infection by the contagion—both literal and figurative—that the immigrant body

---

* Lisa Lowe, *Immigrant Acts: On Asian American Cultural Politics* (Durham, NC:
Duke University Press, 1996), 4. Emphasis in the original.

† David Palumbo-Liu, *Asian/American: Historical Crossings of a Racial Frontier* (Stanford,
CA: Stanford University Press, 1999), 24.

represents.* [Julia] Kristeva draws a similar metaphoric relation between the body and cultural formation in her formulation of abjection. Ostensibly elaborating a theory of culture, Kristeva argues that the quintessential experiences of abjection are decidedly rooted in the body; "as in true theatre ... refuse and corpses *show me* what I permanently thrust aside in order to live. My body extricates itself, as being alive, from that border ... If dung signifies the other side of the border, the place where I am not and which permits me to be, the corpse, the most sickening of wastes, is a border that has encroached upon everything."†

The corpse is, for Kristeva, "the utmost of abjection" precisely because it cannot be categorically or permanently "jettisoned": our bodies are continually approaching that state, and waste marks the presence of mortality and decay within us—evidence of the impossibility of successfully or permanently achieving "radical exclusion" of the abject: "It is death infecting life. Abject. It is something rejected from which one does not part."‡ This paradoxical recognition of the abhorrent as already internalized marks a second aspect of abjection relevant to the present study: for as radically other/foreign to U.S. Americanness as courts (often reflecting more widely held cultural politics) have insisted Asianness is, there has been a consistent, simultaneous rhetoric (both legal and cultural) of "melting pot"/"multicultural" inclusion that envisions Asians as assimilable (or unavoidably assimilated) to U.S. Americanness ...

This seeming contradiction—a history of expulsion and exclusion of Asianness and the discourse of multiculturalism/diversity and inclusion of Asians and other nonnormative subjects—is captured by the dilemma posed by abjection: it is through abjection that stable borders/subjects are constituted; but by definition that process of constitution can never be complete because, in Kristeva's words, the process of abjection "does not radically cut off the subject from what threatens it—on the contrary, abjection acknowledges it to be in perpetual danger." And because the process is never fully successful or complete, the "deject" ("one by whom the abject exists") must repeatedly reinforce those boundaries: "[a] deviser of territories, languages, works, the deject never stops demarcating

---

* For a detailed rhetorical analysis of the Proposition 187 debate, see Kent Ono and John Sloop, *Shifting Borders: Rhetoric, Immigration, and California's Proposition 187* (Philadelphia: Temple University Press, 2001).

† Julia Kristeva, *The Powers of Horror: An Essay on Abjection*, trans. Leon S. Roudiez (New York: Columbia University Press, 1982), 3. Emphasis in the original.

‡ Kristeva, *Powers of Horror*, 4.

his universe whose fluid confines—for they are constituted of a non-object, the abject—constantly question his solidity and impel him to start afresh."* It is this dynamic and unstable aspect of abjection that makes it a peculiarly apt model for charting Asian Americanness. For if "Asianness" is what must be radically jettisoned in order to constitute "Americanness," it is also (has always been) a source of "contamination." If an element of abjection is the impossibility of wholly or finally differentiating it from the deject, what I am suggesting is that it is an (in)ability shared by the nation in its attempt to concretize national boundaries and that it is this inability that positions Asian Americans as a site of national abjection within U.S. American culture. Racialized as (always potentially) foreign, we nevertheless cannot be differentiated from the "legitimate" U.S. American subject with an exclusion carrying the force of law and therefore cannot be openly, completely, or permanently expelled; thus, to maintain the legitimacy of the dominant racial/national complex, the process of abjection must continually be reiterated or re-presented.

The contradictory impulses of abjection were driving forces in the internment of mainland Japanese Americans during World War II.† Ostensibly on the basis of "military emergency" (the rationale of the Supreme Court's finding of constitutionality), in 1941 nearly 120,000 people of Japanese descent (along with their non-Japanese spouses and multiracial children in some cases) were evacuated from their homes on the West Coast (many forced to abandon homes, farms, and other livelihoods) per President Franklin D. Roosevelt's Executive Order 9066. The evacuees were relocated inland to "camps" (military outposts fenced and secured with armed guards). Of course, as Gordon Hirabayashi and other defendants who challenged the constitutionality of internment (and lost) pointed out, many of the internees were U.S. citizens; that is, the very entity being concretized/defended in the expulsion of a "foreign" threat ("American" lives, values, and property) included, indeed, required inclusion of that which was being expelled. The democratic principles ostensibly being defended abroad— freedom from racist genocide and colonial/nationalist brutalities—led directly to

---

* Kristeva, *Powers of Horror*, 9, 8.

† I am not suggesting that abjection represents a (sole) *cause* of the internment; rather, as in the case of model minority discourse and the examples to follow, I am arguing that abjection provides a lens through which we can understand how these instances of racist oppression were/are articulated and, perhaps, how or why they often take these paradoxical or seemingly contradictory forms.

racist-nationalist oppression and property theft at home. The internment camps themselves can be seen as spatializations of abjection: their locations chosen precisely on the basis of their interiority (remoteness from the West Coast), the camps were fenced and patrolled by armed guards to keep a foreign threat out by, paradoxically, drawing it further in …

In his account of the contradiction that marks Asian/Americanness (which he characterizes as "a tenuous, historicized, provisional, and contingent consolidation of a nation against 'itself'"), Palumbo-Liu suggests that "the deployment of the model minority myth is an exemplary instance of [the] negotiations of social and political subjectivity."* Indeed, the popular depiction of Asian Americans as a "model minority" illustrates the very contradictions that characterize abjection. Praised and valued for their ability (and inclination) to assimilate into the "mainstream" (with an eye toward eventually disappearing in/as it)—indeed, to surpass even "normal" Americans (that is, whites) at being ideal manifestations of American success and self-determination at a particular historical moment (the early period of the civil rights movement), Asian Americans were singled out for their aptitude for conforming to dominant models of "proper" American citizenly values and practices (including subjection to the law, heteronormative and patriarchal "family values," and especially the pursuit of higher education), over and against what were seen as other, less tractable, more anti-hegemonic racialized minorities.[†] The ambivalence of abjection is coded into the oxymoronic term itself, which embraces Asian Americanness as exemplary of the correct embodiment of Americanness even as it marks that group out as distinguishable from "normal" Americanness by virtue of its racialized minority status[‡] …

---

* Palumbo-Liu, *Asian/American*, 170–1.

† For example, see William Petersen, "Success Story, Japanese-American Style," *New York Times Magazine*, January 9, 1966.

‡ For a more detailed discussion of the contradictions inherent in model minority discourse, as well as the measures by which "success" is assessed in these articles, see Sucheng Chan, *Asian Americans: An Interpretive History* (Boston: Twayne Publishers, 1991), 167–71; Keith Osajima, "Asian Americans as the Model Minority: An Analysis of the Popular Press Image in the 1960s and 1980s" in *Reflections on Shattered Windows: Promises and Prospects for Asian American Studies*, eds. Gary Okihiro et al. (Pullman, WA: Washington State University Press, 1988), 165–74; Bob H. Suzuki, "Education and Socialization of Asian Americans: A Revisionist Analysis of the 'Model Minority' Thesis," *Amerasia* 4, no. 2 (1977), 23–51; and Ronald Takaki, *Strangers from a Different Shore: A History of Asian Americans* (New York: Penguin, 1989), 474–84.

Because the radically excluded abject is not wholly objectifiable (cannot be definitively differentiated from "real" Americanness), the image constantly wavers, attempting to reconcile itself to that condition/dilemma and thereby resulting in often diametrically opposed stereotypes, both purporting to represent "Asian Americanness."

More accurately, these opposing stereotypes are often invoked in order to represent Asianness (in the guise of Asian Americanness); to the degree Asian Americans are abjected in representation, they are frequently conflated with Asian foreigners. Abjection, in other words, functions to make Asian Americanness into Asianness. If Asian American identity functions as a site of racial/sexual/national abjection, then it can only be represented (objectified) once it has been radically excluded; as "ordinary" Americans, Asian Americans are often simply incomprehensible or invisible. This, finally, is the dynamic that largely dictates Asian American representation: if (paraphrasing Kristeva) the nation must abject itself within the same motion through which it claims to establish itself, it does so by abjecting Asian Americanness, by making it other, foreign, abnormal, not-American.

Countless other historical examples of Asian American abjection could be included in this list—the preceding discussion is intended to be illustrative rather than exhaustive. What I hope becomes clear through these examples is a pattern of contradiction on the part of the U.S. government and mainstream culture with respect to various Asian American communities—at times embracing/ingesting them, at other times violently (if often symbolically) expelling/excluding/segregating them—and that these "contradictions" may be understood as a product of the continually collapsing project of abjection as a fundamental element of national identity formation.

Claire Jean Kim, "Racial Triangulation Theory" (1999)

In contrast to scapegoat theories of Asians as foreign invaders, political theorist Claire Jean Kim has come up with a working theory to better understand the conflicts of Korean American small shop owners in African American communities in New York City and Los Angeles beyond a simple suggestion of Black anti-Asian racism. This graph is an example of a practical theory that gets closer to the complex, relational dynamics of racial formations in the U.S. Her theory of racial triangulation intervening within the standard Black/White binary paradigm is key to understanding contemporary political culture as it is played out.

Figure 58. "Field of Racial Positions." Claire Jean Kim, "The Racial Triangulation of Asian Americans," *Politics & Society*, vol. 27, no. 1 (March 1999), 108.

The Turban Tide (1908)[16]

On September 2, 1907, the Japanese-Korean Exclusion League demanded all South Asians evacuate Bellingham, Washington. When that did not happen, 1,500 people roamed factories and apartment buildings rounding up immigrants to expel "the Turban Tide." In the wake of this violence, The Overland Monthly *published two conflicting views on the South Asian immigration issue, one from an Indian student, and another from an exclusionist. The wave of transnational anti-Asian immigrant violence that targeted Chinese, Japanese, and South Asian communities in California, Washington, and Vancouver led to Theodore Roosevelt's brokering a "Gentlemen's Agreement" with Japan to reduce immigration in exchange for civil rights. Ten years later, Congress created an "Asiatic Barred Zone" that allowed the U.S. to restrict the immigration of British subjects from Asian colonies. Terri Yuh-lin Chen argues that vigilante hate violence is one component of the broader social and legal formation of "border patrol."[17]*

Girindra Mukerji, "The Hindu in America"

Five centuries ago Columbus started out for India; the nuggets of India had been the great attraction of the ambitious merchants, mariners and monarchs of Europe. The wealth of India has been the theme of the poets—Milton, in his famous epic, "Paradise Lost," talks of "the wealth of Ormuz and Ind." After years of adventures, Columbus struck on land which, though not India, more than satisfied the cravings for gold. Columbus, mistaking this land as the long-searched-for India, named the aborigines Indians. Thus, America, from the day of her discovery, becomes associated with India ...

With the years, America grew as a civilized country, and finally became an independent State, and during this period, India fell completely a victim to English dominance. India continued to exist only to be exploited and all but destroyed. America became one of the great nations of the earth. The varied destinies of these two nations went on with time, until today each represents the opposite pole of advancement ...

In India, the peasantry is groaning under the most exorbitant land tax system on earth. As a result, the peasantry is beginning to look for profitable employment outside of India. For many years, they have migrated to Australia and South Africa, where generally they found the peddling of Indian articles or selling of their labor profitable. But the rigid exclusion acts in Australia, and the forfeiture of the right of holding landed property in South Africa, under the new regime of the "Republic," made their struggle for existence a strenuous one ...

Of late, the emigration has been reaching such an alarming point that great consternation has been felt by the British, and in the United States threatens to bring on another racial and international complication. The laboring class sees the great danger of low wages as a result of competition with Asiatic labor, and the probability is not remote that the Indian will be ousted from the means of earning a livelihood in factories and on the railroads. The American, especially the inhabitant of this Western coast, sees the spectre of another "yellow peril," and one prominent newspaper declared the Hindus "outlaws" in this country. The public mind seemed to be in such a disordered state that the better class of the Hindus here blushed for shame for their fellow man. The law courts declared the Hindus as "undesirable," not fit to become citizens of the State. The riot in Bellingham was the culminating point of the Hindus' distress.

Perhaps the greatest maltreatment they received in Canada. Retired English soldiers and officers, from the Indian services, now passing a very luxurious and idle life on the pensions filched from the Indian people by heavy taxation, mercilessly harassed the Hindu immigrants and shot one man and with impunity. Canada has declared "Canada for Canadians:" saying that the Hindus have no business to come to this country to work, to hoard money and then take it back to India. The poor Canadians have no apology to offer for the English who have gone to India only to systematically drain her, and then go back to England to live like lords? That is the reply of the Hindus to the Canadians.

The Hindus in the United States and in Canada are learning the lessons of adversity in their dire economical distress. Their emigration is not in any way based or backed by an organized immigration or colonization company. Their presence here has been due to the organized American or Canadian capitalist, demanding labor for the upbuilding of railroads and other industries. The mob vented their unthinking revenge on the Hindus, but little did they think for had they stopped for thought they would not have failed to see that it is their own people at home who were responsible for the presence of Asiatic labor, now, as in the past.

AGNES FOSTER BUCHANAN, "THE WEST AND THE HINDU INVASION"

California gave to the country the Chinese question. Californians of the Denis Kearney days will remember the street riots which followed each fresh arrival of Celestials. The Geary Act was the result of these agitations. Then followed a few years of comparative quiet. Coolies ceased from troubling, and the country was at rest. The quiet was, however, a temporary one. While the Chinese stood knocking at our outer doors, which had been barred and closed by legislation, their neighbors, not waiting for permission, crept stealthily past the suppliants, entered and took possession. When San Francisco awoke from her short sleep, she found herself face-to-face with the Japanese question, infinitely greater and more insidious in its influence than the Chinese problem had ever threatened to be, for while the yellow men had raised a labor question, their brown brothers have created an industrial one. And then, while the Western press inflamed, and the Eastern journals calmed, neither wholly right nor wholly wrong, another stranger sought the Western coast—the land of promise. He is tall of stature, straight of feature, swarthy of color. But unlike the other visitors, this last is a brother of our own race—a full-blooded Aryan, men of like progenitors with us.

The Hindus and the Hindu Invasion is the latest racial problem with which we of the West have to deal. Not that it is as yet fully recognized as such. As in the cases of the two previous invasions of the coast by Orientals, it is only for the close observer that coming events cast their true shadows ...

They have come to this coast eager, more than eager, to do any and all kinds of work. They are to be found in our iron factories, they are picking fruit, railroads engage them as section hands. And right here comes in the problem of cheap labor which is forever and always the same in similar situations. Asiatics are, by their manner of life and living, able to subsist on incomes that would be prohibitive to the white man. This is a trite truism, but it is the hinge upon which the open or shut door of immigration must hang. The Hindus live together in colonies, a number in a house, and their living expenses are purely nominal. They do not exceed $3 a month per capita. It requires no statistics to demonstrate that a white man must starve on such an allowance.

Then, too, the Hindus have no families to support—that is, there are no women among the newcomers, nor are there likely to be. Among other insignia of conquest, the Mohammedans forced upon the Hindus the "pardah nashin" or drawn veil, which relegated the women of the higher classes to close confinement in their homes, while those of the higher classes, who were compelled to go abroad, were heavily veiled. Not even with the establishment of the British rule has this custom been abandoned, and it is this dislike of the Hindu to expose his womankind to the eyes of the world that has brought to the United States only bachelors and widowers ...

So California and the West give to the Powers that be in Washington another question for legislation, for it must needs be by legislation that the present crisis is to be bridged. The small cloud on the horizon, now no larger than a man's hand, is threatening because misunderstood, but grows larger and larger as each wind that blows from the East brings it nearer.

The sacred writings of the Vedas say: "I gave the earth to Arya." This is a propitious moment for the State Department to adopt an amendment to the Vedas and to tell our brothers of the East that while the earth is large enough for us all, there is no one part of it that will comfortably accommodate both branches of the Aryan family.

"Save Our State from Oriental Aggression" (1918)

James D. Phelan (1861–1930) served two terms as Mayor of San Francisco before being elected to the U.S. Senate in 1913. In 1907 Phelan argued, "Japanese now occupy valleys in California by lease or purchase of land to the exclusion not only of whites but Chinese, and if this silent invasion is permitted by the Federal Government, they would at the rate at which they are coming, a thousand a month, soon convert the fairest State in the Union into a Japanese colony. If they were naturalized they would outvote us. "[18]

Figure 59. "Save Our State From Oriental Aggression," *Sunset, the Pacific Monthly* (1918), 79. Yoshio Kishi/Irene Yah Ling Sun Collection of Asian Americana made possible in large part in memory of Dr. Wei Yu Chen, MSS 292, Series II, Box 9, folder 19. Fales Library and Special Collections, New York University.

The Mongol in Our Midst (1924)

Francis Graham Crookshank (1873–1933) argued "Mongoloid idiotism" (now referred to as Down's syndrome) was a form of racial degeneration. These arguments led to racial sterilization movements and the 1924 Johnson Reed Act favoring immigration from the purported superior race of Nordic Europeans and greatly limiting "inferior" "Alpine" (central and eastern) and "Mediterranean" Europeans from entering the U.S. Note the pose of the young man in a Buddhist type "lotus" position in the photo. Such visual meanings were powerful signs of a great bio-racial divide. With the much greater familiarity with Buddhism today, such representations chosen for the frontispiece of Crookshank, and of Knackfuss's drawing for Kaiser Wilhelm II, seem laughable. But such present day shifts do not diminish how foreign such a bodily position was perceived by Westerners not so long ago.

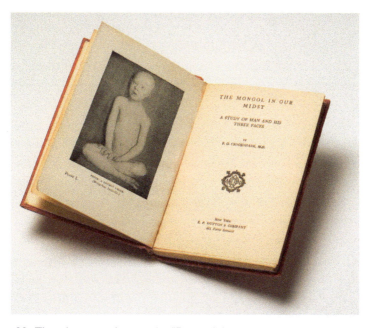

Figure 60. The photo caption reads: "Peter: A London Child (Mongolian Imbecile)." F. G. Crookshank, *The Mongol in Our Midst: A Study of Man and His Three Faces* (New York: E. P. Dutton, 1924). Yoshio Kishi/Irene Yah Ling Sun Collection of Asian Americana made possible in large part in memory of Dr. Wei Yu Chen. Fales Library and Special Collections, New York University.

Randolph Bourne, "A Future America" (1916)[19]

Randolph Bourne (1886–1918) was a Progressive-era essayist and, along with Jane Addams, an anti–World War I activist. His concept of a "Trans-National America" continues to challenge common sense notions of assimilation and the U.S. as a "melting pot." Writing just at the time 100 percent Americanism was surging and anti-immigrant organizing was taking place culminating in the 1924 immigration restrictions limiting "inferior" Europeans' entry to the U.S., Bourne turns the tables on Anglo American nationalism and criticizes their ongoing heritage biases. He identifies a new type of American identity defined as fluid, dynamic, and in process.

The discovery of diverse nationalistic feelings among our great alien population has come to most people as an intense shock. It has brought out the unpleasant inconsistencies of our traditional beliefs …

As the unpleasant truth has come upon us that assimilation in this country was proceeding on lines very different from those we had marked out for it, we found ourselves inclined to blame those who were thwarting our prophecies. The truth became culpable. We blamed the war, we blamed the Germans. And then we discovered with a moral shock that these movements had been making great headway before the war even began. We found that the tendency, reprehensible and paradoxical as it might be, has been for the national clusters of immigrants, as they became more and more firmly established and more and more prosperous, to cultivate more and more assiduously the literatures and cultural traditions of their homelands. Assimilation, in other words, instead of washing out the memories of Europe, made them more and more intensely real. Just as these clusters became more and more objectively American, did they become more and more German or Scandinavian or Bohemian or Polish.

To face the fact that our aliens are already strong enough to take a share in the direction of their own destiny, and that the strong cultural movements represented by the foreign press, schools, and colonies are a challenge to our facile attempts, is not, however, to admit the failure of Americanization. It is not to fear the failure of democracy. It is rather to urge us to an investigation of what Americanism may rightly mean. It is to ask ourselves whether our ideal has been broad or narrow—whether perhaps the time has not come to assert a higher ideal than the "melting-pot." Surely we cannot be certain of our spiritual democracy when, claiming to melt the nations within us to a comprehension of our free and democratic institutions, we fly into panic at the first sign of their own will and tendency. We act as if we wanted Americanization to take place only on our own terms, and not by the consent of the governed ... This is the condition which confronts us, and which demands a clear and general readjustment of our attitude and our ideals.

To think of earlier nationalities as culturally assimilated to America, while we picture the later as a sodden and resistive mass, makes only for bitterness and misunderstanding. The truth is that no more tenacious cultural allegiance to the mother country has been shown by any alien nation than by the ruling class of Anglo-Saxon descendants in these American States. English snobberies, English religion, English literary styles, English literary reverences and canons, English ethics, English superiorities, have been the cultural food that we have drunk in from our mothers' breasts ...

If freedom means the right to do pretty much as one pleases, so long as one does not interfere with others, the immigrant has found freedom, and the ruling element has been singularly liberal in its treatment of the invading hordes. But if freedom means a democratic cooperation in determining the ideals and purposes and industrial and social institutions of a country, then the immigrant has not been free, and Anglo-Saxon element is guilty of just what every dominant race is guilty of in every European country: the imposition of its own culture upon the minority peoples. The fact that this imposition has been so mild and, indeed, semi-conscious does not alter its quality. And the war has brought out just the degree to which that purpose of "Americanizing," that is, "Anglo-Saxonizing," the immigrant has failed.

For the Anglo-Saxon now in his bitterness to turn upon the other peoples, talk about their "arrogance," scold them for not being melted in a pot which never existed, is to betray the unconscious purpose which lay at the bottom of his heart. It betrays too the possession of a racial jealousy similar to that of which he is now ... accusing the so-called "hyphenates." Let the Anglo-Saxon be proud enough of the heroic toil and heroic sacrifices which moulded the nation. But let him ask himself, if he had had to depend on the English descendants, where he would have been living today ...

The failure of the melting-pot, far from closing the great American democratic experiment, means that it has only just begun. Whatever American nationalism turns out to be, we see already that it will have a color richer and more exciting than our ideal has hitherto encompassed. In a world which has dreamed of internationalism, we find that we have all unawares been building up the first international nation. The voices which have cried for a tight and jealous nationalism of the European pattern are failing. From that ideal, however valiantly and disinterestedly it has been set for us, time and tendency have moved us further and further away. What we have achieved has been rather a cosmopolitan federation of national colonies, of foreign cultures, from whom the sting of devastating competition has been removed …

We cannot Americanize America worthily by sentimentalizing and moralizing history. When the best schools are expressly renouncing the questionable duty of teaching patriotism by means of history, it is not the time to force shibboleth upon the immigrant. This form of Americanization has been heard because it appealed to the vestiges of our old sentimentalized and moralized patriotism. This has so far held the field as the expression of the new American's new devotion. The inflections of other voices have been drowned. They must be heard. We must see if the lesson of the war has not been for hundreds of these later Americans a vivid realization of their trans-nationality, a new consciousness of what America meant to them as a citizenship in the world. It is the vague historic idealisms which have provided the fuel for the European flame. Our American ideal can make no progress until we do away with this romantic gilding of the past.

All our idealisms must be those of future social goals in which all can participate, the good life of personality lived in the environment of the Beloved Community. No mere doubtful triumphs of the past, which redound to the glory of only one of our trans-nationalities, can satisfy us. It must be a future America, on which all can unite, which pulls us irresistibly toward it, as we understand each other more warmly.

To make real this striving amid dangers and apathies is work for a younger intelligentsia of America. Here is an enterprise of integration into which we can all pour ourselves, of a spiritual welding which should make us, if the final menace ever came, no weaker, but infinitely strong.

W. E. B. Du Bois, "The Shape of Fear" (1926)[20]

The end of World War I, "the war to end all wars," wrought fear in America—the resumed fear of African Americans exercising their democratic rights. W. E. B. Du Bois (1868–1963), the preeminent American and international intellectual of the mid-nineteenth to mid-twentieth century, analyzes the rise of the Ku Klux Klan after World War I in the context of the rise of fascism and what must be done. This North American Review *piece gets at the root of the culture exploiting everyday fears wrought by international war where "The wages of War is Hate; and the End, and indeed the Beginning, of Hate is Fear." Du Bois's Pulitzer Prize–winning biographer David Levering Lewis wrote, "'The Shape of Fear' describes the national chrysalis from which southern violence and southern malevolence unmysteriously emerged ... As a sort of National Association for the Advancement of Anglo-Saxon People, the Klan was the last best hope of genteel racists—educated folk too ashamed 'to do and say' what the KKK says and does."[21] Hate crimes today, emboldened by hate radio, may be understood as a contemporary version of this secreted exercise of violence in relation to what has become a seeming permanent war against the constant and vague threat of "terrorism" anywhere and everywhere.*

Faced by the fact of the Ku Klux Klan, the United States has tried to get rid of it by laughing it off. We have talked of masquerading "in sheets and pillow cases"; we have caricatured the Klan upon the stage; we have exposed its silly methods, the dishonesty of some of its leaders, and the like. But we have not succeeded in scaring it away by ridicule ...

In the East, New England and New Jersey, the Klan has been mobilized; and need one mention the South?

What is the cause of all this? There can be little doubt but that the Klan in its present form is a legacy of the World War. Whatever there was of it before that great catastrophe was negligible and of little moment. The wages of War is Hate; and the End, and indeed the Beginning, of Hate is Fear ... The Shape of Fear looms over them. Germany fears the Jew, England fears the Indian, America fears the Negro, the Christian fears the Moslem, Europe fears Asia, Protestant fears Catholic, Religion fears Science. Above all, Wealth fears Democracy. These fears and others are ancient or at least long-standing fears. But they are renewed and revivified today because the world has at present a severe case of nerves; it feels it necessary to be nervous because the Unexpected [World War I] has happened.

For years we talked of the possibility of European War with bated breath; then we talked of it jauntily; and then we almost joked about it. While here was a Fear, it was one so far away that it did not seem possible for it ever to materialize, at least not in our day. And then suddenly it became a terrible fact, horrible beyond the dream of men. So that all our other fears today have become portentous. Abd-el Krim may be the vanguard of the launching of Asia against Europe; Ghandi and Das may be at the point of destroying the British Empire; the American Negro, despite all precautions, may force himself into a place where he will enter Congress, storm Wall Street, and marry white women.

Now against such fears as these there are three possible attitudes. One is the attitude of reason and examination. What does the ferment in the colored world mean and how far is our fear of it but a reflex of its fear of us? What do colored folk really want, and do their wants interfere with and oppose the just desires of the white world? How far is free, scientific inquiry going to undermine religious sanction? What is there in the objects of the Bolsheviki which should not appear in ... the objects of American social reformers? These questions indicate one attitude, mental, moral, and practical, toward great pending questions; but it is not the attitude which we are disposed to take today in the world.

On the contrary so imminent does our danger seem to some people that they turn to one of two other methods. They are both forms of Force; one an open appeal to force; Fascismo, either in its bold, physical form as it is appearing in Italy and Spain or in its more spiritual form as it appears in American Fundamentalism; in the determination to drive out of the Church every person who will not honestly or by perjury subscribe to a certain, narrow, outworn, and partially false creed.

The other method is the method of Force which hides itself in secrecy, and that is the method of the Ku Klux Klan. It is a method as old as humanity. The kind of thing which men are afraid or ashamed to do openly and by day, they accomplish secretly, masked, and at night. The method has certain advantages. It uses Fear to cast out Fear; it dares things at which open methods hesitate; it may with a certain impunity attack the high and the low; it need hesitate at no outrage of maiming or murder; it shields itself in the mob mind and then throws over all a veil of darkness which becomes glamor. It attracts people who otherwise could not be reached. It harnesses the mob. How is it that men who want certain things done by brute force can so often depend upon the mob? Total depravity, human hate and *schadenfreude,* do not explain fully the mob spirit in this land. Before the wide eyes of the mob is ever the Shape of Fear. Back of the writhing, yelling, cruel-eyed demons who break, destroy, maim, and lynch … and burn at the stake is a knot, large or small, of normal human beings and these human beings at heart are desperately afraid of something, Of what? of many things but usually of losing their jobs, of being de-classed, degraded or actually disgraced; of losing their hopes, their savings, their plans for their children; of the actual pangs of hunger; of dirt, of crime. And of all this, most ubiquitous in modern industrial society is that fear of unemployment.

It is this nucleus of ordinary men that continually gives the mob its initial and awful impetus. Around this nucleus, to be sure, gather snowball-wise all manner of flotsam, filth, and human garbage and every inhibition of alcohol and current fashion. But all this is the horrible covering of this inner nucleus of Fear … How shall we meet this situation? Again we revert to the three paths: first and foremost by the spread of wider and deeper understanding among the masses of men of the modern industrial process and the method of distributing income, so that intelligently we may attack Production and Distribution and re-make industrial society. Or, a second method, by hue and cry and propaganda to stop all criticism and desire for change by dubbing every reformer "Bolshevik" and by frightening the wage earner with loss of the very foundation of his wage. And this is the kind of attack that again easily sinks to the [third path:] whispering courses underground and attempts to save modern industry through mobs engineered by the secret Ku Klux Klan …

Without doubt, of all the dangerous weapons that civilized man has attempted to use in order to advance human culture the secret mass lie is the most dangerous and the most apt to prove a boomerang. This is the real thing that we are to fear in the Ku Klux Klan.

"The Marching Chinese" (1929)

*Europeans and Americans have long fixated on the large number of Chinese.
This cartoon was one of the earliest and most recognizable in the influential*
Ripley's Believe It or Not! *series. Historian Matthew Connelly has argued that
the emergence of the idea of "overpopulation" was directly tied to fears of Asians
in the early twentieth century.*[22]

Figure 61. "The Marching Chinese," *Ripley's Believe It or Not!* (New York: Simon
and Schuster, 1929). © Ripley's Entertainment, Inc. 2013.

Theodor Seuss Geisel, "Waiting for the Signal from Home ..." (1942)

*Theodor Seuss Geisel (1904–1991), or "Dr. Seuss," was chief editorial cartoonist
for the visual magazine* PM *before World War II and before his more famous
book career. Seuss drew this cartoon a few weeks after the Japanese attack on
Pearl Harbor and the declaration of war, and a mere few days before President
Franklin Delano Roosevelt issued Executive Order 9066 authorizing the*

evacuation of all "persons of Japanese ancestry" from the West Coast into military internment camps—including 110,000 U.S. citizens of all ages. Though no
evidence of sabotage or treason was ever found, many Americans believed local
Japanese Americans had participated in the Pearl Harbor attacks. Decades of
anti-Japanese political organizing fanned the belief that Japanese immigrants,
some many generations removed from Japan, were by their ancestry a faceless mass
loyal only to their emperor and therefore unassimilable to American society. No
similar precautions were taken against German or Italian Americans. The State
Department–commissioned Munson Report (1940) and the Navy-commissioned
Ringle Report (1941) both concluded that Japanese Americans posed no significant security threat. Nevertheless, pressure from California politicians including
Attorney General Earl Warren (the future chief justice of the Supreme Court,
then running for governor) resulted in the mass incarceration.[23]

Figure 62. Theodor Seuss Geisel, "Waiting for the Signal From Home …," (February 13, 1942). The Dr. Seuss Collection, Mandeville Special Collections Library,
University of California, San Diego.

Edward Duran Ayres, "The Nature of the Mexican American Criminal" (1942)

This report, produced by the Los Angeles County Sheriff's Foreign Relations Bureau on the biological aspects of Mexican American criminality, served as crucial evidence in the conviction of seventeen Mexican American young men in the killing of José Díaz. The convictions of the "Sleepy Lagoon" murder case, and the press surrounding them, helped spark the "Zoot Suit Riots" in Los Angeles the following year. During those riots, U.S. Army and Navy servicemen roamed Mexican-, African-, and Filipino American neighborhoods, destroying the flashy clothes of those they considered to be "gangsters" and cutting their hair. Psychohistorian Mauricio Mazón argues that in a climate of widespread fears of Japanese and Mexican American conspiracies against the U.S., servicemen sought to "symbolically annihilate" Mexican Americans as proxy-enemies in order to gain control over their own anxieties and anger about the regimented and unfree life of military service in wartime.[24]

There are a number of factors contributing to the great proportion of crime by a certain element of the Mexican population. Among the contributing factors are those of economics, lack of employment, and small wages that cause certain ones to commit theft and robbery for the purpose of obtaining the means to own and drive automobiles and to have money to spend on their girlfriends, liquor, clothes, etc., also to obtain the wherewithal to live ...

But to get a true perspective of this condition we must look for a basic cause that is even more fundamental than the factors already mentioned, no matter how basically they may appear. Let us view it from the biological basis—in fact, as the main basis to work from. Although a wild cat and a domestic cat are of the same family they have certain biological characteristics so different that while one may be domesticated the other would have to be caged to be kept in captivity; and there is practically as much difference between the races of man as so aptly recognized by Rudyard Kipling when he said when writing of the Oriental, "East is East and West is West, and never the twain shall meet," which gives us an insight into the present problem because the Indian, from Alaska to Patagonia, is evidently Oriental in background—at least he shows many of the Oriental characteristics, especially so in his utter disregard for the value of life.

When the Spaniards conquered Mexico they found an organized society composed of many tribes of Indians ruled by the Aztecs who were given over to human sacrifice. Historians record that as many as 30,000 Indians were sacrificed on their heathen altars in one day, their bodies being opened by stone knives and their hearts torn out while still beating. This total disregard for human life has always been universal throughout the Americas among the Indian population, which of course is well known to everyone ... For 400 years the Mexican people, including their forefathers from Spain, have been confronted with the same problem that we are confronted with today, and they have given just as much study and thought to the problem as we have. In fact, the revolution that started in Mexico under Madera in 1910 had as its objective the freeing and betterment of the Indian, and also much of the Mextizo element, from peonage. Many social experiments were tried out, some of them running to the extreme in their good intentions, but all ending in apparent failure. Mexican authorities state that in spite of every well-meant social reform and leniency shown to a certain element under the program of rehabilitation the said element has not responded to their hopes, and that even from the economic standpoint, when higher wages are given and an opportunity for a higher standard of life is opened to them, instead of availing themselves of that opportunity they prefer to work half a week instead of a whole week, and we find that same condition here in a great many instances among this same element ...

Representatives of the Mexican colony may claim that the contributing factors mentioned, and others, are the sole cause of this crime wave by this particular Mexican element, and they will loathe to admit that it is in any way biological—for reasons one can quite understand, pride of race, nationality, etc., but the fact remains that the same factors, discrimination, lack of recreation facilities, economics, etc., have also always applied to the Chinese and Japanese in California, yet they have always been law-abiding and have never given our authorities trouble except in that of opium among the Chinese, and that of gambling among both the Chinese and Japanese, but such acts of violence as now are in evidence among the young Mexicans has been entirely unknown among these two Oriental peoples. On the other hand, among the Filipinos crime of violence in proportion to their population is quite prevalent, and practically all of it over women. This is due to the fact that there are so few Filipino women here, and also the biological aspect enters into it, as the Filipino is a Malay, and ethnologists trace the Malayan people to the American Indian, ranging from the southwestern part of the United States down through Mexico, Central America, and into South America. The Malay is even more vicious than the Mongolian—to which race the Japanese and Chinese, of course belong. In fact, the Malay seems to have all the bad qualities of the Mongolian and none of the good qualities.

Carlos Bulosan, "Goddamn Brown Monkeys" (1946)[25]

Carlos Bulosan (1913–1956) left the Philippines to work on farms on the West Coast where he became a journalist and labor organizer. His memoir, excerpted below, became a classic of Filipino and Filipino American literature. After the U.S. "march of the flag" west to annex the Philippines, 50,000 Filipino workers migrated east to fill the demand for labor resulting from a booming economy and immigration restriction legislation in the 1920s. As "U.S. nationals," Filipinos could move freely, but after many California municipalities passed local laws to exclude Filipinos, and dozens of race riots left scores of Filipinos dead in 1930, California congressmen began to support calls for Philippine independence, and eventually attempted to subsidize their "repatriation."[26]

It was now the year of the great hatred: the lives of Filipinos were cheaper than those of dogs. They were forcibly shoved off the streets when they showed resistance. The sentiment against them was accelerated by the marriage of a Filipino and a girl of the Caucasian race in Pasadena. The case was tried in court and many technicalities were brought in with it to degrade the lineage and character of the Filipino people.

Prior to the *Roldan vs. The United States* case, Filipinos were considered Mongolians. Since there is a law which forbids the marriage between members of the Mongolian and Caucasian races, those who hated Filipinos wanted them to be included in this discriminatory legislation. Anthropologists and other experts maintained that the Filipinos are not Mongolians, but members of the Malayan race. It was then a simple thing for the state legislature to pass a law forbidding marriage between members of the Malayan and Caucasian races. This action was followed by neighboring states until, when the war with Japan broke out in 1941, New Mexico was the nearest place to the Pacific Coast where Filipino soldiers could marry Caucasian women.

This was the condition in California when José and I arrived in San Diego. I was still unaware of the vast social implications of the discrimination against Filipinos, and my ignorance had innocently brought me to the attention of white Americans. In San Diego, where I tried to get a job, I was beaten upon several occasions by restaurant and hotel proprietors. I put the blame on certain Filipinos who had behaved badly in America, who had instigated hate and discontent among their friends and followers. This misconception was generated by a confused personal reaction to dynamic social forces, but my hunger for the truth had inevitably led me to take an historical attitude. I was to understand and interpret this chaos from a collective point of view, because it was pervasive and universal.

From San Diego, José and I traveled by freight train to the south. We were told, when we reached the little desert town of Calipatria, that local whites were hunting Filipinos at night with shotguns. A countryman offered to take us in his loading truck to Brawley, but we decided it was too dangerous. We walked to Holtville where we found a Japanese farmer who hired us to pick winter peas.

It was cold at night and when morning came the fog was so thick it was tangible. But it was a safe place and it was far from the surveillance of vigilantes. Then from nearby El Centro, the center of Filipino population in the Imperial Valley, news came that a Filipino labor organizer had been found dead in a ditch.

I wanted to leave Holtville, but José insisted that we work through the season. I worked but made myself inconspicuous. At night I slept with a long knife under my pillow. My ears became sensitive to sounds and even my sense of smell was sharpened. I knew when rabbits were mating between the rows of peas. I knew when night birds were feasting in the melon patches.

One day a Filipino came to Holtville with his American wife and their child. It was blazing noon and the child was hungry. The strangers went to a little restaurant and sat down at a table. When they were refused service, they stayed on, hoping for some consideration. But it was no use. Bewildered, they walked outside; suddenly the child began to cry with hunger. The Filipino went back to the restaurant and asked if he could buy a bottle of milk for his child.

"It is only for my baby," he said humbly.

The proprietor came out from behind the counter. "For your baby?" he shouted.

"Yes, sir," said the Filipino.

The proprietor pushed him violently outside. "If you say that again in my place, I'll bash in your head!" he shouted aloud so that he would attract attention. "You goddamn brown monkeys have your nerve, marrying our women. Now get out of this town!"

"I love my wife and child," said the Filipino desperately.

"Goddamn you!" The white man struck the Filipino viciously between the eyes with his fist.

Years of degradation came into the Filipino's face. All the fears of his life were here—in the white hand against his face. Was there no place he could escape? Crouching like a leopard, he hurled his whole weight upon the white man, knocking him down instantly. He seized a stone the size of his fist and began smashing it into the man's face. Then the white men in the restaurant seized the small Filipino, beating him unconscious with pieces of wood and with their fists.

He lay inert on the road. When two deputy sheriffs came to take him away, he looked tearfully back at his wife and child.

12 Chinamen and a Woman (1950)

James Hadley Chase (1906–1985) was a prolific and popular British author considered to have pioneered the detective thriller genre. In this novel, even though Glorie Leadler "could have had a dozen men at her feet for the asking, it was a solitary Oriental that made her heart beat fast." When her lover, Chang, is killed by Cubans smuggling Chinese laborers into Florida, Leadler's quest for revenge leads her to join the criminal underworld. She poses as an inno-cent victim to manipulate rival gang members into killing each other. After a private investigator confronts Leadler about the truth, she breaks down in tears

*about the debased and dangerous consequences of falling in love with a man like
Chang. Despite this cover's allusion to rape by a degraded horde, the text itself
contains no such suggestion.*

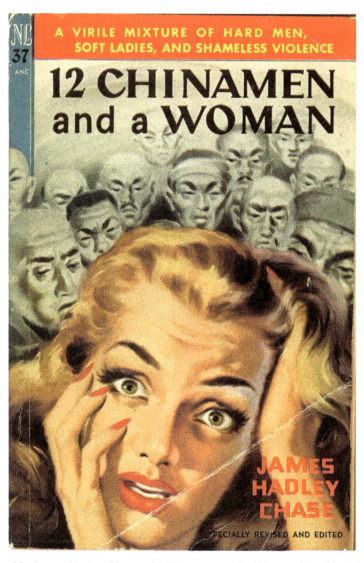

Figure 63. James Hadley Chase, *12 Chinamen and a Woman* (New York: Novel
Library, 1950), cover. Yoshio Kishi/Irene Yah Ling Sun Collection of Asian Ameri-
cana made possible in large part in memory of Dr. Wei Yu Chen. Fales British
Collection, Fales Library and Special Collections, New York University.

Helen Zia, "AutoWorld" (1984)

Writer and activist Helen Zia took this photo (Figure 64) at Six Flags Auto World in Flint, Michigan, in 1984, a short-lived theme park in the heartland of the U.S. car manufacturing industry. She writes: "I was there as a journalist to cover the opening. I found this poster among old Chevys and 1930s gas stations." The theme park, designed for family visitation, was with this poster also teaching stereotypes to the next generation. Featuring a car/bomber with buckteeth and slanted eyes, the yellow and red poster was approximately 5' by 5'. Michael Moore caught the tearing down of AutoWorld in his film Roger and Me *(1997). Helen Zia, in noting how limited the documentation of such images tends to be, writes: "I have no idea if there are any more images of the poster. There was no artist identification or whatever."*

Figure 64. AutoWorld exhibition poster, Flint, MI (1984). Photo: Helen Zia. Courtesy of Helen Zia.

Robert B. Reich, "Is Japan Really Out to Get Us?" (1992)[27]

Robert B. Reich, U.S. Secretary of Labor (1993–97) wrote this article to counter widespread fears about "Japan, Inc." Throughout the 1980s, politicians and industry leaders such as Lee Iacocca blamed Japan for the failures of U.S. industry. Despite the enormous influence of the U.S. over Japanese policy (including 100,000 U.S. troops based in Okinawa), and the Reagan and Carter administrations' "hands-off" policies implicitly supporting deindustrialization, many Americans believed the Japanese were attacking U.S. jobs. Pundits offered major union concessions as the only solution for making the U.S. more "competitive," blaming U.S. workers for not being as industrious and loyal as they imagined the Japanese to be. Amid this climate of insecurity and scapegoating, Vincent Chin, a young Chinese American in Detroit, was beaten to death with a baseball bat the evening of his bachelor party by two white auto-workers who yelled "It's because of you motherfuckers that we're out of work."[28]

"We are definitely at war with Japan," says John Connor, the venerable detective in Michael Crichton's *Rising Sun*, as he guides his junior officer through the intricate web of Japan's evil conspiracy to take over America. Here is the latest, and least subtle, of a great tide of books demonizing the Japanese. Almost all are classified as nonfiction; a few like *Rising Sun*, as fiction. But in this genre the distinction blurs. Mr. Crichton's characters frequently deliver short lectures on the subject of Japan's insidious design, mixing established fact with fantasy. The result is a thriller that doubles as a crude polemic. Just in case the reader misses his point, Mr. Crichton warns in an afterword of Japan's "adversarial trade, trade like war, trade intended to wipe out the competition," and encourages readers to verify the claims his characters make by consulting several recent works of nonfiction, which he lists.

But the nonfiction books Mr. Crichton cites also tend to mix factual analyses of Japan's economic strength with hyperbolic visions of Japan's plot to run the United States. High on the list is *Agents of Influence* (1990) by Pat Choate, which is partly a thoughtful examination of influence-peddling by all large corporations, but also partly a paranoid fantasy about Tokyo's alleged payoffs to influential Americans to achieve "effective political domination over the United States" ...

Mr. Crichton might have added many other recent works to his list, books that similarly blend fiction and nonfiction as they conjure up a Japan intent on controlling America: William S. Dietrich's *In the Shadow of the Rising Sun* (1991), claiming that Japan "threatens our way of life and ultimately our freedoms as much as past dangers from Nazi Germany and the Soviet Union"; Robert Zielinski and Nigel Holloway's *Unequal Equities* (1991), arguing that Japan's big corporations have rigged their capital markets in ways that undermine American corporations; Daniel Burstein's *Yen! Japan's New Financial Empire and Its Threat to America* (1988), asserting that Japan's growing control over our financial markets puts the United States at risk of falling prey to a "hostile Japanese ... world order"; and William J. Holstein's *Japanese Power Game* (1990), contending that Japan is motivated by raw power and parochialism, which threaten the United States. I have located over thirty-five recent books in this genre—many with bellicose titles like *The Coming War With Japan, Zaibatsu America: How Japanese Firms Are Colonizing Vital U.S. Industries, The Silent War, Trade Wars*, and so on.

There are several possible explanations for this outpouring, but Japan's recent behavior is not one. Japan still has a long way to go before its economy is truly open, and it can be (and should be) faulted on many grounds, but the big story since the mid-1980s is how far Japan has come in so short a time from its protectionist ways of the 1960s and 1970s. By 1990, Japan was the world's third-largest importer with each Japanese citizen purchasing, on average, about $1,900 worth of imports—not much less than the average American's purchase of $2,050 of imported products. Japanese imports of manufactured goods have climbed steeply, from less than a quarter of the total in 1980 to over 60 percent last year—including many high-tech items like space satellites and telecommunications equipment. Since 1985, manufactured imports from the United States to Japan have almost doubled.

Nor do Japanese investments in the United States suggest a conspiracy. For the most part, those investments have been big losers, which is one reason why Japan is cutting back on them. The Treasury bills the Japanese have liked to acquire have declined in value as the dollar has dropped since 1985; the prices of real estate, another Japanese favorite, have fallen since 1989. Only a tiny portion of Japan's total investment has gone to successful

American companies; more has been directed at relatively *unsuccessful* companies in Rust Belt industries like tires and steel. Other investments have taken the form of new factories, where American workers are learning to become more productive and create higher-quality goods than in many American-owned factories.

It is hard to find much of a plot in any of this. Mitsubishi's purchase of a substantial interest in Rockefeller Center, Sony's purchase of Columbia Pictures and Nintendo's recent flirtation with the Seattle Mariners make the headlines, but in almost every case, it has been the American owners who have initiated the deal. The British still own more of the United States than the Japanese do ... But if Japan is not really plotting against us, what accounts for this wave of fearmongering?

Perhaps American sensitivities are running high in light of the 50th anniversary of Pearl Harbor. Memories of the attack can be detected in the metaphors with which the Japanese challenge is described in many of these books: Japan is "targeting" our key industries (Holstein); it is "raiding" our technologies (Dietrich); we are "outgunned ... in the battle for control of world financial resources" (Burstein); Japan is mounting a "planned attack" on the United States through a "new kind of invasion" (Crichton) ...

Yet memory of the disaster fifty years ago is only a small part of the explanation. The fears expressed in these books would not be as intense as they are were it not for America's own economic doldrums. Although several of the books were published before the current recession, low productivity gains and deepening debt have been eating away at the foundations of the American economy for years. The reasons for these long-term ills have been well chronicled: a capital market that resembles a casino and demands immediate profits; and educational system that leaves almost 80 percent of our young people unable to comprehend a news magazine and many others unprepared for work; managers who award themselves princely sums while laying off their workers at the slightest hint of a downturn; a collapsing infrastructure of unsafe bridges and potholed roads; and more generally, a social norm—which reached its zenith during the 1980s—of overconsumption and underinvestment ...

But I think there is something else going on here as well. Most of these books seek not only to explain our problems in terms of Japan's aggressiveness, but also to incite a response from the reader. These books are calls to arms. Their authors want America to join together against the perceived threat. *Join together:* American government, American business, American labor. *Join together:* wealthy Americans, poor Americans, Americans of every creed and ethnicity. In *Trading Places*, Clyde Prestowitz asks rhetorically whether the American motto will be " 'every man for himself,' or 'all for one and one for all?' " and answers that "*E Pluribus Unum* (out of many, one) needs to be reaffirmed." William Dietrich urges us to "develop a national consensus of our own."

James Fallows, a Washington-based journalist and among the most thoughtful critics of Japan, develops the unity theme most fully in his book *More Like Us* (1989). After surveying the differences between Japanese and American society, Mr. Fallow urges us to "revive the idea that America is one coherent society, with bonds that are stronger than its internal differences. We understood this instinctively during World War II, but not often enough since then."

The ostensible purpose of joining together is to meet the Japanese challenge. But I think that the real logic—the deep message of these books, hidden perhaps even from the purveyors of the warnings—is precisely the reverse. The purpose of having a Japanese challenge is to give us a reason to join together. That is, we seem to need Japan as we once needed the Soviet Union—as a means of defining ourselves, our interests, our obligations to one another. We should not be surprised that this wave of Japan-as-enemy books coincides exactly with the easing of cold-war tensions ...

This is the real specter haunting these Japan books: not the specter of Japan's dominance, but of an America that no longer coheres. Japan's extreme homogeneity—racial, cultural, linguistic—intensifies, by contrast, our feared loss of identity. They *do* join together; they do seem tightly bound to one another. They know who they are. But who are we? ...

The central question for America in the post-Soviet world—a diverse America, whose economy and culture are rapidly fusing with the economies and cultures of the rest of the globe—is whether it is possible to rediscover our identity, and our mutual responsibility, without creating a new enemy. The authors under review think not. I hope they are wrong.

Dylan Yeats, "Chinese Professors" (2013)

Playing politics with China is an American political tradition. Democratic President Harry Truman sold U.S. involvement in the Korean War in 1950 as responding to Chinese aggression, even as his Republican opponents like Senator Joseph McCarthy tried to argue Truman's advisors were pro-Chinese Communist spies. Democratic President Lyndon Johnson sought to bolster flagging support for the Vietnam War in 1967 by trying to link Vietnamese Communists to the People's Republic of China, despite their well-known opposition to each other. In the 1990s Republicans manufactured scandals about Chinese campaign donors and security leaks at Los Alamos National Laboratories to discredit President Bill Clinton.

Politicians rarely, if ever, challenge this China-baiting, instead competing for who can seem tougher on America's "enemies." In 2012, both President Barack Obama and Republican challenger Mitt Romney sought to portray the other as betraying America by being "soft" on China. Obama challenged Romney's investments in Chinese companies and history of supporting outsourcing. Romney claimed Obama's security and economic policies bowed to Chinese "cheaters" and asserted that it wasn't worth "borrowing from China" to fund PBS.[29] This sort of bipartisan rhetoric exacerbates the seemingly ever-escalating post–Cold War fantasy that the U.S. and China are on a collision course.

"Why do great nations fail?" asks a Chinese Professor in Beijing in 2030. "The Ancient Greeks … the Roman Empire … the British Empire … and the United States of America. They all make the same mistakes, turning back on the principles that made them great. America tried to tax and spend itself out of a great recession. Enormous so-called 'stimulus' spending, massive changes to health care, government takeover of private industries, and crushing debt. Of course, we owned most of their debt," the Professor states as he chuckles, "so now they work for us." At this a mass of Chinese students sitting in a futuristic lecture hall bursts into laughter, and a narrator concludes, "America can determine our future, but only if we own it."

Such was the script of "The Chinese Professor" Political Action Committee ad first released during the 2010 Midterm elections and then again in the final weeks of Republican Mitt Romney's flailing 2012 presidential election bid. The Americans for Prosperity Foundation (AFP), chaired by

libertarian-leaning oil and pharmaceutical industrialist David Koch, produced "The Chinese Professor." Koch helped found AFP in the waning days
of George Bush's presidency as part of a broader strategy to reinvigorate the
Republican Party. AFP and its "Tea Party" conservative offshoots oppose
"big" government regulation and global warming "alarmism." The ad opens
and closes with a wide shot of a futuristic Chinese lecture hall decorated with
portraits of Mao Zedong. The ad contrasts this visage to that of Abraham
Lincoln whose monument flashes on screen as the Professor notes how the
great nation of America turned back on its principles. Ironically, Lincoln
was no advocate of limited government, but juxtaposing this American icon
against what seems in the ad to be continued Chinese dedication to Mao
suggests that against an intractable unchanging foe like China, Americans
must stay the course and support the status quo.

The history lesson in "The Chinese Professor" is quite dubious, but it is
part of an important and under-recognized tradition in American politics
and culture. Since the late 1990s politicians have tried to use the threat of
China to tarnish their political opponents. As part of a broader attack on
president Bill Clinton, who sought to expand government provisions for
healthcare and to cut the defense budget, Republican senator (and former
Law & Order television star) Fred Thompson used campaign finance hearings in 1997 to argue that improper Democratic contributions accounting
was part of a Chinese plot to purchase influence in Washington. In the
wake of these accusations, the *National Review* described Clinton as well as
First Lady Hillary Clinton and Vice President Al Gore, then gearing up for
the 2000 presidential campaign, as "Manchurian Candidates" and depicted
them on the magazine's cover as buck-toothed and yellow-faced in caricatured Asian costumes.*

As the campaign finance scandal faded, Newt Gingrich and House
Republicans convened a commission under California Republican
Christopher Cox to expand the investigation of "Chinagate" to include
espionage. Secret Cox Commission materials were leaked to the *New York*

---

* Darrell Y. Hamamoto, "White and Wong" in *Image Ethics in the Digital Age*, eds.
Larry P. Gross, John Stuart Katz, and Jay Ruby (Minneapolis, MN: University of
Minnesota Press, 2004), 247–67; David Palumbo-Liu, "Out of Place: Trans-
nationalism, Race, and the New Cold War," *Stanford Journal of International Relations*
1, no. 1 (Summer/Fall 1998) sjir.stanford.edu; *National Review*, March 24, 1997.

Times in March 1999, which published what were later revealed to be fabricated reports that an unnamed Chinese American scientist at Los Alamos National Laboratory had provided the "crown jewels" of America's nuclear program to China. The *Times* reported that under Clinton's watch security had grown lax and the administration had let the supposedly suspected "Chinese spy" who "stuck out like a sore thumb" operate with impunity so as not to jeopardize diplomatic and trade relations with China. This publicity prompted the FBI to interview Wen Ho Lee, an American citizen originally from Taiwan working on scientific research related to missile technology at Los Alamos. While the investigation uncovered no espionage, the Department of Energy decided to terminate Lee's position, which the *Times* publicized by claiming Lee was likely the "prime suspect" in passing classified nuclear secrets to China, a crime the paper (and the FBI) argued was the biggest breach of security since Julius Rosenberg's capital treason in the 1950s. *Times* columnist William Safire declared, "Our nuclear genie is out of the bottle."[*]

The Cox Commission published its findings in May 1999 criticizing the national security risks associated with American academic exchanges with China.[†] However, experts and journalists widely dismissed the vague accusations of the Commission as playing politics with national security.[‡] Nonetheless, fearing a brewing scandal, the FBI arrested Lee, who spent 278 days in what U.S. District Attorney James A. Parker later described as "demeaning" and "unnecessarily punitive" solitary confinement before he was charged with minor crimes associated with violating laboratory protocol. No evidence ever surfaced that Lee sought to share his data with anyone. During the trial, agents revealed that Lee's ethnicity was the primary factor

---

[*] Robert Scheer, "No Defense: How the New York Times Convicted Wen Ho Lee," *Nation*, October 23, 2000; Jeff Gerth and James Risen, "Breach at Los Alamos," "U.S. Fires Scientist Suspected of Giving Bomb Data," and "A Visit from China," *New York Times*, March 6 and 9, April 8, 1999; William Safire, "The Deadliest Download," *New York Times*, April 29, 1999.

[†] *U.S. National Security and Military/Commercial Concerns with the People's Republic of China, Select Committee*, U.S. House of Representatives (May 1999), house.gov/coxreport.

[‡] *The Cox Committee Report: An Assessment*, ed. M. M. May (Stanford, CA: Center for International Security and Collaboration, 1999).

making him a suspect for a crime they couldn't determine had actually been committed, and for which neither Lee nor anyone else was ever charged. Parker officially apologized to Lee for the "unfair manner [Lee] was held in custody by the Executive branch." Parker stated the "highest levels" of the Clinton administration deliberately misled him about Lee's threat to national security to keep him in prison, and that the Executive's behavior "embarrassed our entire nation and each of us who is a citizen of it."*

Civil rights activists, the scientific community, Lee's lawyers, and a few crusading journalists picked apart the racial profiling, scapegoating, and political manipulation at the heart of the case. Lars Erik-Nelson claimed the Lee episode was a spy scandal without a spy. Robert Scheer compared the Lee case with the Dreyfus Affair. Legal scholar Frank Wu argued the case was a classic example of the "perpetual foreigner syndrome" plaguing Asian Americans, stating "the 'Chinese look for spies among Chinese Americans' argument as a justification for selecting Lee is identical to that presented for the Japanese American Internment."†

Political operatives and their colleagues in the press manufactured a compelling story with typecast characters that left an innocent man in prison for most of a year. In point of fact, fiction hangs around the entire "Chinagate" episode. Supposed exposés and even the Cox Commission Report itself read like spy novels. During Lee's imprisonment Cox's aide Chuck DeVore even self-published a future-war novel entitled *China Attacks* (1999) in which the People's Republic of China uses stolen U.S. military technology to attack Taiwan and then the U.S. Clinton's former Secretary of Defense William Cohen also used fiction to casually confirm the Chinese theft of missile technology in his political thriller *Dragon Strike* (2006). The Bureau of Atomic Scientists and the President's Foreign Intelligence Advisory Board, on the other hand, have consistently challenged the validity of the supposed Chinese theft of U.S. nuclear secrets.

Peeling back some of this history (and fiction) helps illustrate that

* Frank H. Wu, *Yellow: Race in America Beyond Black and White* (New York: Basic Books, 2002), 104–16, 176–90.

† Lars-Erik Nelson, "Washington: The Yellow Peril" *New York Review of Books* 46, no. 12 (July 15, 1999), 6–10; Frank H. Wu, "Profiling Principle: The Prosecution of Wen Ho Lee and the Defense of Asian Americans," *UCLA Asian Pacific American Law Journal* 7 (Spring 2001), 52–6.

widespread discussions about China's inevitable threat to America are not merely rational responses to current geopolitical and economic conditions. Let's peel back further still. Almost 125 years ago, politically connected patrician New Yorker Arthur Dudly Vinton invented his own future "Chinese Professor" to make sense of contemporary politics. In 1890, Vinton penned a fantastic 2023 lecture of Won Lung Li. Li lectured that late nineteenth-century Americans had also abandoned the principles that made them great. Vinton's fictitious Li stated, "owing to the short-sightedness of your remote ancestors you had permitted your country to be overrun with emigrants from the slums of other nations; they had been given equal rights, socially and politically, and they had intermarried with your native stock until it became so debased that, one hundred years ago, your ancestors were as ready as the Frenchmen of the eighteenth century to abandon everything for the sake of an idea." Li narrated Vinton's own dystopic fantasy: immigrant voters would build a welfare state that would weaken "individual initiative" and national resolve and give the imagined Chinese an opportunity to invade and enslave America.[*]

At the turn of the twentieth century, Americans used the threat of China to argue against each other. Free-trade Republicans attacked protectionist Democrats as akin to those Chinese who sought to close themselves and their country off from the world. Democrats seeking white working-class votes depicted the Republicans as seeking to turn American laborers into robotic Chinese Coolie slaves.[†] The staying power of such rhetoric helps us see beyond today's supposedly common-sense logic of the threat from China. In Vinton's time China was wrought with internal division and was about to be carved up into quasi-colonial spheres of interest by the Europeans, Japanese, and Americans, not the other way around. This geo-political situation gave Vinton's invasion fantasy an air of absurdity, and the similarities between his story and the Koch PAC ad help us see the long, but unacknowledged, tradition of the Chinese Threat as a politicized trope, not an assessment of reality.

---

[*] Arthur Dudly Vinton, *Looking Further Backward* (Albany, NY: Albany Book Co., 1890), 31, 93.
[†] Michael Hunt, *The Making of a Special Relationship: The United States and China to 1914* (New York: Columbia University Press, 1983).

Jasbir Puar and Amit Rai, "Monster, Terrorist, Fag" (2002)[30]

The terrifying and traumatic attacks of September 11, 2001, provoked a quest for meaning among many Americans. Jasbir Puar and Amit Rai analyze how the figure of the terrorist, developed to make sense of those events, relied upon and bolstered broader cultural constructs of "normalcy" that shaped official and popular understanding. While many asserted that 9/11 "changed everything," in the wake of the attacks, conservative commentators used the confusion and despair to assert a "traditional" martial masculinity against purportedly discredited "feminism." At the level of formal politics, the shock of the attacks justified the rapid enactment of controversial economic, military, and domestic surveillance policies with little discussion. "Common sense" approaches reduced the complicated and vexed geopolitical context of the attacks to a civilizational clash between American righteousness and those who "hate freedom."[31]

Sexuality is central to the creation of a certain knowledge of terrorism, specifically that branch of strategic analysis that has entered the academic mainstream as "terrorism studies." This knowledge has a history that ties the image of the modern terrorist to a much older figure, the racial and sexual monsters of the eighteenth and nineteenth centuries. Further, the construction of the pathologized psyche of the terrorist-monster enables the practices of normalization, which in today's context often means an aggressive heterosexual patriotism …

To begin, let us consider the monster. Why, in what way, has monstrosity come to organize the discourse on terrorism? First, we could merely glance at the language used by the dominant media in its interested depictions of Islamic militancy. So, as an article in the *New York Times* points out, "Osama bin Laden, according to Fox News Channel anchors, analysts and correspondents, is 'a dirtbag,' 'a monster' overseeing a 'web of hate.' His followers in Al Qaeda are 'terror goons.' Taliban fighters are 'diabolical' and 'henchmen.' "* Or, in another Web article, we read: "It is important to realize that the Taliban does not simply tolerate the presence of bin Laden and his terrorist training camps in Afghanistan. It is part and parcel of the

---

* Jim Rutenberg, "Fox Portrays a War of Good and Evil, and Many Applaud," *New York Times*, December 3, 2001.

same evil alliance. Al-Qa'ida and the Taliban are two different heads of the same monster, and they share the same fanatical obsession: imposing a strict and distorted brand of Islam on all Muslims and bringing death to all who oppose him"* ...

Foucault tied monstrosity to sexuality through specific analyses of the deployment of gendered bodies, the regulation of proper desires, the manipulation of domestic spaces, and the taxonomy of sexual acts such as sodomy. As such, the sexualized monster was that figure that called forth a form of juridical power but one that was tied to multiform apparatuses of discipline as well.[†]

We use Foucault's concept of monstrosity to elaborate what we consider to be central to the present war on terrorism: monstrosity as a regulatory construct of modernity that imbricates not only sexuality, but also questions of culture and race. Before we tie these practices to contemporary politics, let us note two things: First, the monster is not merely an other; it is one category through which a multiform power operates. As such, discourses that would mobilize monstrosity as a screen for otherness are always also involved in circuits of normalizing power as well: the monster and the person to be corrected are close cousins. Second, if the monster is part of the West's family of abnormals, questions of race and sexuality will have always haunted its figuration. The category of monstrosity is also an implicit index of civilizational development and cultural adaptability. As the machines of war begin to narrow the choices and life chances people have here in America and in decidedly more bloody ways abroad, it seems a certain grid of civilizational progress organized by such keywords as "democracy," "freedom," and "humanity" have come to superintend the figure of the monster. We turn now to this double deployment of the discourse of monstrosity in "terrorism studies" ...

Counterterrorism is a form of racial, civilizational knowledge, but now also an academic discipline that is quite explicitly tied to the exercise of state power. This knowledge, moreover, takes the psyche as its privileged site of investigation. As [an] article in *Studies in Conflict and Terrorism* put it,

---

* Rand Green, "Taliban Rule in Afghanistan Is a Horrible Reign of Terror," September 24, 2001, www.perspicacityonline.com/109/Talibanrule10924.htm.

† Michel Foucault, "The Abnormals," trans. Robert Hurley, in *Ethics: Subjectivity and Truth*, ed. Paul Rainbow (New York: New Press, 1997), 51–2.

Models based on psychological concerns typically hold that "terrorist" violence is not so much a political instrument as an end in itself; it is not contingent on rational agency but is the result of compulsion or psychopathology. Over the years scholars of this persuasion have suggested that "terrorists" do what they do because of (variously and among other things) self-destructive urges, fantasies of cleanliness, disturbed emotions combined with problems with authority and the Self, and inconsistent mothering.* ...

We should note how white mythologies such as "inconsistent mothering" (and hence the bad family structure apparently common in the East) are presented as psychological compulsions that effectively determine and fix the mind of the terrorist ...

What all these models and theories aim to show is how an otherwise normal individual becomes a murderous terrorist, and that process time and again is tied to the failure of the normal(ized) psyche. Indeed, an implicit but foundational supposition structures this entire discourse: the very notion of the normal psyche, which is in fact part of the West's own heterosexual family romance—a narrative space that relies on the normalized, even if perverse, domestic space of desire supposedly common in the West. Terrorism, in this discourse, is a symptom of the deviant psyche, the psyche gone awry, or the failed psyche; the terrorist enters this discourse as an absolute violation. So when Billy Collins (the 2001 poet laureate) asserted on National Public Radio immediately after September 11: "Now the U.S. has lost its virginity," he was underscoring this fraught relationship between (hetero) sexuality, normality, the nation, and the violations of terrorism.

Not surprisingly, then, coming out of this discourse, we find that another very common way of trying to psychologize the monster-terrorist is by positing a kind of failed heterosexuality. So we hear often the idea that sexually frustrated Muslim men are promised the heavenly reward of sixty, sixty-seven, or sometimes even seventy virgins if they are martyred in jihad. But As'ad Abu Khalil has argued, "In reality, political—not sexual—frustration constitutes the most important factor in motivating young men, or women, to engage in suicidal violence. The tendency to dwell on the sexual motives

---

* David Brennan et al., "Talking to 'Terrorists': Towards an Independent Analytical Framework for the Study of Violent Substate Activism," *Studies in Conflict and Terrorism* 24 (2001), 6.

of the suicide bombers belittles these sociopolitical causes."* Now of course, that is precisely what terrorism studies intends to do: to reduce complex social, historical, and political dynamics to various psychic causes rooted in childhood family dynamics. As if the Palestinian Intifada or the long, brutal war in Afghanistan can be simply boiled down to bad mothering or sexual frustration! In short, these explanatory models and frameworks function to (1) reduce complex histories of struggle, intervention, and (non)development to Western psychic models rooted in the bourgeois heterosexual family and its dynamics; (2) systematically exclude questions of political economy and the problems of cultural translation; and (3) attempt to master the fear, anxiety, and uncertainty of a form of political dissent by resorting to the banality of a taxonomy.

Our contention is that today the knowledge and form of power that is mobilized to analyze, taxonomize, psychologize, and defeat terrorism has a genealogical connection to the West's abnormals, and specifically those premodern monsters that Western civilization had seemed to bury and lay to rest long ago. The monsters that haunt the prose of contemporary counterterrorism emerge out of figures in the eighteenth and nineteenth centuries that have always been racialized, classed, and sexualized. The undesirable, the vagrant, the Gypsy, the savage, the Hottentot Venus, or the sexual depravity of the Oriental torrid zone shares a basic kinship with the terrorist-monster. As we know, in the twentieth century these disparate monsters became case studies, objects of ethnographies, and interesting psychological cases of degeneracy. The same Western, colonial modernity that created the psyche created the racial and sexual monster. In other words, what links the monster-terrorist to the figure of the individual to be corrected is first and foremost the racialized and deviant psyche ...

Posters that appeared in midtown Manhattan only days after the attacks show a turbaned caricature of bin Laden being anally penetrated by the Empire State Building. The legend beneath reads, "The Empire Strikes Back" or "So you like skyscrapers, huh, bitch?" Or think of the Web site where, with a series of weapons at your disposal, you can torture Osama bin Laden to death, the last torture being sodomy; or another Web site that

---

* As'ad Abu Khalil, "Sex and the Suicide Bomber," November 13, 2001, www.salon. com/sex/feature/2001/11/07/islam.

shows two pictures, one of bin Laden with a beard, and the other without—and the photo of him shaven turns out to be O. J. Simpson.* What these representations show, we believe, is that queerness as sexual deviancy is tied to the monstrous figure of the terrorist as a way to otherize and quarantine subjects classified as "terrorists," but also to normalize and discipline a population through these very monstrous figures.

Though much gender-dependent "black" humor describing the appropriate punishment for bin Laden focuses on the liberation of Afghan women (liberate Afghan women and send them to college or make bin Laden have a sex change operation and live in Afghanistan as a woman—deeply racist, sexist, and homophobic suggestions), this portrayal suggests something further still: American retaliation promises to emasculate bin Laden and turn him into a fag. This promise not only suggests that if you're not for the war, you're a fag, it also incites violence against queers and specifically queers of color. And indeed, there have been reports from community-based organizations throughout New York City that violent incidents against queers of color have increased. So on the one hand, the United States is being depicted as feminist and gay-safe by this comparison with Afghanistan, and on the other hand, the U.S. state, having experienced a castration and penetration of its capitalist masculinity, offers up narratives of emasculation as appropriate punishment for bin Laden, brown-skinned folks, and men in turbans …

Another historical memory must organize our practice. As we begin to unearth these historical and discursive reticulations, we must not lose sight of the shared histories of the West's abnormals. All of these examples, and more, function to delimit and contain the kinds of responses that LGBTQ (lesbian, gay, bisexual, transgender, queer) communities can articulate in response to September 11. If we are to practically resist the "war effort" and the Us/Them and "you're either with us or against us" rhetoric, we must disarticulate the ties between patriotism and cultural and sexual identity. We must pose questions that allow us to construct practical solidarities with domestic and international communities and movements.

---

* www.gzero.net/osamatron.html (link no longer active, but I found it here: www. newgrounds.com/portal/view/35844) and www.funblaze.com/media/osama/osama. shtml. Accessed March 2013.

6

The Coming War

"Why do they hate our freedoms?" "What have we done to deserve such terror?" These were the questions asked after the attack on the Twin Towers and the Pentagon in 2001. The following chapter illustrates how the inherited tradition of racialized fears, desires and identifications has skewed American conceptualizations of their role in the world since World War II.

After the 9/11 attacks, the Bush administration argued the inconceivable nature of the plot made it impossible to prevent. However, numerous news commentators, including former government officials. However, skeptically noted that techno-thriller pioneer Tom Clancy had depicted just such a spectacular attack in his popular 1994 future-war novel *Debt of Honor.* This collective reference to Clancy betrayed the place of yellow perilist fiction at the heart of U.S. foreign policy rhetoric.

In Clancy's novel, a Japanese kamikaze pilot flies a plane into the Capitol building, killing the nation's leaders, to avenge the U.S. atomic bombing of Hiroshima and Nagasaki. The eerie insistence that this plotline "predicted" the 9/11 attacks helped make sense of 9/11 as part of a discourse of civilizational clash between America and a barbarous East. Pundits repeatedly compared the 9/11 attacks to the Japanese "sneak attack" on Pearl Harbor, and many hoped such grizzly terrorism would catalyze naïve Americans into supporting another unequivocal fight against enemies of freedom.

The rapid appropriation of "Ground Zero"—the term for the epicenter of an atomic explosion—as the name for the destroyed World Trade Center further connected the 9/11 attacks to the "good war" against Japan, though of course in that war it was the good guys, not the Japanese, who dropped the atomic bombs. "Ground Zero" registered a collective sense of ambivalence about escalating cycles of violence and the terror of modern war, but also seemed to relieve America, now the victim, of any moral obligation to investigate its own role in fostering global conflict.[1] Instead of looking inward for answers, the Bush administration prepared Americans for yet another round of the apocalyptic contest of Good vs. Evil, us versus *them*. Untangling the history of American militarism between World War II and the War on Terror helps demonstrate the impact of multiple generations of yellow perilism in shaping American perception of global conflicts.

Today's military Orientalism continues the Cold War anti-Communist logic that preceded it. In fact, outside Europe the Cold War never ended. Instead, the Cold War in many ways extended the policies and rivalries of the earlier imperialist Great Game under new guises.[2] The U.S. never left the Pacific theater of World War II after occupying Japan, and technically the Korean War, which in many ways institutionalized U.S. Cold War policies, is still ongoing. State-sponsored popular understanding about the succession of American enemies and a refusal to think of the U.S. as an empire have blocked Americans from understanding the relationships between U.S. foreign policies and domestic policies. This chapter suggests how Yellow Peril fears promote an American culture of war-making.

This tradition blurs the line between fact and fantasy, policy and fiction. Clancy has been a darling of the U.S. military since the Naval Academy published his first novel, and his unprecedented access give his books an air of authenticity. In *Executive Orders* (1996), his sequel to *Debt of Honor*, Clancy channels the U.S. military's desperate grasping for a global enemy to define itself against after the fall of the Soviet Union. In this novel, China and India join to support the creation of an Iranian-Iraqi-led United Islamic Republic that stretches from Egypt to Bangladesh. If this scenario seems absurd given the political, economic, and religious divisions across that broad swath of Asia, famed political scientist and advisor to five U.S. presidents Samuel Huntington proposed just such a "realignment" in his influential *Clash of Civilizations and the Remaking of World Order* (1996). In that book Huntington argued that after the Cold War, transnational "cultural" units would replace the Cold War of superpowers. Huntington posited a crass set of arbitrary and ahistorical "civilizations" modeled after Blumenbach's early nineteenth-century classification of the "five races of mankind." Huntington even concluded his oft-cited book with a possible future-war vignette in which Hispanic immigration erodes American patriotism to the point where China feels secure in finally invading the U.S.

Such schemas of civilizational clash mask the actual power politics and contradictory alliances of U.S. empire building. During the late Cold War, the U.S. harnessed and fostered Islamic fundamentalism alongside support for brutal dictators in the Middle East as part of their fight against what President Ronald Reagan termed the "Evil Empire." U.S. leaders argued the Taliban were freedom fighters on par with America's Founding Fathers, and that brutal dictators like Saddam Hussein in Iraq and General Muhammad Zia in Pakistan were necessary to keep their local constituencies in line. When times changed, and these pawns were no longer necessary, some analysts claimed that such Oriental brutality was always antithetical to the American project. Civilizational clash became a new way to sell an old war.[3]

Like the imperial conflicts a century ago, belief in the U.S. as exceptional and detached from world events is the necessary precondition for accepting the logic of civilizational clash. *They* (not us) keep threatening our future because that's what *they* always do. Narratives excusing horrifying civilian death rates and the erosion of basic liberties in the name of preserving a way of life serve only to distance ourselves from our own complicity in such cycles of violence. The more we do that, the more we dehumanize our victims in order to defend our fantasies, the deeper our dependence upon such violence will become. With each turn of the cycle we forget the tragic lessons of the generations that came before. Dr. Martin Luther King Jr. summed up this situation in his speech announcing his opposition to the Vietnam War: "when machines and computers, profit motives and property rights, are considered more important than people, the giant triplets of racism, materialism, and militarism are incapable of being conquered."[4] But this time the war is real. This time we know what we're doing.

Jean-Paul Sartre's analysis of mid-century French anti-Semitism sheds light on America's foreign policy blinders today. Sartre argued that rooting all Jewish behavior in the supposedly immutable clannishness, deviousness, and jealousy of the Jewish "race" prevented anti-Semites from recognizing Jews as rational people who made strategic decisions from their own subject positions.[5] In America this has a long history. Self-proclaimed Anglo Americans have imagined that the ability to deliberate reasonably is their own precious racial superpower, and have tried to dismiss the political tumult of their times on the unrestrained passions of the horde. First, it was Southern and Eastern European left and labor activists that seemed excessively worked up. Then, misguided multiculturalists. Now, it's the Muslims, inheritors of that same Oriental blood, that seem overly upset about Western empire-building.

Osama bin Laden was not a new Fu Manchu. But there were many resonances. Both were reputed shadowy and elusive terrorist-masterminds organizing the world's hordes. They used underground networks to smuggle weapons through porous borders. Their fanatical and vengeful race hatred targeted civilizational progress and freedom. However, approaching foreign policy challenges as pulp novels doesn't make sense. And, as we know, it doesn't really work. This chapter lays out the recent history of yellow peril-ist fantasy to make manifest America and the West's collective tendency to uncritically support expansionist wars in different parts of Asia. By acknowledging this weakness, hopefully we can begin to move beyond it.

"Tomorrow" (1939)

Arthur Leo Zagat (1896–1949) wrote dozens of science fiction stories in various "pulp" magazines in the 1930s and 1940s. "Tomorrow," written before the German invasion of Poland sparked war in Europe, was the first in a series re-counting the future invasion and occupation of America by the "yellows." As the story unfolds we learn that the main character, Dikar, was born Dick Carr, but has suffered civilizational degeneration in the absence of parents and technology. Dikar hunts for food with a bow and arrow, wears animal skins, and lives in trees. He discovers that blacks under the direction of yellows have enslaved the whites of America into concentration camps. Dikar recovers memories of being evacuated to the forest while many others decided to kill themselves rather than live ruled by the invading yellows. "Dikar knew that the white-faced men and women were his people and this green land belonged to them and him, and that the black and yellow men were they whom the voice in his dream had said, 'have come out of the East to make this world a Hell,'" and he plots to retake his land.

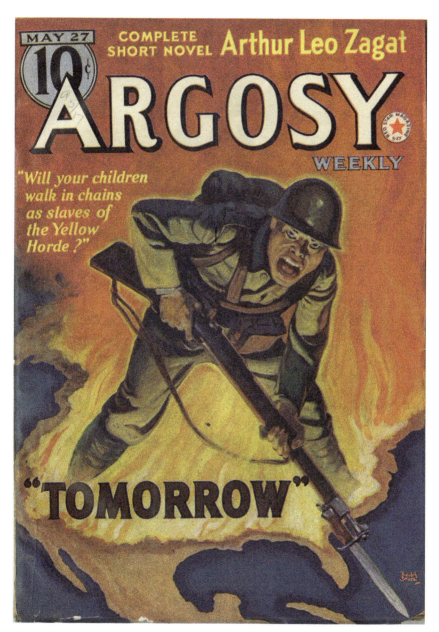

Figure 65. *Argosy* (May 27 1939). Yoshio Kishi/Irene Yah Ling Sun Collection of Asian Americana made possible in large part in memory of Dr. Wei Yu Chen, MSS 292, Series V, Box 17, folder 5. Fales Library and Special Collections, New York University.

"Is This Tomorrow?" (1947)

*Father Louis Gales's Catechetical Guild Educational Society of St. Paul,
Minnesota, distributed this comic as a public service to awake Americans to the
"menace of Communism" in their midst by depicting New York City Communist
Party members' plan for a coup. They create a front group, The League to Oppose
Intolerance, which secretly exacerbates class and religious divisions. They pose as
Catholics delivering fiery speeches against Jews and provoke race riots by planting white women to accuse African Americans of harassment. At the same time
they push workers to strike and support loyal politicians to capitalize on the
growing unrest. Then, they assassinate the president and use their influence to
gain control. Once in power, the Communists establish concentration camps for
Catholics, censor newspapers, and burn books. The comic warns, "The average
American is prone to say, 'It can't happen here.' Millions of people in other countries used to say the same thing. Today, they are dead."*

Figure 66. *Is This Tomorrow: America Under Communism!* (St. Paul, MN: Catechetical Guild Educational Society, 1947). Liturgy and Life Collection, John J.
Burns Library, Boston College.

John W. Dower, "Patterns of a Race War" (1986)[6]

While often described as "The Good War," World War II was a brutal affair in both Europe and the Pacific, yet with an important difference—Americans have historically been uncomfortable questioning the strategic decisions of the Pacific theater of the war, in particular the decision to use nuclear weapons against the Japanese city of Hiroshima on August 6 and then again on Nagasaki on August 9, 1945. John W. Dower was one of the first U.S. historians to investigate the role of race in the differences between U.S. military strategy in Europe and Asia.

World War II changed the face of the globe. It witnessed the rise and fall and rise again of empires—the swiftly shifting fortunes of the European powers and the Axis allies, the emergence of the American and Soviet super-powers—and no policymaker was unaware of the stakes involved. Control of territory, markets, natural resources, and other peoples always lay close to the heart of prewar and wartime planning. This was certainly true of the war in Asia, where nationalist aspirations for genuine liberation and inde-pendence met resistance from Europeans, Americans, and Japanese alike. In Asia, the global war became entangled with the legacies of Western impe-rialism and colonialism in a manner that proved explosive, not only at the time but for decades thereafter.

To scores of millions of participants, the war was also a race war. It exposed raw prejudices and was fueled by racial pride, arrogance, and rage on many sides. Ultimately, it brought about a revolution in racial con-sciousness throughout the world that continues to the present day ... The Germans pointed to the status of blacks in America as proof of the validity of their dogma as well as the hollowness of Allied attacks on Nazi beliefs. The Japanese, acutely sensitive to "color" issues from an entirely different perspective, exploited every display of racial conflict in the United States in their appeals to other Asians (while necessarily ignoring the white suprema-cism of their German ally). Racism within the Allied camp was, however, a volatile issue in and of itself regardless of what enemy propagandists said. Although only a few individuals spoke up on behalf of the persecuted Japanese Americans, both the oppression of blacks and the exclusion of Asian immi-grants became political issues in wartime America. Blacks raised questions about "fighting for the white folks," and called for "double victory" at home and abroad. Asians, especially Chinese and Indians, decried the humiliation of being allied to a country which deemed them unfit for citizenship; and for a full year in the midst of the war, the U.S. Congress debated the issue of revising the suddenly notorious Oriental exclusion laws. In such ways, World War II contributed immeasurably not only to a sharpened awareness of racism within the United States, but also to more radical demands and militant tactics on the part of the victims of discrimination.

This was equally true abroad, especially in Asia, where the Allied struggle against Japan exposed the racist underpinnings of the European and American colonial structure. Japan did not invade independent countries in southern Asia. It invaded colonial outposts which the Westerners had dominated for generations, taking absolutely for granted their racial and cultural superiority over their Asian subjects. Japan's belated emergence as a dominant power in Asia, culminating in the devastating "advance south" of 1941–42, challenged not just the Western presence but the entire mystique of white supremacism on which centuries of European and American expansion had rested. This was clear to all from an early date: to the Japanese; to the imperiled European and American colonials; and, not least, to the politically, economically, and culturally subjugated peoples of Asia.*

Japan's Pan-Asiatic slogans played upon these sentiments, and the favorable response of many Asians to the initial Japanese victories against the Americans, British, and Dutch intensified Western presentiments of an all-out race war in Asia … The Tokyo conference of November 1943 was designed to be an inspiring symbol of Pan-Asian idealism and the demise of white colonial rule in Asia; and although it was ultimately a hollow exercise, it fueled both Asian racial dreams and Western racial fears. Officials in the West took the rhetoric of Asian solidarity painfully to heart. During the first year of the war, for example, Admiral Ernest King worried about the repercussions of Japanese victories "among the non-white world" while Roosevelt's chief of staff Admiral William Leahy wrote in his diary about the fear that Japan might "succeed in combining most of the Asiatic peoples against the whites." William Phillips, Roosevelt's personal emissary to India

---

* Christopher Thorne, *Allies of a Kind: The United States, Britain, and the War Against Japan, 1941–1945* (New York: Oxford University Press, 1978); "Racial Aspects of the Far Eastern War, 1941–1945," *Proceedings of the British Academy* 66 (1980), 329–77.

in 1943, sent back deeply pessimistic reports about a rising "color consciousness" that seemed to be creating an insurmountable barrier between
Oriental and Occidental peoples. In March 1945, a month before he died,
President Roosevelt evoked in a negative way much the same image of Pan-
Asian solidarity that the Asian leaders had emphasized in Tokyo in 1943.
"1,100,000,000 potential enemies," the president told a confidant, "are
dangerous."*

The media in the West were frequently even more apocalyptic in their
expression of such fears. Thus, the Hearst newspapers declared the war in
Asia totally different from that in Europe, for Japan was a "racial menace" as
well as a cultural and religious one, and if it proved victorious in the Pacific
there would be "perpetual war between Oriental ideals and Occidental."
Popular writers described the war against Japan as "a holy war, a racial war
of greater significance than any the world has heretofore seen." Spokesmen
for the cause of China and a free Asia like Pearl Buck and Lin Yutang were
so appalled and alarmed by the way Westerners instinctively saw the fight
against Japan in sweeping racial terms that they warned of a Third World
War between whites and nonwhites within a generation† ...

Where the Western Allies were concerned, the visceral hatred of the
Japanese inevitably tapped Yellow Peril sentiments that, before the turn of
the century, had been directed mainly against the Chinese. The coarseness
and pervasiveness of plain anti-"yellow" race hate throughout the war is as
shocking in retrospect as is the popularity of simian imagery; but the Yellow
Peril sentiment was itself rooted in earlier centuries. The war words and race
words which so dominated the propaganda of Japan's white enemies—the
core imagery of apes, lesser men, primitives, children, madmen, and beings
who possessed special powers as well—have a pedigree in Western thought
that can be traced back to Aristotle, and were conspicuous in the earliest

---

* Thorne is excellent on these pervasive racial fears. For Admiral King, see Ernest
J. King and Walter Muir Whitehall, *Fleet Admiral King, A Naval Record* (New York:
W. W. Norton, 1952), 382. See also U.S. Department of State, *Foreign Relations of
the United States, 1943*, 4 (Washington, D.C.: Government Printing Office, 1964)
217–31; Ibid. *1945*, 6 (1968), 249–51.
† "Peril Exposed," *San Francisco Examiner*, January 25, 1943; Walter B. Clausen,
Blood for the Emperor: A Narrative History of the Human Side of the War in the Pacific
(New York: D. Appleton-Century, 1943).

encounters of Europeans with the black peoples of Africa and the Indians of the Western Hemisphere. The Japanese, so "unique" in the rhetoric of World War II, were actually saddled with racial stereotypes that Europeans and Americans had applied to nonwhites for centuries: during the conquest of the New World, the slave trade, the Indian wars in the United States, the agitation against Chinese immigrants in America, the colonization of Asia and Africa, the U.S. conquest of the Philippines at the turn of the century. These were stereotypes, moreover, which had been strongly reinforced by nineteenth-century Western science ...

It was a common observation among Western war correspondents that the fighting in the Pacific was more savage than in the European theater. Kill or be killed. No quarter, no surrender. Take no prisoners. Fight to the bitter end. These were everyday words in the combat areas, and in the final year of the war such attitudes contributed to an orgy of bloodletting that neither side could conceive of avoiding, even though by mid-1944 Japan's defeat was inevitable and plain to see. As World War II recedes in time and scholars dig at the formal documents, it is easy to forget the visceral emotions and sheer race hate that gripped virtually all participants in the war, at home and overseas, and influenced many actions and decisions at the time. Prejudice and racial stereotypes frequently distorted both Japanese and Allied evaluations of the enemy's intentions and capabilities. Race hate fed atrocities, and atrocities in turn fanned the fires of race hate. The dehumanization of the Other contributed immeasurably to the psychological distancing that facilitates killing, not only on the battlefield but also in the plans adopted by strategists far removed from the actual scene of combat. Such dehumanization, for example, surely facilitated the decisions to make civilian populations the targets of concentrated attack, whether by conventional or nuclear weapons. In countless ways, war words and race words came together in a manner which did not just reflect the savagery of the war, but contributed to it by reinforcing the impression of a truly Manichaean struggle between completely incompatible antagonists. The natural response to such a vision was an obsession with extermination on both sides—a war without mercy.

And yet, despite this, the two sides did have things in common, including not only race hate and martial fury but also battlefield courage and dreams of peace ... In the heat of war, such points of common ground were lost sight of and the behavior of the enemy was seen as unique and peculiarly odious, with the issue of atrocities playing an exceptionally large role in each side's perception of the other. Savage Japanese behavior in China and throughout Southeast Asia, as well as in the treatment of Allied prisoners, was offered as proof of the inherent barbarity of the enemy. In a similar way, the Japanese stimulated hatred of the Allies by publicizing grisly battlefield practices such as the collection of Japanese skulls and bones, and responded with profound self-righteousness to the terror bombing of Japanese civilians ... Such acts, and the propagandizing of them, became part of the vicious circle of war hates and race hates and contributed to the deaths of hundreds of thousands of individuals—millions, if the civilian deaths of the Japanese as well as other Asians are counted—long after Japan's defeat was a foregone conclusion ...

To a conspicuous degree, the racial and racist ways of thinking which had contributed so much to the ferociousness of the war were sublimated and transformed after August 1945. The merciless struggle for control of Asia and the Pacific gave way, in a remarkably short time, to an occupation in which mercy was indeed displayed by the conquerors, and generosity and goodwill characterized many of the actions of victor and vanquished alike. That vicious racial stereotypes were transformed, however, does not mean that they were dispelled. They remain latent, capable of being revived by both sides in times of crisis and tension. At the same time, these patterns of thinking also were transferred laterally and attached to the new enemies of the cold-war era: the Soviets and Chinese Communists, the Korean foe of the early 1950s, the Vietnamese enemy of the 1960s and 1970s, and hostile third-world movements in general. The patterns persist, even as specific circumstances change. They are only part of the picture, but still a telling and potentially tragic part.

Remember Pearl Harbor (1942)

Emily Rosenberg has argued that when the Japanese attacked Pearl Harbor on December 7, 1941, Americans had already been prepared to see war with Japan as a civilizational clash. The fear of a Japanese attack had been brewing for decades. But image-makers quickly placed this new conflict within a much broader tradition of Manifest Destiny—connecting the Mexican American War, Indian Wars, Spanish-Philippine-American War, and the fight with Japan into one long progression of conflicts between brave individuals and treacherous hordes. Remember the Alamo! Remember Custer! Remember the Maine! Remember Pearl Harbor! Historicizing the already scary attacks exacerbated American anxieties, and hardened resolve, but also might account for the particular brutality of the war in the Pacific.[7]

Figure 67. *Remember Pearl Harbor* (New York: Street & Smith, 1942). Comic Art Collection, Special Collections, Michigan State University Libraries.

Rey Chow, "The Age of the World Target" (1998)[8]

The use of nuclear weapons and the embrace of Mutually Assured Destruction as a means of global stability profoundly shaped American culture. Historian Tom Engelhardt has argued that dropping the bomb provoked a profound national sense of unease about what he terms "victory culture" that still reverberates. Cultural critic Rey Chow wrote the essay excerpted here before the attacks on the World Trade Center, but her analysis helps frame Engelhardt's contention that naming the site of those attacks "Ground Zero," the name for the center of a nuclear explosion, as well as the fabricated threat of Iraq's weapons of mass destruction taking the form of a "mushroom cloud" over a U.S. city, illustrates how America's unresolved relationship to the destructive power of the military still animates national culture.[9]

For most people who know something about the United States' intervention in the Second World War, there is one image that predominates and seemingly preempts the rest: the dropping of the atomic bomb on Hiroshima and Nagasaki, pictorialized in the now familiar image of the mushroom cloud, with effects of radiation and devastation of human life at a scale never before imaginable.[*] Alternatively, we can also say that our knowledge about what happened to Hiroshima and Nagasaki is inseparable from the image of the mushroom cloud. As knowledge, "Hiroshima" and "Nagasaki" come to us inevitably as representation and, specifically, as a picture. Moreover, it is not a picture in the older sense of a mimetic replication of reality; rather it has become in itself a sign of terror, a kind of gigantic demonstration with us, the spectators, as the potential target …

In a well-known essay, "The Age of the World Picture," Martin Heidegger argues that in the age of modern technology, the world has become a "world picture." However, he adds, this "does not mean a picture of the world but the world conceived and grasped as a picture."[†] By this, Heidegger means

---

[*] For an account of the immediate consequences of the dropping of the bombs in Hiroshima, see John Hersey, *Hiroshima* (New York: Alfred A. Knopf, 1946). For accounts of the censorship of information about the atomic bomb in the aftermath of the Second World War, see Monica Braw, *The Atomic Bomb Suppressed: American Censorship in Occupied Japan* (Armonk, NY: M. E. Sharpe, 1991).

[†] Martin Heidegger, *The Question Concerning Technology and Other Essays*, trans. William Lovitt (New York: Harper Colophon Books, 1977).

that seeing and objectification have become so indispensable in the age of modern technology that understanding—"conceiving" and "grasping" the world—is now an act inseparable from visuality. Supplementing Heidegger, we may say that in the age of bombing, the world has been transformed into—is essentially conceived and grasped as—a target. To conceive of the world as a target is to conceive of it as an object to be destroyed ...

Among the most important elements in war, writes Karl von Clausewitz, are the "moral elements."* From the U.S. point of view, this phrase does not seem at all ironic. The bombings of Hiroshima and Nagasaki, for instance, were considered pacific acts, acts that were meant to save lives, and save civilization in a world threatened by German Nazism. (Though, by the time the bombs were dropped in Japan, Germany had already surrendered.) Even today, some of the most educated, scientifically knowledgeable members of U.S. society continue to believe that the atomic bomb was the best way to terminate the hostilities.† And, while the media in the United States are quick to join the media elsewhere in reporting the controversies over Japan's refusal to apologize for its war crimes in Asia or over France's belatedness in apologizing for the Vichy government's persecution of the Jews, no U.S. head of state has ever visited Hiroshima or Nagasaki or expressed regret for the nuclear holocaust.‡ In this—the perpetual conviction and self-legitimation of its own superiority, leadership, and moral virtue—lies perhaps the most deeply ingrained connection between the dropping of the atomic bombs and the foundation myth of the United States as a nation, as well as all its subsequent interventions in nationalist struggles in Asia, Latin America, and the Middle East.

In the decades since 1945, whether in dealing with the Soviet Union, the People's Republic of China, Korea, Vietnam, countries in Central America, or during the Gulf War, the United States has been conducting war on the

---

* Karl von Clausewitz, *On War*, eds. and trans. Michael Howard and Peter Paret (Princeton, NJ: Princeton University Press, 1976).

† Ian Buruma, *The Wages of Guilt: Memories of War in Germany and Japan* (New York: Farrar, Straus, Giroux, 1993), 105. See also Mary Palevsky Granados, "The Bomb 50 Years Later: The Tough Question Will Always Remain," *Los Angeles Times Magazine*, June 25, 1995, 10–11.

‡ Robert Jay Lifton and Greg Mitchell, *Hiroshima in America: Fifty Years of Denial* (New York: Grosset/Putnam, 1995), 211–22.

basis of a certain kind of knowledge production and producing knowledge on the basis of war. War and knowledge enable and foster each other primarily through the collective fantasizing of some "foreign" or "alien" body, usually communist or Muslim that poses danger to the "self" and to the "eye" that is the nation. Once the monstrosity of this foreign body is firmly established in the national consciousness, the United States feels it has no choice but war.* War, then, is acted out as a moral *obligation* to expel an imagined dangerous otherness from the United States' self-conception as the global custodian of freedom and democracy. Put in a different way, the "moral element," insofar as it produces knowledge about the "self" and "other"—and hence "eye" and "target"—as such, justifies war by its very logic. Conversely, the violence of war, once begun, fixes the other in its attributed monstrosity and confirms the idealized image of the self.

As in the scenario of aerial bombing, the elitist and aggressive panoramic "vision" in which the other is beheld means that the sufferings of the other matter much less than the transcendent aspirations of the self. And, despite being the products of a particular culture's technological fanaticism, such transcendent aspirations are typically expressed in the form of selfless universalisms. As [Michael] Sherry puts it, "The reality of Hiroshima and Nagasaki seemed less important than the bomb's effect on 'mankind's destiny,' on 'humanity's choice,' on 'what is happening to men's minds,' and on hopes (now often extravagantly revived) to achieve world government."[†]

Once the relations between war, racism, and knowledge production are underlined in these terms, it would no longer be possible to assume, as many still do, that the recognizable features of modern war—its impersonality, coercion, and deliberate cruelty—are "divergences" from the "antipathy" to violence and to conflict that characterize the modern world.[‡] Instead, it would be incumbent upon us to realize that the pursuit of war—with its use of violence—and the pursuit of peace—with its cultivation of knowledge—are the obverse and the reverse of the same coin, the coin that I have

---

* Jacqueline Rose, *Why War?—Psychoanalysis, Politics, and the Return to Melanie Klein* (Cambridge, MA: Blackwell, 1993), 15–40.

† Michael Sherry, *The Rise of American Air Power: The Creation of Armageddon* (New Haven, CT: Yale University Press, 1987), 351.

‡ See, for instance, the discussion of the "inhuman face of war" in John Keegan, *The Face of Battle* (London: Jonathan Cape, 1976), 319–34.

been calling "the age of the world target." Rather than being irreconcilable opposites, war and peace are coexisting, collaborative functions in the continuum of a virtualized world …

As long as knowledge is produced in a self-referential manner, as a circuit of targeting or *getting* the other that ultimately consolidates the omnipotence and omnipresence of the "self" and the "eye" that is the United States, the other will have no choice but to remain just that—a target whose existence justifies only one thing, its destruction by the bomber. As long as the focus of our study of Asia remains the United States, and as long as this focus is not accompanied by knowledge of what is simultaneously happening elsewhere, such study would ultimately confirm once again the already self-referential function of virtual worlding that was unleashed by the dropping of the atomic bomb, with the United States always being the bomber and the other cultures being the military and information target fields …

The truth of the continual targeting of the world as a fundamental form of knowledge production is, as I already suggested, xenophobia, the inability to handle the otherness of the other beyond the orbit of the bomber's own visual path. For the xenophobe, every effort must be made to sustain and secure this orbit—that is, by keeping the place of the other-as-target always filled. Hence, with the end of the Cold War and the disappearance of the Soviet Union, the United States, by necessity seeks other substitutes for war. As it has often been pointed out, drugs, poverty, and illegal immigrants have since become the new targets. Like the communists and the Muslims, drugs, poverty, and illegal immigrants now occupy the place of that ultimate danger which must be "deterred" at all costs.

Even then, xenophobia can still backfire. When the anxiety about the U.S. loss of control over its own target fields—and by implication its own boundaries—becomes overwhelming, bombing takes as its target the United States itself. This is because, we remember, bombing the other was the means to end the war, the violence to stop violence, and, most important of all, the method to confirm moral virtue. Why, then, when the United States is perceived to be threatened and weakened by incompetent leadership, should bombing not be the technique of choice for correcting the United States itself? And so, in spite of all the racist conspiracy suspicions about "foreigners," it was U.S. minutemen who were revealed to have been, apparently, the bombers of the federal office building in Oklahoma City on

April 19, 1995. Spurred by a moral determination to set things right, the targeting of "others" turned into the targeting of innocent American men, women, and children, with a violence that erupted from within the heart of the country. The worst domestic terrorist incident in U.S. history, the bombing of Oklahoma City, took place with the force of an emblem. The vicious circle of "the world as target" had returned to its point of origin.*

William Pietz, "Orientalist Totalitarianism" (1988)[10]

The rhetoric of "Oriental Despotism" accompanying the nineteenth-century anti-Chinese movement and twentieth-century critiques of Japan also shaped how Americans understood the "unfreedom" of Russian culture and Soviet Communism. This "East versus West" framing helped define American notions of freedom as freedom of expression, and made the Manichean logic of the Cold War easy to understand.

The idea of totalitarianism is the theoretical anchor of cold war discourse. As such, its abstract conceptual core—that of a society in which all arrangements are directly administered through state institutions—becomes secondary to its expression of the concrete, historical idea that communism and fascism are the same thing, and that they—or rather it—represent a fundamentally new political phenomenon … American Cold War discourse about totalitarianism served a double function: in regard to the Soviets, it justified a policy of global anti-communism by reinterpreting all struggles for national self-determination in terms of the geopolitical contest for zones of power against totalitarian Russia (thereby also rejecting the case for a continuation of the British colonial empire made by Churchill in his famous "Iron Curtain" speech in favor of a non-colonial "Pax Americana"); in regard to Nazi Germany, it saved the traditional prewar faith concerning "the values of Western civilization" held by post-war foreign-policy "wise men"†

---

* See the exclusive prison interview with the prime suspect, Timothy McVeigh, in David H. Hackworth and Peter Annin, "The Suspect Speaks Out," *Newsweek*, July 3, 1995, 23–6.

† For the cultural presuppositions of key proponents of containment policy, whose clean Eurocentric spheres-of-power logic ultimately bogged down and disintegrated

by displacing the human essence of fascism into the non-Western world …

The basic argument is that "totalitarianism" is nothing other than traditional Oriental despotism plus modern police technology. The appearance of the first truly totalitarian state in the heart of Europe was thus an accident, explainable by the fact that the technology permitting totalitarianism was invented by Western science and was thus first accessible in the West. Moreover, Germany's totalitarian moment is characterized by [George] Kennan as a "relapse" into barbarism; far from showing a flaw in Western culture, it proved the need for constant alertness in preserving our distinctly Western values.

These interpretive moves are evident in Kennan's two key tests of the time: his famous secret cable from Moscow in February, 1946, in which he formulated the policy of containment which within the next year became the basis of official U.S. policy as expressed in the Truman Doctrine;* and his anonymous 1947 article in *Foreign Affairs*, which was the most articulate justification of the new commitment to a Cold War policy, a policy which programmatically ruled out the very possibility of dialogue and negotiation with the Soviets. In both the cable and his essay, Kennan supported his argument by pointing to what he called "the natural outlook of the Russian people." "At [the] bottom of [the] Kremlin's neurotic view of world affairs," Kennan's cable states, "is [the] traditional and instinctive Russian sense of insecurity." Kennan goes on to characterize Russian psychology (which he views as the basis of Russian policy) in terms Edward Said has taught us to recognize as the colonialist language of Orientalist. "The natural and instinctive urges of the Russian rulers," argues Kennan, cause the Russian government to be pervaded by an "atmosphere of oriental secretiveness and conspiracy."† …

---

in the Third World mire of Vietnam, see the early chapters of Walter Isaacson and Evan Thomas, *The Wise Men: Six Friends and the World They Made* (New York: Simon and Schuster, 1986).

* See Barton J. Bernstein, "American Foreign Policy and the Origins of the Cold War" in *Politics and Policies of the Truman Administration*, ed. Barton J. Bernstein (Chicago: Quadrangle Books, 1970), 53–5.

† "Kennan's Cable on Containment," in *The Truman Administration: A Documentary History*, eds. Barton J. Bernstein and Allen J. Matusow (New York: Harper and Row, 1966), 200, 202, 203.

It is the notion of ideology that permits Kennan to link modern totalitarianism with the traditional Oriental psyche, with its alleged neurotic
sense of insecurity and lack of faith in human dignity. Kennan explains
that in "Marxist dogma" the Russians had found "a perfect vehicle for the
sense of insecurity"* which he earlier proposed as the central characteristic
of the Russian-Asiatic mind. Kennan, and Cold War ideologues in general,
justified a policy based on the rejection of the very possibility of communication, negotiation, and compromise with communist totalitarians by
presenting a double picture of the way the Russian-Oriental mind corrupts
the very process of truthful language and reason by embracing an ideology which panders to their neurotic insecurity. On the one hand, Kennan
writes that Russian communists are completely hypocritical, using Marxism
merely as "the fig leaf of their moral and intellectual respectability."† Any
use of rational thought or principled justification is merely the cover for
an irrationally paranoid and immoral pragmatism which has no allegiance
to reason and honesty. But at the same time, according to Kennan, they
follow absolutely the logic and dictates of Marxist dogma. "Like the white
dog before the phonograph," Kennan writes, "they hear only the 'master's
voice.' "‡

Thus communist totalitarians are doubly irrational and untrustworthy:
they are irrational in their hypocritical, nihilistic pragmatism, which makes
rational speech a mere vehicle for hidden, irrational motives; and they are
irrational in their blind obedience to the logic of Marxist ideology, which
makes rational speech the vehicle of overrationalistic motives detached from
pragmatic reality. Totalitarian irrationality is thus simultaneously subrational and hyper-rational. Kennan explains the possibility of this paradox
by appealing to the Russian-Oriental capacity for denial and detachment
from the real world, which permits a kind of "self-hypnotism":§

---

* "Kennan's Cable on Containment," 202.
† Ibid., 202.
‡ George Kennan, "The Sources of Soviet Conduct," *Foreign Affairs*, 25, no. 4 (July,
1947), 574.
§ "Kennan's Cable on Containment," 203. In "The Sources of Soviet Conduct,"
Kennan speaks of the "Russian capacity for self-delusion," 580.

The very disrespect of Russians for objective truth—indeed their disbelief in
its existence—leads them to view all stated facts as instruments for further-
ance of one ulterior purpose or another.*

This ultimate explanation of the psychological ground of totalitarianism
and ultimate justification of Cold War policy by appealing to an apparently unprecedented (and yet all too familiar) capacity for irrationality and
contradiction in the communist-Oriental mind based on a lack of all sense
of the truth of objective reality is not peculiar to Kennan, but rather is
characteristic of the other great forgers of the Cold War discourse about
totalitarianism ...

In 1942, [Arthur] Koestler published an essay in *Horizon* magazine
entitled "The Yogi and the Commissar," which later became the title for a
popular collection of his essays published in 1947.† It was Koestler's constant thesis that the non-Western, non-civilized, non-democratic part of the
world could be viewed along a single "sociological spectrum" whose extreme
policies of social behavior were represented by the communist Commissar
(an activist who believes that his revolutionary end justifies even the most
immoral means) and the mystical Yogi (a totally passive type who doubts
all ends and thinks that means alone count) ... Either the Yogi abandons
logical, non-contradictory thought in favor of direct mystical experience and
irrational poetic language, or the Commissar becomes a hyper-rationalistic
puppet of ideology, abandoning his capacity for reality-testing. Either way
there is a loss of connection with what Koestler is pleased to call "objective
reality." Like Kennan, Koestler finds at the root of non-Western psychology
"the feeling of insecurity."‡

In some essays, Koestler makes his point about the self-contradicting, "ide-
ologized" nature of all non-Western thought by proclaiming the uniqueness
of the Western "scientific" mentality. Here he appeals to the anthropologist,
who is to the colonialist discourse about "primitives" what the Orientalist is
to the discourse about "Orientals." In "Anatomy of a Myth," Koestler seeks

---

* Ibid., 202.
† Arthur Koestler, *The Yogi and the Commissar, and Other Essays* (New York:
MacMillan, 1947).
‡ Ibid., 219.

to explain "the magic aura of the Soviet myth."[*] Koestler (appealing also to the science of psychology) posits that "the human mind is basically schizophrenic ... The hot stream of belief and the ice block of reason are packed together inside our skulls."[†] Koestler's primary example of the "socially approved split mind patterns" characteristic of all non-Western cultures is the fetishism of "the Primitive":

> The Primitive knows that his idol is a piece of carved wood, and yet believes in its power to make rain; and though our beliefs underwent a gradual refinement, the dualistic pattern of our minds remained basically unchanged.[‡]

Western science, Koestler argues, puts us for the first time beyond the split-mindedness normal to humans (though even for us, a relapse into pre-scientific "schizophrenia" is always possible, since this is an organic condition overcome only by the intellectual discipline unique to Western science). His innovation here is to map the familiar "magic versus science" argument of the human sciences, which functioned to distinguish Westerners from primitives, onto current political arguments seeking to distinguish "ideology" from the mode of political reasoning proper to those Cold War intellectuals who had arrived at "the end of ideology"[§] ...

[C]old War discourse mapped certain traditional Orientalist stereotypes onto the Russians (not only did this justify the practical policy of containment, but it contributed to a new theory of the neurotic psychological basis of all "ideology," that is, of all left political argument); in addition,

---

* Ibid., 129.

† Ibid., 117.

‡ Ibid.

§ In 1960 Koestler turned his dualizing analytic grid onto non-communist Asia alone; his book entitled *The Lotus and the Robot* (New York: Harper and Row, 1960), now finds the same polar extremes expressed in India (the lotus) and Japan (the robot), the sub-rational Yogi or the hyper-rational technocratic potential commissar. Writes Koestler: "Common to both [cultures] is a type of reasoning indifferent to the 'laws' of contradiction and excluded middle, to the distinction between subject and object, between the act of perception and the thing perceived ... an approach to Reality which is intuitive and a prioristic rather than rational and empirical, and relies on fluid analogies rather than well-defined concepts." (227)

primitivist stereotypes were used to explain the component of state-backed social terror so prominent in twentieth-century European history …

"[T]echnology," as the physical sign of "Progress," was essential to the myth of the West through which politicians and intellectuals alike understood themselves and their role in world history. Yet the unprecedented evil of the Nazi concentration camps, and of the Gestapo and the S.S. as police institutions, was characterized by the rational application of sophisticated Western technology. How to save the myth of the West, with its essential ideological component of "technology," in the face of Nazi Germany? The theory of totalitarianism, with its adoption of accepted colonialist "ideology" was the answer. Fascism and Nazism could be identified as examples of totalitarianism, whose Russian version revealed the unprecedented use of technologically sophisticated police terror by twentieth-century European states to be, in essence (that is, in its social and human truth) nothing but traditional Oriental despotism. In a complementary fashion, the new component in state terror of the radical and violent assault on subjectivity could be attributed to the savagery of "prehistoric" primitives. In this way, the ideology of "Western civilization" was preserved among Cold War intellectuals.

Dan Gilbert, "Why the Yellow Peril Has Turned Red!" (1951)[11]

Dan Gilbert (1911–1962) was an influential evangelical Christian writer who wrote a column for the monthly anti-Communist illustrated magazine The National Republican, *the director of the affiliated Christian Press Bureau, and the author of numerous books and pamphlets such as* Crucifying Christ in Our Colleges *(1933) and* The Conspiracy Against Chastity *(1939). The* National Republican *was edited by Walter S. Steele who provided research on radicals and subversives to government agencies and testified before the House Committee on Un-American Activities in favor of banning radical political parties. Like many anti-Communists in the McCarthy era, Gilbert saw "losing" China and the decision to pursue "limited" war in Korea as evidence of a corruption of national spiritual resolve. Gilbert regularly toured the country promoting his beliefs, and was an early advocate for General Douglas MacArthur's aborted presidential campaign after Truman dismissed him for insubordination.*

Then the sixth angel poured out his bowl on the great river Euphrates, and its water was dried up, so that the way of the kings from the east might be prepared. And I saw three unclean spirits like frogs coming out of the mouth of the dragon, out of the mouth of the beast, and out of the mouth of the false prophet. For they are spirits of demons, performing signs, which go out to the kings of the earth and of the whole world, to gather them to the battle of that great day of God Almighty. *Revelation 6:12–14*

In my book published ten years ago, on the YELLOW PERIL, I pointed out—on the basis of Bible Prophecy—the error of concentrating on Europe, and neglecting Asia. Billions upon billions of dollars have been poured into the "defense" of Europe, while even the pathetic trickle of help to anti-Communist forces in Asia was shut off. The Acheson State Department idea was, we were told, let Asia be "written off as a loss"—while Europe is fortified against the Red Tide. This was a monumental mistake.

Bible prophecy teaches that the Red advance in Europe will be POWERED FROM OUT OF ASIA. From out of Asia, the power of the North—Russia—will get the men and materials for the assault on southern and western Europe, and finally on Palestine itself. There can be no Soviet drive to the Holy Land, UNTIL ASIA IS SECURELY IN THE HOLLOW OF THE CLENCHED FIST OF THE BOLSHEVIK.

President Theodore Roosevelt sounded a warning against the "yellow peril." He was the friend of all Orientals. But he feared that out of the Orient would come a godless barbarian force that would sweep over so-called Christian civilization. He loved Asiatic peoples. But he feared the ignorance and cruelty and terrorism that flow forth from any people that know not Christ. Communism is an Asiatic theory of government. It grows out of heathenism and barbarism. Now that the "yellow peril" has turned *red,* it is a million times the menace that Theodore Roosevelt warned it might become ...

By the "yellow peril," we mean the organizing of Orientals into a force that seeks to destroy all white men from the face of the earth. In his famous conversation with the Japanese ambassador, Joseph Stalin said, "We Orientals must stick together." Stalin *is* an Asiatic. Part of Russia is in Europe—part is in Asia. There are *white Russians,* of course. But the Bolshevik element that rules identifies itself with the Orient—racially, politically, socially ...

Communism is anti-God. When Communism takes over, it simply means that the Devil takes over. Religious liberty is suppressed. The Bible becomes an outlawed Book. Christians are murdered. Churches are burned. The Bible instructs that in the last days, there shall be a "great falling away." Our Lord Jesus Christ said, "the love of many shall wax cold." In the Old Testament, we are told of a "famine for the Word of God." People shall grow cold and indifferent in their love for the Gospel. Many churches shall become dead—and lose their missionary vision.

Communism has swept over the Orient, because of this "falling away"; this failure to carry out the Great Commission: "go ye into all the world—and preach the Gospel to every creature." The churches of America could have sent hundreds of thousands of missionaries into Asia during the past half-century. Instead, they have sent a few hundred. Billions of dollars could have been spent in spreading the Gospel, instead of a paltry few hundred thousand ...

The "yellow peril" would destroy Christianity and Judaism, while establishing a pagan religion of *materialism*. Materialism is the basis of Bolshevism. God does not exist, said Karl Marx. Material things and material forces control the destiny of the world. The army of 200,000,000 men, described in Revelation, flows forth from the empire of the "yellow peril" which consists of people who "WORSHIP DEVILS, AND IDOLS OF GOLD, AND SILVER, AND BRASS, AND STONE, AND OF WOOD: WHICH NEITHER CAN SEE, NOR HEAR, NOR WALK." This is the religion of "pantheism"—which denies a personal God. *Pantheism* worships things, material things, rather than a Living God.

Confucianism—better spelled and pronounced *confusionism*—is still the dominant form of superstition in China. This "religion" is very much like that of *Shintoism* in Japan. While Christianity has made amazing progress in Japan since the war, millions are still the slave-subjects of the superstitions of *Shintoism*. All Oriental religions are cut from the same cloth and according to substantially the same pattern. Personality is denied any importance or reality. When an individual dies, his personality is lost. He is "merged" with material and non-personal forces and things. This is especially true of Buddhism. It is true of all the Asiatic religious cults. God is denied personality. God is thought of not as a Person, but as a *thing*. Some forms of pantheism make the material universe an object of worship. Others deify a blind material force.

Even by hairsplitting, it is impossible to discover any important difference between the materialism of Marxian Communism and the superstitions of the Oriental religions. It is true, of course, that Marx put "scientific" labels upon his materialistic rantings. He announced his materialism as the product of a scientific age and scientific brain. But, boiled down, it is just age-old heathenism.

We are told in Revelation that the rampaging *Yellow Peril* will launch mass slaughters that will take the lives of one-third of the human race: the "third part of men" shall be killed. Amongst the survivors, this heathen cult shall be strong. There will be the large-scale worship of "devils, and idols of gold, and silver, and brass, and stone, and of wood: which neither can see, nor hear, nor walk." Of these doers of murder and the deeds of the devil, it is written, "Neither repented they of their murders, nor of their sorceries, nor of their fornication, nor of their thefts." Communism sanctions fornication, murder, sorcery, and theft.

There will be no turning back, let alone "repenting." The Yellow Peril will sweep on, reinforced by the Red Terror, to spread the deeds of the devil and the crimes of Communism all over the world. But, thank God, this onward sweep of evil *will be stopped* in God's own time. The Antichrist, and all the workers of iniquity, shall be dealt with by our Almighty Lord Himself. All that lives and moves under the banner of Satan's Wickedness shall be brought under the judgment described in II Thessalonians 2:8: "And then shall that wicked be revealed, whom the Lord shall consume with the sprit of His mouth, and shall destroy with the brightness of His coming."

Red China's Fighting Hordes (1952)

The Truman administration's decision to roll back the North Koreans past the 38th Parallel in November 1950 provoked the recently victorious Chinese People's Liberation Army into entering the Korean War. Although Truman privately acknowledged that he regretted exacerbating the situation in Korea, publically he depicted the Chinese Communists as the aggressors and claimed they were the "inheritors of Genghis Khan and Tamerlane, who were the greatest murderers in the history of the world." Newspapers across the nation ran headlines such as "Red Hordes Swarm South Korea!" as the Chinese pushed American troops back south. Popular press accounts claimed that the Chinese troops were mere cannon fodder, but their sheer numbers made them invincible. The following year, Lt. Col. Robert B. Rigg published his experiences and analysis of the "countless masses of uninformed robots" who had captured him in Korea, stating, "There is a sadism and brutality inherent in many Asiatics, that is not commonly found within men of the better educated areas of the world."[12]

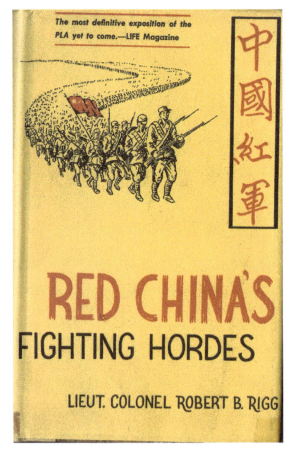

Figure 68. Lt. Col. Robert B. Rigg, *Red China's Fighting Hordes: A Realistic Account of the Chinese Communist Army, by a U.S. Army Officer* (Harrisburg, PA: Military Service Publishing Co., 1952). Courtesy of the Wong Ching Foo Collection.

Matthew Jacobson and Gasper Gonzales, "Orientalism and Brainwashing in *The Manchurian Candidate*" (2006)[13]

The Manchurian Candidate (1962), directed by John Frankenheimer and starring Frank Sinatra, premiered during the Cuban Missile Crisis, the closest the U.S. and the Soviet Union ever came to war. In the widely popular film, adapted from a novel of the same title by Richard Condon, Communists brainwash American soldiers captured during the Korean War to assassinate a presidential candidate and manipulate the U.S. political process. The CIA was so sure that Soviet mind-control plots explained the popularity of Communism that they began to fund research and propaganda promoting the tenets of capitalism.[14]

The Manchurian Candidate and the war it presumes to depict were produced during a period of especially heightened Orientalist concern. As Harold Isaacs wrote in the wake of the Korean War and on the eve of Vietnam, "Asia has become important above all because it has become dangerous. For most of those to whom Asia is newly discovered, a strong feeling of uneasiness, apprehension, or imminent peril overhangs all the immensity, complexity, unintelligibility of it." (One might be inclined to flip the argument here, attributing Asia's "danger" to its "importance" rather than vice versa; but the general marriage of import and danger still holds.) Although newsman Eric Sevareid underscored the enduring continuities of the "Oriental" character—"The Chinese Reds did not invent official Chinese indifference to human life ..."—still such images took on new meanings and achieved a new degree of menace in the years between the war in the Pacific and the Cold War engagements in Korea and Vietnam.[*]

Pearl Harbor, of course, inaugurated neither the brutal anti-Asian imagery nor the brutal military tactics that would characterize U.S. efforts in Japan, Korea, and Vietnam: in America's first land war in Asia, the oft forgotten Philippine-American War (1899–1902), one field general had promised to reduce the entire province of Samar to a "howling wilderness," and he advocated killing as combatants all *Filipinos over the age of ten.*

---

[*] Harold Isaacs, *Scratches on Our Minds: American Views of China and India* (Armonk, NY: M.E. Sharpe, 1980 [1958]), 55, 105.

"It is not civilized warfare, but we are not dealing with a civilized people," one Philadelphia paper had explained. "The only thing they know and fear is force, violence, and brutality, and we give it to them." Our brutality is attributable to *them,* in other words; they are nothing like us—never the twain shall meet. Estimates of the Filipino death toll in this forgotten war range upwards of 220,000.*

But by the mid-twentieth century, when the United States had become more thoroughly integrated into the global system on the terms of a major economic and military power, analogues would multiply. In Japan, the fire-bombing of Tokyo (in which nearly a hundred thousand civilians in a sixteen-square-mile area were "scorched and boiled and baked to death," in Major General Curtis LeMay's words) and the atomic bombing of Hiroshima and Nagasaki raised the specter of "total war" to levels undreamed of by previous generations.† In Korea, where Americans resisted the nuclear temptation, the unleashing of napalm and the intentional bombing of northern dams nonetheless resulted in the remarkable civilian death toll of two million (the civilian-to-soldier kill ratio, which had been 40 percent in World War II, was 70 percent in Korea).‡ And the Vietnam War—from systematic U.S. search-and-destroy missions, "Zippo raids," and carpet bombings, to aberrations such as My Lai—has been famously summed up in phrases like "We had to destroy the village in order to save it," or "Then the village, which was no longer a village, was our village." The United States destroyed thousands of villages and hamlets, twenty-five million acres of farmland, twelve million acres of forest, and 1.5 million farm animals.

---

* Matthew Frye Jacobson, *Barbarian Virtues: The United States Encounters Foreign Peoples at Home and Abroad, 1876–1917* (New York: Hill and Wang, 2000), 243–7; Stuart Creighton Miller, *Benevolent Assimilation: The American Conquest of the Philippines, 1899–1903* (New Haven, CT: Yale University Press, 1982), 220, 230. [Orientalism's most famous jingle employs the refrain, "East is East and West is West, and never the twain shall meet." Rudyard Kipling, "The Ballad of East and West," *Rudyard Kipling: Complete Verse* (New York: Anchor, 1988), 233.]

† John Dower, *War Without Mercy: Race and Power in the Pacific War* (New York: Pantheon Books, 1986), 40–1.

‡ Bruce Cummings, *Korea's Place in the Sun: A Modern History* (New York: W. W. Norton, 1997), 289–90 and *Parallax Visions: Making Sense of American-East Asian Relations* (Durham, NC: Duke University Press, 2002), 64.

The war also left in its wake more than 879,000 orphans and one million widows*...

All of these mid-century military operations were carried out amid a pervasive and fairly casual American discourse of Asian treacheries and short-comings. The Japanese were "vermin," "lice," "monkey-men," "cockroaches or mice," "vipers," a "yellow serpent," "a veritable human beehive or anthill," whose total "extermination" or "annihilation" was consistently favored by some 10 to 13 percent of the U.S. population when polled.† The Koreans were "yellow bastards," "apes," and "gooks" who "scorn all the rules of civi-lized warfare." By "occidental standards," according to one military report in 1945, "Koreans are not ready for independence"; and a CIA personality study of Syngman Rhee, the United States' handpicked *ally*, concluded that his behavior was "irrational and even childish."‡ The Vietnamese, too, were "little yellow bastards," "gooks," "slopes," and "slants" who did not "value human life" ...

In representing the "Oriental" enemy of the Korean 1950s for an American audience at the dawn of the Vietnam era, then, *The Manchurian Candidate* could not exactly claim political innocence or detachment ... In terms of both its overarching Orientalism and its ideological work on the Korean War, one of the film's most significant but easily overlooked scenes is the opening sequence at a Korean brothel. After the opening legend, "Korea 1952," two soldiers whom we will later know as Raymond Shaw and Bennett Marco pull up in a military truck and park in front of a small, poorly lit clapboard building, Miss Gertrude's. Marco remains in the truck, smoking and reading, while Shaw gets out and enters the building. Once inside, we hear the blare of a jazz record and the muffled, inarticulate hubbub of some kind of party; Shaw makes his way past a disheveled couple who have come into the entry hall from a side room (obviously a bedroom), and now pause, necking in the hallway, as Shaw passes. He slides open an Oriental screen to reveal a smoky room full of revelers—uniformed (but partly undressed) American soldiers, and Asian women in various suggestive states of attire ...

* Marilyn Young, *The Vietnam Wars, 1945–1990* (New York: Harper, 1991), 301–2; Gabriel Kolko, *Anatomy of War: Vietnam, the United States, and the Modern Historical Experience* (New York: Pantheon Books, 1985), 200.

† Dower, *War Without Mercy*, 53–4, 78, 80, 83, 161, 182, 185.

‡ Cummings, *Korea's Place in the Sun*, 271, 287, 198, 215.

Among the structuring dualisms that Edward Said attributed to Orientalist thinking was that of a masculine West and a feminine Orient—indeed, this might be said to be the founding dualism of them all: "the Orient was routinely described as feminine, its riches as fertile, its main symbols the sensual woman, the harem and the despotic—but curiously attractive—ruler."* The implication of this sensual notion is profound, and it is twofold. First, East-West economic or geopolitical relations are scripted as an encounter whose "natural" systems of dominance and submission borrow their authority from the "natural" order of patriarchal sexual relations. East and West are made for each other, just like the "opposite sexes." The West has the will to conquer, to possess; the East, no more than a will to *be possessed* (or, in the parlance of neocolonialism, to be "penetrated"). It is thus inevitable that the male/West will "have" the female/East, just as it is natural that, for the female/East, such possession will represent fulfillment itself. Second, then, the psychodrama of sexualized East-West relations is scripted back upon the living, breathing bodies of "Western" and "Oriental" people: the Asian woman (in this case Korean) *stands for* the submissive East, assuming in fantasy the image of the hyperfeminine-hypersubmissive-hypersexualized object—the geisha, the comfort woman, the concubine, the harem girl … Here, as elsewhere, the sexual availability and subservience of the Asian woman strangely "proves" the availability and subservience of Asia itself, and vice versa …

This Orientalist, sexualized opening gambit not only frames the U.S. presence in East Asia, but it provides the foundation for the film's ensuing renditions of Oriental villainy. It is against the backdrop of the brothel's hospitality that, in the very next scene, we see Chunjin sell out "Cholly Company" and hand them over to the Sino-Soviet plotters. The visual cues of this next sequence are important and familiar—the inscrutable but seemingly trustworthy "native guide" leading the men across unfamiliar terrain; then, after their sacking, his handshake with an enemy officer and an almost leering mid-shot of Chunjin's duplicitous and self-satisfied face. The duplicity

* Quoted in Mathew Bernstein, "Introduction" in *Visions of the East: Orientalism in Film*, eds. Matthew Bernstein and Gayln Studlar (New Brunswick, NJ: Rutgers University Press, 1997), 3. For Korea specifically, see Katherine H. S. Moon, *Sex Among Allies: Military Prostitution in U.S.-Korea Relations* (New York: Columbia University Press, 1997).

here—like the sensuality of the Oriental woman—was ready-made in U.S. culture and already had thousands of well-known precedents, Fu Manchu, the white slaver, and Japanese Emperor Hirohito among them. But so does Frankenheimer's rendering of Chunjin's duplicity both depend on, and flow from, the sociopolitical equation established moments ago in the brothel. If there is any room at all to think of the Korean conflict as a civil war—if we are aware in the least of Koreans fighting Koreans for the soul and future of the nation—then Chunjin's treachery might read as, say, patriotism; one person's traitor is another's freedom fighter. But because the Koreans' affinity for, and lusty desires toward, America are already "known" in the film, Chunjin can only be serving Chinese and Soviet, not Korean, interests: he is not only a sellout to his American allies, but a turncoat to his country as well, a pattern of despicable political disloyalties that lie safely hidden behind his inscrutable Oriental eyes.

GIDRA

These two excerpts are from GIDRA, *an early Asian American Movement magazine published in Los Angeles. Norman Nakamura, himself a U.S. soldier who served in Vietnam, represented the growing antiwar movement that culminated in the 1971 Winter Soldier hearings sponsored by Vietnam Veterans Against the War in Detroit and later submitted to Congress. The brutality of the war in Vietnam led Nakamura and Evelyn Yoshimura to understand their own positions as Asian Americans as part of a global Third World Peoples' Movement. The Asian American critique Nakamura and Yoshimura helped develop connected racist stereotypes, discrimination, and social invisibility at home to imperialism and inhuman brutality abroad.[15]*

NORMAN NAKAMURA, "THE NATURE OF GI RACISM" (1970)[16]

One finds it hard not to sarcastically laugh when he hears that the United States is fighting in Vietnam to save and maintain the Vietnamese people, while many American GIs do not treat the Vietnamese as people but as animals. How can we be fighting and supporting a war when the very people who we are supposed to be helping by this costly action begin hating us because of the racist antagonisms of the U.S. soldier?

For some GIs in Vietnam, there are no Vietnamese people. To them the land is not populated by people but by "Gooks," considered inferior, unhuman animals by the racist-educated GI. Relieved in his mind of human responsibility by this grotesque stereotype, numerous barbarities have been committed against these Asian peoples since "they're only 'Gooks.'"

Out on the roads of Vietnam the GI more overtly exhibits antagonisms against the Vietnamese civilians, for there he is more or less free from the direct restraints of military control that exist in the main base camps. He also has the security in the knowledge that other GIs consider these people as "Gooks" and will not deal with him too severely if he should be caught antagonizing "Gooks." Furthermore, the GI does not seem to be subject to Vietnamese law, so any civilian's complaint would have to be executed through the U.S. military if he could identify his antagonizer and if he felt that justice would be done.

Throwing empty cans at children along the roadside is so common that GIs are told not to do this over the radio. Although they have been told otherwise, I have seen this more and more. Driving alongside Vietnamese on motorcycles to either hit them on the head or steal their hats is a daily practice of a courier on Q.L.13. Having acquired tear gas canisters for his grenade launcher, one officer shot tear gas into a group of Vietnamese as he drove through their village during a non-military action. He also shot tear gas into a Lambretta mini-bus filled with civilians. Obscene gestures and phrases are also hurled at the Vietnamese along the roads, especially at any Vietnamese girl, for many GIs believe that all Vietnamese women are whores. Meaningless petty thefts by GIs also occur on the roads. One GI in his dump truck asked a roadside seller to hand her tray of miscellaneous goods up to him for close examination. When she did this, he took off with everything without paying her a cent. In a group effort, some GIs surrounded a roadside seller and kept her busy by examining various products. While she was looking at one GI, the others would slip some of her goods into their pockets. In both of these cases, the thefts were not done out of need but were done to play a clever trick on a "Gook."

Unfortunately, some GIs get malevolent on the roads. One GI threw a piece of lumber into the windshield of a moving Vietnamese bus from his vehicle for no apparent reason. Some GI drivers recklessly drive at high speeds, running motor scooters and ox carts off the road. Furthermore, they drive this way through villages, which have no signals so that the civilians in these villages must be cautious. The regard for these people is so low that in Lai Khe Base Camp you may hear a driver say to a new driver that it is better to run over a "Gook" than a chicken, because when you kill a chicken, you have to pay for the number of eggs that this chicken would have layed in a year. I saw a Vietnamese mother in the road through her village squatting in front of a small object covered with a gunny sack covered in a pool of blood; she had her face covered with her hands and was rocking back and forth crying. Upon seeing the driver of the murder vehicle with an expression of guilt and horror on his face, I am sure that he would have rather killed a chicken.

For no apparent reason, a child was shot to death and another wounded by a drunken American GI In Lai Khe Base Camp on day tower guard duty. In no way could one interpret the actions of these Vietnamese children as hostile. The soldier, who had spent at least eleven months in Vietnam as an engineer in a construction engineer unit, was not a combat fatigued soldier. Had there not been a stereotype that pictured Vietnamese to be inferior, unhuman animals, this and other atrocities in Vietnam would not have happened. I do not believe that this drunken soldier actually felt he was shooting at human beings; he was "only shooting at 'Gooks' " ...

"You can't trust a 'Gook' " is a common expression among GIs. During the GI's Vietnam orientation training, he is told by the Army not to trust any Vietnamese, because any one of them may be a Viet Cong terrorist or sympathizer. When out of the confines of military installations, the GI is told to carry a weapon and to avoid contact with Vietnamese, for there may be terrorists lurking about. In addition, the GI is told that many V.C. are civilians during the day doing their regular work and guerillas at night planting mines and booby-traps or firing rockets into military targets. Since one cannot physically tell who is a civilian or V.C. due to guerilla warfare and since one's life is at stake, the GI is suspicious of all Vietnamese ...

"Why do they cheat and steal from us; they should be grateful that we're here to help them" is another familiar exclamation by GIs in reference to both Vietnamese civilians and soldiers. Having seen too many war hero movies, the GI seems to expect the Vietnamese to show appreciation for the

U.S. presence in Vietnam by being the humble and honest Oriental. The Vietnamese seem to treat the GI as another entity and not as a super-hero, which embitters the GI ego …

Since there is tendency in the United States to equate poverty with intellectual or moral weakness on the part of the impoverished people, many GIs feel superior to the Vietnamese and feel that they are inherently stupid and immoral. The fact that many Americans measure cultural level by the quality and quantity of material goods and technology also reinforces this viewpoint. Rather than see a non-technological culture, many GIs see the Vietnamese as people who are too dumb to ever be technological.

The sum total of this ethnocentric and racist negative stereotype is summarized in the term "Gook." The ugly sound of this word indicates the feeling of many GIs that the people and culture of Vietnam are ugly. The word is impersonal and does not connote human beings, which goes along with the fact that many GIs do not consider the Vietnamese to be human beings but animals. Furthermore, it makes the people seem so impersonal that one could commit barbarous acts upon them from malice or military expediency without feeling guilty of committing crimes against human beings. The word "Gook," which is used by most GIs instead of the word "Vietnamese," is definitely a racist term in Vietnam.

The GI in Vietnam is a frustrated individual and takes out his frustrations upon the Vietnamese either in derogatory words or in malicious acts. Many GIs have used this physically, culturally, and linguistically distinct group to take out their frustrations upon since the Vietnamese have been negatively stereotyped in an impersonal manner by the GI.

The GI feels culturally and physically superior to the Vietnamese, yet they are being killed or wounded by some of these people. Since the enemy does not fight out in the open but plants mines and booby-traps, fires rockets or mortar rounds into the base camps, and usually does most of his fighting under the cover of darkness, the GI is always in danger of his life, which is quite a frustrating thing to have on one's mind. Since he cannot easily strike out at the enemy to rid himself of this frustration, the GI strikes out at the closest thing to the enemy that is readily available …

Since guerilla warfare depends upon the support of the people and since many GIs are antagonizing the people, it seems that the presence of such GIs in Vietnam is perpetuating the war. It seems ridiculous and hypocritical to be antagonizing the very people you are supposed to be aiding if such is the case. There can only be a military victory in Vietnam, for rather than bringing civilization to Vietnam, the American GI has brought syphilization and racism to the Vietnamese people.

EVELYN YOSHIMURA, "GIS AND ASIAN WOMEN" (1971)[17]

The Vietnam war has touched the lives of the American people in many ways, and the Asian American community has not been immune. Our brothers have been drafted into the military to face fighting and possibly dying in a war that even the legislators of our country cannot wholly support; and for Asian American brothers, there is the added contradiction of killing other Asian people in the name of a country that itself is divided in its support for the war. The drafting of our brothers into the military, and the taxes that we must pay for this war are two very concrete ways in which we are touched. There are other ways in which we feel the ugliness of that war.

GIs are sent to Vietnam by the U.S. government and its military armed with martial training, sophisticated weapons and a view of Asian people as sub-human beings. A vast number of Asian American GIs have unpleasant memories of being called *Gook, Charlie, Jap, Chink, Ho Chi Minh* by superior officers and fellow GIs in their basic training. And the phrase *Asians have no value for human life* has been used too often to detract from the horror of rumored and proven atrocities against Vietnamese civilians.

Because of the lack of self-motivation and justification on the part of the GIs to fight against the Vietnamese people, it is necessary for the U.S. Military to psychologically break down GIs so they can instill the values and mentality that is necessary to become effective killers. One method employed by the military toward this end is the use of women, or more correctly, the sexual symbol of women, which proves very effective because of the long and complete separation from women that GIs experience, especially in basic training. This use of women to oppress GIs many times manifests itself in the way GIs relate to women they come in contact with after boot-camp. Because of World War II, the Korean War and now, the Vietnam War, many times these women are Asian women. An Asian American brother recalls his experiences in boot-camp:

INDISPENSABLE ENEMIES

"In Marine Corps boot-camp, the military goes through a psychological and physical breakdown trip of the men so they (the military) can instill their values. And a heavy part of that trip is the mentioning of women in certain sexual contexts.

"Some guys really believed this shit too. Like when you get overseas afterwards, you kind of trip on the jokes you heard and look for things you remember from the jokes.

"We had these classes we had to go to taught by the drill instructors, and every instructor would tell a joke before he began class. It would always be a dirty joke usually having to do with prostitutes they had seen in Japan or in other parts of Asia while they were stationed overseas. The attitude of the Asian woman being a doll, a useful toy or something to play with usually came out in these jokes, and how they were not quite as human as white women. For instance, a real common example was how the instructor would talk about how Asian women's vaginas weren't like a white woman's, but rather they were slanted, like their eyes."

By using Asian women in this manner, the military gains in two ways. First, they use Asian women as a symbolic sexual object. The military knows that the GIs aren't able to seek sexual satisfaction during basic training and a large part of their combat time, so they use this knowledge to keep the men down. They continually remind them of their desire by talking about women all the time, yet they keep the gratification of this desire from their reach. Again, the psychological breakdown …

The second way the military gains from using the symbol of Asian women is by the racism against Asians that it encourages and perpetuates. The image of a people with slanted eyes and slanted vaginas enhances the feeling that Asians are other than human, and therefore much easier to kill. More than a few Vietnam veterans tell of incidents of GIs who spend time in combat; then during their Rest and Recuperation periods, suddenly and with no apparent provocation, will kill a Vietnamese civilian out of a paranoid concept of *Gooks*. And according to many vets, civilian massacres like My Lai are not exceptional happenings …

And there is another dimension in the use of Asian women as sexual objects. The view that Asian women are less than human helps perpetuate another myth—that of the White women "back home" being placed on a pedestal. (This is not to say that the White woman's position is to be

envied. Her position on that pedestal is also an oppressive situation.) …
As long as there are U.S. troops in Asia, as long as the U.S. government and the military wage wars of aggression against Asian people, racism
against Asians will serve the interest of this country. And that racism will
be perpetrated. We, as Asian Americans cannot divorce ourselves from this
reality, and we as Asian American women cannot separate ourselves from
our Asian counterparts. Racism against them is too often racism against
us. The stereotype fits us much too easily. The mentality that keeps Suzy
Wong, Madame Butterfly, and gookism alive; the mentality that turns
human beings into racist, murdering soldiers, also keeps Asian Americans
from being able to live and feel like human beings. We must destroy the
stereotypes of Asian women, and Asian people, as a whole, so we can define
ourselves, and be free to realize our full and total potential. Just as the U.S.
government, through forced control, denies the Vietnamese people of their
right to self-determination and self-definition, the racism needed to maintain that control cripples us as Asians in America.

H. Bruce Franklin, "Reimaging Vietnam" (2000)[18]

*There is a long American tradition of screening U.S. wars as their opposite.
In Westerns, Indians ambush wagon trains, and in war films about U.S. oc-
cupations, indigenous enemies ambush American soldiers. Cultural historian
H. Bruce Franklin has shown how American culture has transformed the U.S.
war in Vietnam into various myths and fantasies, describing the U.S. role in
Vietnam as a form of "science fiction." In this excerpt he analyzes one filmic representation of that conflict. As the situation in Vietnam deteriorated, President
Lyndon Johnson framed America's role in terms easy to understand: "There are
three billion people in the world and we have only 200 million of them. We are
outnumbered 15 to 1. If might did make right they would sweep over the U.S.
and take what we have. We have what they want."[19]*

One of the most shocking, influential, and enduring single images from
the Vietnam War exploded into the consciousness of millions of Americans
in February 1968 when they actually watched, within the comfort of the
own homes, as the chief of the Saigon national police executed a manacled

Figure 69. General Nguyen Ngoc Loan, head of South Vietnam's police force and intelligence, executing a prisoner in 1968. Photograph by Eddie Adams. © Associated Press 2013.

Figure 70. In *The Deer Hunter* (1978), General Loan's revolver becomes a North Vietnamese officer's revolver, and his NLF prisoner is replaced by U.S. prisoners forced to play Russian roulette. © NBC/Universal.

NLF* prisoner. In a perfectly framed sequence, the notorious General Nguyen Ngoc Loan unholsters a snub-nosed revolver and places its muzzle to the prisoner's right temple. The prisoner's head jolts, a sudden spurt of blood gushes straight out of his right temple, and he collapses in death. The next morning, newspaper readers were confronted with AP photographer Eddie Adams's potent stills of the execution. The grim ironies of the scene were accentuated by the cultural significance of the weapon itself, a revolver, a somewhat archaic handgun symbolic of the American West.

Precisely one decade later, this image, with its roles now reversed, was transmuted into the dominant metaphor of a lavishly financed Hollywood production crucial to reimaging the history of the Vietnam War: *The Deer Hunter*. After being designated the best English-language film of 1978 by the New York Film Critics Circle, this celluloid displacement of reality within illusion was sanctified by four Academy Awards, capped by Best Picture—an award presented appropriately enough by John Wayne, the World War II draft dodger who received a Congressional Gold Medal for playing a warrior hero in the movies. *The Deer Hunter* succeeded not only in reversing key images of the war but also in helping to canonize U.S. prisoners of war as the most significant symbols of American manhood for the 1980s, 1990s, and beyond.

The reimaging was blatant, though most critics at the time seemed oblivious to it. The basic technique was to take images of the war that had become deeply embedded in America's consciousness and change them into their opposites. For example, in the film's first scene in Vietnam, a uniformed soldier throws a grenade into an underground village shelter harboring women and children, and then with his automatic rifle mows down a woman and her baby. Although the scene resembles the familiar TV sequence of GIs in Vietnamese villages, as well as *Life's* photographs of the My Lai massacre, the soldier turns out to be not American but North Vietnamese. He is then killed by a lone guerrilla—who is not a "Viet Cong" but our Special Forces hero, played by Robert De Niro. Later, when two

---

* National Liberation Front, correct term for "Viet Cong," a derogatory epithet roughly translated as "Viet Commies." The NLF, though Communist-led, was a broad coalition of forces opposed to U.S. and U.S.-backed forces in the southern half of Vietnam.

men plummet from a helicopter, the images replicate a telephotographic sequence once seen by millions of Americans that showed a Vietnamese prisoner being hurled from an American helicopter to make other prisoners talk*; but in the movie the falling men are American POWs attempting to escape their murderous North Vietnamese captors.

The structuring metaphor of the film is the game of Russian roulette the sadistic Asian communist guards force their prisoners to play. The crucial torture scene consists of sequence after sequence of images replicating and replacing that infamous historical sequence in which General Loan placed a revolver to the right temple of his NLF prisoner and killed him with a single shot. In the movie the American captives are kept in tiger cages, another image that reverses reality; the actual tiger cages, also overseen by General Loan, were used by the Saigon government to torture thousands of Vietnamese political prisoners. The movie shows American prisoner after prisoner being hauled out of the tiger cages and forced by the demonic North Vietnamese officer in charge, who always stands to the prisoner's right and our left, to place a revolver to his own right temple. Then the image is framed to eliminate the connection between the prisoner's body and the arm holding the revolver, thus bringing the image closer to the famous execution image. One sequence even replicates the blood spurting out of the victim's right temple …

The brazen reversal of this image was a spectacular success, as I discovered while giving lectures about it on college campuses in 1992. I would begin by projecting a slide of the original AP photo. Then I would ask, "How many people here are familiar with this image?" Almost every hand would go up. Then I would ask, "What is this a picture of?" Almost invariably, at least three fourths of those who had raised their hands would declare that it was a picture of "a North Vietnamese officer" or "a communist officer" executing "a civilian" or "a prisoner" or "a South Vietnamese."

---

* "How Helicopter Dumped a Viet Captive to Death," *Chicago Sun Times* (November 29, 1969); "Death of a Prisoner," *San Francisco Chronicle*, November 29, 1969.

Myra Mendible, "Post-Vietnam Syndrome" (2008)[20]

Psychoanalyst Myra Mendible explores some of the psychosocial dimensions of the continuing "culture wars" over memory of the U.S. defeat in Vietnam. As Mendible mentions, the experience of Vietnam veterans fittingly prompted the diagnosis of Post Traumatic Stress Disorder. Chiam F. Shatan identified what he termed "Post-Vietnam Syndrome" during grassroots "rap sessions" with Vietnam Veterans who had been denied mental health counseling by the Veterans Administration. Shatan challenged military training techniques that he claimed brutalized recruits and encouraged a militarized form of mourning for the loss of freedom, ego, and friends that typifies war. He claimed this psychological conditioning led to an erotic discharge of emotion onto surrogate enemies on the battlefield. Shatan cautioned that "unshed tears shed blood," warning that soldiers harassed by their superiors and prevented from displaying emotion were more likely to commit brutal atrocities, and that this condition stayed with soldiers even after they returned home.[21]

In a victory speech following the 1991 Persian Gulf War, President George H. W. Bush proclaimed it a proud day to be American. The president's speech officially heralded a new structure of feeling in America, one more suited to an imperial power's spectacular reemergence on the world stage, it pronounced an official end to the "Vietnam syndrome," a malaise that had presumably stricken the American psyche for over sixteen years. The war had been the antidote for what ailed us, Bush's speech assured us, the means to restore the nation's honor and reclaim its rightful status. Americans could finally trade in the sackcloth of humiliation for the mantle of pride. By God, we had "kicked the Vietnam syndrome once and for all."* …

Coined by none other than Henry Kissinger, the term Vietnam syndrome has become an integral part of our political lexicon, shaping attitudes and predispositions more than three decades later. The term aspires to a kind of quasi-psychological legitimacy, but actually reflects a semantic sleight of hand. The term Post-Vietnam Syndrome was first used to describe the trauma experienced by soldiers who served in Vietnam. Later known as

---

* George H. W. Bush, Remarks to the American Legislative Exchange Council (March 1, 1991), *Public Papers of the Presidents of the United States.*

Post-Traumatic Stress Disorder (PTSD), this condition received attention in 1970 as a result of work by a handful of psychiatrists, especially Robert Jay Lifton and Chaim Shatan, who conducted extensive interviews with Vietnam veterans suffering from flashbacks, paranoia, and other symptoms of trauma. The term "Vietnam syndrome" turns the soldier's traumatic experience of war into a story of national humiliation.*

The psychology of PTSD has been highly politicized, while a ring of scientific authenticity has masked the politics of the Vietnam syndrome.† No longer signifying a nation, "Vietnam" functions as metaphor for America's humiliation. This trope has served U.S. presidents from Richard Nixon to George W. Bush, each of whom has relied on its compelling themes to garner support for military interventions and "preemptive" strikes. It frames America's political rhetoric whenever leaders seek to stifle political dissent at home, "harden" national borders, or rally nationalistic strains in the American character. Recalled in this way, the legacy of Vietnam becomes a story about "our" humiliation, about the "wrong" committed against *us*. As Vietnam vet W. D. Ehrhart aptly remarked on NPR's "Talk of the Nation": "You know, the Vietnam War, we imagine it's this thing that happened to us when, in fact, the Vietnam War is this thing we did to them."‡ ...

Stories about America's humiliation have circulated widely through popular lore and familiar images. They often play out through Hollywood film stereotypes of the Vietnam veteran, whose wounded body and psyche sign for the nation's crisis of honor. Spat upon by ungrateful antiwar protestors, lied to by their presidents, shackled by the policies of civilian whiz

---

* During WWI, PTSD was known as "shell shock," while the term "combat fatigue" became popular during and after WWII. The American Psychiatric Association (APA) finally recognized PTSD in 1980. See Boyce Rensberger, "Delayed Trauma in Veterans Cited; Psychiatrists Find Vietnam Produces Guilt and Shame," *New York Times*, May 3, 1972.

† For the politicizing of PTSD, see Allan Young, *The Harmony of Illusions: Inventing Post-Traumatic Stress Disorder* (Princeton, NJ: Princeton University Press, 1995); W. J. Scott, "PTSD in DSM-III: A Case in the Politics of Diagnosis and Disease," *Social Problems* 37 (1990), 294–310; Ben Shepard, *A War of Nerves: Soldiers and Psychiatrists in the Twentieth Century* (Cambridge, MA: Harvard University Press, 2001).

‡ W. D. Ehrhart, "Former Senator Bob Kerry and Vietnam," *Talk of the Nation*, National Public Radio, Washington, D.C., May 2, 2001.

kids in Washington, America's protagonists in these tales form a sad cast of dishonored men, defeated warriors, forgotten sons and husbands …

As a basis of national feeling, humiliation or its perception exacerbates collective feelings of vulnerability or powerlessness in the citizenry. It can lead to brutal retaliations and mass bloodshed, triggering cycles of violence that can persist for generations. Social psychologist Evelin Gerda Lindner argues that when a group is convinced of their humiliation, "Terror, war, and genocide can result if this belief is fed by 'humiliation entrepreneurs' who exhort their followers to exact revenge with grand narratives of humiliation and retaliation."[*]

Yet official versions of the Vietnam Syndrome tell us that Americans had not been spurred into violent retaliation as a result of our "humiliating" defeat. We had not sought new enemies or become entangled in cycles of violence that follow in humiliation's wake. Instead, Americans had fallen victim to a debilitating "syndrome" of passivity and weakness. Humiliation had made us "soft," afraid to wield our power or influence on the world stage. The post-Vietnam generation presumably suffered from what Norman Podhoretz diagnosed as a "sickly inhibition against the use of military force." Similarly, Ernest Lefever blamed the Vietnam syndrome on our "culture of shame, guilt and self-flagellation," which presumably "paralyzed America from using military force abroad." William Safire, President Nixon's speechwriter during the War, revived this narrative in a 2001 *New York Times* piece, referring to the Vietnam syndrome as "that revulsion at the use of military power that afflicted our national psyche for decades after our defeat." The syndrome's symptoms are widely known and accepted as common knowledge: a breakdown of national will, a loss of confidence, and an unwillingness to engage in protracted conflicts abroad. This narrative identifies Americans' aversion to war as a sign that America had been feminized by defeat, turned into a nation of wimps and pacifists[†]…

When groups or nations are forced to recognize the humanity of their enemies, witnessing serves to produce competing moral visions and

---

[*] E. G. Linder, *Making Enemies: Humiliation and International Conflict* (Westport, CT: Praeger Security International, 2006), xv.

[†] Podhoretz quoted in Noam Chomsky, *Deterring Democracy* (New York: Verso, 1991), 86; Ernest Lefever, "Vietnam's Ghosts," *Wall Street Journal*, May 21, 1997; William Safire, "Syndrome Returns," *New York Times*, April 30, 2000.

appraisals. Most importantly, recognizing the other's status as "worthy" victim can move subjects toward the experience of shame. Unlike humiliation, which entails a response directed against an external object, shame involves "a reflection upon the self by the self."* In other words, we believe we deserve our shame because of some moral failing or lapse in judgment, but humiliation never entails a victim's culpability. While we own our shame, we can feel humiliated without having done anything to warrant censure or blame. It is therefore not surprising that the Vietnam syndrome has played such a critical role in deflecting feelings of shame or guilt in the citizenry.

By invoking the logic of humiliation, the story of Vietnam works to deny the shame that might otherwise take shape in the nation's conscience. As victim, this subject is constituted as innocent and thus spared accountability or blame for negative outcomes. The well-intentioned victim of this tale bears no moral responsibility for the nation's actions in Vietnam—or for the deaths of over 58,000 American soldiers and 3 million Vietnamese civilians. Thus Nixon rejected the possibility that the U.S. should feel any shame as a result of our actions in Vietnam or because of the chaos that followed our retreat: "Of all the myths about the Vietnam War, the most vicious one is the idea that the United States was morally responsible for the atrocities committed after the fall of Cambodia in 1975." Similarly, after the disclosure in 2001 that American soldiers had massacred civilians at Thanh Phong during a mission in 1969, influential writers like William Safire moved quickly to deflect any sense of shame or accountability. Assuming a sermonizing tone of righteous anger, Safire asks, "Are there no voices left, after that costly loss of life, to reject the Syndrome's humiliating accusation of national arrogance—and to recall a noble motive?"†

Shame compels the self to recognize another's moral legitimacy. Internalizing blame, it undermines the kind of retaliatory impulse leaders seek in garnering support for war. Thus questions about the rationale for waging war or the cost of victory must always be averted, as these may induce subjects to identify with the "wrong" victim and to confront ensuing feelings of shame. The denial of shame in a community, Thomas Scheff argues, leads to its coded expression. Shame conceptions emerge as

---

* S. B. Miller, *Shame in Context* (Hillsdale, NJ: The Analytic Press, 1996), 42.
† Nixon, *No More Vietnams*; Safire, "Syndrome Returns."

narratives of honor, humiliation, and revenge. In nations that have suffered military defeat, "stab-in-the-back" myths emerge as a defense against shame. Defeat functions in these myths as a "dramatic signal of unworthiness or inadequacy. The stab-in-the-back legend is a justification of self or group: It is not our fault, we are worthy, but we were betrayed. When such a falsehood is enshrined as official history, it can be an emblem of complete denial of shame in a society as a whole."[*]

In the U.S., the Vietnam syndrome incorporates the stab-in-the-back myth as a way to secure the nation's positive self-image. Deflecting attention from leaders' misjudgments or policy decisions and towards those who opposed them, the stab-in-the-back motif reassures the body politic, as Nixon did in 1969, that only Americans can defeat or humiliate the United States. Kevin Baker suggests that the stab-in-the-back myth "has been the device by which the American right wing has both revitalized itself and repeatedly avoided responsibility for its own worst blunders. Indeed, the right has distilled its tale of betrayal into a formula: Advocate some momentarily popular but reckless policy. Deny culpability when that policy is exposed as disastrous. Blame the disaster on internal enemies who hate America"[†]...

America's ongoing participation in this tit for tat cycle of humiliation may well be our Achilles heel in the "war on terror." Expressing her opposition to the invasion of Iraq in 2002, *New York Times* columnist Maureen Dowd had argued, "Extirpating Saddam is about proving how tough we are to a world that thinks we got soft when that last helicopter left the roof of the American embassy in Saigon in 1975."[‡] But five years later, George W. Bush is no longer able to claim Saddam, WMDs, or even democracy as rationale for prolonging the war in Iraq. Thus the need to avert humiliation is invoked again, conjured as a means to deflect questions about negative outcomes or exit strategies. As one representative said recently on the floor of the House, "President Bush is sending 20,000 more American lives into mortal danger, and spending $100 million a day just to avoid the humiliation of admitting

---

* Thomas Scheff, *Bloody Revenge: Emotions, Nationalism, and War* (Boulder, CO: Westview Press, 1994), 140.

† Richard Nixon, Silent Majority Speech, November 3, 1969, *Public Papers of the Presidents of the United States*, 901–9; Kevin Baker, "Stabbed in the Back! The Past and Future of a Right Wing Myth," *Harper's*, June 2006, 31–41.

‡ Maureen Dowd, "Culture War with B-2s," *New York Times*, September 22, 2002.

that his policy has been fundamentally flawed from the very beginning."[*] And so it is that long after Vietnam—long after Grenada, Libya, Panama, and Gulf I, we Americans find ourselves cast in a Sartrean tale of "no exit," bound to a never-ending story of humiliation and war.

Jesse Springer, "On Our Knees" (2004)

A cousin of Yellow Peril, the Arab-as-villain has dominated Western popular culture since the so-called Arab Oil Embargo. Springer's cartoon visualizes the pervasive sense that the U.S., embodied by Uncle Sam, is shamefully dependent and subservient to Oriental despots. In today's iconography the costume of the sheik signifies racial difference, sexuality, and power, rendering America the victim.

Figure 71. Jesse Springer, "On Our Knees" (October 24, 2004). © Jesse Springer 2004. Courtesy of the artist. www.springercreative.com.

---

* L. Woolsey, "Repeating the Mistakes of Vietnam," January 18, 2007, House of Representatives, *Congressional Record.*

John Esposito, "Islam and the West:
A Clash of Civilizations?" (1999)[22]

This excerpt, written before 9/11 or the "Arab Spring," reminds us that the disinformation about Islamic "jihads" against the "West" was not simply a popular reaction to the attacks, but a symptom of deeper U.S. academic and policy assumptions. Throughout U.S. history, elites have promoted the "cultural" and "biological" origins of conflicts rather than acknowledge the division of resources as a proper subject of politics. Colonial and neocolonial administrators have justified their rule by portraying the populations they speak for as unfit for self-government, decrying indigenous demands for democratic control as threats to the global order. Such thinking shapes the very policies it was invented to justify.

Fear often issues in the demonization of an enemy or threat. For decades, international relations were conducted within the context of a superpower rivalry, between East and West, the Soviet Union and the United States. In the post–Cold War period, many who seek new demons warn of an Islamic threat to Western civilization or of an impending clash of civilizations. Increasingly, voices in America and Europe proclaim, "The Muslims are coming, the Muslims are coming!"[*] ...

There are lessons to be learned from the Cold War. Celebration of the unraveling of communism and the victory of democracy has been tempered by questions that go to the heart of our ability to understand, analyze, and formulate policy. Delight at the triumph of democracy was accompanied by a growing realization of the extent to which fear and the demonization of the enemy blinded many to the true condition and extent of the Soviet threat. Viewing the Soviet Union through the prism of the "evil empire" was ideologically reassuring and emotionally satisfying, justifying the expenditure of enormous resources and the support of a vast military-industrial complex. However, our easy stereotypes of the enemy and the monolithic nature of the communist threat also proved costly in other respects. Despite an enormous amount of intelligence and analysis, few seemed to know until

---

[*] When I first wrote this phrase, I feared some might think the statement a bit outrageous. I discovered subsequently that the *National Review* had published Daniel Pipes's "The Muslims Are Coming! The Muslims Are Coming!" November 19, 1990, 28–31.

the end that the emperor had no clothes. Neither government agencies nor academic think tanks predicted the extent and speed of the disintegration of the Soviet empire. The exaggerated fears and static vision that drove us to take Herculean steps against a monolithic enemy blinded us to the diversity within the Soviet Union and the profound changes that were taking place.

In understanding and responding to events in the Muslim world, we are again challenged to resist easy stereotypes and solutions. There is an easy path and a hard path. The easy path is to view Islam and Islamic revivalism as a threat—to posit a global Pan-Islamic threat, monolithic in nature, a historic enemy whose faith and agenda are diametrically opposed to that of the West. This attitude leads to support for secular regimes at almost any cost (regardless of how repressive) rather than risk an Islamically oriented government's coming to power ...

The confrontation is often portrayed as a clash of civilizations. Two pieces have been particularly influential: Bernard Lewis's "The Roots of Muslim Rage" and Samuel P. Huntington's "The Clash of Civilizations."* Both have been seminal in defining the parameters of a debate that has gripped diplomats, policymakers, journalists, and academic analysts ...

The selective approach of most analyses of Islamic activism omits, downplays, or dismisses the reasons given by activists (and indeed many Arabs and Muslims) for their criticism and rejection of the West: imperialism, America's tilt toward Israel, Western governments' support for oppressive regimes (the Shah's Iran, Tunisia, Nimeiri's Sudan, Lebanon). The reader is never challenged to consider the reasons behind the attitudes and actions of activists rather than simply dismiss them as the product of a clash of civilizations or a blind, irrational clinging to faith ... [Lewis claims,]

> we are facing a mood and a movement—far transcending the level of issues and policies and the governments that pursue them. This is no less than a clash of civilizations—perhaps irrational but surely historic reaction of an ancient rival against our Judaeo-Christian heritage, our secular present, and the worldwide expansion of both.[†]

---

* Bernard Lewis, "The Roots of Muslim Rage," *Atlantic Monthly*, September 1990; Samuel P. Huntington, "The Clash of Civilizations," *Foreign Affairs* 72, no. 3 (Summer, 1993).
† Lewis, "Roots of Muslim Rage," 56–60.

Stereotypical dichotomies are reinforced to obscure a complex reality: Islam against the West, fundamentalism against modernity, static tradition versus dynamic change, the desire to simply return to or preserve the past versus adaptation to modern life. All "fundamentalist leaders" are lumped together, obscuring the fact that many Islamists are modern, educated people who hold responsible professional positions and participate in the democratic process. Moreover, the causes of conflicts are facilely reduced to a clash of civilizations. The primacy of competing political interests, policies, and issues is dismissed or eclipsed by the vision of an age-old rivalry between "them" and "us." Once again, history witnesses Islam pitted against the West, against "our Judeo-Christian and secular West," a confrontation of competing and conflicting global visions and missions. This approach is as valid and useful as the attempts of Saddam Hussein (like the Ayatollah Khomeini before him) to reduce the West's antagonism toward him to Crusader imperialism against the oppressed masses of the Arab and Muslim worlds.

Denying the need to address specific political or socioeconomic issues also negates any notion of shared responsibility. How can the West respond to what is obviously emotional and "irrational," an assault upon it by peoples who are peculiarly driven by their passions and hatred? As James Piscatori observed:

> Whether it was the Ottoman attempt to thwart Christian nationalists or the Muslim attempt to gain independence from the West, Islam was fanatical because it ran counter to imperial interests. But it was the converse formulation that became the standard explanation of Muslim conduct: Islam was hostile to the West because it was fanatical ... Consequently, Muslims came to be seen as a uniformly emotional and sometimes illogical race that moved as one body and spoke with one voice.*

The pattern persists. As many in the past dismissed the political realities of Muslim-Christian relations by retreating to the bogeyman of "Muslim fanaticism," so Muslims today are described as a people and civilization who, though courteous and possessing a rich religious tradition and civilization, harbor a propensity to hatred and rage when angered ...

---

* James Piscatori, *Islam in a World of Nation-States* (Cambridge: Cambridge University Press, 1986), 38.

The clearest, most provocative, and influential articulation of this position is Samuel P. Huntington's *Clash of Civilizations* ... Belief in a monolithic notion of civilization results in the contention that some civilizations are diametrically opposed (the West versus Islamic and Confucian civilizations), which creates the possibility of a clash of civilizations. In order to support his position, Huntington, astonishingly, is not content, as are many others, to see "Islamic fundamentalism" as a threat to the West but rather identifies Islam itself: "The underlying problem for the West is not Islamic fundamentalism. It is Islam, a different civilization whose people are convinced of the superiority of their culture, and are obsessed with the inferiority of their power." Here again, "Muslim" or "Islamic civilization" rather than "Islam" would be the more comparable terminology, since Islam refers more properly and specifically to the religion of Islam, which is an important component of Muslim or Islamic civilization but is only one component of it. Over and against Islam, Huntington posits a monolithic West, whose difference puts it on a collision path with Islam: "The problem for Islam is not the CIA or the U.S. Department of Defense. It is the West, a different civilization whose people are convinced of the universality of their culture and believe that their superior, if declining, power imposes the obligation to extend that culture throughout the world. These are the basic ingredients that fuel the conflict between Islam and the West"* ...

The perception of a monolithic "Islamic threat" often motivates the United States to support repressive governments in the Muslim world and thus to a self-fulfilling prophecy. Governments that thwart a participatory process by canceling elections or repressing populist Islamic movements that prove effective in electoral politics, as they have in Tunisia, Algeria, Egypt, and Turkey, encourage or risk the radicalization of moderate movements and the emergence of new forms of radicalism and extremism ... Official U.S. or Western silence or economic, political, and military support for such regimes is read as complicity and a sign of the West's double standard for the implementation of democracy. Repressive regimes and the violation of human rights, along with a compliant Western policy toward such actions, can create conditions that lead to political confrontation and violence. They

---

* Samuel P. Huntington, *The Clash of Civilizations and the Remaking of World Order* (New York: Simon and Schuster, 1997), 217, 218.

enable governments in the Muslim world and some Western policy makers to seemingly validate their prior contention and prophecy that Islamic movements are inherently violent and antidemocratic and constitute a threat to national and regional stability ...

From North Africa to Southeast Asia, Islamic movements participated in electoral politics and, relative to the expectations of some, scored stunning successes. This created a political and analytical dilemma. The justification for the condemnation and suppression of Islamic movements was that they were violent extremists, small nonrepresentative groups on the margins of society that refused to work within the system and thus posed a threat to both society and regional stability. The vision of Islamic organizations working within the system ironically made them an even more formidable threat to regimes in the Muslim world and to some in the West. Those who once dismissed their claims as unrepresentative and denounced their radicalism as a threat to the system now accused them of an attempt to "hijack democracy." This charge became the excuse for governments in Egypt, Turkey, Algeria, Tunisia, and Jordan to slow down or back away from political liberalization and democratization ...

For many governments in the Muslim world whose legitimacy is tenuous and whose power is based upon force and coercion, the combination of "uncontrolled democracy" and Islam is indeed a formidable threat. For Western governments, long accustomed to pragmatic alliances with regimes which, however undemocratic or repressive, were dominated by Western-oriented elites, the leap into the unknown of a potential fundamentalist government is far from attractive. This is especially true in light of the example of the Islamic republics of Iran, Afghanistan, and Sudan. As a result, the challenge of contemporary Islamic revivalism to the political and intellectual establishment is easily transformed into a threat ...

Our challenge is to better understand the history and realities of the Muslim world and to recognize the diversity and the many faces of Islam. This approach lessens the risk of creating self-fulfilling prophecies that augur the battle of the West against a radical Islam or a clash of civilizations. Guided by its stated ideals and goals of freedom and self-determination, the West has an ideal vantage point for appreciating the aspirations of many in the Muslim world as they seek to define and forge new paths for their future.

"Militancy Considerations: Violence and Adherence
to the Torah, Bible, and Koran" (2010)

This slide from an FBI training session illustrates a view of Islam, and the threat of "Islamic fundamentalism," that exacerbates conflict and justifies brutality. Such logic is reflected in mainstream news outlets like Newsweek, *which in 2012 chose to distill the evolving politics in the Middle East into a simple cover story: "Muslim Rage." What were the screaming young men on the cover mad about? Who knows? Who cares? They're Muslims, of course they're angry.*[23]

The Center for Security Policy, a prominent neoconservative think tank, helped produce the inflammatory documentaries Obsessed *(2006) and* The Third Jihad *(2008). Portions of the films aired on CNN and Fox News. They were screened across the U.S., and were used in anti-terrorism training for police and law enforcement officials. The films suggest that the Muslim sharia, a religious code of conduct, demands that the devout in America dedicate themselves to the overthrow of the U.S. government and all other "infidel" institutions.*[24]

In 2010, the Center commissioned an independent investigation of American Muslims to challenge the contentions of mainstream security agencies that Muslim American communities did not pose a threat to U.S. security and regularly cooperate with law enforcement. Retired Lt. Gen. William G. "Jerry" Boykin, who argued publicly and in uniform that the War on Terror was a Christian crusade against Islam (and was subsequently promoted under President George W. Bush), co-chaired the investigation, and former CIA Director R. James Woolsey served as a coauthor.[25]

The resulting report argues that Muslim sharia law is a "more insidious ideological threat" than Communism was during the Cold War and that "Immigration of those who adhere to sharia must be precluded, as was previously done with adherents to the seditious ideology of Communism." The report even proposes that American advocates of sharia should be deported, and that every Muslim is a potential sharia adherent.[26]

The last chapter of the report concludes:

The growth of Muslim populations in the West augurs the inexorable spread of sharia into Western societies—less by violence than by dint of natural procreation, unchecked immigration, and the incessant demands of an aggressive minority that refuses to assimilate. Logic should tell us, then,

that the growth of sharia in the West threatens Western-style liberty: threatens freedom of expression, freedom of conscience and upends religious and
sexual equality. But we are at a point where we, the children of Athens, fear
and deny that logic.

We do so because logic would lead ineluctably to the perception that
the beliefs of sharia Islam and the beliefs of the West are at irreconcilable
odds. It is not just sharia's place in the West that would then become an
acknowledged threat to the survival of the West. The multicultural mirage
of interchangeable diversity and "universal values" necessarily vanishes
as well.

In its place would arise an inevitable hierarchy of differentiation: Not
all religions are equally benign; not all religions are equal. Not all cultures
have made equal contributions; not all cultures are equal. To our elites, this
would be a bad thing because it would set into motion a rite of passage—a
painful, difficult awakening from a dream world of sunny universalism and
pale indecision into a stark reality of black and white, good and evil, win or
lose, do or die.

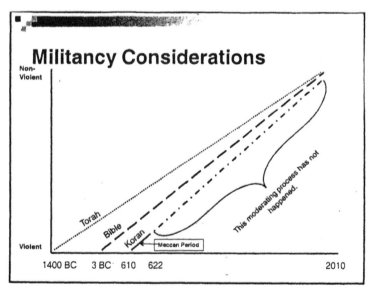

Figure 72. "Militancy Considerations: Violence and Adherence to the Torah,
Bible, and Koran," *Islam 101* (Quantico, VA: Federal Bureau of Investigation,
2010).

Eve Bennett, "Orientalisms Old and
New in *Battlestar Galactica*" (2012)[27]

This excerpt traces the logic of the modern horde and its relationship to race, gender, and sexuality in a popular American science fiction television series. While seemingly futuristic, this trope is also abundantly invested in the past, and has existed for at least a century.

Since its "very origins" in the adventure stories of such authors as Jules Verne, H. G. Wells and H. Rider Haggard, science fiction "has been part and parcel of imperialism."[*] It has always "engage[d] in real world political and colonial parallels" and while "post–World War II" science fiction texts do not necessarily "promot[e] imperialism," as almost all earlier exponents of the genre did, they "continue ... to explore the meeting of cultures and the variety of violent and military responses to that meeting" in a way that "mirrors the intercultural and intersocietal relations of our world."[†] This is epitomised by the premise of the 'reimagined' *Battlestar Galactica* (US 2003–09). A community of humans once colonised twelve apparently unoccupied adjacent planets and built a society very similar to present-day terrestrial Western ones. The Colonials—as the settlers unashamedly refer to themselves—built a race of slave-robots, the Cylons, to act as soldiers, servants and labourers. Forty years before the series' narrative begins, the Cylons rebelled against their masters and, as an intertitle in the pilot "Miniseries" (December 8, 2003) informs us, "after a long and bloody struggle, left for another world to call their own." The events of the miniseries see the Cylons—many now "evolved" to the stage where they are indistinguishable from humans—return and mount a surprise nuclear attack on the Twelve Colonies, instantly killing most of the population. The handful of survivors are forced to flee for their lives, protected only by the one remaining warship, the eponymous *Galactica*. While some Cylons relentlessly pursue the human escapees, the others take on the role of colonisers, occupying the Twelve Colonies and, later—at the end of the programme's second season,

---

* Kevin J. Wetmore, Jr., *The Empire Triumphant: Race, Religion and Rebellion in the Star Wars Films* (Jefferson, NC: McFarland, 2005), 29.
† Ibid., 29, 32.

in "Lay Down Your Burdens, Part Two" (March 10, 2006)—another planet, New Caprica, on which some of the humans have settled ...

I want to consider how *BSG* engages with what Edward Said refers to as the "imperial perspective." That is, the ways in which imperial powers represent the people of the countries they wish to colonise or otherwise exert authority over in order to justify and enhance that authority. The groundwork in this area was, of course, laid by Said's *Orientalism: Western Conceptions of the Orient* (1978), which describes in detail the West's strategies for "dominating, restructuring, and having authority" over the lands they colonised or sought to colonise during the eighteenth and nineteenth centuries, particularly those countries of the Eastern Mediterranean—commonly referred to at the time as the Orient—where Islamic empires had historically often "dominated or effectively threatened European Christianity"* ...

However, my primary focus will not be on Said's Orientalism but on its development by David Morley and Kevin Robins as they seek to elucidate the discourses and stereotypes relating to East Asia, which as European exploration and colonial expansion advanced steadily eastwards, had by the end of the nineteenth century begun to usurp the label "the Orient." Writing in 1992, they suggest that the West, particularly America, has become troubled by Japan's success in the international business arena, especially in the field of new technologies, and the rising level of Japanese investment in Western corporations. The result, they argue, is a new kind of orientalism, wherein Japan has replaced the Eastern Mediterranean as the place against whose supposed "difference, the West fortifies and defends what it sees as its superior culture and identity"† ... [The] long-standing Western myth of Japan's "irreducible difference"—of a culture that is supposedly "cold, impersonal [and] authoritarian," but also "exotic, enigmatic and mysterious"—has, more recently combined with anxiety about its technological advancements, resulting in a perception of the Japanese as a race of "machine-like," identical people who are fixated with incomprehensible technology and "lack ... emotional connection to the rest of the world."‡

---

* Quoted in Wetmore, *The Empire Triumphant*, 19; Edward W. Said, *Orientalism: Western Conceptions of the Orient* (London: Penguin, 1978), 2, 74.

† David Morley and Kevin Robins, *Spaces of Identity: Global Media, Electronic Landscapes, and Cultural Boundaries* (London: Routledge, 1995), 172.

‡ Ibid., 161, 169, 170.

Morley and Robins call this new image "techno-orientalism" … My analysis centres on the Cylon model Eight, especially the two most important copies, Boomer and Athena. While many facets of techno-orientalist discourse can be linked to the Cylons in general, there are certain elements of it—specifically those related to the representation and fetishisation of Asian women—that become especially obvious, and worrying, when focused on characters played by Korean-Canadian actress Grace Park …

Boomer is the first member of the *Galactica* crew to be revealed as a Cylon, a revelation that occurs for the audience at the end of the miniseries. Boomer's shipmates, on the other hand, do not become aware of her true identity until the climax of season one when, in "Kobol's Last Gleaming, Part Two" (January 24, 2005), she shoots the Commander of the *Galactica*, Bill Adama (Edward James Olmos). Prior to this, Boomer had lived as a human for several years, rising through the ranks to become a respected pilot and forming strong bonds of friendship with her *Galactica* crewmates. Her Cylon programming first starts to come into action in "Water" (October 25, 2004), leading her to sabotage the ship's water supplies, and then later to secretly assist a Five (Matthew Bennett) in carrying out a suicide bombing in "Litmus" (November 22, 2004). Boomer thus represents an enemy who works from within, carefully infiltrating the very heart of society in order to attack it, behaviour that brings to mind the anxiety "about the 'stealth' of Japanese corporations" which buy into Western businesses. Having "gain[ed] 'insider' status within regional and local markets" Morley and Robins suggest, "Japanese interests appear to work behind the scenes … manipulating Western concerns … [with a] perceived … robot-like dedication to achieving world hegemony."[*]

Boomer's shooting of Adama just as he is warmly congratulating her on completing a mission is arguably the most shocking thing we ever see an individual Cylon do throughout *BSG*. It seems worse than, for example, a Six murdering a baby in the miniseries because Adama is a character

---

* Ibid., 150–3. Morley and Robins cite a number of "ninja" characters in American popular cultural texts as manifestations of this anxiety. Boomer is somewhat different to these as, as a "sleeper" agent, she operates mostly in plain sight. She is perhaps more reminiscent of the brainwashed American soldier, Sgt. Raymond Shaw (Laurence Harvey), "programmed" to kill by sinister Chinese, North Korean, and Russian Communists in *The Manchurian Candidate* (Frankenheimer, U.S., 1962).

that the audience knows well and because so much emphasis is placed on the betrayal of Adama's trust and paternal feelings towards his pilots that the shooting represents. In "The Farm" (August 12, 2005), a convalescent Adama visits the now-dead Boomer's body in the morgue and asks "Why?" before breaking down in tears. This scene implies that Boomer's act cannot be understood in normal human terms, but only as the result of inhuman programming. Morley and Robins argue that techno-orientalism combines an ancient stereotype of the Japanese as "brutal" and "barbaric," with the idea that their society is now one "where technology and rationalisation have fused perfectly" leaving no place for "emotions" or "humanity" and where every person is trained from birth in such a way as to "ensure predictable and disciplined behaviour ... The barbarians have now become robots."[*]

The belief that Japanese society is "conformist," with little ethnic diversity or pluralism, can easily be linked to the Cylons in general, of which there are only twelve models, each one with many identical copies. However, even this trait is repeatedly visually connected with Boomer and the Eights in that, throughout the first season, the pre-title sequence which briefly explains the nature of the Cylons uses a split-screen image of Boomer next to the other principal Eight, Athena, to illustrate the line of text "There are many copies." Furthermore, the first large group of identical humanoid Cylons the audience ever sees are dozens of Eights, whom a horrified Boomer encounters aboard a Cylon baseship shortly before she shoots Adama. The Eights are naked, making them impossible to distinguish from one another, and they finish each other's sentences, thereby highlighting that they are essentially the same person.[†]

Boomer's encounter with the Eights aboard the baseship not only emphasises their "sameness" but is obviously also intended to cast them as an erotic spectacle: there is no narrative explanation for their nakedness as Cylons generally wear human-style clothes. However, Westerners have always found the supposed "irreducible difference" of Asia a source

---

* Morley and Robins, *Spaces of Identity*, 173.

† A pan across the Eights' faces taken from this scene subsequently illustrates "There are many copies" in seasons two and three's pre-title sequences. Another big group of (clothed) Eights approach Athena in the episode "Faith" (May 9, 2008). Number Eight is the only Cylon model we ever see in such large numbers as this.

Figure 73. "Kobol's Last Gleaming, Part Two," *Battlestar Galactica*. © NBC / Universal 2013.

of "fascination" as well as "anxiety" and are therefore liable to "indulge … in unashamed aestheticism, eroticisation and idealization." This Far Orientalism is given a specifically contemporary inflection by Darrell Y. Hamamoto, who notes that "since the late 1960s" Western cultures have had a tendency to "fetishi[se] all things Asian." This includes not only cultural exports such as *anime* but also Asian women, who may be subject to the "racist love" of white men[*] …

Looking beyond these possible manifestations of "Asiaphilic White desire," the fact that the Cylon model most closely associated with techno-orientalist attitudes is female is also significant in terms of the hostility towards technological advancement that the discourse implies.[†] A number of critics have already suggested that it is common for science fiction texts to conflate anxieties about technology with an apparent mistrust of women, especially those who do not conform to traditional feminine roles. For example, Cornea and Doane both analyze several films in which female

---

[*] Morley and Robins, *Spaces of Identity*, 163–4; Darrell Y. Hamamoto, "Introduction: On Asian American Film and Criticism," *Countervisions: Asian American Film Criticism,* eds. Darrell Y. Hamamoto and Sandra Liu (Philadelphia: Temple University Press, 2000), 11, 12.

[†] Hamamoto, "Introduction," 12.

cyborgs or androids are represented as threatening, such as *Metropolis* (Lang, Germany, 1927), *Eve of Destruction* (Gibbins, U.S., 1991) and *Star Trek: First Contact* (Frakes, U.S., 1996), and note that these films often foreground the idea of technological, "motherless" or otherwise unnatural reproduction as a source of horror* ...

The second principal Eight, Athena, initially appears to be cast in a similar mould, seducing marooned human pilot Helo (Tahmoh Penikett) in order to conceive a hybrid baby in "Six Degrees of Separation" (November 29, 2004). However, she soon comes to realise she has fallen in love with him and consequently betrays her fellow Cylons by fleeing with him back to *Galactica* ("The Farm") ... Athena's final symbolic rejection of her own "Cylon-ness" accords with one of the main criticisms that Geoff Ryman levels at the ending of *BSG*: that it replicates the powerful American myth of the "melting pot," the idea that cultural identities other than that belonging to the "white folk ... in power" get "assimilated completely" to the extent that they cease to exist.† ... In these terms, as Matthew Gumpert observes, Helo and Athena's daughter Hera is not, in fact, a "mixture" of Cylon and human but a completely new type of entity whose "true hybridity signifies the end of race itself"‡ ... [The] very last sequence of *BSG* indicates its most recent evolution. During a flash-forward to present-day New York, a news item captioned "Advances in Robotics" plays on a television in a shop window. The final and most advanced-looking robot in the montage is in the form of an East Asian woman in high-heeled boots and a PVC mini-dress, who blinks her long eyelashes seductively as a cut reveals that her image is also being displayed on two of the giant screens on Times Square ...

---

* Christina Cornea, *Science Fiction Cinema: Between Fantasy and Reality* (Edinburgh: Edinburgh University Press, 2007), 145–74; Mary Ann Doane, "Technophilia: Technology, Representation and the Feminine" in *Liquid Metal: The Science Fiction Film Reader,* ed. Sean Redmond (London: Wallflower, 2004), 186.

† Geoff Ryman, "Adama and (Mitochondrial) Eve: A Foundation Myth for White Folks" in Battlestar Galactica: *Investigating Flesh, Spirit and Steel,* eds. Roz Kaveney and Jennifer Stoy (London: I.B. Tauris, 2010), 47.

‡ Matthew Gumpert, "Hybridity's End," *Cylons in America: Critical Studies in Battlestar Galactica,* eds. Tiffany Potter and C.W. Marshall (London: Continuum, 2008), 152–3.

Epilogue:
Uncle Sam and the Headless Chinaman

Progress was embodied by a mechanical man. The 1893 Chicago Columbian Exposition featured a ten-foot Uncle Sam talking automaton standing above the gathered throngs. Attributed to inventor Thomas Edison, this anthropomorphic thing reportedly gave 40,000 speeches during the fair. Phonographs were hidden inside, blaring at the gawkers. For many, this machine embodied the boundless, expansive spirit of industrial America, the realization of John Gast's "American Progress."

The trade card (Figure 74) advertising Hub Gore "elastic for shoes" depicts national caricatures from around the world, including a Chinaman with a proto–Fu Manchu mustache next to an American Indian with a generic feather headress. All are looking up, marveling at American progress in action, used here to sell Hub Gore products.

Five decades later, Professor Fei Xiaotong, a founder of Chinese sociology, was walking through the hallowed halls of the University of Chicago noting that America was "a land without ghosts."[1] With the critical vantage of a trained scholar from outside a culture, he observed that Americans, rather than living with the past, kept their gaze fixed forward with a faith in progress. By this date in 1943, Fei's slice of the U.S. was obsessed with a figure other than the mechanical Uncle Sam. The new fascination was with the "man of steel"; Superman was Fei's symbol of an America abundant with material uplift and righteousness. He thought, here "life is free and easy." In this land, "American eyes can gaze straight ahead." Such was the hope and the promise. The promise keeps the spirited growth machine fueled for more growth.[2] "Keep those passions invested!" we are exhorted.

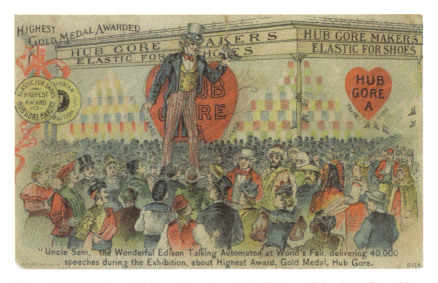

Figure 74. Uncle Sam talking automaton, 1893 Chicago Columbian Exposition. Hub Gore was a Boston-based maker of elastic for shoes. Part of the mass production of shoes, they advertised supplying 1,000 makers of "good shoes" sold by 100,000 dealers and guaranteeing stretchiness for 18 months. *Scribner's Magazine*, vol. 4 (1889), advertisements, 56. "Hub Gore's elastic shoes," trade card (c. 1893–95). Photographed by Phillip Chen. Courtesy of the Lenore Metrick-Chen Collection.

In the best of all worlds, the machine, the spirit of capitalism, the Protestant work ethic, and the promise hummed along in perfect harmony—each adjusting to the shifts in the other.[3] In theory, it's a wondrous system. In this fantasized world, Manifest Destiny had become "truth, justice, and the American way."

Fei might or might not have been aware that Superman was dreamed up by two Russian Jewish immigrants. They carried on the American dream of "life, liberty, and the pursuit of happiness." "The American Way of Life is individualistic, dynamic, pragmatic. It affirms the supreme value and dignity of the individual; it stresses incessant activity on his part, for he is never to rest but is always to be striving to 'get ahead'; it defines an ethic of self-reliance, merit, and character, and judges by achievement: 'deeds, not creeds' are what count."[4]

At the same time, 100 percent Americanism still reigned in many universities and public institutions. America had been deeply impacted by fears of "racial degeneration" and the 1924 Johnson Reed Act. Eugenicists

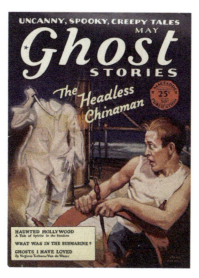

Figure 75. *Ghost Stories* (May 1929), cover art by Jean Oldham. Courtesy of pulpcovers.com.

such as Cold Spring Harbor's Eugenics Research Office, and popularizers Madison Grant and Lothrop Stoddard, alarmed Americans about the
civilizational dangers of so-called inferior races mixing with white, Anglo
American Protestants.[5] The long century of *de jure* Jim Crow segregation
in the post–Civil War South was linked to immigration restriction and
exclusion laws defining the United States as a white republic.[6] Anti-Chinese
and anti-"Oriental" racism constitute a key part of how Americans defined
themselves as citizens against those deemed unassimilable, foreign others.
For the purposes of understanding Yellow Peril in this larger context, we'll
frame this connection to the larger dynamics in U.S. history as an era of Jim
Crow segregation and exclusion.

Fei was accurate in sensing American's faith in progress, but the realm
of popular culture told a far more ambivalent story to a far more haunted
public. From 1882 to 1943 to 1965, the period of racially defined anti-
Chinese and anti-Asian immigration laws played out social and political
issues in the powerful, emergent mass media. Out on the streets, on the
newsstands, in the films, and in the archives, spooks were creeping and frol-
icking the mediascape—here exemplified by the pulp fiction *Ghost Stories*
"The Headless Chinaman" (Figure 75) and this 1882 political cartoon

Figure 76. George Frederick Keller, "Impending Retribution," *The Wasp*, vol. 9, no. 323 (October 7 1882), centerfold. Courtesy of The Bancroft Library University of California, Berkeley.

"Impending Retribution" (Figure 76). In the latter, a Columbia-like figure is leading victims of a deadly railway land dispute at Mussel Slough, California to rid the land of monopolists Stanford, Huntington, and Crocker.[7] The dead shall have their justice over the powerful. The fleet-footed Mercury, with a cheering crowd, presided above the carcass of a derailed steam locomotive. Perhaps not haunting the lecture halls of academe, spectres, ghosts, and the undead were omnipresent everywhere else in this Gothic-infused landscape.[8]

Other than dismissing this phenomenon as "superstition," how might we understand haunted America in relation to yellow perilism? Understanding, in this volume, leads to an historical recognition. And recognition to reckoning and action. This epilogue explores what we must do to counter yellow perilism and other practices of racial scapegoating. What are these American hauntings about? At their core, we can gain insights about yellow perilism and the political culture of American society.

The visual ephemera of the Jim Crow era offers us valuable insights into how this system of dehumanization and scapegoating was possible. It exemplifies a violent dismembering and obsessive manipulation with the racialized Chinaman's body via the new visual print media of popular commercial culture. These visual fragments give us hints about what happened in the actual historical enactment of these wild, passionate fantasies onto the lives of real, living people.

PLAYING JIM CROW

This following series of anti-Chinese Yellow Peril images document a playful violence, a willful dismemberment of a scapegoated people. But can we stand looking at ourselves so honestly? Can we hold the gaze to remember that past? Can we face history and learn about ourselves?

We begin with the playfulness of visual representations that can be easily fictionalized. In this trade card advertisement for "Malt Bitters" a visual

Figure 77 (left). Malt Bitters trade card "puzzle" asking "Who is the coming man?" Malt Bitters was advertised as "The purest, safest and most powerful restorative in medicine for feeble and exhausted constitutions, nervous and general debility, consumption and wasting diseases." Malt Bitters, trade card (c. 1870s). Photo by Phillip Chen. Courtesy of the Lenore Metrick-Chen Collection.

Figure 78 (right). The "Chinaman" is "the coming man"! Detail, Malt Bitters, trade card.

puzzle is created asking "Who is the coming man?" (Figure 77). The gentleman, head obscured in a cloud of his own cigarette smoke, presumably a white male, a visual figure representing the normative (white) American patriarch-consumer.

The artist cleverly tricks the eye to see smoke. But when tipped, reveals the swollen, seemingly "negroid" featured Chinese man (Figure 78). Indeed, Chinese immigrants to California were commonly referred to as "The coming man." This disembodied, ghostly head clearly belongs on "The headless Chinaman." Such visual puns expressed the new freedom certain artists could express with cheap print technology. While racial and ethnic mix-ups were common on the nineteenth-century American stage, visual mix-ups were common in the visual print culture.

The object of this encased pocket toy (Figure 79) is to gently roll the beads, the missing teeth, into position, thus completing the Chinaman's buck-toothed smile. This head could also be cut out and put onto the "headless Chinaman"!

A Chinaman snacking on a rat is featured also in Figure 80. Though part of the American palate today, when Chinese food was first introduced to

Figure 79. The object of this small hand toy is to gently roll the small white beads into the holes in the mouth of the "Chinaman," restoring the grotesque's teeth, "Ball in Hole" Game, handmade (c. 1870s). Photo by Phillip Chen. Courtesy of the Lenore-Metrick Chen Collection.

the American streetscape doubts were raised about what kinds meats were used. Showing a Chinaman eating rats, on the New Jersey–based product "Rough on Rats," clearly helped company sales. The boundaries of what carnivores in the U.S. would eat and not eat—muskrats yes, dogs no—were sorted out in the free play of the advertising world. But why stop at rats!? See the detail from "The Problem Solved" (Figure 81), shown earlier in Chapter 5, with the voracious Chinaman eating the Irishman who had just shared a meal devouring Uncle Sam. Chinamen were clearly cannibalizing the American body politic.

Figure 82 shows the disfigured profile of Lon Chaney in the silent film classic *Shadows* (1922). Chaney, "the man of a thousand faces,"

Figure 80. "Rough on Rats" (arsenic) at fifteen cents a box was advertised as ridding houses of "Rats, Mice, Moths, Ants, Mosquitoes, Bed Bugs, Insects, Skunk, Weasel, Gophers, Chipmunks, Moles, Musk Rats, etc." Druggist Ephraim S. Wells of Jersey City made "Rough on Corns" for calluses, "Rough on Toothache," "Mother Swan's Worm Syrup," and other medicines. "Rough on Rats," trade card (c. 1880s). Photo by Phillip Chen. Courtesy of the Lenore-Metrick Chen Collection.

Figure 81. Ultimately, the voracious Chinaman eats the Irishman, who earlier joined him in eating Uncle Sam. See Figure 57 for full illustration.

sympathetically plays the ill-treated Chinaman Yen Shen, who is scripted as a bent-over, self-sacrificing laundryman. Even when played as a "positive" stereotype, the Chinese male body was represented and seen as grotesque.

As medical science refined their understanding of human anatomy, it became commonplace for skeletons and skulls to be drawn in the burgeoning print culture. This skull of a monstrous Chinaman (Figure 83) is staring down at a surprised and frightened Uncle Sam in this close up of Glackens's political cartoon shown in the Introduction.

And this disembodied hand, "the yellow claw" (Figure 84), threatens to turn off the lights. The visual heroine retreats in fear. Such bony fingers with sharpened fingernails attached to the bodies of evil Asian male bodies were a common way to represent queered, perverse sexuality as discussed in the introduction. The yellow disembodied "claw" was also evocative of the shape of the reviled octopus and spider.[9]

The Chinaman was and remains a fantastic figment of the American and Western imagination. Serving multiple purposes in multiple places and multiple moments. So conjured, he is also symbolically and ritually tortured. Add up all these visual stigmas and a visual common sense of non-normative, queer disgust is formulated, serialized, and looped. This floating Chinaman's head (Figure 85) emerging from a magical Oriental

Figure 82. The Chinaman as a grotesque figure was portrayed sympathetically by Lon Chaney, "the man of a thousand faces," in the silent film *Shadows* (1922). He played "Yen Shen" a self-sacrificing laundryman based on the short story "Ching, Ching, Chinaman" by Wilbur Daniel Steele (1917). *Ching, Ching, China-man*, sheet music cover (1922). Yoshio Kishi/Irene Yah Ling Sun Collection of Asian Americana made possible in large part in memory of Dr. Wei Yu Chen, MSS 292, Oversize Series II, Subseries C, Box 45, folder 16. Fales Library and Special Collections, New York University.

Figure 83. The skull of Chinese exclusion frightens Uncle Sam. Can there be a historical reckoning with the meaning of racial exclusion from American life? Detail, Louis Glackens (see Figure 15 for citation details).

Figure 84. Horrid, terrifying body parts, the clawed, creeping hand, the voracious yawning mouth, appeared ever-ready in the visual, commercial culture to consume all that America and the West hold dear. The Yellow Peril male grotesque has been the "bad object" of comedy, derision, and worse. "The Yellow Claw," *Detective Story*, vol. 5, no. 1 (Oct. 5, 1916). Courtesy of the Wong Ching Foo Collection.

Figure 85. The spectral disembodied head emerges from a magic lamp. It must belong to "The Headless Chinaman"! *Money vs. Muscle, or, Chinese Emigration. To the Workmen and Trade Unions of America* (New York: The "Season" Press, 1870). Courtesy of the New York Public Library.

vase captures this deep Western civilizational association—an Orient with fantastical body parts.

Even the visual representation of brutality and violation becomes burlesqued. "They are pretty safe there, when politicians do agree, their unanimity is wonderful" (Figure 86). Once reassembled, we can begin to reconstruct the visual language of disgust attached to these drawn lines commonly recognizable as the Chinaman's despicable and iconic body parts. This is the logic of a system of bullies. It produced a necessary, indispensable visual Other where the stigmatized grotesque deserves violation; indeed the Chinamen bring violence onto themselves. "Give it to him, he's got no votes nor no friends."

Glackens's haunting skull (Figure 83) is of the disappeared Chinaman, hidden away and forgotten, returning to frighten the forgetful, and hence

Figure 86. The logic of a system of bullies produced a necessary other where the stigmitized grotesque deserves violation, and indeed, brings violence onto itself. The original caption continues: "They are pretty safe there: when politicians do agree, their unanimity is wonderful." Bernhard Gillam, "They Are Pretty Safe There," *Puck*, vol. 11, no. 265 (April 5, 1882), 75. Courtesy of the New York Public Library.

"innocent," Uncle Sam. Facing our ghosts suggests the imperative of Americans looking deeply into Uncle Sam eyes—to look at him rather than his misdirected gaze at the ghostly other. His scapegoats, now long forgotten, come back as the "return of the repressed" disembodied from the memory of the Chinese Exclusion Act, the legacy of which is still in effect. National identity, embodied by Uncle Sam, keeps his sense of integrity and goodness by forgetting its misdeeds. Misremembering, here, should not only be understood as faulty recall but also the incorrect piecing together, the mistaken re-assembly of severed members of the body politic, literally mis-re-member-ing.

This "American innocence" is what haunts us all. This elusive yet omnipresent and omnipotent spectral presence, after all, is what we must retrieve from dusty, long-disavowed storage shelves. This remembering formulated our mission in hauntological studies. It is easier to obsess about the woes of the present rather than reckon with the past. It is easier to promise the future will be better if we only obsess about a scapegoated Other to embody what poisons the body politic. But can we reckon with repressed past injustices?

VISUALIZING RACIAL CAPITALISM

The protests of the July 1877 sandlot riots, from which the Workingmen's Party of California emerged, shouted for "Cooperation" and also waged two demands: "Down with monopolies!" and "The Chinese Must Go!"[10] The following three images from the weekly San Francisco–based satirical publication *The Wasp* illustrated the Party's concerns for a broader public.

"Down with Monopolies" was the first demand of Denis Kearney, the leader of the Workingmen's Party. This 1882 "Curse of California" (Figure 87) depicts a rapacious giant octopus hording its wealth on Nob Hill while its tentacles grab up all businesses and means of independent livelihoods including wheat, mining, lumber, farmers, fruit growing, and wine making. Stanford and Crocker, Southern Pacific Railroad magnates, are the monster's eyes. The Big Four railroad-building financiers, Leland Stanford, Colis P. Huntington, Charles Crocker, and Mark Hopkins, came to symbolize the thwarting of individual white workers being able to make a decent living. Artist George Frederick Keller, himself a recent Prussian immigrant, used the European American motif of the octopus to capture the despotism of this corporate grab.

Keller illustrates the visceral reasons for the second demand, "The Chinese Must Go!" (Figure 88). A multi-armed, grotesque Chinaman is working all industries at once epitomizing "unfair competition" and sending the money back to China. Outside are the white boys left idle and policed. The Chinese caricature is a human octopus on steroids, at once able to take on multiple skilled trades. Indeed, "they" are machine-like and imagined to be model industrial workers from the point of view of employers.

The next graphic (Figure 89) transforms the octopus into a smoke-spewing automaton. It illustrates "raw material" fed down a chute into the machinic monster of "progress." It spews out, like so much vomit, manufactured goods of all kinds. Again, idled men and a mother with child stand by watching. A man facing the newspaper reader is waving his arm as if declaiming to readers. Two hidden messages add layers to this political illustration.

Figure 87. Here, the consolidation of power and greed is represented as a giant, grasping octopus. Stanford and Crocker are the eyes of the smiling monster stripping the landscape of hard-working, free laborers. The graveyard is all that remains, represented by the Mussel Slough martyrs (lower left). George Frederick Keller, "The Curse of California," *The Wasp*, vol. 9, no. 316 (August 19, 1882), centerfold. Courtesy of the Bancroft Library, University of California, Berkeley.

Figure 88. "The Chinese Must Go!" conflates the anti-monopoly octopus with the ugly, inhuman, work monster with many arms, each working tirelessly. Such "unfair competition" causes young white men to be idle and prone to mischief. But who can blame them?! George Frederick Keller, "What Shall We Do With Our Boys?", *The Wasp*, vol. 8, no. 292 (March 3, 1882), centerfold. Courtesy of the Bancroft Library, University of California, Berkeley.

In a shadowy recess, center right, we can spy the outline of a figure controlling the machine—the silhouette of a Chinaman pulling the lever. Is he the true culprit behind the machine (Figure 90, left)? Yet, the cartoon plays out one more layer of meaning. Above the Chinaman and the billowing smoke: "The real Chinaman who is at the root of all evil" is said to be another culprit (Figure 90, right). The machine replacing the manly producer is the evil. It produces a way of life full of machinic-generated progress but leaving passive spectators in its wake.

The sandlots and *The Wasp* contested the overwhelming power of the Nob Hill power brokers. Within British settler colonial republics, such as the United States, the older ruling verities of the wisdom of the few and the mob ignorance of the many, expressed throughout this volume, chafed and opened raw wounds. New ideals of participation, many radicals demanding a vote for non–property owning men, threatened even yesterday's agitators.

Figure 89. George Frederick Keller, "Machinery Monopolizes Labor," *The Wasp*, vol. 4 (August 30, 1879). Courtesy of the Bancroft Library, University of California, Berkeley.

Figure 90. *Left*: In a shadowy recess we can spy the outline of a controlling figure, the silhouette of a "Chinaman" pulling the lever. The true culprit behind the machine! Or is he? *Right*: But perhaps "The real Chinaman who is at the root of all evil" is the machine itself. Details, "Machinery Monopolizes Labor."

Who could be included was always a process of triangulating a group who would and could be othered. *The Wasp*'s brilliant artists expressed and evoked palpable connections being made in this countercultural sphere and played out this triangulated system of uniting and othering. Such visual phantoms embodied the fears felt by all—but ultimately supported the compromise solution of excluding Chinese in the formulation of a white republic in which white workingmen and white bosses could both flourish.

Abracadabra! *That horrid, pestilent other is causing all our problems.* Indeed, scapegoating is a time-tested form of episodic, short-term risk management. If the political culture can't quite deliver its promises, it will appease the white working class by creating an external enemy and blaming the victim. From the 1880s onwards, the decades in which Chinese and then other racialized "Oriental" workers were excluded and marginalized, the system of the machine could survive by redirecting class injustices and inequities through repeated rounds of stereotyping others from various parts of Asia and the Pacific, and scapegoating the stereotypes. The 1870-80s sandlot protests and the passage of the 1882 Chinese Exclusion Act are but a case study of these dynamics in action. Siphoning off anger directed at the monopolies reduced the risk of further disruption, indeed the rhetoric of class war itself had to be hedged against.

The progress machine fed exponentially rising expectations. Such expectations of materially delimited "happiness" can never quite be contained by the promises of inclusion and rising expectations. The machinic spirits are far too self-serving, too passionate, and too greedy to ever be controllable.[11] At each crisis point in which legitimacy and the system is called into question, stopgap measures have been improvised, with lots of duct tape, to work out temporary fixes with plenty of compromises. Amid this instability, pointing the finger of blame outside of the straining system buys time. This spirit of scapegoat capitalism was able to form an unholy amalgam of free territorial and economic expansion, unfettered commerce, and racial hierarchy in the name of keeping the growth machine going. This practice of racial capitalism was formulated and refined against various Chinese Americans and Mexicans, against Japanese Americans, Filipino Americans, Korean Americans, South Asian Americans, Pacific Islanders, against Soviet and Chinese Reds, *ad nauseam* until the civil rights movement ended a century of Jim Crow and racially defined exclusion.

This ghost of a historical past, conveniently forgotten in U.S. history, is part of what we need to learn how to reckon with. Sociologist Fei delineated a dimension of social life referred across generations, often neglected in the emphasis on American individualism and progress. Looking forward and not dealing with the past had become a mode of being during the Jim Crow/Chinese Exclusion era. For Fei, living with the past was to live with memories and meanings, continuities as well as shifts. By ignoring this past, Asian American and other Othered faces, names, bodies, signifying this expelled, alien-ized difference, are forever deemed non- and un-American, forever foreign. Can Americans learn to deal with this abjected ghost that does not fit the normative mythos? Or will the national history and memory refuse to re-attach, literally re-member, the body politic? Can "we, the people" only be racially-defined as white male non-queer in this pluralist democratic republic?

Never a land without hauntings, today our culture is overrun with the juvenilia of superheroes but with a difference. An untroubled, corn-fed Superman is not the dominant mythos. Today, with a far more gothic sensibility, we know even superheroes must have flaws. Today, we are far less certain about America's future, present, and past.

HOW SHOULD WE RESPOND?

Today, emergent local economies and interests are often outflanked by multinational conglomerate strategies and power plays. Through highs and lows, wealth continues to concentrate at the top within nations and across. Linked to rigid notions of a fundamentalist Protestant nationalist and civilizational Self, the Anglo American world remakes the world as its domain in which all other sovereign worldviews are assumed competitive and non-compatible unless proven otherwise. As various sovereign political economies continue to grow in different parts of Asia, the Westernized Global North faces stiff competition. Now that the growth machines of India, China, and other industrializing and digitizing societies are producing and consuming, the contest for resources and labor, what European and American empires had once taken for granted, has intensified. With a national mythos still framed by Manifest Destiny and the right to "life, liberty, and happiness," the free and easy access to energy, rare earths (for high technology), raw materials, and other "necessities" to keep the American Way of Life is commonly believed to be sacrosanct. All resistance can be construed as a threat to Homeland Security. Meanwhile, the media is rife with stories about China's failure to develop industry in environmentally sustainable ways, that China copies and steals, that China is hacking away America's wealth, ad infinitum. How many of us repeat the inaccurate statement gone viral that China owns the U.S. debt? (Google or Bing "U.S. debt" to see how viral this mythology has become. U.S. law mandates that the U.S. owns the majority of its own debt.) Without this tautology, what has become a secular fundamentalist belief of the U.S. citizenry, businessman Peter Kiernan's brazen, catchy title *Becoming China's Bitch* (2012) would make no sense. Peter Navarro's *The Coming China Wars: Where They Will Be Fought and How They Can Be Won* (2008) asserts, "China is on a collision course with the rest of the world." "China's conquest of so many of the world's export markets has vaporized literally millions of manufacturing jobs and driven down wages from the heartland of America and the *maquiladoras* of Mexico to the slums of Bangladesh, the shores of Indonesia, and the once teeming textile factories of Africa."[12] Surely this is not anti-Asian, the literal reader might rightfully query. Surely if the author includes China harming other parts of Asia it would be unfair to make such accusations. Yet

Figure 91. Here a muscle-bound beach bully, the People's Republic of China, is shown intimidating a scrawny Uncle Sam. Robert Sikoryak was commissioned by *Fortune* to illustrate the cover story "Can Americans compete?" He chose to do a parody of the classic Charles Atlas comic book advertisement. Cover illustration for "America the 97 Lb. Weakling?," *Fortune* (August 1, 2005). © Robert Sikoryak 2005. Courtesy of the artist.

the racial triangulation of the coalition of the good American with the good Other versus the bad Other is the same. In the geopolitics of post–Civil Rights racial capitalism, there is always the good, self-sacrificing Chinaman and the evil, monomaniacal Chinaman. This is the fundamentalist West's practice of the repressed bully within, projected outward onto whatever Oriental Other best fits the "bad boy" needs of the moment (Figure 91). Such schoolyard hubris fuels conceits of American innocence, purity, and exceptionalism.

Indeed the rise of the regime of neoliberal "shop till you drop" globalization means that the world need subscribe to the Westernization process started centuries ago. The purchase of Westernizing stories, histories, and mythos of progress and modernity is to be chosen over the othered's own traditions. The right to unfettered happiness through shopping has become the new standard of universal freedom and happiness. *But be careful not to buy and believe this "progress" can be gained from "cheap" Asian-made fakes!* The 99 percent should all want to buy the promise at retail prices.

Yellow perilism is neither misinformation nor the figment of overactive imaginations. It is a structured tradition of concepts and practices hardwired into the political culture of Western Enlightenment modernity itself. Globalized especially by British and Anglo American expansionism, its patterning is a relational and recurrent process of identity formation and disidentification.

How can this binary-driven, fundamentalist, deeply traditional yellow perilist political culture be challenged and changed? Our goal in creating this book was to provide a starting point. We have sought to make visible what has been silenced and disappeared by making facts, archives, stories, and histories present and accessible. We've teased and taunted at the binaries with the language of reversal: Europe is a peninsular subcontinent, Europe as having been Westernized, and how the "barbarians" catalyzed the Renaissance and modernity. At the more foundational level, we've sought to change the spirit that drives the passions and the interests of the divisive political culture of racial capitalism. The question that remains is how might we effect similar changes in the broader culture?

What must we do? Rather than scapegoating the Other, displacing and escaping, we must become hauntologists. We must face our ghosts.

We need to track down what shadows us and engage with what our compulsive, manic-obsessive preoccupation is all about. "[W]e have to learn how it speaks ... we have to grasp the fullness of its life-world, its desires and its standpoint."[13] This necessitates a forensic stance. "When I am a spooky phantom you want to avoid, when there is nothing but the shadow of a public civic life, when bedrooms and boardrooms are clamorous ghost chambers, deep 'wounds of civilization' are in haunting evidence."[14] With cyclic bouts of perilism, we've been serialized and distracted, fooled and foolish; but this is not the way it has to be.

Lawyer and activist scholar Eric Yamamoto offers a useful way to organize the necessary intervention. In his study of groups working on healing the wounds of racism, he has identified a process of group-to-group, community-to-community dialogue, communication, and reconciliation, along with "Four R's" to follow (recognition, responsibility, reconstruction, reparation). We've translated this valuable set of practices into ways of de-scripting and dis-membering the overwhelming power of the Yellow Peril living archive within the political culture of the U.S., drawing on the "civilizing mission" of "the West." The instances of violation are particular to a time and place, as we have analyzed, but the deeper issue of scapegoating has been everywhere. Yet, as the world becomes more interlinked, largely driven by the United States through the passions and the interests of market capitalism, the ghosts in the machines foment more systemwide scapegoating. Fighting perilism is local, regional, national, and global. It is a foundational issue of human rights and social justice. It is a struggle that has to begin at the grass roots: people to people, group to group.

> What is interracial justice? In brief, interracial justice entails hard acknowledgment of the historical and contemporary ways in which racial groups harm one another, along with affirmative efforts to redress justice grievances and rearticulate and restructure present-day relations. So conceived, interracial justice is often integral to building (or rebuilding) relationships among communities of color—the establishment of "right relationships, the healing of broken relationships."[15]

Recognition: The Bigger Picture

Randolph Bourne (1886–1918) was a Progressive-era essayist and, along with Jane Addams, an anti-WWI activist. Bourne's concept of a "Trans-National America" continues to challenge commonsense notions of assimilation and the U.S. as a "melting pot." Written just at the time "100 percent Americanism" was surging and anti-immigrant organizing was taking place, culminating in the 1924 immigration restrictions limiting "inferior" Europeans entry to the U.S., Bourne turned the tables on Anglo American nationalism and criticized their ongoing ethnic heritage biases. Bourne identified a new type of American identity defined as fluid and dynamic, and in process.[16]

Yellow perilism is part of a matrix of historically embedded practices and beliefs, materialized over the centuries as what Michael Omi and Howard Winant call "racial formations" in notions of Western Civilization and European American political culture. It might be helpful to think of formations operating on different scales, from local to regional to national to intra-national, to larger scales of reference, and across scales, hence translocal, transregional, transnational. Recognition entails recognizing the harm and injustice done to the targets of Yellow Peril historically and in the present.

Recognition "asks racial group members to recognize and empathize with the anger and hope of those wounded; to acknowledge the disabling social constraints imposed by one group on another and the resulting group wounds; to identify related justice grievances often underlying current group conflict; and to critically examine stock stories of racial group attributes and interracial relations ostensibly legitimating those constraints and grievances."[17]

Responsibility: Naming Injustice

Naming injustice is the beginning of taking responsibility as a social process. It is necessarily a grassroots, group-making process, and cannot emerge simply from reading a book, though that can help. It happens from being with people and understanding what is happening to them, and could mean explicitly and carefully assessing the power dynamics between individuals of different races within a particular group. It means really listening to one another—and especially those who have been othered—and sharing the authority of naming. It may also mean imposing disabling constraints on those with racial privileges, and accepting group responsibility for healing any resulting wounds.

Reconstruction: Reframing Stories

Reconstruction is a process of "reframing stories of group interrelations and group identities." The peoples' culture-making process of copying best practices and commons-making are part and parcel to the rediscovery of the social within all individuals and freeing the propagandized, scripted individuals to critically think for themselves.

Fear and scapegoating on behalf of elite interests, which defines Yellow Peril practices, derives from a zero-sum notion of who can achieve a good life, or in other words, the idea that Americans only have access to the good life if we cut off "Oriental" workers. As Anglo American neoliberal globalization drives the privatization of basic resources, such as clean air and water once shared and common by local peoples around the globe, the conditions for the competition and accumulation of natural resources will become the new battleground. Reconstruction means changing how we evaluate the terms of threat, self, and otherness, and it means creating a vision for a different future, either drawing upon a lost past or different from the past. The central question is how we might transform the present. Speculative fiction, used much in yellow perilist discourse, can also be mobilized to contest such visions.

Reparation: An Ethics of Care

Reparation is making long-term material and cultural changes in the big picture. Reparation "seeks to repair the damage to the material conditions of racial group life in order to attenuate one group's power over another." This means material changes in the structure of the relationship (social, economic, political) to guard against "cheap reconciliation," in which healing efforts are "just talk." The reparations campaigns of America's first nations peoples have been long fought and continue. And important victories have been won finally recognizing the sovereignty of many violated nations.

Is it possible to speak of material reparations to those wronged by yellow perilism? After organizing for redress, Japanese Americans placed in WWII concentration camps gained an "apology" from President Reagan and a symbolic payment of $20,000 for damages done. After Chinese Canadians organized national protests, the Canadian Parliament has recently apologized for the anti-Chinese Head Tax and supported the formation of a digital archive to support scholarship and education about this past racist policy and practice. Chinese Americans in the U.S. recently organized to gain a Congressional statement of "regret" for the Chinese Exclusion Act. However, this vote has proven meaningless with no comparable research and educational funds alerting a public that doesn't know and appears not to care about this history.

Still, government "regrets," "apologies," and financial reparations are important, no matter how superficial and insincere. Such official statements become part of the record of the national body politic, and ethically, even the unrealized rhetoric of higher juridical standards for all have to be asserted time and again. However, unless reparation campaigns mobilize larger and larger grassroots educational efforts such governmental statements have little public impact and meaning. The Japanese American campaign was successful because the younger generations wanted to hear the stories and end the silencing of the past. Having mobilized tens of thousands to sign petitions and circulate the stories of what happened, the organizing campaign became a Redress Movement. The script was rewritten once people began to speak out beyond the confines of private households. A new public was created. Many of the reparations payments were donated directly to the building of the Japanese American National Museum in Los Angeles. The architecture, wall of donors, exhibits, and archives have become emblems of the Redress Movement. The Mashantucket Pequot Museum and Research Center is a magnificent, additional example of reparations sustaining ongoing public education.

It is only fitting that we end with a working-through of these questions by pioneering scholar-activist Edward Said. We here engage his unpacking of his ideal of realizing "home," anywhere in the universe but especially one's own.

I find myself returning again and again to a hauntingly beautiful passage by Hugo of St. Victor, a twelfth-century monk from Saxony:

> It is therefore, a source of great virtue for the practiced mind to learn, bit by bit, first to change about in visible and transitory things, so that afterwards it may be able to leave them behind altogether. The person who finds his homeland sweet is still a tender beginner; he to whom every soil is as his native one is already strong; but he is perfect to whom the entire world is as a foreign place. The tender soul has fixed his love on one spot in the world; the strong person has extended his love to all places; the perfect man has extinguished his.

> Erich Auerbach, the great German scholar who spent the years of World War II as an exile in Turkey, cites this passage as a model for anyone—man *and* woman—wishing to transcend the restraints of imperial or national, or provincial limits. Only through this attitude can a historian, for example, begin to grasp human experience and its written records in all their diversity and particularity; otherwise one would remain committed more to the exclusions and reactions of prejudice than to the negative freedom of real knowledge.[18]

Said's haunting is that of a deep connecting with a loving sentiment of the past. The meaning he makes in collaboration with a twelfth-century Saxony monk is especially poignant when we recall that Said himself was a Palestinian Christian New Yorker who has wrongly been accused by peril-ists of being an anti-Semitic terrorist. We are complicated creatures. Said, a lover of and deeply knowledgeable about Western classical music, also wrote regular reviews of this elite European enlightenment musical tradi-tion. Decolonizing for Said was a multiple parsing and working-through of our daily engagements—for him as a classical music critic, as a Columbia University professor, as one of Palestinian Christian heritage, as a lover of home.

Historian Thomas Bender uses Todorov's rephrasing of Said's interpreta-tion of Hugo to offer readers the ideal figure of the "cosmopolitan," making a lyrical and very useful point: "The true cosmopolitan must cultivate a doubleness that allows both commitment and distance, an awareness at once of the possible distance of the self and of the possibility of dialogical knowledge of the other."[19] Meanwhile, this Du Boisian "doubleness" Bender refers to is actually a tripleness, and quadrupleness, if not more. As third-wave feminist critics have pointed out, the abstractions of "the nation" and "women" have to be broken down in order to understand the particularity of subject positions. We are all subject to positions of citizenship and to the world through powerful classificatory grids of intersecting serialized positions—what Foucault called power/knowledge. It's tempting for many to decry those claiming particularist positions as "Balkanizing" and splintering off. But Said is clear on this point. Rather than abstractly rising above such local attachments, he advocates a "working-through."

> No one today is purely *one* thing. Labels like Indian, or woman, or Muslim, or American are not more than starting points, which if followed into actual experience for only a moment are quickly left behind. Imperialism consolidated the mixture of cultures and identities on a global scale. But its worst and most paradoxical gift was to allow people to believe that they were only, mainly, exclusively, white, or Black, or Western, or Oriental. Yet just as human beings make their own history, they also make their cultures and ethnic identities. No one can deny the persisting continuities of long traditions, sustained habitations, national languages, and cultural geographies, but there seems no reason except fear and prejudice to keep insisting on their separation and distinctiveness, as if that was all human life was about.

This larger, more generous, comparative and ethical understanding constitutes a larger reckoning with our own multiplicity within ourselves, with those we love, and with the multiplicity outside our immediate selves, those still "foreign."

Psychotherapist and writer Alan Roland has suggestively framed the migratory process of Asians and Asian Americans in a global era as a "journey to foreign selves."[20] Sociologist Paul Chan Pang Siu documented the stories of Chicago Chinese hand laundry workers in the 1940s. In the front of the shop customers called him "Charlie." In the back where he slept, he dreamt of his village home. Everyday he skirted the Chinese Exclusion Laws as a "paper son." Everyday while wielding an eight pound iron, he fantasized about not having to live furtively and perhaps becoming an American citizen.[21] Can we, the customer, bearing the laundry ticket to pick up an ironed shirt, be in touch with the foreign within ourselves in order to relate to this different experience? Can we, the customer, visit this "mysterious" place and encounter it also as a home behind the counter? Or is this encountered difference and mystery a bit too much, and a source of unease and disidentification?

The challenge for us all, whatever side of the counter we find ourselves on, is whether we can take that journey to foreign selves within and without (Figure 92).

Can we become limber and flexible enough to regularly engage with otherness, enlarge our sense of connectedness, and reintegrate our own sense of well-being? Roland writes: "The complex layering of the self is particularly important in this era of rapid social change" that could spark "considerable unconscious conflicts but also contain the possibility of an expanding self."[22] "It's a self that goes beyond it's original rootedness in another culture. At the same time it can also be rife with conflict. But that doesn't negate a robust new development."[23]

With decolonization and struggles against other vicious divides, we are on the verge of formulating a series of connecting stories of possible shared ways of living through practical, everyday actions. We need both engaged philosophizing and engaged songwriting. We need multiple connecting stories that necessarily become a more accurate set of histories constantly needing retelling. Critiquing yellow perilism and other forms of orientalphobia are necessary in this larger engaged project of enlarging what we mean by "We, the people."

Stay tuned.
To be continued …

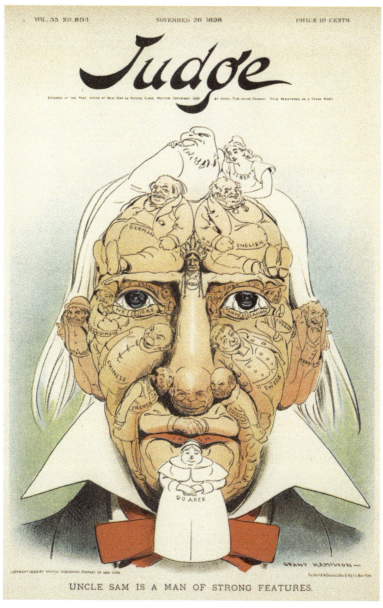

Figure 92. Here Uncle Sam is shown to be a composite of many different peoples. As typical of the times, all these figures are caricatured as national and racial types. Yet, they are portrayed as constituting the strength of the U.S. Grant Hamilton, "Uncle Sam Is a Man of Strong Features," *Judge*, vol.35, no.893 (November 26, 1898). The Ohio State University Billy Ireland Cartoon Library & Museum.

Acknowledgments

We dedicate this volume to the memories of three pathbreaking, independent-spirited scholars, largely unsung. Yoshio Kishi and Him Mark Lai built collections and archives to understand the history of the Americas differently and more completely. Alexander Saxton, born into the Anglo American Protestant culture, offered a way for Western-trained academics to critically "know thyself" with immense integrity. All three understood that the prevailing scholarship, opinion, and practices of their times had to be radically changed and opened up. Their work set a solid foundation upon which generations today are building.

Edward Said's influences are evident throughout this volume. Thanks to William F. Wu, Jack Shaheen, Philip Choy, and Roger Shimomura, collectors and ethnographers of "oriental" otherness—also making bedrock for ongoing and future work. We also want to recognize the edited collections and cooperative spirit of Yorimitsu Hashimoto. We also want to recognize the visionary and foundational progressive scholarship-building work of publisher and editor Janet Francendese.

This project first took shape at the Asian/Pacific/American Institute, New York University. In many ways it is a long-term, collaborative research endeavor that is rarely supported in today's individualized, privatized academic climate. The A/P/A Institute initially focused on the phenomenon of Yellow Peril, in part, to raise funds for the acquisition of the Yoshio Kishi and Irene Yah-ling Sun Collection. The purchase was made possible, in large part, by the Chen Family donation to the memory of Dr. Wei Yu Chen. The catalogue *Yellow Peril: Collecting Xenophobia* (2007) and the undergraduate seminar "Yellow Peril: Understanding Xenophobia" emerged as dialogic joint projects that shaped the development of this book. Institute Deputy Director Laura Chen-Schultz has been at the core of this collections development initiative, as well as many other initiatives. Her steady hand at the rudder, during times both stormy and at dead calm, has made all the difference.

Jack Tchen wants to thank John Dower and the late Paul Chan Pang Siu for their inspiration and support. And thanks to Phillip Chen and Lenore Metrick-Chen in sharing their home, collections, and insights. Thanks to my many generous colleagues. Among them are Tom Bender, Kyoo Lee, Randy Martin, George Shulman, Carolyn Dinshaw, Valerie Forman, Andy Romig, Myles Jackson, Stephen Duncombe, Ruthanne Lum McCunn, Frank Wu, Henry Sapoznik, and especially Lars Amenda and Ruth Mayer. As always, my work is only possible with the help and love of those closest to my heart: Judy Susman and Sara Tchen-Susman. It's been great working with you, Dylan. Thanks for your work with Kishi. And thanks for slogging this project all the way through!

Dylan Yeats wants to thank Jack, the Asian/Pacific/American Institute, and Verso Books for the opportunity to co-edit a volume like this. While the process was at times quite harrowing, it was a true privilege to have the freedom and support to build such a creative and innovative project. Thanks also to the Mortal Kombat writing group for their insights in the early stages of this work and to Philip Choy for sharing his inspirational collection and expertise with me. Emotional support from Suzanne Loughlin, Ed Yeats, Andrew Yeats, Bus Loughlin, Stephanie Hsu, Mike Fassil, David Kim, Carmen Soliz, and Richard Eichler was indispensible. I would also like to recognize some very important people lost along the way: Tish Loughlin, Trav Richmond, and Yoshio Kishi.

Key faculty and administrators have supported this work and made it possible, they include: Ulrich Baer, Susanne Wofford, Joy Connolly, Fran White, Andrew Ross, and Mary Louise Pratt. We've been privileged to work with the faculty, librarians, and archivists at the NYU Library, including Michael Stoller, Marvin Taylor, Peter Wosh, Andrew Lee, and the late Michael Nash.

Thank you to the numerous authors and artists who gave us permission to use their work for free. In this age of profiteering off the knowledge commons, it's refreshing for colleagues and artists to allow free access to their work. Thanks also to the many librarians at the multitude of repositories we consulted. We were sometimes frantic in our pursuit of deadlines and appreciate your patience and willingness to help. In particular we would like to acknowledge the commitment to the democratization of knowledge of the staff at the New York Public Library and the Skidompha Library.

Andrew Hsiao of Verso has been a rock-solid supporter from the very beginning. And it's been a pleasure working with Audrea Lim and Mark Martin.

The Yellow Peril Project team has made this book possible. They include Ji Han, Alexis Perlmutter, Hans Weinreich, Robin Sand, and especially the many quality hours put in by Noah Fuller and Nancy Ng Tam. Thanks also to our terrific crew of Archives MA archivists. Besides Dylan Yeats and Nancy Tam Ng, they also include I. Emily Chu, Amita Manghnani, Daniel Kim, and Janice Liao. And thanks for the amazing and wonderful A/P/A Institute family in addition to LCS: Ruby Gomez, Alexandra Chang, and the same Amita Manghnani.

Finally, we wish to thank the great students we've worked with in the NYU seminar "Yellow Peril: Understanding Xenophobia"—five semesters of smart, creative, and insightful gleaners, documentarians, and analysts. You are too many to list here but you have taught us a great deal and kept us going.

We hope this volume will inspire more projects. It's only together that we can identify and analyze the yellow perilist and Islamophobic archive, and undo the ugly ongoing legacy of violent, toxic power.

Notes

Introduction

1 Schilling was an admirer of Adolf Hitler and continued drawing throughout the Fascist period. After Hitler's suicide in 1945, Schilling too committed suicide. Ulrich Appel, *Satire als Zeitdokument: der Zeichner Erich Schilling* [Satire As a Contemporary Document: The Drawings of Erich Schilling] (Bonn: Verlag M. Wehle, 1995).

2 Michael Keevak, *Becoming Yellow: A Short History of Racial Thinking* (Princeton, NJ: Princeton University Press, 2011).

3 Yoko Wada, Introduction, in *A Companion to* Ancrene Wisse, ed. Yoko Wada (Rochester, NY: D.S. Brewer, 2003), 16–17.

4 *Oxford English Dictionary*, online. Accessed March 2013.

5 Eric Hobsbawm, *The Invention of Tradition* (Cambridge: Cambridge University Press, 1992).

6 Walter Benjamin, "On the Concept of History" in *Selected Writings,* vol. 4, eds. Howard Eiland and Michael W. Jennings, trans. Edmund Jephcott et al. (Cambridge, MA: Harvard University Press, 2003).

7 Rudyard Kipling, *The Letters of Rudyard Kipling, 1890–99,* vol. 2, ed. Thomas Pinney (London: Macmillan, 1970), 350.

8 Michel-Rolph Trouillot, *Silencing the Past: Power and the Production of History* (Boston: Beacon, 1995), 26.

9 Nicholas Mirzoeff, *The Right to Look: A Counterhistory of Visuality* (Durham, NC: Duke University Press, 2011), xiv.

10 Jürgen Habermas, *The Structural Transformation of the Public Sphere: An Inquiry into a Category of Bourgeois Society,* trans. Thomas Burger and Frederick Lawrence (Cambridge, MA: MIT Press, 1989).

11 David Howes, Introduction, in *Empire of the Senses*, ed. David Howes (Oxford: Berg, 2004), 1–17.

12 Charles W. Mills, *The Racial Contract* (Ithaca, NY: Cornell University Press, 1997).

13 Pierre Bourdieu, *Distinction: A Social Critique of the Judgment of Taste*, trans. Richard Nice (Cambridge, MA: Harvard University Press, 1984).

14 Eve Kosofsky Sedgwick, *Epistemology of the Closet* (Berkeley, CA: University of California Press, 1990).

15 As pogroms were waged against Jews in Russia, the American Jewish Congress organized and lobbied for the U.S. to protest such violence. Glackens was pointing out the U.S. policies and practices of violence, segregation, and exclusion in U.S. history. Carole Fink,

Defending the Rights of Others: The Great Powers, the Jews, and International Minority Protection, 1878–1938 (Cambridge: Cambridge University Press, 2004), 39–61.

16 Jane Leung Larson, "The 1905 Anti-American Boycott as a Transnational Movement," *Chinese America: History and Perspectives*, 2007, xx, 10.

17 Ibid., 11.

18 Marc Bloch, *Feudal Society, Volume 1: The Growth of Ties of Dependence*, trans. L. A. Manyon (Chicago: University of Chicago Press, 1964), 30; Shankar Raman, *Framing "India": The Colonial Imaginary in Early Modern Culture* (Stanford, CA: Stanford University Press, 2001), 4–5.

19 Jacqueline Kaye, "Islamic Imperialism and the Creation of Some Ideas of 'Europe,'" in *Europe and Its Others*, eds. Francis Barker et al. (Colchester, England: University of Essex, 1985), 66; Raman, *Framing "India,"* 5.

20 Committee of 100, *2007 Report & 2012 Report, Public Perceptions & Opinion Survey*. Online: http://survey.committee100.org, accessed April 2013.

21 Raman, *Framing "India,"* 11. All parenthetical citations in this section, unless otherwise indicated, are from Raman.

22 Jonathan Gil Harris, "Introduction: Forms of Indography" in *Indography: Writing the "Indian" in Early Modern England*, ed. Jonathan Gil Hams (New York: Palgrave Macmillan, 2012), 1–2.

23 Ibid., 14.

24 Special issue on Hans Blumenberg, *TELOS* 158 (Spring 2012).

25 Jonathan Gil Harris, "Introduction: Forms of Indography" in *Indography*, 14–15, also footnote 26, 295.

26 Ibid., 14.

27 Walter D. Mignolo, *The Darker Side of the Renaissance: Literacy, Territoriality, and Colonization* (Ann Arbor, MI: University of Michigan Press, 1995).

28 Ibid., 15.

29 Ibid., 72.

1. Decolonizing Scholarship

1 Giambattista Vico, *The New Science*, 1744 edition (Ithaca, NY: Cornell University Press, 1984), 125.

2 J. G. A. Pocock, *The Machiavellian Moment: Florentine Political Thought and the Atlantic Republican Tradition* (Princeton, NJ: Princeton University Press, 1975).

3 Boaventura de Sousa Santos, "Introduction: Opening Up the Canon of Knowledge and Recognition of Difference" in *Another Knowledge Is Possible: Beyond Northern Epistemologies*, ed. Boaventura de Sousa Santos (New York: Verso, 2008).

4 The pre-1800s scholarship of what is still awkwardly termed the "premodern" West has exploded with stunning insights that move well past the set frames textbooks have segmented as "classical," "medieval," "middle ages," "Renaissance," and "modern." Within a Eurocentric narrative, the "modern" becomes the reprise of the "classical" after the long night of the "dark ages." Instead, recent research elucidates a far more historically situated understanding of the dynamic nature of regional identity formations and consolidation over the centuries. R. I. Moore, *The Formation of a Persecuting Society: Authority and Deviance in Western Europe, 950–1250* (New York: John Wiley & Sons, 2007) and Robert Bartlett, *The Making of Europe: Conquest, Colonization, and Cultural Change, 950–1350* (Princeton, NJ: Princeton University Press, 1993) are key pivotal studies complicating and moving prior framings.

5 Karl Kerényi, *The Heroes of the Greeks* (London: Thames and Hudson, 1959), 80.
6 This is an expanded excerpt from an earlier published essay. John Kuo Wei Tchen, "Asian," in *Keywords for American Cultural Studies*, eds. Bruce Burgett and Glenn Hendler (New York: New York University Press, 2007), 22–6. © 2013 John Kuo Wei Tchen. Reprinted by permission of New York University Press.
7 Jack Goody, *The Theft of History* (Cambridge: Cambridge University Press, 2006), 13–15, 20–1. © 2000 Jack Goody. Reprinted by permission of Cambridge University Press.
8 Recent scholars discuss this issue in terms of "The Great Divergence." For a far more comparative example of grappling with the history of science and technology, see Francesca Bray, "Only Connect: Comparative, National, and Global History as Frameworks for the History of Science and Technology in Asia," *East Asian Science, Technology and Society: An International Journal* 6 (2012): 233–41. Bray, for example, asks, "When it comes to the *Cambridge World History*, and to the early modern era, could I surprise and educate my readers by using China as the touchstone for Europe, rather than the other way around?" (239).
9 Martin W. Lewis and Kären E. Wigen, "The Spatial Constructs of East and West," in *The Myth of Continents: A Critique of Metageography* (Berkeley, CA: University of California Press, 1997), 49–55. © 1998 the Regents of the University of California. Reprinted by permission of the University of California Press.
10 Europeans had almost no knowledge of East Asia until the Mongol period in the thirteenth and fourteenth centuries. Subsequent knowledge of the area again diminished: "[T]o Europeans in the sixteenth century, Cathay remained a mystery"; Seymour Phillips, "The Outer World of the European Middle Ages," *Implicit Understandings: Observing, Reporting, and Reflecting on the Encounters Between Europeans and Other Peoples in the Early Modern Era* (Cambridge: Cambridge University Press, 1994), 42.
11 Schwab, *The Oriental Renaissance*, 71.
12 Linda Tuhiwai Smith, *Decolonizing Methodologies: Research and Indigenous Peoples* (London: Zed Books, 2012), 62–7. © 2012 Linda Tuhiwai Smith. Reprinted by permission of Zed Books.
13 Fernando Coronil, "Beyond Occidentalism: Toward Nonimperial Geohistorical Categories," *Cultural Anthropology* 11, no. 1 (Feb. 1996), 76–80. Reprinted by permission of the American Anthropological Association. Not for sale or further reproduction.
14 For example, Fred Cooper and Ann Stoler "Tensions of Empire: Colonial Control and Visions of Rule," in special issue of *American Ethnologist* 16 (1989), 609–21.

2. Westernizing Europe

1 Richard C. Lewontin, *The Genetic Basis of Evolutionary Change* (New York: Columbia University Press, 1974).
2 On the *longue durée*, see Fernand Braudel, *The Mediterranean and the Mediterranean World in the Age of King Philip II*, 3 volumes (Berkeley, CA: University of California Press, 1996).
3 Spencer Wells, *The Journey of Man: A Genetic Odyssey* (Princeton, NJ: Princeton University Press, 2002), 55.
4 Nicholas K. Kiessling, "Antecedents of the Medieval Dragon in Sacred History, *The Society of Biblical Literature* 89, no. 2 (June 1970), 167.
5 David W. Anthony, *The Horse, the Wheel, and Language: How Bronze-Age Riders from the Eurasian Steppes Shaped the Modern World* (Princeton, NJ: Princeton University Press,

2009), 459–62. © 2007 by Princeton University Press. Reprinted by permission of Princeton University Press.

6 See Jared Diamond, *Guns, Germs, and Steel: The Fates of Human Societies* (New York: W. W. Norton, 1997).

7 Irene J. Winter, "Homer's Phoenicians: History, Ethnography, or Literary Trope," in *The Age of Homer: A Tribute to Emily Townsend Vermeule*, eds. Jane B. Carter and Sarah P. Morris (Austin, TX: University of Texas Press, 1995), 247, 262–4. © 1995 University of Texas Press. Reprinted by permission of the University of Texas Press.

8 Benjamin Isaac, *The Invention of Racism in Classical Antiquity* (Princeton, NJ: Princeton University Press, 2004), 285–8. © 2004 Princeton University Press. Reprinted by permission of Princeton University Press.

9 Adam Kuper, *The Reinvention of Primitive Society: Transformations of a Myth* (New York: Routledge, 2005), 20–2. © 2005 Adam Kuper. Reprinted by permission of Taylor & Francis Ltd, www.tandfonline.com.

10 R. I. Moore, *The Formation of a Persecuting Society: Power and Deviance in Western Europe, 950–1250* (Oxford: Basil Blackwell, 1987).

11 Shankar Raman, *Framing "India": The Colonial Imaginary in Early Modern Culture* (Stanford, CA: Stanford University Press, 2002), 5.

12 Hall, *Inventing*, 5.

13 Robert Bartlett, *The Making of Europe: Conquest, Colonization and Cultural Change, 950–1350* (Princeton, NJ: Princeton University Press, 1993), 2.

14 Jacques Bongars, *Gesta Dei per Francos*, 1, 382 f., trans. in *A Source Book for Medieval History*, eds. Oliver J. Thatcher and Edgar Holmes McNeal, (New York: Scribner, 1905), 513–17.

15 Matthew Paris, *Matthew Paris's English History: From the Year 1235 to 1273*, vol. 1, trans. the Rev. J. A. Giles, (London: George Bell and Sons, 1889), 312–14.

16 J. A. Giles, Introduction, *Paris's English History*, v.

17 Robert Graves, *The Greek Myths*, vol. 1 (New York: Penguin, 1990).

18 Saracen was the term used for Islamic Arabs.

19 Paragraphs divided by editor.

20 Scott D. Westrem, "Against Gog and Magog" in *Text and Territory: Geographical Imagination on the European Middle Ages*, eds. Sylvia Tomasch and Sealy Gilles (Philadelphia: University of Pennsylvania Press, 1998), 55–7, 65–6. © 1998 University of Pennsylvania Press. Reprinted by permission of the University of Pennsylvania Press.

21 Suzanne Conklin Akbari, "Placing the Jews in Late Medieval English Literature," *Orientalism and the Jews*, eds. Ivan Davidson Kalmar and Derek J. Penslar (Waltham, MA: Brandeis University Press, 2002), 32–3, 36–7, 44–5, 47–50. © 2002 University Press of New England, Lebanon, NH. Reprinted by permission of the University Press of New England.

22 Alex Bein, *The Jewish Question: Biography of a World Problem* (Rutherford, NJ: Fairleigh Dickinson University Press, 1990), 594.

23 On purity see Mary Douglas, *Purity and Danger: An Analysis of Concepts of Pollution and Taboo* (London: Routledge Press, 1966). On the process of disidentification, though used differently here from the viewpoint of the dominating society, see the key formulation giving agency to those subject to disempowerment: José Esteban Muñoz, *Disidentifications: Queers of Color and the Performance of Politics* (Minneapolis, MN: University of Minnesota Press, 1999).

24 Allan and Helen Cutler, *The Jew as Ally of the Muslim: Medieval Roots of Anti-Semitism* (Notre Dame, IN: University of Notre Dame Press, 1986), 97; Jeremy Cohen, "The Muslim Connection, or On the Changing Role of the Jew in High Medieval Theology" in *From Witness to Witchcraft: Jews and Judaism in Medieval Christian Thought*, ed.

Jeremy Cohen (Wiesbaden, Germany: Harrassowitz, 1996), 141–62, quotation from 162.

25 John V. Tolan, *Saracens: Islam in the Medieval European Imagination* (New York: Columbia University Press, 2003), 275–8, 281, 283. © 2003 Columbia University Press. Reprinted by permission of Columbia University Press.

26 Ana Echevarria, *The Fortress of Faith: The Attitude Towards Muslims in Fifteenth-Century Spain* (Leiden, Netherlands: Brill, 1999); Richard William Southern, *Western Views of Islam in the Middle Ages* (Cambridge, MA: Harvard University Press, 1962), 83–103; Darío Cabanelas Rodríguez, *Juan de Segovia y el problema islámico* (Madrid: Maestre, 1952).

27 Frances Gardiner Davenport, *European Treaties Bearing on the History of the United States to 1648* (Washington, DC: The Carnegie Institution of Washington, 1917), 8.

28 Gerard Delanty, *Inventing Europe: Idea, Identity, Reality* (London: Macmillan, 1995), 30–1, 41–3. © 1995 Gerard Delanty. Reprinted by permission of Palgrave Macmillan.

29 Paul Valéry, "The Crisis of the Mind," 1919, in *Paul Valéry: An Anthology*, ed. James R. Lawler (London: RKP, 1977), 102.

Part Two: Manifest Destinies

1 Henry Steele Commager, *The Empire of Reason: How Europe Imagined and America Realized the Enlightenment* (New York: Anchor, 1977).

2 Albert O. Hirschman, *The Passions and the Interests: Political Arguments for Capitalism Before Its Triumph* (Princeton, NJ: Princeton University Press, 1997), 130–1.

3 John Locke, *Two Treatises of Government* II, paragraph 22, quoted in Hirschman, *The Passions and the Interests*, 53.

4 Uday Singh Mehta, *Liberalism and Empire: A Study in Nineteenth-Century British Liberal Thought* (Chicago: University of Chicago Press, 1999); Charles W. Mills, *The Racial Contract* (Ithaca, NY: Cornell University Press, 1997).

5 Ashis Nandy, *The Intimate Enemy: Loss and Recovery of Self Under Colonialism* (Dehli: Oxford University Press, 1983), 14.

6 Alexander Saxton, *The Rise and Fall of the White Republic: Class Politics and Mass Culture in Nineteenth-Century America* (New York: Verso, 2003); Cheryl Harris, "Whiteness as Property," *Harvard Law Review* 106:8 (1993), 1707–91.

7 For an analysis of this in the U.S. see Ronald Takaki, *Iron Cages: Race and Culture in Nineteenth-Century America* (New York: Knopf, 1979); Gail Bederman, *Manliness and Civilization: A Cultural History of Gender and Race in the United States, 1880–1917* (Chicago: University of Chicago Press, 1996).

8 Peter Hopkirk, *The Great Game: The Struggle for Empire in Central Asia* (New York: Kodansha International, 1990).

9 Ikura Akira, "The 'Yellow Peril' and Its Influence on Japanese-German Relations," in *Japanese-German Relations, 1895–1945: War, Diplomacy, and Public Opinion*, eds. Christian W. Spang and Rolf-Harald Wippich (New York: Routledge, 2006), 80–97.

10 René Pinon, "La Guerre Russo-Japonaise et l'Opinion Européenne," *Revue des Deux Mondes* 21 (May 1, 1904), 218–19.

3. Geo-Racial Mapping

1 Bruno Latour, "Drawing Things Together" in *Representations in Scientific Practice*, eds. Michael Lynch and Steve Woolgar (Cambridge, MA: MIT Press, 1990), 9–68. Virey cited in Reginald Horsman, *Race and Manifest Destiny: The Origins of American Racial Anglo-Saxonism* (Cambridge, MA: Harvard University Press, 1981), 49.

2 Susan Buck-Morss, "Hegel and Haiti," *Critical Inquiry* 26, no. 4 (Summer, 2000), 821–65.

3 *The Doctrine of the Unity of the Human Race Examined on the Principles of Science* (Charleston, SC, 1850), 212.

4 Francis Parkman, *The Old Regime in Canada* (Boston: Little, Brown, 1874), 201.

5 "Mammalia, order 1. Primates." Carl von Linné (Linnaeus), *A General System of Nature* (London: Lackington, Allen, and Co., 1806).

6 George M. Fredrickson, *Racism: A Short History* (Princeton, NJ: Princeton University Press, 2002), 57; Marvin Harris, *The Rise of Anthropological Theory: A History of Theories of Culture* (Lanham, MD: AltaMira Press, 2001), 84; Nell Irving Painter, *The History of White People* (New York: W. W. Norton, 2010) 72–90.

7 Robert Chambers, *Vestiges of the Natural History of Creation* (London: John Churchill, 1844).

8 Ann Fabian, *The Skull Collectors: Race, Science, and America's Unburied Dead* (Chicago: University of Chicago Press, 2010), 1–119; Samuel George Morton, *Crania Americana; or, A Comparative View of the Skulls of Various Nations of North and South America* (Philadelphia: J. Dobson, 1839), 5; Stephen Jay Gould, *The Mismeasure of Man* (New York: W. W. Norton, 1996), 62–104.

9 *Types of Mankind*, 81; Reginald Horsman, *Josiah Nott of Mobile: Southerner, Physician, and Racial Theorist* (Baton Rouge, LA: Louisiana State University Press, 1987); Frederick Douglass, "The Claims of the Negro, Ethnologically Considered," address before the literary societies of Western Reserve College, at commencement July 12, 1854 (Rochester, NY: Lee, Man & Co., Daily American Office, 1854), 20–1, cited in Fabian, *The Skull Collectors*, 118.

10 *Phrenology Journal* 19 (July 1846), 214.

11 Ronald Rainger, *An Agenda for Antiquity: Henry Fairfield Osborn and Vertebrate Paleontology at the American Museum of Natural History, 1890–1935* (Mobile, AL: University of Alabama Press, 2004).

12 G. W. F. Hegel, *The Philosophy of History*, trans. John Sibree (London: Henry G. Bohn, 1861), 180–232.

13 Brendan O'Leary, *The Asiatic Mode of Production: Oriental Despotism, Historical Materialism, and Indian History* (Cambridge: Basil Blackwell, 1989), 41–2, 67–70, 72. © 1989 Brendan O'Leary. Reprinted courtesy of the author.

14 There are also some references to despotism and oriental despotism in *The Philosophy of Right*; G. W. F. Hegel, *The Philosophy of Right*, trans. T. M. Knox (New York: Oxford University Press, 1967), 173, 180, 188.

15 Robert Kurfirst, "John Stuart Mill's Asian Parable," *Canadian Journal of Political Science* 34, no. 3 (September 2001), 601–19. Copyright © 2001 Canadian Political Science Association (l'Association canadienne de science politique) and / et la Sociéte québécoise de science politiquel. Reprinted by permission of the publisher.

16 Edward S. Herman and Noam Chomsky, *Manufacturing Consent: The Political Economy of the Mass Media* (New York: Pantheon, 2002).

17 Gregory Blue, "Gobineau on China: Race Theory, the 'Yellow Peril,' and the Critique of Modernity," *Journal of World History* 10, no. 1 (1999), 116–9, 133–4. ©1999 University of Hawaii Press. Reprinted courtesy of the author and by permission of University of Hawaii Press.

18 Nell Irving Painter, *The History of White People* (New York: W. W. Norton, 2010), 222–7; William Z. Ripley, "Races in the United States," *The Atlantic* (December 1908) and "Acclimatization," *Popular Science Monthly* 48 (March 1896).

19 Mary Ann Stevens, *The Orientalists: Delacroix to Matisse: The Allure of North Africa and the Near East* (New York: Thames and Hudson, 1984).

20 Richard Slotkin, *The Fatal Environment: The Myth of the Frontier in the Age of Industrialization, 1800–1890* (New York: Atheneum, 1985), 371–475.

21 Sam DeShong Ratcliffe, *Painting Texas History to 1900* (Austin, TX: University of Texas Press, 1992), 32–4.

22 Mark Twain, "To the Person Sitting in the Darkness," *North American Review* 81 (February 1901), 161–76.

23 Baron von Falkenegg (pseudonym), *Japan Die Neue Weltmacht* (Berlin: Boll & Pickardt, 1905), 17.

24 H. J. Mackinder, from "The Geographical Pivot of History," *The Geographical Journal* 23, no. 4 (April 1904), 421–37.

25 Brian W. Blouet, "The Imperial Vision of Halford Mackinder" *The Geographical Journal* 170, no. 4 (December 2004), 322–9; "Sir Halford Mackinder as British High Commissioner to South Russia, 1919–1920" *The Geographical Journal* 142, no. 2 (July 1976), 228–36; Gerry Kearns, *Geopolitics and Empire: The Legacy of Halford Mackinder* (Oxford: Oxford University Press, 2009).

26 "With faces like the snouts of dogs," Theodore Roosevelt, "Foreword" in Jeremiah Curtin, *The Mongols: A History* (Boston: Little, Brown, 1908), ix–xv.

27 Curtin, *The Mongols*, 412.

28 H. B. Segel, "Sienkiewicz's First Translator, Jeremiah Curtin," *The Slavic Review*, vol. XXIV, no. 2 (June 1965).

29 Jack London, "The Yellow Peril," *San Francisco Examiner*, September 25, 1904.

30 Ian Mugridge, *The View from Xanadu: William Randolph Hearst and United States Foreign Policy* (Montreal, Canada: McGill-Queen's University Press, 1995), 46–59; Jack London, "The Unparalleled Invasion," *McClure's Magazine* (May 1910), also reprinted in *The Strength of the Strong* (New York: Macmillan, 1914); Colleen Lye, *America's Asia: Racial Form and American Literature, 1893–1945* (Princeton, NJ: Princeton University Press, 2005), 12–94.

4. Anglo America's "Great Game"

1 Edmund Wilson, "The Kipling That Nobody Read" in *Kipling's Mind and Art*, ed. Andrew Rutherford (Stanford, CA: Stanford University Press, 1964), 17–69.

2 Thomas R. Hieatala, *Manifest Design: Anxious Aggrandizement in Late Jacksonian America* (Ithaca, NY: Cornell University Press, 1985); Bruce Cumings, *Dominion From Sea to Sea: Pacific Ascendancy and American Power* (New Haven, CT: Yale University Press, 2009).

3 Shelley Streeby, *American Sensations: Class, Empire, and the Production of Popular Culture* (Berkeley, CA: University of California Press, 2002); Stuart Creighton Miller, *Benevolent Assimilation: The American Conquest of the Philippines, 1899–1903* (New Haven, CT: Yale University Press, 1982); Amy Kaplan, *The Anarchy of Empire in the Making of U.S. Culture* (Cambridge, MA: Harvard University Press, 2002).

4 Washington Irving, *A History of New York from the Beginning of the World to the End of the Dutch Dynasty* (Philadelphia: M. Thomas, 1809), 65–85.

5 Gerald Horne, *Race War!: White Supremacy and the Japanese Attack on the British Empire*

(New York: New York University Press, 2004), 187–219; Thomas Eich, "Pan-Islam and 'Yellow Peril': Geo-Strategic Concepts in Salafi Writings Prior to World War I" in *The Islamic Middle East and Japan: Perceptions, Aspirations, and the Birth of Intra-Asian Modernity*, ed. Renee Worringer (Princeton, NJ: Markus Wiener Publishers, 2007), 121–36.

6 Christopher Herbert, *War of No Pity: The Indian Mutiny and Victorian Trauma* (Princeton, NJ: Princeton University Press, 2007).

7 Pranav Jani, "Karl Marx, Eurocentrism, and the 1857 Revolt in British India," *Marxism, Modernity and Postcolonial Studies*, eds. Crystal Bartolovich and Neil Lazarus (Cambridge: Cambridge University Press, 2002), 81–98; Brendan O'Leary, *The Asiatic Mode of Production: Oriental Despotism, Historical Materialism, and Indian History* (New York: Basil Blackwell, 1989).

8 Karl Marx, "The Indian Revolt," *New York Tribune*, September 16, 1857.

9 William Ward Crane, "The Year 1899," *Overland Monthly*, June 1893, 579–81.

10 William Ward Crane, "Fanciful Predictions of War," *Lippincott's Monthly Magazine*, vol. 62 (November 1898), 716–17.

11 H. Bruce Franklin, *War Stars: The Superweapon and the American Imagination* (Amherst, MA: University of Massachusetts Press, 2008), 19–53; Floyd Gibbons, *The Red Napoleon* (New York: J. Cape and H. Smith, 1929).

12 Ashis Nandy, "The Psychology of Colonialism" from *The Intimate Enemy: Loss and Recovery of Self Under Colonialism* (Oxford: Oxford University Press, 1988), 30–41. ©1988 Oxford University Press. Reprinted courtesy of the author and by permission of Oxford University Press.

13 Rudyard Kipling, "The Ballad of East and West," *Macmillan's Magazine* (December 1889), and "The White Man's Burden: The United States and the Philippine Islands" *McClure's Magazine* (February, 1899).

14 Richard Slotkin, *Gunfighter Nation: The Myth of the Frontier in Twentieth-Century America* (New York: Atheneum, 1992), 29–62; Gail Bederman, *Manliness and Civilization: A Cultural History of Gender and Race in the United States, 1880–1917* (Chicago: University of Chicago Press, 1996), 170–216; Mrinalini Sinha, *Colonial Masculinity: the "Manly Englishman" and the "Effeminate Bengali" in the Late Nineteenth Century* (Manchester: Manchester University Press, 1995).

15 Gary Okihiro, "Perils of the Body and Mind" in *Margins and Mainstreams: Asians in American History and Culture* (Seattle: University of Washington Press, 1994), 118–40. © 1994 University of Washington Press. Reprinted by permission of the University of Washington Press.

16 Albert Jeremiah Beveridge, "The March of the Flag" in *The Meaning of the Times* (Indianapolis, IN: Bobbs-Merrill, 1908), 47–57.

17 John Braeman, *Albert J. Beveridge: American Nationalist* (Chicago: University of Chicago Press, 1971); *Vestiges of War: The Philippine-American War and the Aftermath of an Imperial Dream, 1899–1999*, eds. Angel Velasco Shaw and Luis H. Francia (New York: New York University Press, 2002).

18 This quote is from Gillam's cartoon "Hands Across the Sea," *Judge*, June 11, 1898, depicting Uncle Sam and John Bull reaching toward each other over an Atlantic Ocean full of warships. Paul Kramer, "Empires, Exceptions, and Anglo-Saxons: Race and Rule Between the British and United States Empires, 1880–1910," *Journal of American History* 88, no. 4 (March 2002), 1315–553.

19 Laura Wexler, *Tender Violence: Domestic Visions in an Age of U.S. Imperialism* (Chapel Hill, NL: University of North Carolina Press, 2001); James Bradley, *The Imperial Cruise: A Secret History of Empire and War* (New York: Back Bay Books, 2009).

20 Yorimitsu Hashimoto, "Germs, Body-Politics and Yellow Peril: Relocation of Britishness in The Yellow Danger," *Australasian Victorian Studies Journal* 9 (2003), 52–66.

21 William Wu, *The Yellow Peril: Chinese-Americans in American Fiction, 1850–1940* (Hamden, CT: Archon Books, 1982).

22 James L. Hevia, "The Archive State and the Fear of Pollution: From the Opium Wars to Fu-Manchu," *Cultural Studies* 12, no. 2 (1998), 234–64. © 1998 Routledge. Reprinted by permission of Taylor & Francis Ltd, www.tandfonline.com.

23 Jeffrey Richelson and Thomas Blanton, "Electronic Surveillance from the Cold War to Al-Qaeda," *National Security Archive Electronic Briefing Book* 178, February 4, 2006, www.gwu.edu/~nsarchiv.

24 Donald Rumsfeld, Department of Defense briefing, February 12, 2002, www.defense.gov/transcripts.

25 In the full article, Hevia terms the British Empire an "archive state" to signify that British fantasies of total knowledge and accompanying bureaucratic practices served as a form of epistemological power crucial to colonial dominance.

26 Urmila Seshagiri, *Race and the Modernist Imagination* (Ithaca, NY: Cornell University Press, 2010), 53, 59, 60, 61–2, 66, 71, 75–6. © 2010 by Cornell University Press. Reprinted by permission of Cornell University Press.

27 Jonathan Freedman, "Transgressions of a Model Minority," *Shofar: An Interdisciplinary Journal of Jewish Studies* 23, no. 4 (2005), 69–97.

28 Yorimitsu Hashimoto, "Germs, Body-Politics and Yellow Peril: Relocation of Britishness in The Yellow Danger," *Australasian Victorian Studies Journal* 9 (2003), 52–66; Colleen Lye, *America's Asia: Racial Form and American Literature, 1893–1945* (Princeton, NJ: Princeton University Press, 2005).

29 Philip Francis Nowlan, "Armegeddon 2419" and "Airlords of Han," *Amazing Stories* 3:5/3:12 (August 1928/March 1929). Patrick B. Sharpe, *Savage Perils: Racial Frontiers and Nuclear Apocalypse in American Culture* (Norman, OK: University of Oklahoma Press, 2007), 107–20; Carter Hanson, "1920's Yellow Peril Science Fiction: Political Appropriations of the Asian Racial 'Alien,'" *Journal of the Fantastic in the Arts* 6 (1995): 312–29.

30 Hadley Cantril, *The Invasion from Mars: A Study in the Psychology of Panic* (Princeton, NJ: Princeton University Press, 1940), 153–64.

Part Three: Indispensable Enemies

1 Michael Rogin, *Ronald Reagan: the Movie; and Other Episodes in Political Demonology* (Berkeley, CA: University of California Press, 1987).

2 Alexander Saxton, *The Indispensable Enemy: Labor and the Anti-Chinese Movement in California* (Berkeley, CA: University of California Press, 1971).

3 Walter LeFeber, "Zelig in U.S. Foreign Relations: The Roles of China in the American Post-9/11 World" in *Iraq and the Lessons of Vietnam*, eds. Lloyd C. Gardner and Marilyn Young (New York: The New Press, 2007), 201–15.

4 Carey McWilliams, *Prejudice: Japanese Americans: Symbol of Racial Intolerance* (Boston: Little, Brown, 1944).

5 *Personal Justice Denied: Report of the Commission on Wartime Relocation and Internment of Civilians* (Seattle: University of Washington Press, 1997), 222.

6 Robin Kelly, *Race Rebels: Culture, Politics, and the Black Working Class* (New York: The Free Press, 1996), 161–182; Gerald Horne, *Race War!: White Supremacy and the Japanese Attack on the British Empire* (New York: New York University Press, 2004), 43–59; Luis Alvarez, *The Power of the Zoot: Youth Culture and Resistance During World War II* (Berkeley, CA: University of California Press, 2008).

7 "Malcolm X Scores U.S. and Kennedy," *New York Times* (December 2, 1963), 21.
8 See Rogin, 44–80.
9 Joan Wallach Scott, *The Politics of the Veil* (Princeton, NJ: Princeton University Press, 2010).

5. The Enemy Within

1 Moon-ho Jung, "Seditious Subjects: Race, State Violence, and the U.S. Empire," *Journal of Asian American Studies* 14, no. 2 (June 2011), 221–47; William Preston, *Aliens and Dissenters: The Federal Suppression of Radicals, 1903–1933* (Cambridge, MA: Harvard University Press, 1963); *The Fear of Conspiracy: Images of Un-American Subversion from the Revolution to the Present*, ed. David Brion Davis (Ithaca, NY: Cornell University Press, 1971).
2 Paul A. Gilje, *The Road to Mobocracy: Popular Disorder in New York City, 1763–1834* (Chapel Hill, NC: University of North Carolina Press, 1987).
3 Samuel F. B. Morse, *Foreign Conspiracy Against the Liberties of the United States* (New York: Leavitt, Lord & Co., 1835), 71.
4 Alphonso Wetmore, *Gazetteer of the State of Missouri* (New York: Harper & Brothers, 1837), 94.
5 *Twelfth Annual Report of the Bureau of Statistics of Labor* (Boston: Rand, Avery, & Co., 1881), 469.
6 Mae Ngai, *Impossible Subjects: Illegal Aliens and the Making of Modern America* (Princeton, NJ: Princeton University Press, 2004).
7 *United States Attorney General A. Mitchell Palmer on Charges Made Against the Department of Justice by Louis F. Post and Others: Hearings before the Committee on Rules.* House of Representatives, Sixty-Sixth Congress, Second Session (Washington, DC: Government Printing Office, 1920), 27.
8 Michael Sherry, *In the Shadow of War: The United States Since the 1930s* (New Haven, CT: Yale University Press, 1995).
9 "Islamophobia: Anatomy of an American Panic," *Nation,* July 2–9, 2012.
10 David Campbell, *Writing Security: United States Foreign Policy and the Politics of Identity* (Minneapolis, MN: University of Minnesota Press, 1992).
11 Saum Song Bo, "A Chinese View of the Statue of Liberty," *The American Missionary* 39, no. 10 (October 1885), 290.
12 "The Chinese Exclusion Case," from Chae Chan Ping v. United States, No. 1448, argued March 28–9, 1889, Decided May 13, 1889, 130 U.S., 581–611.
13 Lucy E. Salyer, *Laws Harsh as Tigers: Chinese Immigrants and the Shaping of Modern Immigration Law* (Chapel Hill, NC: University of North Carolina Press, 1995).
14 Karen Shimakawa, "National Abjection," from *National Abjection: The Asian American Body Onstage* (Durham, NC: Duke University Press, 2002), 1–16. © 2002 Duke University Press. All rights reserved. Republished by permission of the Duke University Press, www.dukeupress.edu.
15 Nayan Shah, *Contagious Divides: Epidemics and Race in San Francisco's Chinatown* (Berkeley, CA: University of California Press, 2001).
16 *Overland Monthly* 51, no. 4 (April 1908): 303–13.
17 Erika Lee, "The 'Yellow Peril' and Asian Exclusion in the Americas," *Pacific Historical Review* 76, no. 4 (Fall 2007), 537–62; Terri Yuh-lin Chen, "Hate Violence as Border Patrol: An Asian American Theory of Hate Violence," *Asian Law Journal* 7, no. 69 (2000), 69–100.
18 "Says Jap Trouble is Only Labor Question, Will Not Tolerate Invasion of California Even if It Is Peaceful," *Boston Sunday Herald,* June 16, 1907.

19 Randolph Bourne, "Transnational America," *Atlantic Monthly* 118 (July 1916), 1–4, 6, 10.

20 W. E. B. Du Bois, "The Shape of Fear," *North American Review* 223 (June 1926), 291–2, 294, 297, 304.

21 David Levering Lewis, *W. E. B. Du Bois: The Fight for Equality and the American Century, 1919–1963* (New York: Henry Holt and Company, 2000), 194.

22 Matthew Connelly, *Fatal Misconception: The Struggle to Control World Population* (Cambridge, MA: Harvard University Press, 2010).

23 Richard H. Minear, *Dr. Seuss Goes to War* (New York: The New Press, 1999); Roger Daniels, *The Politics of Prejudice: The Anti-Japanese Movement in California and the Struggle for Japanese Exclusion* (Berkeley, CA: University of California Press, 1962).

24 Mauricio Mazón, *The Zoot-Suit Riots: The Psychology of Symbolic Annihilation* (Austin, TX: University of Texas Press, 1984).

25 Carlos Bulosan, *America Is in the Heart: A Personal History* (Seattle: University of Washington Press, 1973), 143–6.

26 Mae Ngai, *Impossible Subjects: Illegal Aliens and the Making of Modern America* (Princeton, NJ: Princeton University Press, 2004), 96–126; Ruby C. Tapia, "Just Ten Years Removed from a Bolo and a Breech-cloth" in *Positively No Filipinos Allowed: Building Communities and Discourse*, eds. Antonio T. Tiongson, Jr. et al. (Philadelphia: Temple University Press, 2006), 61–71.

27 Robert B. Reich, from "Is Japan Really Out to Get Us?" *New York Times Book Review*, February 9, 1992. © 1992 Robert Reich. Reprinted courtesy of the author.

28 Helen Zia, *Asian American Dreams: The Emergence of an American People*, (New York: Farrar, Straus and Giroux, 2000), 55–81.

29 On September 14, 2012, the Romney campaign released "Failing America's Workers" and the Obama campaign released "The Cheaters," two of many ads attacking the opposing candidate for failing to confront China.

30 Jasbir Puar and Amit Rai, from "Monster, Terrorist, Fag: The War on Terrorism and the Production of Docile Patriots," *Social Text* 20, no. 3 (2002), 117–48. © 2002 Duke University Press. All rights reserved. Republished by permission of Duke University Press, www.dukeupress.edu

31 Susan Faludi, *The Terror Dream: Fear and Fantasy in Post-9/11 America* (New York: Metropolitan Books, 2007); Naomi Klein, *The Shock Doctrine: The Rise of Disaster Capitalism* (New York: Picador, 2008), 355–88.

6. The Coming War

1 John Whittier Treat, "Hiroshima, Ground Zero," *PMLA* 124, No. 5 (October, 2009), 1883–5; Amy Kaplan, "Homeland Insecurities: Some Reflections on Language and Space," *Radical History Review* 85 (Winter, 2003), 82–93; Donald E. Pease, *The New American Exceptionalism* (Minneapolis, MN: University of Minnesota Press, 2009), 1–67, 153–79.

2 Odd Arne Westad, *The Global Cold War: Third World Interventions and the Making of Our Times* (Cambridge: Cambridge University Press, 2005); Chalmers Johnson, "The Three Cold Wars" in *Cold War Triumphalism*, ed. Ellen Schrecker (New York: The New Press, 2004), 237–61.

3 Mahmood Mamdani, *Good Muslim, Bad Muslim: America, the Cold War, and the Roots of Terror* (New York: Pantheon, 2004).

4 Martin Luther King, "Beyond Vietnam: A Time to Break Silence," speech delivered to Clergy and Laity Concerned at Riverside Church, New York, April 4, 1967.

5 Jean-Paul Sartre, *Anti-Semite and Jew* (New York: Schocken, 1948).

6 John W. Dower, "Patterns of a Race War," in *War Without Mercy: Race and Power in the Pacific War* (New York: Pantheon, 1986), 3, 5–6, 10, 12–13. © 1986 by John Dower. Reprinted courtesy of the author.

7 Emily S. Rosenberg, *A Date Which Will Live: Pearl Harbor in American Memory* (Durham, NC: Duke University Press, 2003).

8 Rey Chow, "The Age of the World Target," in *America's Wars in Asia: A Cultural Approach to History and Memory*, eds. Philip West et al. (Armonk, NY: M. E. Sharpe, 1998), 205, 208, 212–13, 215. © 1998 The Maureen and Mike Mansfield Center. Reprinted with permission of M.E. Sharpe, Inc.

9 Tom Engelhardt, *The End of Victory Culture: Cold War America and the Disillusioning of a Generation* (Amherst, MA: University of Massachusetts Press, 2007).

10 William Pietz, "The 'Post-Colonialism' of Cold War Discourse," *Social Text* 19, no. 20 (Autumn, 1988), 55, 58–9, 65, 69–70. © 1988 Duke University Press. All rights reserved. Republished by permission of Duke University Press, www.dukeupress.edu

11 Dan Gilbert, *Red China: The Yellow Peril in Bible Prophecy* (Washington, DC: Evangelist Dan Gilbert, 1951).

12 Paul P. Kennedy, "Truman Calls Reds Present-Day Heirs of Mongol Killers," *New York Times*, December 24, 1950; Frank Tremaine, "Red Hordes Swarm into South Korea," *The Deseret News*, April 24, 1951, 1; Rigg, *Red China's Fighting Hordes*, 19, 2, 6, 104–41.

13 Matthew Jacobson and Gasper Gonzales, "Orientalism and Brainwashing in *The Manchurian Candidate*" in *What Have They Built You to Do?: The Manchurian Candidate and Cold War America* (Minneapolis, MN: University of Minnesota Press, 2006), 109, 111–12, 114–15, 117. © 2006 the Regents of the University of Minnesota. Reprinted by permission of the University of Minnesota Press.

14 David Seed, *Brainwashing: The Fictions of Mind Control* (Kent, OH: Kent State University Press, 2011).

15 Evelyn Yoshimura, "How I Became an Activist and What it All Means to Me," *Amerasia Journal* 15, no. 1 (1989), 106–9; Lori Kido Lopez, "The Yellow Press: Asian American Radicalism and Conflict in *GIDRA*," *Journal of Communication Inquiry* 35, no. 3 (July 2011), 235–51; Laura Pulido, *Black, Brown, Yellow, and Left: Radical Activism in Los Angeles* (Berkeley, CA: University of California Press, 2006); Daryl J. Maeda, *Chains of Babylon: The Rise of Asian America* (Minneapolis, MN: University of Minnesota Press, 2009). *Asian Americans: The Movement and the Moment*, eds. Steve Louie and Glenn Omatsu (Los Angeles: UCLA Asian American Studies Center Press, 2000).

16 Norman Nakamura, "The Nature of G.I. Racism," *GIDRA*, June/July 1970. © 1970 Norman Nakamura. Reprinted courtesy of the author.

17 Evelyn Yoshimura, "GIs and Asian Women," *GIDRA*, January 1971. © 1971 Evelyn Yoshimura. Reprinted courtesy of the author.

18 H. Bruce Franklin, *Vietnam and Other American Fantasies* (Amherst, MA: University of Amherst Press, 2001), 14–17. © 2000 H. Bruce Franklin. Reprinted courtesy of the author.

19 Lyndon B. Johnson, "Remarks to American and Korean Servicemen at Camp Stanley, Korea. November 1, 1966" in *Public Papers of the Presidents of the United States*.

20 Myra Mendible, "Post Vietnam Syndrome: National Identity, War, and the Politics of Humiliation," *Radical Psychology* 7 (Summer 2008), www.radicalpsychology.org. © 2008 Myra Mendible. Reprinted courtesy of the author.

21 Chiam F. Shatan, "Bogus Manhood, Bogus Honor: Surrender and Transfiguration in the U.S. Marine Corps," *Psychoanalytic Review* 64, no. 4 (1977), 585–610.

22 John L. Esposito, "Islam and the West: A Clash of Civilizations?" in *The Islamic Threat: Myth or Reality?* (New York: Oxford University Press, 1999), 213–14, 219, 222, 226,

228–9, 272–3, 285, 287, 289. © 1999 John L. Esposito. Reprinted by permission of Oxford University Press.

23 "Muslim Rage," *Newsweek*, September 17, 2012.

24 Spencer Ackerman, "FBI Teaches Agents: 'Mainstream' Muslims are 'Violent, Radical,'" *WIRED*, September 14, 2011; Trevor Aaronson, "The Informants," *Mother Jones*, September/October 2010; Thomas Cincotta, *Manufacturing the Muslim Menace: Private Firms, Public Servants, and the Threat to Rights and Security* (Somerville, MA: Political Research Associates, 2011); Wajahat Ali et al., *Fear, Inc.: The Roots of the Islamophobia Network in America* (Washington, DC: The Center for American Progress, 2011); Tom Robbins, "NYPD Cops' Training Included Anti-Muslim Horror Flick," *The Village Voice*, January 19, 2011.

25 R. James Woolsey et al., "Second Opinion Needed on Sharia: Our Political Establishment Wears Blinders and Ignores the Threat," *The Washington Times*, September 14, 2010; Seymour M. Hersh, "Moving Targets: Will the Counter-Insurgency Plan in Iraq Repeat the Mistakes of Vietnam?", *The New Yorker*, December 15, 2003; Gary Wills, "A Country Ruled by Faith," *The New York Review of Books*, November 16, 2006.

26 *Sharia: The Threat to America (An Exercise in Competitive Analysis—Report of Team 'B' II)* (Washington, DC: The Center for Security Policy Press, 2010), 6–9, 125–9.

27 Eve Bennett, "Techno-butterfly: Orientalism Old and New in *Battlestar Galactica*," *Science Fiction Film and Television*, vol. 5, no. 1 (Spring 2012), 23–46. © 2012 Liverpool University Press. Reprinted courtesy of the author and by permission of Liverpool University Press.

Epilogue

1 Fei Xiaotong, "The Elimination of Ghosts," in *Land Without Ghosts: Chinese Impressions of America from the Mid-Nineteenth Century to the Present*, eds. R. David Arkush and Leo O. Lee (Berkeley, CA: University of California Press, 1990).

2 Here I adapt Molotch's formulation. Harvey Molotch and John Logan, *Urban Fortunes: The Political Economy of Place* (Berkeley, CA: University of California Press, 1987).

3 Benjamin Lee and Edward LiPuma, "The Foundations of Finance: Charisma, Aura, and Uncertainty" in *Rethinking Capitalism*, Issue 3 (April 2012), 2–4.

4 Will Herberg, *Protestant, Catholic, Jew: An Essay in American Religious Sociology* (Chicago: University of Chicago Press, 1955).

5 Jonathan Peter Spiro, *Defending the Master Race: Conservation, Eugenics, and the Legacy of Madison Grant* (Burlington, VT: University of Vermont Press, 2009).

6 Alexander Saxton, *The Rise and Fall of the White Republic: Class Politics and Mass Culture in Nineteenth-Century America* (New York: Verso, 1990); Eric Foner, *Reconstruction: America's Unfinished Revolution, 1863–1877* (New York: HarperCollins, 1988).

7 "The President in San Francisco: How He Spent Sunday—An Address from the Mussel Slough Settlers," *The New York Times*, September 13, 1880.

8 Avery F. Gordon, *Ghostly Matters: Haunting and the Sociological Imagination* (Minneapolis, MN: University of Minnesota Press, 2008); Christopher Peterson, *Kindred Specters: Death, Mourning, and American Affinity* (Minneapolis, MN: University of Minnesota Press, 2007); Ivy G. Wilson, *Specters of Democracy: Blackness and the Aesthetics of Politics in Antebellum U.S.* (New York: Oxford University Press, 2011).

9 John Kuo Wei Tchen, "The Yellow Claw: The Optical Unconscious in Anglo American Political Culture," *Oxford History of Popular Print Culture, 1860–1920*, ed. Christine Bold (Oxford: Oxford University Press, 2010).

10 Neil Larry Shumsky, *The Evolution of Political Protest and the Workingmen's Party of California* (Columbus, OH: Ohio State University Press, 1991).

11 Albert O. Hirschman, *The Passions and the Interests: Political Arguments for Capitalism Before Its Triumph* (Princeton, NJ: Princeton University Press, 1977).

12 Peter Navarro, *The Coming China Wars: Where They Will Be Fought, How They Can Be Won* (Upper Saddle River, NJ: Financial Times Press, 2008), xv.

13 Gordon, *Ghostly Matters*, 207–8.

14 Ibid., 207.

15 Eric K. Yamamoto, *Interracial Justice: Conflict and Reconciliation in Post–Civil Rights America* (New York: New York University Press, 1999), 9–13.

16 Randolph Bourne, "Transnational America," *Atlantic Monthly* 118 (July 1916), 1–4, 6, 10.

17 Yamamoto, *Interracial Justice*, 10.

18 Edward W. Said, *Culture and Imperialism* (New York: Knopf, 1993), 335.

19 Thomas Bender, *Rethinking American History in a Global Age* (Berkeley, CA: University of California, 2002), 11.

20 Alan Roland, *Journeys to Foreign Selves: Asians and Asian Americans in a Global Era* (New York: Oxford University Press, 2011).

21 Paul Chan Pang Siu, *The Chinese Laundryman: A Study of Social Isolation*, ed. John Kuo Wei Tchen (New York: New York University Press, 1987).

22 Roland, *Journeys*, 222–3.

23 Alan Roland, email correspondence with John Kuo Wei Tchen, August 28, 2012.